Going to Heaven
The Life and Election of Bishop Gene Robinson

Blessing on you!

+ V. Gene Robinson

Going to Heaven
The Life and Election of Bishop Gene Robinson

by Elizabeth Adams

Soft Skull Press
Brooklyn, NY
2006

Going to Heaven
The Life and Election of Bishop Gene Robinson
©2006 Elizabeth Adams

ISBN-13: 978-1-933368-22-1
ISBN: 1-933368-22-5

Cover Design: Intermedia Communications
Cover Photo: Jonathan Sa'adah
Book Design: Luke Gerwe

Photography Credits:

Pages xii, 32, 58, 82, 85, 87, 100, 112, 148, 151, 168-206, 213, 215, 222, 224, 230, 266: © 2003-2006 Jonathan Sa'adah
Pages 8-30, 34, 44-47, 65-77, 154, 211, 218, 221, 255, 264: Gene Robinson Family Archives
Pages 98, 128: © 2003 Ben Garvin/*Concord Monitor*
Page 250: © 2005 Michael Barwell

Published by Soft Skull Press
55 Washington St., Suite 804
Brooklyn, NY 11201
www.Softskull.com

Distributed by Publishers Group West
www.pgw.com 1-800-788-3123

Printed in Canada

Library of Congress Cataloging-in-Publication Data for this title available from the Library of Congress.

Will you strive for justice and peace
among all people, and respect the dignity
of every human being?

I will, with God's help.

The Baptismal Covenant
The Book of Common Prayer

Contents

Acknowledgements

A book of this scope does not come about without the cooperation and encouragement of many people. First and foremost among them is Bishop Gene Robinson himself. He gave me his undivided attention whenever we were together and answered my questions with depth, humor, warmth, knowledge, and thoughtfulness. He has taught me a great deal about living with grace while under pressure and enlarged my own faith and deepened my commitment to social justice. I am honored by the trust and confidence he has placed in me, and will always be immensely grateful to him for granting me extraordinary access to his ministry, thought, and daily life at a time when his personal privacy was precious and very difficult to maintain.

Likewise, this book would not have been possible without the confidence and determined support of my publisher and editor, Richard Eoin Nash. Not only am I grateful for Richard's decision to publish the manuscript and wholeheartedly support it, but also for his partnership throughout the writing and editing process. He has made this a much better book through his penetrating questions, astute editing and clear grasp of this story's importance in the current political and religious debate. I would also like to thank Anne Horowitz, the book's copy-editor, for her very close reading of the text and the many corrections and improvements she suggested.

At the Diocese of New Hampshire, Paula Bibber, the bishop's executive assistant, has facilitated my communication and scheduling, helped me with countless details, and generally made my life easier throughout the writing of this book in hundreds of ways, always in the most gracious manner. I would also like to say a special thank you to the Rev. Canon Tim Rich, who on several occasions gave me a better background on events affecting the bishop's office, and to the Rt. Rev. Douglas Theuner for sharing his unique and extensive knowledge of this period in the life of the diocese and the Episcopal Church.

I am indebted to all the people who graciously consented to be interviewed at length for this book, and extend to them my heartfelt thanks: the Rev. Canon Henry Atkins, Michael Barwell, Paula Bibber, Marge Christie, Dr. Louie Crew, the Rev. Randy Dales, Judith Esmay, the Rev. David Jones, the Rev. Hays Junkin, the Rt. Rev. Douglas Theuner, the Rev. Canon Tim Rich, Ella Robinson, Deane Root, the Rev. Nancy Wittig, and the Rev. Nancy Vogele.

I would like to thank my friends in the choir and on the Second Sunday Forum Committee at St. Thomas Episcopal Church, Hanover, New Hampshire, for supporting me as a writer on religion, spirituality, and contemporary culture, and for the long conversations we have shared about issues of social justice and the future direction of the church—discussions which were formative as I began my work on this book. I would also like to thank the members of that parish for electing me to serve on their vestry: an experience which was challenging and eye-opening, and through which I learned many things that contributed to this project. My new friends among the clergy and congregation at Christ Church Cathedral, Montréal, have likewise been most supportive, and have added a Canadian perspective that has greatly expanded my knowledge and thinking about the North American churches and their place within Anglicanism as a whole.

In addition to the members of the clergy who were interviewed for this book, I would like to thank my other friends in the clergy who have helped me, throughout a lifetime of animated conversations, to understand so much more about Christian theology and history, as well as the politics of the Episcopal Church and Anglican Communion, and who have encouraged me to write about those topics, not in an academic fashion, but in connection to everyday life: the Rev. James Adams, the Rev. Canon Henry Atkins, the Rev. Dr. Roger Balk, the Rev. Sarah Hague, the Rev. Beth Hilgartner, the Rev. John Conbere, the Rev. Willard Cook, the Rev. Andrew Kline, the Rev. Mounir Sa'adah, the Rev. Noel Sokoloff, the Rev. Susan Stiles, the Rev. James McDermott, the Very Rev. Michael J. Pitts, the Rev. Joyce Sanchez, and the Rev. Dr. Elizabeth Rowlinson.

I am fortunate to be surrounded by a community of family and friends who have encouraged this project, listened to its ups and downs, and put up with extended absences during the periods when I was working intensively. Among them are many gay and lesbian friends without whose trust and sharing about their lives I would be incapable of writing this book; thank you. There are too many personal friends to mention everyone individually, but I would like to extend particular thanks to Nardi Campion, Chris Clarke, Natalie d'Arbeloff, Lorianne DiSabato, Cheryl Elinsky, Kingsley Ervin, Judith Esmay, Dale Favier, Gay Gellhorn, Bill Gordh, Mark Hibbs, Alison Kent, Jennifer Lewis, Bob and Merle Linnell, Veronica McDermott, Tom Montag, Jean Morris, Yemi Onafuwa, Rhonda Rockwell, David and Gretchen Sa'adah, Mounir Sa'adah, Robert Strauss, Nancy Vogele, and Patrick Wedd, all of whom have (probably without knowing it) said a right word at the right time and helped me to overcome discouragement and difficulties. Marjorie Gellhorn Sa'adah, in particular, has been a steadfast cheerleader for this project, believing in me through the worst times and rejoicing with me at the best with her special humor and love: she deserves special thanks and credit in bringing this book to completion. Finally, I would like to thank my friend and fellow writer Dave Bonta for offering to be a first outside reader; his comments on my writing were, as always, insightful, very helpful and greatly appreciated.

As I began my search for a publisher, two people gave me generous and special assistance, and I would like to thank them here: Peregrine Wittlesey, for her comments on the manuscript and her knowledge of the publishing world, and Jane Garrett, for understanding the book within the context of the Episcopal Church, and for putting me in contact with Richard Nash.

On the most personal level, I want to offer my thanks to my own immediate family. My paternal grandfather, the Rev. Charles Wesley Adams, was a Methodist minister; from him and from my grandmother, Mabel Adams, I learned what it meant to live a life dedicated to the church. My maternal grandparents, Floyd and Elizabeth Miner, taught me what it meant to be an Episcopalian and to practice "radical hospitality." But it was my own parents, Howard and Martha Adams, who encouraged my interest in religion, politics, and social justice, and helped me think about how to apply ethical teachings to my own life. They also encouraged me, from an early age, to develop the discipline necessary for undertaking large projects. Their belief in me throughout my life has allowed me to believe in myself: a gift so precious that I will never be able to acknowledge it sufficiently.

Finally, without the love, encouragement, unfailing support and considerable personal sacrifice of my husband, Jonathan Sa'adah, this book would never have come into being. In addition to being my partner in the project by photographing the major events and people of this story, and acting as the photo editor for the book itself, he has been a sounding board, a first reader, an advisor, a steady comforter during the project's low points and a happy companion at the high ones. To him, and to all of you, this work is dedicated.

Elizabeth Adams
Montréal, Québec
April 4, 2006

Gene Robinson during a quiet moment at his formal investiture as bishop of New Hampshire.

Prologue

On May 24, 1964, wearing a white cotton eyelet dress, white ankle socks, patent leather shoes, and a white, waist-length tulle veil, I knelt at the altar rail of Christ Church, Sherburne, New York, and was confirmed as a member of the Episcopal Church.

It startles me to realize how vividly I remember that moment: the pressure of the bishop's hands pressing down on my head, as if he were trying to push me through the floor; the itchiness of the too-tight plastic headband with its sharp, grippy prongs securing the veil; my worry about holding the card with my name on it so the bishop could read it properly. As for the six weeks of confirmation classes I'd attended over the late winter: I remember little. What I recall are the boredom and barely-contained rudeness of twelve-year-olds who had been coerced into a process that mattered far more to their parents than to them, and the tension that erupted into tittering behind the back of the beleaguered, well-meaning priest and, on our release, into huge snowball fights outside the parish hall, often with the boys heaving snowballs at the shrieking girls.

I was interested, though, in church doctrine and in matters of faith and belief, and during the classes I had asked questions—questions that hadn't always received satisfactory answers. Here I was, an idealistic twelve-year-old, vowing my consent to something I already wasn't sure I believed. What *was* this institution of the church, which a part of me loved, and a part of me wanted to run from forever? What did it stand for? I knew that belonging to the church came with responsibilities, but what would that mean in *my* life? Like my mother and grandmother, would my role be serving on the altar guild, pressing and embroidering the fine linens, or typing the church newsletter and making breakfast for the bishop when he came to stay in our house—because the rectory, across the street, was too full of boys to have a guest room?

At the time, I did what I was allowed to do: I sang in the choir, watching from the back balcony as those beloved neighbor boys served as acolytes. I helped my mother snap wax drippings off the cream-colored candles, polished the silver chalice so that not a fingerprint remained in its gleaming surface, and learned how to turn the crosses on the glass cruets so that they faced in exactly the same direction. I made carefully crustless egg salad sandwiches for church lunches and learned how to pour tea.

Men—like my grandfather—served on the vestry or took long terms as wardens, caring for the church finances and property. Men were the ushers, the delegates to convention; with long serious faces they carried the casket when someone died, and with the same solemnity they decided how the money would be spent and who would go to seminary. Men were the only ones allowed to read the Scripture.

Women taught Sunday School, trained the junior choir, put on the luncheons and coffee hours, prayed and visited the sick and the shut-ins, dressed the children in elaborate angel and sheep and shepherd costumes for the Christmas pageant, raised money through endless bazaars and suppers and bake sales, collected boxes of beads and rick-rack to send to the Indians somewhere in the southwest, and pennies to send to China. But they had no vote in church policy, no seat on the vestry, no voice at the lectern or pulpit, and certainly no hand to raise and consecrate the wafers my mother and I had placed in the polished, round, silver box with its standing silver cross.

Already, at twelve, I sensed the storm brewing over gender roles and sexuality without knowing what it would mean. Nothing in my earlier childhood—those calm years of the fifties—prepared me for the enormous changes that would sweep our society or the Episcopal Church during the next decade, let alone during the forty-plus years between my confirmation, in 1964, and today. What I did know was that integrity was important and that I didn't want to be a hypocrite. I made my confirmation vow, but on that day I began to move away from a church that told me what to believe and whom to obey, and onto a path of discovering what that meant for myself. I grew up in the fifties but came of age in the sixties. That confirmation day was the last time I would ever wear a white veil, and I would not make an unconditional promise to obey anyone or anything again until I made my way back to the church and to a differently-understood God many, many years later.

But something did happen at that altar rail, something I could not undo or escape. I felt it happen when the bishop laid his hands on my head and said:

Defend, O Lord, this thy child Beth with thy heavenly grace, that she may continue thine for ever, and daily increase in thee more and more, until she comes to thy everlasting kingdom.

I had no idea what that prayer meant. I responded to its poetic language and cadence, and to its calm formality, but sensed something more: a covenant, a promise. Even though the bishop moved on, repeating the same prayer for every one of my friends kneeling at the altar rail, I knew something indelible had happened to me: that when his hands pressed my head the prayer had been for me alone, and that I had assented to something that would not let me go. In the days afterward I feigned a cool indifference, but in secret I memorized the prayer and repeated it to myself. "*Defend*"—I liked the strange choice of that powerful word and the way it was phrased almost as a command. "*That she may continue thine*"—I belonged to someone other than my parents. Who was this, whose child was I? "*Daily increase in thee more and*

2

more"—this was the most curious part, the inescapable part, implying both a lifelong relationship, and continuing change.

In 1964 I had never heard the phrase, "the priesthood of all believers." Like all the other children in my confirmation class, I had been baptized before I could remember, and certainly before I could speak for myself or understand the pledges made in my name. Confirmation, on the cusp of adolescence, was the time of taking responsibility for oneself in the church and confirming one's baptismal vows, but the idea of children, especially female children, sharing in "priesthood" would have been as radical a concept as calling my grandmother's life of teaching by that name, or my grandfather and father's kind, honest, and egalitarian work as businessmen and community leaders, or my mother's artwork and unconditional, patient love for her family and friends. Nevertheless, I now understand that what happened to me that day was the descent of the mantle of my own priesthood. I eventually left the church for a long time of wandering and spiritual exploration, during which I called myself an agnostic.

During the late sixties and seventies, those years of political and social turmoil, the church felt irrelevant and retrograde to me. Except for a few strong voices—the Berrigans, or William Sloane Coffin, whom I heard speak at Cornell University's Sage Chapel during the Vietnam years—I didn't see the church changing, or effectively engaging the struggles of the day. Of course it was—or to be more accurate, some people within the institution were trying to push change forward, dragging the church itself along behind them like a very heavy anchor. I was not particularly aware of the significant Christian efforts to stop the nuclear arms race, end racism, and give women equal rights, perhaps because in my small-town parish back home these particular struggles were not being engaged. The societal changes I felt connected to were happening on city streets and in the dorms and student unions of college campuses. Fervor and passion for a different future without racism, sexism and classism pulsed in *our* veins, or so we thought, not in the cold, slowly-running veins of institutions and governments.

The way back home can be a very long one. Over the next twenty years I poked my head into churches a number of times, singing in a choir here or there, listening to a good preacher. I joined an Episcopal Church for one two-year period, during which time I still struggled with the Nicene Creed and, as a young single person, felt less than welcome in a New England community of longtime church "pillars" and families with children. It wasn't until the early 1990s when I finally reluctantly heeded an insistent voice in my head that said, "Go take communion."

The church I re-entered had utterly changed. There were girls serving as acolytes, women lectors reading the lessons and holding the chalice, women on the vestry and all the committees, and a woman priest preaching and celebrating Communion. There was a new hymnal, and a new prayer book with gender-inclusive language. People were talking not only about women's ordination, but about gay and lesbian rights, new roles for both laity and clergy, and about social justice ministry. Gradually I realized that there was open discussion here about faith and doctrine; that there was room for doubt, debate, and questioning, as well as deeply committed engagement with the world; that signing one's name on a dotted line under the creeds was not what this community was about. This openness mattered to me, and within it I would eventually find my own calling and ministry. But what made the tears flow, during those first weeks in the back pew, were the things that *hadn't* changed—the old hymns, the power of the liturgy, the Eucharist, and in it, a rediscovered faith that I didn't have to fully understand. I had been found by "a love that would not let me go," or to be more accurate, I had rediscovered the love that had been there all along, defending me with its grace.

Like so many other Episcopalians in the Diocese of New Hampshire, I already knew Gene Robinson when he was elected bishop in 2003. As an active member of a congregation, I had previously worked with Gene as the assistant to then-Bishop Douglas Theuner during some particularly trying times in our home parish. Our rector (priest) and members of the parish and staff were struggling over questions of authority, lay and clerical roles, and conservative/liberal theology. During this painful process, I was impressed with Gene's low-key but firm manner of facilitating discussion, his consistent charge to all of us to "speak the truth in love," his quick intelligence and awareness of subterfuge, manipulation, and other psychological game-playing, and his insistence that we take responsibility for our own issues and patterns rather than expecting the bishop to come in and "fix" parish problems with a wave of his crook.

As Theuner's assistant for seventeen years, Gene Robinson worked with virtually every parish in the diocese, and became a familiar, well-loved, and respected figure; my experience with him was typical. His sexual orientation was known but regarded as a non-issue by most people; his skills as priest, facilitator and administrator and his personal qualities of approachability, enthusiasm, warmth, and unshakable faith were the characteristics people focused on and which led, eventually, to his election as the successor to the beloved, charismatic, and progressive Douglas Theuner.

Yet in the space of one momentous afternoon, at the diocesan election at St. Paul's Church in Concord, the name of this small, unassuming man catapulted into world awareness. The Diocese of New Hampshire, knowing and loving the man who had served them so well as canon to the ordinary for the past seventeen years, had chosen him on the second ballot to be their next bishop. And out of that Episcopal sanctuary in a small northern city, filled with a great deal of joy and a few tears, came the word that someone named Gene Robinson had just been elected: the first openly gay bishop in the history of the Anglican Communion.

Because the sexual issue simply had not been in the forefront of either their decision or their prior relationship, neither the New Hampshire Diocese nor the bishop-elect fully anticipated the huge amount of energy that would be generated, both positively and negatively, by his election. Two intertwined stories began to emerge: the unusual trajectory of Gene's own life, leading to his call to the episcopate and his historic election, and that of a small, rural diocese rising to the challenge of enormous pressure on the world's religious stage.

The controversy and media onslaught at the General Convention of the Episcopal Church, where the election had to be ratified, and the subsequent, extraordinary Lambeth gathering of Anglican primates to discuss the election, called by the Archbishop of Canterbury, were highly-charged events; so was the solemn, joyful, and deeply moving consecration of Bishop Robinson in New Hampshire a month later. But the controversy would not abate: the re-election of George W. Bush and the growing debate over the proper place of religion in American politics seemed to mirror the polarization within Episcopal and other American denominations, while vocal opposition to progressive Western attitudes toward homosexuality (and sexuality in general) from African Christians and Islamic fundamentalists would become ever more strident.

As a milestone in the history of the Anglican Church, the election of Gene Robinson is a dramatic enough story. Yet, as its worldwide ramifications show, it is much more than a singular event, and he is more than a symbol for gay and lesbian rights. Of course his election is a benchmark for that community, which has been struggling for years to be considered equal children of God, accepted participants in the life of the church, and for the freedom to be honest and open within it. But Gene himself has been amazed by the positive response his election has received from other, less predictable quarters, among people who are *not* the traditional constituency of the Episcopal Church or, for various reasons, have felt marginalized or rejected by some traditional Christian communities. These include young people, people from other traditions who have been looking for greater honesty and integrity in a church, conservatives who for the first time are struggling to accept their children's homosexuality, and people he has touched through prison ministry. But the largest group includes people who, like me, left the church of their youth because it didn't speak to them, or felt too rigid, or seemed only interested in preserving itself and the status quo.

Perhaps even more than his black and female forerunners in church leadership, Bishop Robinson represents the "other": the person who has been persecuted, shamed, feared, and rejected for being different, told that he or she is not worthy of God's love or of inclusion in the community of believers, or that his or her ideas about justice are not welcome there—and thus has had to find a relationship with God apart from the institutional church. Although the progressive movement has been active within Christianity and the Episcopal

Church for a number of years, Bishop Robinson's election and his message have been startling exclamation points proclaiming to many that the church truly can be different, that in it all people are welcome, and that it can be a force for love, compassion, and change in a broken and divided world.

From the early days after his election, Gene Robinson has willingly shouldered the burden of being a symbol and a potential martyr. He never sought fame; in fact he speaks longingly of the day when the media spotlight will dim and he will be able to give himself wholly to the task for which he has been elected—being a diocesan bishop to the people of New Hampshire. "However," he repeats, in his folksy way, "as long as I'm getting all this attention, I'm going to use it for God." By that he doesn't mean evangelism of the Christian right variety, but by using every possible opportunity to preach a Gospel of inclusion, equality, and love for all people, following the teaching and life of Jesus Christ.

Two months after his consecration, the new bishop coadjutor invited clergy, congregational leaders, and members of the diocesan parishes to a half-day conference in Concord, New Hampshire, under the title "Re-Imagining the Diocese." In his opening remarks, Bishop Robinson read aloud the passage from Isaiah (61:1-9) that had been read at his consecration and asked everyone present to reflect upon it. "'To give hope to the poor, and set the captive free . . . .' What would your parish, and our diocese, look like, if we really took these words seriously? How would we have to change? What would we need to do?" Asking the members of the diocese to begin a process of discussion and discernment in regard to these questions, he suggested two concepts that he hoped would guide the process, "Infinite Respect" and "Radical Hospitality." He made it clear that the listeners had been given an opportunity to move beyond a mere mention in the Anglican history books. "A lot of eyes are upon us," he said. "It is up to all of us to see this as a call, and an opportunity."

It was clear that Bishop Robinson was talking not about work he could do himself, but about the priesthood of each person in that crowded conference-center ballroom. As one priest remarked later, "99 percent of the work of ministry in this world is done, and has to be done, by people who are not ordained." In subsequent conversations with many people, both clergy and laity, who have been energized and heartened by Gene Robinson's election, I have sensed an emerging excitement, clarity of purpose, and determination to work not only toward dialogue and unity within the Episcopal Church and Anglican Communion, but toward becoming people and faith communities who strive to confront and dismantle all the "isms": racism, sexism, homophobia, classism. As Bishop Robinson often points out, our baptismal covenant includes the vow, "to strive for justice and peace among all people, and respect the dignity of every human being." How different our world, our churches, and our lives would be if we, as a priesthood of believers, truly took that vow to heart.

During the writing of this book, I've been reminded of the prayer spoken at my confirmation. I'm far more aware now of what it means to be "defended by God's grace," but I'm also slowly learning what it means to "increase in Him more and more." Faith and ministry are journeys that require us to move both inward and outward: inward for strength and renewal, outward to engage the world with compassion and justice. Gene Robinson's deep faith and dedicated ministry are examples of that continual inward/outward movement. He has accepted God's call to a unique role with courage and hope, and in the process been transformed into greater humility and selflessness. Just as he never anticipated the unique position in history he would occupy, he undoubtedly did not anticipate the halting, demanding, ultimately joyful process that "increasing in God" has meant for him. Perhaps most importantly, by being a person of humility, compassion, and love, Gene Robinson is both a leader and fellow pilgrim for whom hierarchy and title are far less important than the priesthood, responsibility, and hope we all share.

Gene in front of his childhood home. The cistern where the family drew their water is barely showing at right; the outhouse is just outside the margins of the photograph.

Chapter I
A Kentucky Childhood

"You now have my undivided attention," said the bishop-elect, his bright eyes sparkling behind round wire-rimmed glasses as he shut the heavy, old oak doors of the conference room behind him. Gene Robinson, wearing a black shirt, clerical collar and a cross, shook hands and sat down at the big table in the former formal dining room of an old New England house that is now the headquarters of the Diocese of New Hampshire. "I'm so excited about this!" he said, clapping his hands together and grinning like a kid about to jump on a hayride. "Where shall we start?"

Gene laughs a lot: a delighted laugh that emerges from him as naturally as his concern when he hears of a problem. He is an extrovert who thrives on being with people, whether they are old friends and close colleagues or individuals he's never met. As he confers with his staff, hearing about upcoming phone calls and appointments, he is joking one minute, serious the next. But in the early days following his election, amid increasing pressure and publicity, everyone close to him wondered whether he'd be able to keep the warmth, humility, and personal touch that had endeared him to the diocese. Would he be able to juggle the job he'd been elected to do with his new role as an icon for gay rights and all that came with it: the speaking engagements, the awards, the glamour of celebrity, the travel schedule? Would fame go to his head? Or worse, would he crumble under the spotlight and the strain of scrutiny? How would he handle the effect on his family? Could one man really bear the vilification, the physicals threats, and the personal exposure of being at the center not only of the debate over homosexuality, but of a schism that could split the Episcopal Church and the Anglican Communion at large?

What lay ahead?

At that early date, no one knew. There was a clue, however, in those first words he spoke. We *did* have his undivided attention, and that attention never faltered. A priest who knows him well put it this way, "When you're with Gene, you feel like you're the most important person in the world. And even though you know that he's going to make the next person feel exactly the same way, it's fine—because you also know it's absolutely sincere."

Only a person who is extremely calm and secure about himself can step aside and listen to others in that way. At the time of his election, Gene had no idea of the storm that was gathering, the toll it would take, or the story that it would eventually write. He had no idea what would be said about him, about gay people and God, or what his election would mean—either to those who vehemently disagreed, or to those for whom it was a gateway to life-changing acceptance and affirmation. What he did have was the sure, calm center he needed not only to survive, but to grow, to help, and to lead. That center had begun to develop long before, in a very different world.

Gene Robinson grew up in Fayette County, which surrounds Lexington, Kentucky. He was not born into a world of privilege and affluence—his parents were poor tenant farmers who worked in the tobacco fields all day long. Their house didn't have running water until Gene was ten years old. "It's kind of amazing even for me to look back on," he said, "but it was pretty basic: if you wanted cold water you cranked it out of a cistern, if you wanted hot water you put it on the stove and heated it up."

The life Gene entered, on May 29, 1947, was hard enough in itself, but he had barely survived an extremely difficult birth which had left him temporarily paralyzed and his head misshapen. The pediatrician, certain that the baby wouldn't survive, massaged Gene's head into a more normal shape so that his young mother—only twenty years old at the time—wouldn't be horrified when she saw her child in his coffin. The Robinsons had hoped for a girl, and when the hospital asked them to indicate a name for the birth and—as they thought likely—death certificates, they named the baby Vicki Gene Robinson, after his father, Victor, and his mother, Imogene.

When the baby did survive, he was given to his parents to take home—"to watch me die or become a vegetable," said Gene. "My dad was poor and uneducated. I can't imagine what this would have felt like to him at age twenty or twenty-one, except I suspect it was awful."

Fotomat picture of Gene as a young baby, 1947.

The young parents didn't know what to expect, except that the doctors had told them the baby would probably die soon. When he didn't die, they were told he would stop developing, that he would never walk, talk, or have any use of himself. Many years later, Gene's father told him, "I couldn't take any joy in you and your development because I always thought each step was going to be the last thing. So you rolled over; that was as far as you were ever going to go. Okay, so you sat up; that was as far as you were ever going to go." He said he was never able to rejoice because he was too focused on, "Well, that's the last thing."

But the baby grew into a boy who could not only walk and talk but was curious and eager. He was under the care of a pediatrician who became an important influence on Gene's young life. "He took care of me until I was way too old to be going to a pediatrician," Gene said, "and I idolized him to the point where I was convinced that that was what I wanted to be myself."

Somehow, Gene feels, his father's early fears for his son became translated into excessive strictness. "I don't ever remember being beaten, but I do remember the terror that he could put in my heart by just touching his belt buckle. If we were out in public somewhere, and I was doing something that he didn't want me doing, he would just touch his belt buckle, and I would just freeze. So probably deep in my subconscious somewhere are memories that have not surfaced. I don't have any memories of being beaten, but I can't imagine why I'd be that terrified if something hadn't preceded it."

Gene with his mother.

As the son of tobacco sharecroppers, Gene knew what it was like to be poor. He also had, from childhood, a heightened sensitivity to "otherness": in segregated Kentucky in the forties, fifties, and sixties, otherness was everywhere.

"I remember a hot summer day in Lexington, Kentucky," he said. "My mother had taken me swimming. We were at a public swimming pool, and my mother saw a black family get in the pool, at the other end, and I remember, like it was yesterday, being taken out of that pool and driven all the way across

Lexington to a segregated swimming pool." He shook his head in disbelief. "That segregated pool was in an amusement park which was called 'Joyland.'"

"When we'd go to the movies, the ticket office was on a corner. And the woman selling tickets sat on a chair that rotated. And she'd turn around to the window that sold tickets for whites, and then turn around to the ticket-window on the other side of that corner, on the side street, to sell tickets to blacks. And then they went upstairs and sat in the balcony, and we sat downstairs." It was one thing, and bad enough, that blacks were forced to take the worst theater seats and sit in the backs of buses. But racism goes to another level when "contamination" is implied: pool water can't be shared; drinking fountains must be separate. It's a short step from there to the presumption of guilt: Gene remembered a Saturday afternoon in Nicholasville, Kentucky, when a jury was in the courthouse making a decision about a black man who had allegedly accosted a white woman. "I can remember the smell of lynching in the air," he recalled with a shudder.

Gene sometimes calls himself "a recovering racist"; he feels it's impossible to grow up white in America and not be racist at all, because racism has such a strong background in the culture. He remembers members of his own family calling Martin Luther King, Jr. a communist. But his grandfather, whom he calls his "most beloved grandparent," was different. For a time, he served as a policeman in that same town of Nicholasville, Kentucky. "I don't think he ever arrested anyone, he just couldn't bring himself to do it," Gene said. "I can remember him saying, shaking his finger at me, 'Don't ever let me catch you saying the word "nigger."' And I remember, at his funeral, all the black people who showed up to honor him."

Because of Gene's very difficult birth, his mother was advised not to get pregnant again, but ten years later she did, and gave birth, without complications, to his sister Karen. Because the two siblings were so far apart in age, they didn't play together much or become close friends until later in life.

The hard life of the tobacco fields, combined with poverty, didn't leave a lot of time for other activities beyond keeping the family going. What the Robinsons did have was a tightly-knit community centered on religion. Gene's parents were, and still are, members of a small Disciples of Christ congregation. He describes his upbringing as "very religious."

"The church was probably the only community anybody had outside of blood kin," he remembered. "The blood kin thing was really strong, and, because families have fights and stuff, church was nearly as strong, if not in some ways stronger. Church is still what my parents do."

"The thing that I loved and respected about it was that it was so second nature and unselfconscious. If someone in that community—I'm talking about maybe sixty or seventy people—if somebody's sick, somebody's in the hospital, somebody has a relative that dies, nobody has to think about, 'Do we go see them?' Well, of course, you go see them! You might wonder whether you should take the vanilla wafer pudding, banana pudding, or a chess pie, but that would be about the only decision. It would not be about should you go see them? Should you offer to help? Should you offer to get their tobacco stripped while they're doing the funeral, or all that kind of stuff."

"It strikes me, in most of the churches that I've been in, you really have to push people to *go* and *do* and be the hands and feet of the Lord. And that is just not the case back where I came from. My parents are the most amazing Christians I've ever known. Now, they don't do a lot of talking about Jesus, actually, except at Sunday School. They didn't talk all about that, but in every moment of their lives, they're just doing it. It's really astounding."

Top: Gene with a beagle puppy, while the mother dog watches.

Above: "Granddaddy," Gene's maternal grandfather, lets his grandson "ride" his workhorse.

Gene himself entered church life willingly. The Sunday services were very long, starting with hymns and prayers, and then moving to an hour of Christian education for everyone—children and adults. That was followed by another hour of worship. There was youth group every Sunday night. Gene had thirteen years of perfect attendance at Sunday School and is still amused when he recalls the formidable woman who ran the Sunday School and allowed no excuses, even for sickness. "I think you could have gotten hit by a car and it wouldn't have mattered," he said, laughing. "I remember going once and then telling my mother that I thought I had measles right after. I probably gave the entire class measles because I was just not going to miss," he said, shaking his head ruefully. "So that thirteen years of perfect attendance pins really means that I did not miss a single Sunday."

Gene in 1957, wearing his Sunday School perfect attendance pin.

The sharecroppers worked in the fields all day and then went to revivals at night in the summertime. These tent meetings took place during August, the hottest month of the year, when the farmers were bringing in the tobacco. Gene describes tobacco harvesting as "ungodly work" in Kentucky's heat and humidity, and speculated that maybe it helped people identify with the fire-and-brimstone preaching by the itinerant preachers who led the revivals. "Everyone would sit there fanning themselves with one of those funeral home fans with a picture on it of Jesus knocking on the door of your heart," he said. At the age of twelve, during one of those revivals, Gene took Jesus Christ as his Lord and Savior and was baptized.

The Disciples of Christ denomination is not well known in the Northeast, but it is actually a substantial Christian denomination in North America, with over 800,000 members in the United States and Canada. It was founded as part of the "great awakenings," the series of religious revivals that swept through the formerly Puritan eastern states in the late eighteenth and early nineteenth centuries. The revival movement was characterized by flamboyant and highly emotional preaching that led to widespread conversions, and it planted the roots for what we call evangelicalism today.

At the time, Kentucky and Ohio were the "Western Frontier." The denomination's origins go back to a Presbyterian minister, Barton W. Stone, who was born in Port Tobacco, Maryland in 1772. Stone served as minister in Cane Ridge, Kentucky, where he hosted a famous revival in 1801. Along with several others, he formed a group that dissolved its ties to all denominations, rejected all creeds, and took the Bible as its sole authority. They called themselves simply "The Christians," believing that the body of Christ was and should be united as one.

Thomas Campbell and his son Alexander were both born in Ireland and came to America from Scotland—Thomas in 1807, and his son two years later. In Pennsylvania, they, too, refused to use the Presbyterian creeds, taking the motto, "Where the Scriptures speak, we speak; where the Scriptures are silent, we are silent." Their movement, which was allied for a time with the Baptists, became known as the Restoration Movement. In 1830, the Campbells and their followers became independent of the Baptists and took the simple name of "Disciples." The younger Campbell was influenced by, and in great agreement with, the principles of Thomas Jefferson. He wrote a great deal and was an excellent public speaker who engaged in a marathon eight-day debate on Catholicism with the Roman Catholic archbishop of Cincinnati, John Purcell.

In 1832, in Lexington, Kentucky, Stone's "Christians" and the Campbells' "Disciples" united to form the Disciples of Christ.[1]

Gene Robinson explained that the denomination was founded in reaction to churches like the Episcopal Church, in which there was thought to be too much emphasis on ritual. "What they were trying to do was recover the early, New Testament church," he said. "So the only creedal statement required was, 'Do you take Jesus Christ as your Lord and Savior?' It was real simple. And baptism was by full immersion."

The church his parents belonged to was one of the earliest congregations, and a direct ancestor of theirs had been one of the founding members. There has been one son in each generation of Robinsons, and that son has always become an elder of the church.

Dressed up for Easter (1956) with Granny Ella and his mother in front of the local firehouse where Gene's father worked. They had gone there to show off their new clothes.

Today Gene describes the Disciples of Christ as "a pretty great denomination," saying he didn't have much perspective on what it was as a national denomination until he learned more about it after leaving home. "The particular congregation my parents belonged to was more narrow and more tending towards fundamentalist than the denomination as a whole," he said. "I think that probably had to do with the level of education of the people in the congregation, more than anything. These were virtually all poor tobacco farmers, not all of whom—including my father—had finished high school." The ministers in that church were seminarians at the local seminary, whose name at that time was College of the Bible; it's now the Lexington Theological Seminary.

For a church that was supposedly non-liturgical, there was strict adherence to an order of worship. "You ought to try changing the order of any one of those things that took place," Gene recalled, with a laugh. "There would be hell to pay! But those liturgies weren't written down in books anywhere; they were just written down in people's hearts and memories." Another aspect that he finds fascinating (and that is quite different from many reformist Protestant denominations) is that there was Communion every single Sunday. The Communion was presided over by lay deacons and elders, not the minister. "Now they would certainly not espouse any kind of belief in the Real Presence of Jesus in the communion," he added emphatically. "This is just a memorial meal."[2]

"The Disciples claim to be a New Testament church," he went on, "but there was actually nothing that connected them with the New Testament, beyond a couple hundred years of history. As for the evangelical aspect, what I remember growing up is that we were not afraid to talk about Jesus. We sang all kinds of tacky and otherwise horribly bad theological hymns. The hymnbook was divided into liturgical seasons, but we had no idea what they meant; the division was not guided by the ancient Church's ritual at all. Well, we knew Christmas, and we knew Easter. The seasons of Lent and Advent were completely unknown to us, let alone that they were meant to be times of penitence and self-examination."

Denominationally, people tended to stick together, with some cohesiveness between the Protestant churches and a great gulf between Protestantism and anything else. "There were Christians, and then there were Catholics," Gene remembered. "We'd never confuse the two. We had this vague notion that Lent was something that Catholics did. We had absolutely no understanding that Mass in the Roman Catholic Church was Communion. I can remember thinking that 'mass' was short for 'massacre.'"

Once, his paternal grandfather, who had been one of the deacons and elders in this little church, had to go to the wedding of a person who plowed some of the fields. Gene recalled that his grandfather and his wife were nervous wrecks for two months because the wedding was going to be in a Roman Catholic church and they didn't know what to expect. "So the day came, and they went, and then they came home saying, 'Oh my God! It was Communion!' They couldn't believe it."

Besides church, music was the other major focus of Gene's early years. Until his voice changed, he sang in a quartet with his close friend Charles Miller from the Disciples congregation, whom he describes now, with an affectionate smile, as "one of the most literate, articulate people who raises tobacco that you've ever seen." The quartet made it onto television "back when everything was still live and black-and-white."

But the biggest thing in Gene's life was band. High school marching bands were, and still are, a big deal in the south. Gene played clarinet in a band that had about 350 members and a 50-person clarinet section. Depending on the season, this group morphed into a concert band, a marching band that marched 220 people, a Dixieland band, a stage band, and a Black Watch band that performed at basketball games.

His best friend in junior and senior high school was Deane Root, another serious musician and enthusiastic member of "The Pride of the Bluegrass," the name of the band emblazoned across the cover of the LP record they made every year. Root is now a professor of musicology at the University of Pittsburgh.

"I moved to Lexington in 1959 from Atlanta," Deane recalled, "and started at Lafayette Junior High School. Gene and I met there and more or less grew up together through the band." Membership in a band of this caliber was intense and time-consuming as well as a bonding experience for everyone involved, especially when the group was preparing for and performing in competitions. Deane and Gene went to rehearsals that started at five every morning before school, performed in elaborate, precision-marching half-time shows at every football game at home or away, and went to extra rehearsals for the pep band that played in the stands. In the summer, there was a two-week band camp to learn the football half-time show for the fall. The band went

Formal portrait of Gene as member of the Lafayette High School Band.

on weekly trips, such as a big competition in Virginia Beach during their freshman year, and Louisville for the state competition.

"We often won some of these competitions," Deane recalled, "and I can still remember how nervous and excited we were to be there. It was intensely unifying for the whole group to travel and compete together, working with each other to make sure we were all upholding the highest standards: instruments polished properly, feet placed at right angle, posture just so. It wasn't only a bonding experience, but also a deep lesson in being a member of a social group with a common goal."

Seating in the band was highly competitive. Deane explained that once a week or so there would be "challenges": someone seated below could challenge the person ahead of him. Then, in the presence of everyone—and often in a private room behind a screen, to conceal who was who—the two students would have to play a particular piece of music, and the director and the drum majors would act as judges. "That was how you worked your way up," Deane explained. "But there was a sort of code of honor—when someone was so respected as a musician and leader they wouldn't be challenged." By the time they were seniors, he had become first chair of the trumpet section, and Gene was first chair of the clarinets. Deane doesn't remember being challenged during his senior year.

The money for trips, uniforms, and equipment was raised by the students' parents and the band boosters. As a fund-raiser for their trips, the band members sold chocolate-covered "turtles"—and Gene rather sheepishly still remembers the desire to overachieve that made him consistently sell more turtles than anybody else.

While working one's way up to first chair of a section was a high achievement, the very top musical positions were those of the two drum majors—the high-hatted, high-stepping leaders in front of the marching band—and of the student conductor. "Those positions were at least as big as being captain of the football team," Gene explained. Being a fairly short person, he would have been an unlikely candidate for drum major. But he was chosen to be student conductor. "I conducted in front of 10,000 people at an outdoor concert in St. Petersburg, Florida—that kind of thing." Gene practiced his conducting at home, using recordings made by the Eastman Wind Ensemble from the Eastman School of Music in Rochester, New York.

"You basically did nothing but live, eat, and breathe band," he said, with a wry grin, but with obvious delight as he recalled memory after memory. When Gene found out, in one of our first interviews, that I had played glockenspiel in a very competitive marching band throughout my junior high and high school years, he laughed and said, "Then you know!" He admitted that even now he doesn't know a thing about sports but loves the halftime shows: "Everybody always leaves the room at half-time, and of course the network always cuts in with the commercials, but I'm always freaking out and telling my friends, 'But this is what I came to see!'"

The band gave Gene an outlet for his ambition, an opportunity to travel, and developed his musical ability, but its most important contribution to his life was in developing his leadership ability.

"Gene wasn't quite as outgoing in high school as he is now, and of course his chosen career thrives on that aspect of his personality, so he has gone on to develop it more," Deane Root commented. "But he was always a natural leader."

Gene was chosen as president of the National Honor Society their senior year and held other offices before that. Because of its size, the frequency of rehearsals, and the intensity of relationship and familiarity it fostered, the band was a community where students with leadership, academic, and personal skills had an opportunity to help others. "We both became mentors, talking to other members, helping them in sectional rehearsals and with personal concerns," Deane said. "I did a lot of tutoring, helping other kids who might be struggling in a subject. Gene and I were close friends and we were also highly competitive academically."

After school, the boys often studied together. "Gene had a little *Jeopardy* game," Deane remembered, "and we'd often play that and then hit the books. I was often in his house. His mom was usually there—I can still hear her calling from some other room, 'Vicki Gene, come here!' One holiday, she was making very pretty purses out of burlap with horse's heads on them, and I ordered one for my mother. Another time we visited his grandparents and had a typical central Kentucky Sunday meal and talked about the church services everyone had gone to."

Gene and Deane were clearly headed to college and were in a kind of advanced placement track in their class of six or seven hundred. "We had an English teacher, Mrs. Lundy, who got us reading philosophy and theology," Deane said, "and writing deep, deep papers on the philosophy of life, rather than your standard English class essays." Out of that class grew a circle of friends who discussed these issues and tried to come to grips with what their young lives meant. Deane said they talked about why was it important to work together in the band, for instance: what larger goals might it be serving? He traces the beginnings of his own lifelong questions about how he could be of service to others, and what might be the purpose of his life, to those early intense conversations.

Gene's sexual orientation was never discussed between the two friends, which may be a reflection of how much repression surrounded the issue of homosexuality in the Kentucky culture of the time. Deane, who is heterosexual and married, visited Gene a few times after leaving high school, and then the two were out of touch for many years. After hearing about Gene's coming out, Deane reflected on his memories of the earlier years and said simply that he now has "a different understanding and respect for things that were going on in those days" than he did before.

When Gene looks back on that atmosphere of repression, it is with horror and sadness. He sometimes tries to express the changes between then and now when he speaks to current students, saying that when he was young, the slightest suggestion that a boy might be gay was enough to warrant a severe beating in the locker room as well as continual taunting and ostracism. Even though many gays and lesbians today refer to themselves as "queer" as a way of detoxifying the word, the term still remains so loaded for him that he can't use it. The pressure to have relationships with girls was intense, from both peers and family. "What we all tried to do was to persuade ourselves that we were developing in the same way as all the young men our age. There was no other option."

In the early 1960s, the civil rights struggle and Vietnam were both major national issues. For Deane, both issues were somewhat distant until he got to college. "I remember one fellow who played tuba in the band talking to me about this stuff that was going on in Alabama," he said, "and he was thinking of going down there and marching with something called the 'student non-violent coordinating committee'—what was all of that? We were talking amongst ourselves; we felt there was a need to be public and to speak out, but I'm not aware that most of us went to marches, though we did later, in college. In 1965, my first year in college, when we began to interpret these events, how I felt was very much colored by this philosophy that we had been discussing in high school." He said that, compared to the vast majority of their classmates, they were probably liberals, but that they didn't think of themselves that way: "We thought of ourselves as being students of philosophy. Students of writers like Khalil Gibran. It wasn't so much liberal/conservative—but as being people who thought about philosophy and the lives of individuals in the world, and discussing these ideas openly rather than accepting some set of standards that were expected of us by an organization, an institution, a party, a church or whatever."

Senior year of high school (1965).

Both friends remember the summer band camps as having drill-camp intensity, but in the evenings the students would often gather around a bonfire with their friends, to tell stories and sing songs. Deane remembered that Gene was very taken with songs from the inspirational genre of musical theater, which was very popular at the time, and that he'd often share those songs with the rest of the group, encouraging them to sing them and pay attention to the words. One evening, Gene shared the song "The Impossible Dream" from the musical *Man of La Mancha*:

> *And I know, if I'll only be true*
> *To this glorious quest*
> *That my heart will lie peaceful and calm*
> *When I'm laid to my rest.*

"The feeling of those performances that Gene shared with us was one of wonder and deep appreciation at the way the songwriter had crafted these beautiful messages, so giving to humanity and so inspiring to us."

For Deane, the quest for meaning and service that began in high school led him to a music degree, teaching music and humanities in the state prison system, and starting a home-grown band in a senior citizen center in Florida. His career eventually evolved into study and teaching at the University of Pittsburgh about quintessential American music and musicians, such as Stephen Foster, on whom he is the acknowledged American expert. He also studies the role music plays in communities and, most recently, has been compiling the music that surrounds and illustrates the most important events of American history and making it available as a teaching aid for educators.

For Gene, the quest led toward social justice and religion.

Graduating from the University of the South at Sewanee, 1969.

Chapter 2
The Making of a Priest

The bubbly enthusiasm and clarity with which Gene recalls his childhood and youth evaporate as soon as he mentions college. He had wanted to come to school in the North and was offered a half-scholarship by Princeton University, but received a full scholarship at the University of the South, in the city of Sewanee, Tennessee—a liberal arts school which was founded in 1858 by the Episcopal dioceses of ten southern states to provide education and religious training for young men from wealthy southern families. The idea for the school originated with Leonidas Polk, Bishop of Louisiana, who had also been a general in the Confederate army; he was a cousin of U.S. President James Polk. Episcopalianism has always been strong in the American South, especially among the aristocracy. General Robert E. Lee, for instance, was Episcopalian.

The college's setting is beautiful. The poet William Alexander Percy described Sewanee this way: "It's a long way away, even from Chattanooga, in the middle of woods, on top of a bastion of mountains crenelated with blue coves. It is so beautiful that people who have been there always, one way or another, come back . . ."

The college is well-regarded today, ranking thirty-fourth among small liberal arts schools in a list recently compiled by *US News and World Report*. It is both Southern and very Episcopalian; the campus's Gothic buildings are modeled after British boarding schools and universities. All Saints' Chapel, with its vaulted ceiling and stone arches, looks as if it had been lifted directly out of England. The flags that hang from horizontal standards along the sides of the chapel were once the flags of the Confederate states, but those were removed a long time ago. The flag of the university, designed by Bishop Polk, bears a red cross on a white field, with the upper left corner in light blue with eleven white crosses: very similar to the flag of the Episcopal Church itself. However, the eleven crosses on Polk's flag represented the eleven states of the Confederacy.

Gail Jarvis, a visitor to the school during the 1960s, described his impression of the genteel atmosphere:

> We toured the campus and celebrated Eucharist in the college's All Saints' Chapel. One of the monks took us on a tour on the monastery and showed us what a typical monk's cell looks like. Of course, we adhered to the rule of silence in the halls. We were impressed by the

deportment of the students; at the time it was an all male school. The students were always neatly groomed and coats and ties were required for class attendance. The school had quietly integrated a few years before our visit and became coed a few years later.[1]

When Gene matriculated in 1965, that atmosphere was just starting to change. Many of the students were wealthy. "Not only did I not have a fancy car," he says, "I didn't have a car at all!" Gene was a student at Sewanee between 1965 and 1969: years of upheaval for the country, but also a very trying time in his personal life. He entered college thinking that he wanted to be a pediatrician, like the doctor he idolized who had saved his life and taken care of him through the years of his childhood and adolescence. He enrolled in pre-med and began his studies but quickly found out that perhaps this path wasn't the best fit, after all. "I think it was probably the organic chemistry class that did me in," he said. "I did fine in it, but what I realized was that my interest was in people and not in the science of medicine." Ultimately, he decided to major in American Studies, a timely choice for a thoughtful young man in a country that was undergoing the major crisis of Vietnam.

Gene filed with his local Selective Service board as a conscientious objector, a decision that did not sit well with his family. The only time his father ever came to see him alone at school, without his mother, was when he came and begged his son not to do that. He himself had quit high school and lied about his age in order to fight in the Second World War.

During those years there was a national draft lottery. The names of the 365 or 366 days of each year were drawn at random from a large glass bowl, and those dates were assigned a number corresponding to the order in which they were drawn. The draft eligibility of every eighteen-year-old man in the country was then determined by correlating his birthday to the lottery numbers. The lower your number, the more likely it was that you would be called up for military service and sent to Vietnam, where, as American households saw on television every night, thousands of young men were being killed and wounded. Everyone who was eligible then, or loved someone who was of draft age, remembers the lottery. Gene grew grim, thinking about it, and shook his head. "I remember the night of the lottery, sitting in these dorms of men—we had a matron, an elderly woman, who let us watch TV in her apartment. We all gathered around the TV as they drew the numbers and the people who had single digit numbers were just completely horrified. It was just an awful night."

The local Selective Service boards were responsible for granting or denying conscientious objector status to those who applied. Gene's board only acted on the applications if a person was called up for service. "My number was, I think, 221," he said, "so it was never acted upon. But that particular

Selective Service board never granted a single application. It was all locally determined and they never granted one. I had a friend in high school who was called up, and his application was rejected—and he went to Leavenworth."

Gene conducted the "itty bitty" university band at Sewanee and also did some choral conducting. He often wasn't in class and ended up pulling a lot of all-nighters, finishing his work at the last minute.

Gene conducting the Sewanee band.

"I don't know that I realized it then, but I think I was probably clinically depressed. I was fighting so hard to keep down everything around my orientation—remember this is an all-men's school—that I pretty much repressed everything, so consequently I really don't remember much about college. It's a great sadness for me."

As the idea of becoming a doctor waned and he considered what to do with his life, Gene realized that the possibility of ordained ministry had always been somewhere in the back of his mind. "It almost immediately felt right; it felt like a true call," he said. "And once I had figured that out, the only real dilemma for me was choosing whether or not to leave the Disciples and become an Episcopalian."

Even as a young boy, Gene had been theologically curious, and he had worried about some things he was being told by the Disciples of Christ. "As a child I kept saying, 'So now tell me again—you're saying that if I go to bed and say my prayers and ask God to forgive me all of my sins, and I get up in the morning, and while I'm brushing my teeth, I think something bad about somebody, and before I have a chance to even know that I thought something bad and ask forgiveness for it, I fall down dead. No matter what my life has been up to that point, because I have that one piece of unfinished business, I'm gone?'" Gene said he worried about things like that when he was seven or nine, "way younger than I needed to be worrying about such things."

By the time he got to high school, he had begun to read some theology and ask "some pretty embarrassing questions" of the deacons and elders in his church. The only answer he got was, "You know, there are some things you shouldn't ask."

Gene said that he figured there were some questions that probably didn't have answers, but he didn't think there were any questions that shouldn't be asked. So by the time he left for college, he was looking around, if not entirely intentionally, for a different religious home. The theology he had grown up with struck him as "white-knuckling it to the finish line." "One screw-up, one screw-up in timing, and you are a goner," he said. "When you compare what life must be like, lived in that atmosphere, versus, 'Oh my God, what a beautiful day—what can I do with it?'—well, one seems like death to me, and the other one seems like life. So it was at Sewanee that that Episcopal Church got a hold on me, and I was confirmed my senior year, and went off to seminary that fall."

Today, people who think they might be called to the priesthood in the Episcopal church go through a lengthy process of discerning whether the call is genuine and appropriate and then undertake study leading toward ordination, with the sponsorship of a parish and a local committee, approval of the local bishop, and oversight by the Commission on Ministry appointed for the diocese. The process is long and demanding, and many people drop out. But at the time when Gene felt the call to become a priest, the process was simply a matter to be handled by a candidate and his bishop.

At the time when Gene was a young man, nearly half of all clergy in the Episcopal Church had come from another denomination. And about half of those were from the Disciples of Christ. "I think part of the reason that could have happened is that the two share a sense of the centrality of the Eucharist," Gene reflected. That was an important reason for his personal decision, along with the richness and depth of the liturgy, and the long historical tradition of the Episcopal Church.

"I didn't even know who my bishop was!" he said. "That's because I'd never been an Episcopalian in Kentucky. I had been confirmed at college, in Tennessee, so I had to go home and introduce myself to the bishop and to a local rector." For Gene, the most difficult part had been to choose a denomination in which he felt comfortable. He knew that, given his family's history, it would be very difficult for his parents if he left the Disciples of Christ.

"It wasn't like I was becoming a Moonie or a Hare Krishna or something—that would have been a lot worse," he remarked, rolling his eyes, and adding that, for people back home in that very Protestant part of Kentucky, Catholicism was pretty far outside the range of acceptability, and Episcopalianism must have been not too far away. "It was pretty hard for them," he said, "but they got over it."

Gene's sense of his call to the priesthood was one thing that felt stable during a very turbulent time. He graduated from Sewanee and entered General Theological Seminary in New York City in the fall of 1969. "General," as it is informally called, is the oldest Episcopal theological seminary in the country. It was founded in 1817, in Chelsea, the heart of the garment district in Manhattan. When Gene talks about it, he gets a beatific look on his face. The boy from Kentucky clearly loved this venerable place of learning, its tradition-soaked atmosphere, and the oasis-like spot it created in the midst of a teeming city. "It's the best," he says, simply. "The seminary takes up an entire city block: three full sides are buildings, and inside there's 'the close,' an area that's all full of trees and grass and shuts out all the sounds of the city. You'd think you were somewhere in upstate New York. It's just spectacular."

Calm was a relative thing in the late 1960s and early 1970s: the entire country was torn apart over Vietnam. In the spring of Gene's first year at seminary, on April 30, 1970, President Nixon announced the invasion of Cambodia, causing widespread protests on college campuses throughout the United States. A few days later, on May 4, four students were killed when National Guardsmen opened fire on students at Kent State.

"There was this great divide at the seminary," Gene said. "There was one group who were always fighting about—or talking about—what kind of vestments should be worn and how many candles should be at the altar, and all this kind of froufrou, churchy stuff. And then there were others of us who were trying to figure out what it meant to be a priest in those turbulent times. And the two groups really never, never came together. It was a very fragmented community, reflective of what was happening in the country as a whole. I was in seminary with Jack Iker, the current bishop of Fort Worth, one of the most rabidly anti-women bishops. The current bishop of Pittsburgh, Bob Duncan, who has become a leader of arch-conservative Episcopalianism, was in seminary at General when I was."

He looked up and raised an eyebrow. "And we're still having trouble with those divisions. I've always been more on the sort of social gospel side of things, and agreeing with the idea that Jesus couldn't abide churchy types and spent all of his time outwardly-directed. I'm still trying to figure out what it means to be a priest in this world. It's pretty clear to me that it doesn't mean sitting around and playing church all day, in spite of the fact that I've spent most of my life serving the institution."

A lot of the people in Gene's group wound up leaving the institutional church entirely, or doing things like pastoral counseling or institutional chaplaincy. "We were all a bunch of hippies, you know," he admitted. "At Sewanee I was totally clean-cut, with short hair, and by the end of seminary I've got an Afro out to here . . . I actually did have hair then!" Gene's eyes twinkled behind his wire-rimmed glasses as he reached up to rub the thinning top of his head. "We were doing the marching against the Vietnam War and all that stuff, and this other bunch literally never left those four walls. And I have to say neither group much respected the other."

Not far away from General Theological Seminary, another movement was gathering momentum. On June 27, 1969, police had raided a gay bar in New York's Greenwich Village. This was nothing particularly new; the New York City police were adept at raiding the bars, often run or "protected" by the Mafia, and meting out particularly hard force to the more feminine-appearing gay patrons. But what happened that night in June was different: the patrons fought back, spilling out of the bar and into the street. When the police started to advance down the street in formation, arms linked, the gays retreated, but then doubled back around the block and came up on the rear of the police, throwing debris. At one point, the police were horrified to find themselves facing a chorus line of high-kicking patrons, singing gay-pride lyrics. The next evening, there were thousands of demonstrators protesting police brutality and passing out leaflets that read, "Get the Mafia and cops out of gay bars!" These "Stonewall Riots" are often considered the beginning of the organized gay liberation movement; later that summer the Gay Liberation Front was formed by a small group of activists.[2]

Gene Robinson entered seminary in September 1969, a couple of months after the Stonewall Riots, about which he says he was "frankly ignorant" at the time. He was not fighting for gay rights: he was waging an internal and very personal battle. During college, he had been depressed as a result of trying to repress his orientation. During seminary, he set about trying to overcome it.

Gene had grown up in the 1950s in a conservative, southern, Christian background where homosexuality was completely unacceptable. He is quick to point out how difficult it is for young people today to understand what life was like for homosexuals back then, not just in conservative places but everywhere.

"It's such a different world we live in today," he remarked at a meeting with students at Dartmouth College before his consecration as bishop. "As impatient as I can get with the progress we seem not to be making, the world has really changed a lot in that thirty, forty years. When I was young we didn't use or have the word 'gay' meaning what it means today. You would not label yourself as such, or self-identify that way, because there was no good that could come of it." The students were shocked when he described how many homosexuals used to commit suicide, or became alcoholics or drug addicts after being told repeatedly by society, family and religious leaders that they were unacceptable and disgusting in the eyes of God.

"Homosexuality was so abhorred that those who understood how condemned it was by God just did the logical thing and did themselves in. Suicide was something we thought the good homosexuals did." There was literally no other place to be than in the closet: everything in your life—work, relationships, community, family—was at risk if you were honest and open.

"Growing up, there was no one to say, 'Yes, I can be gay, and Christian, and a real contributor to the community, and so on,'" he explained to the students. "So at about the age of twelve or thirteen, I began doing what an awful lot of us of that era did: we started pretending to be someone we weren't. We learned to *pretend* to be developing in the ways other kids were, which leads to a kind of self-isolation and self-alienation that is pretty horrible."

When Gene was in seventh grade, he and some friends were looking at a copy of *Playboy* that one of them had secretly acquired. He vividly remembers two things about that experience: first, that the other boys were reacting to the picures very differently than he was, and secondly, that he had better keep his own feelings secret.[3]

In Rome during the summer of 1971, which Gene spent traveling in Europe.

The hiding, pretending, and repression continued through college, though Gene continued to fear that he might be gay. "I was so terrified that this might be true that I just completely buried it," he said. Although he never mentions that he considered suicide himself, he did become seriously depressed.

That pattern continued into his first year at seminary. "I got pretty sick," he said. "I got mono, and for a while I was in a pattern where I would stay up all night and sleep during the day, rarely going to classes, a kind of a downward spiral. For many years I was angry at my seminary for their inattention to someone who was so obviously depressed and having serious problems. I mean, if someone only shows up for exams and is never in chapel except in the middle of the night, wouldn't you ask if there was something wrong?"

Gene and Boo's wedding, Peterborough, New Hampshire, 1972.

Gene's memory of that first year at seminary is a little fuzzy, but after that his recall improves. "I think it's because that's when I began to both be clearer with myself that this wasn't going to go away, and to redouble my efforts to make it go away. I was able to admit a little more to myself my attraction to men, but I desperately wanted to get married and have kids. So I got into therapy to change myself. Lord knows I'd been praying about it long enough. Prayer hadn't seemed to solve the problem, so I thought maybe therapy would." For the next two years, Gene worked with a therapist twice a week.

After he completed two years of seminary, he spent the next summer traveling in Europe. When he came back, he did an intern year as a chaplain at the University of Vermont, and during that year he met and began dating a woman named Isabella Martin, known to all of her friends as "Boo." About a month into their relationship, Gene explained his background and his fears about his sexuality. He told her that his most significant previous relationships had been with men, but that he'd gotten himself into a place where he felt he could be in a good relationship with her. The following summer Gene did his second quarter of Clinical Pastoral Education at Mass General Hospital in Boston. The relationship continued to flourish, and Gene and Boo decided to marry. About a month before the marriage, Gene again became frightened that, as he puts it, "this thing would raise its ugly head some day, and cause her and me great pain." They talked about it, and decided that if that happened they could face it together.

He and Boo were married at the end of the summer, and the couple returned to New York for his final year of seminary at General. Gene's wife had been an education major at University of Vermont, and when the couple moved to New Jersey, she began commuting back into the city to the Lincoln Center campus of Fordham University, to continue her studies in education and political science.

The Rt. Rev. Barbara Harris, Bishop Suffragan of Massachusetts (retired), the first woman to be ordained bishop.

Chapter 3
Sisterhood

At General Theological Seminary, Gene had started with one class and graduated with another because he took a year off from school to be the chaplain at the University of Vermont. After graduation he took his first job, at Christ Church, Ridgewood, New Jersey, and about two weeks after arriving, on June 9, 1973, he was ordained a deacon at the cathedral in Newark: the final step before his ordination to the priesthood, which would take place six months later.

It was a sizeable church, a bit larger then than the seven to eight hundred parishioners it has now. At the time when Gene arrived, there were only two clergy—the main priest (generally called a "rector" in the Episcopal Church) and the curate (a former term for the associate or assistant rector), which was to be his position.

The Diocese of Newark, where Gene found himself, is arguably the most progressive diocese in the country. Marge Christie was very active there in the early movement for women's ordination and has continued to serve on many diocesan and national committees as an advocate for progressive church politics and the roles of women, both lay and ordained; at the 2004 conference "Justice IS Orthodox Theology," a gathering of Episcopalians committed to working for social justice, she was among the people receiving the "Justice Giants" award for her life of ministry on behalf of women in the church.

"Gene was, as he is now, a very outgoing, personable man," Marge recalled. "As curate, his main role was to work with young people. Gene took all of the other necessary roles as well, such as pastoral calling and preaching, but his main focus was with the teenagers."

In 1970 Marge was vice president of the Episcopal Church Women in the Diocese of Newark. She recalled, "The president, Peggy Gilman, was a wonderful mentor to me, and we were both ardently in favor of the ordination of women and at the same time ardently lay persons. Someone recently asked me, hadn't I ever wanted to be ordained? And I said, no, it never crossed my mind—it's not who I am, it's not the direction in which I see my life."

But other Episcopal women did see their lives going the way of the priesthood, and they were becoming increasingly frustrated about the church's refusal to move forward. In 1970, Peggy Gilman and Marge Christie co-authored a resolution to their diocesan convention that called for the acceptance of women as priests and bishops.

"It passed!" Marge remembered, with delight. "Not easily, but it passed. We did a lot of work. Those were the days of mimeograph and I can remember being up to my armpits in mimeograph ink—there was no way you could do anything without ending up with that ink all over you by the time you were finished. I used to see Gene face-to-face a good deal, because I was using the mimeograph machine at Christ Church, and cranking out statements like 'Stop baptizing women if you won't accept them as full members' and preparing them for distribution at Diocesan Convention. The next year one of the male clergy in the diocese introduced a resolution to rescind what we had done, but it was defeated. So Newark was clearly on record for its support of women's ordination."

Gene's class at General Theological Seminary, 1973. Gene is above and to the right of the Rt. Rev. Stephen Bayne, Bishop of Olympia 1947-1959, and a professor at General.

The history of the struggle for women's rights in the Episcopal Church is long and is in many ways parallel to that of gay rights. Although women priests and bishops have been parts of the Episcopalian landscape for quite a long time now and are accepted nearly everywhere in America, most other parts of the Anglican Communion have lagged far behind the North American churches on this issue. Certain provinces, including some in Africa, declared themselves "out of communion" with the American church as soon as it began to ordain women: the argument about non-straight-male priesthood actually has a long history. Most Episcopalians don't realize that at General Convention and at meetings of the House of Bishops of the Episcopal Church, there are current bishops who for many years have refused to share Communion with the majority, out of conviction that women's ordination is unacceptable, and also for fear that the Communion bread has been touched by the hand of a woman priest and is therefore tainted.

The "contamination language" that first began to be heard in connection with racism in the United States continued as a component of sexism and, of course, has been glaringly apparent in homophobic rhetoric.

The Episcopal Church is governed by two voting bodies: the House of Deputies, made up of elected lay and clergy deputies from each diocese (usually a state, or a large part of a state), and the House of Bishops. All binding votes to change the canons—the governing laws of the church—must be passed by both Houses at the meetings of the General Convention of the Episcopal Church, which take place every three years. The House of Bishops also meets twice yearly, and while they may call for study commissions, issue resolutions, and vote on issues, the bishops cannot vote, on their own, to change the rules of the church. Historically, of course, only men were legally allowed to be ordained as priests in the Episcopal Church. A majority vote in *both* the lay and clergy divisions of the House of Deputies, and in the House of Bishops at a General Convention, was required to change the canons to include the ordination of women.

As a natural progression of the civil rights struggle and women's movement, the issue of women's ordination in the Episcopal Church came to a head in the 1970s. At the 1970 General Convention, women were finally admitted as lay deputies after fighting for that right for more than half a century. It was also voted to allow women to be ordained as deacons: assistants who help with pastoral care, liturgy, and teaching, and who perform some priestly functions but do not have the authority to perform the sacraments such as marriage, baptism, or consecrating the bread and wine at Communion. Like priests, deacons also have the right to receive pensions from the Church Pension Fund.

When the 1970 Convention also took a vote on authorizing the ordination of women to the priesthood, however, the motion was approved by the lay delegates in the House of Deputies but narrowly defeated by the clergy delegates. After that vote, the House of Bishops referred women's ordination "for further study." The Episcopal Women's Caucus, an activist organization, was founded as a result of the intense frustration felt by women in the church: the issue of women's ordination had already been "discussed" within the church for more than half a century.

Meanwhile, women began to be ordained as deacons. One of the first of these female deacons was a young woman named Nancy Wittig who, like Gene, became a deacon in the Diocese of Newark. Nancy had graduated from Virginia Seminary in 1972, and her husband was headed for ordination in the Methodist Church. The Methodists were already ordaining women to be ministers, but Nancy was Episcopalian and wanted to stay in the denomination—even though, at the time, that raised some eyebrows since people expected her to be in the same church as her husband. She first tried to enter the ordination process in the Episcopal Diocese of Virginia, but that diocese had balked at allowing women to become deacons. When the couple moved to northern New Jersey, Nancy wrote to the bishop of the Diocese of Newark, George Rath, and was allowed to continue the process toward the diaconate. She took the National Canonical Exams the second year they were offered, and was ordained a deacon in the fall of 1973, a few months after Gene.

Gene and Nancy were about the same age, both were recently married, and they became good friends. They both had home lives that they were trying to manage in the midst of also being in the church and moving in the direction of ordained ministry. Once Gene had told her, "You know, all I do is spend my day off cleaning!" and added that he and his wife had struggled with this. Nancy had replied, "Yes, I do too, and I've decided just to forget cleaning!"

"These were typical struggles of young clergy and young family people," she recalled. "We were already feeling the pressure that the tradition puts on you, about putting all your energy into things outside your personal life, in terms of ministry."

She also remembered, laughing, that Gene had a full, curly head of hair back then. "Those were the days when African Americans were wearing Afros, and Gene fit right in, except for not being black! It was the seventies, and the energy and enthusiasm we had as young seminary graduates and ordinands was really very, very important. There was an idealism in the air that doesn't exist any longer."

In 1972, during one of their annual meetings, the House of Bishops had tested the women's issue with a vote, and come out 74 to 61 in favor of ordaining women priests, but at the next General Convention, at Louisville in 1973, the ordination of women again failed to pass in the House of Deputies because of a rule which said that if the votes of a diocesan delegation to the House of Deputies was split (such as a "yes" vote from the lay delegation and a "no" vote from the clergy), the vote of the entire delegation would be recorded as a "no." The lay deputies voted in the affirmative, but the clergy vote in Louisville was even more anti-women than at the previous convention.

The progressive women who made up the Episcopal Women's Caucus were, at that time, scattered all around the country. They included young activist women and recent seminary graduates like Nancy Wittig; Suzanne Hiatt, who had gone to the Episcopal Divinity School in Cambridge, Massachusetts and had also gotten a social work degree in community organizing; and Carter Heyward, who would become one of the best-known of the first women priests. Also included in the caucus were some of the original women "deaconesses"; lay women leaders like Marge Christie; several mothers who had already had some experience in the church; and some women who had graduated from Union Seminary and then married clergymen.

In Louisville, these women got together and experienced strong camaraderie, and discussed how they could organize and help one another. "It wasn't really an organized effort yet," Nancy remembered. "There were some of us who were young and shot our mouths off—and I was certainly one of them—who knew some of the history of Phyllis Edwards and Bishop Pike."

"Deaconesses" had in fact been allowed in the Episcopal Church since 1889, but did not have the same authority as male deacons, who were considered members of the clergy. Both the Episcopal Church and the Anglican Communion had stressed this point, that deaconesses were "not clergy," although they had gone back and forth on the question of whether the conferring of deaconess status by the laying-on of hands was, in fact, a conferring of "holy orders." Didn't the church believe that something incontrovertible happened—a permanent change ultimately emanating from God—when someone was ordained by laying-on of hands, rather than being simply appointed? That was the underlying question. In the 1960s this debate gathered steam. In 1964 the General Convention changed the canons to state that deaconesses are "ordered" (like male deacons, priests, and bishops) rather than "appointed." The following year, 1965, the controversial bishop James Pike of San Francisco recognized Deaconess Phyllis Edwards as a regular deacon, setting off tremendous protest within the hierarchy—and it would take five years of argument before the church voted to allow women deacons to be ordained with the same authority as their male counterparts.

"People in power don't easily give over some of that power and authority—it has to be taken," Nancy stated. "I felt that for women's ordination to succeed, it couldn't be a matter of one bishop and one woman. That had been the beginning of the end for Pike—the church pursued him and tried him for heresy—and I am convinced to this day that it was really over the ordination of Phyllis Edwards as a deacon. So the lesson to be learned from that was 'don't do anything by yourself, work as a community.'"

"In the church, women had been attacked and accused of not being able to do things on our own—the big joke, of course, was that we all got up and went to the bathroom together. But the Holy Spirit worked in the feminist movement to educate those of us in the church and outside of the church to realize that we would have to band together to survive. And we did."

In addition to the fight over women's ordination, the Louisville convention had also seen a tremendous struggle in the House of Deputies over the election of John Allin, a conservative, as Presiding Bishop of the Episcopal Church. Bishop Allin succeeded John E. Hines, who had been a staunch supporter of the church's role in the civil rights movement, and perhaps one of the most progressive Presiding Bishops in the church's history.

Allin's election may have been part of what Nancy Wittig called "the beginning of a backlash." It came from the more conservative priests and bishops who finally realized that women were serious about being ordained not just to the diaconate, but to the priesthood—and saw this as simply too much.

"Not only would they have to share," Nancy said, "but it had been a boys' club, with all that boys' clubs do: they had not only been the holders of all the power, but they had also been the holders of a lot of dirty secrets. And I suspect on a gut level that some of them knew that if women began to get wind of this, it was not going to be life as usual. All clubs that are just for the people in power are like that. And that was before we really knew how to talk about the power differentials between men and women emotionally, socially, politically, economically—all of that—and all of those things were mixed up in the argument over women's ordination."

Gene Robinson was ordained to the priesthood by George Rath, the Bishop of Newark, on December 15, 1973. One of Marge Christie's most vivid memories about Gene occurred in the kitchen of the Ridgewood parish on the day he was to be ordained priest. She asked him, "How does it feel for you to be ordained when the women you went to seminary with aren't allowed to be?" This is a memory that Gene shares. "She was all over me about that," he says.

"Now we laugh about that," Marge said, "but he told me later that I really gave him pause that day, and he almost thought about not going forward."

Frustrated and impatient, activists began to consider going outside the institutional procedures and engaging in acts of "disobedience." Just as Rosa Parks had refused to sit in the back of the bus and thereby changed the course of the civil rights struggle, activist women decided that radical action was necessary to break through the stalemate between the progressives and those who opposed women's ordination, or were afraid of the effect it might have on the church and the Anglican Communion and were continuing to recommend the shop-worn but effective delaying tactics of "further study and discussion."

Bishop Paul Moore, who would eventually become a central figure in the struggle for gay rights in the church, was then the bishop of New York (City). He was known to be sympathetic to the ordination of women, but was unwilling to go outside the canons of the church. In 1974, while he was presiding at the ordination of five male deacons to the priesthood, several women deacons also came forward and knelt at the altar rail, as a way of publicly protesting their exclusion from an equal right to be ordained. Bishop Moore did not ordain the women, but he was both shaken and moved by the experience. He later wrote that the women "looked up to me with what seemed the pain of a thousand years." He recognized that they were offering their vocation to their bishop—a person who knew each of them well. In his heart, he knew that each was more than qualified to be a priest, and that each one of them had suffered because her calling to the priesthood was not considered acceptable:

> My hands involuntarily began to move forward to lay upon their heads, upon their lives, the burden and glory of priesthood. I knew I could not; yet in that moment, as the congregation gasped and leaned forward in their seats, a holy silence made us all aware of the presence of God.[1]

Outside the cathedral, a siren suddenly blared, breaking the silence. Bishop Moore rose and began the Creed. The women got up, turned, and walked out of the church.

Then, on July 10, 1974, a group of bishops, priests, women deacons and lay people met in Philadelphia, for the purpose of planning an "illegal" ordination—an event which would surely rock the foundations of the church but which, they hoped, would propel the movement forward. Marge Christie had been on vacation for the entire month of July, and when she came back to New Jersey she read in the *New York Times* that eleven Episcopal women were going to be ordained in Philadelphia—and one of them was Nancy Wittig.

"I let out a whoop of joy," Marge said, "and dashed off a note to my bishop, George Rath, saying 'Congratulations, you're going to be ordaining Nancy!'" But the article hadn't said who the bishops would be, and Rath was definitely not among them. After the event Bishop Rath wrote back and said, "Sorry, not quite true."

Bishop Bob DeWitt, who would be one of the consecrating bishops in Philadelphia, called Paul Moore to tell him that the service was going to take place and that three of the women would be members of Moore's own diocese. Moore was astounded and asked DeWitt if he was crazy, but DeWitt said no, he had every intention of going through with it.

Nancy Wittig had asked Gene Robinson if he would serve as one of her presenters, or sponsors, at the ordination. "Much to my shame," Gene said, decades later, "she asked me to be one of her sponsors at that illegal ordination, and I declined. I still don't know exactly what I think about it. I certainly know that the ordination of women was the right thing, but at the time I couldn't see my way clear to do the illegal ordination because I cared about the canons."

Gene expressed understanding with the plight of bishops like Paul Moore, who were certainly in favor of the ordination of women but were unwilling to go outside the rules of the church. "It's a fear of throwing the baby out with the bathwater," Gene said. "You start dealing that loosely with the canons, and I don't know where it ends. When it came time for my own consecration, all these years later, I was approached about the fact that there were at least three bishops who were willing to consecrate me anyway if my election was not consented to at convention. And I would just have none of it. I felt that my election and consecration had to be done absolutely by the book—and of course that's part of what makes the opposition so angry is that it was absolutely legal, and they have no leg to stand on about that."

"But in terms of women's ordination . . . I've thought about it a lot. If I had it to do over again knowing what I know now, I don't know what I would say. I might be tempted to do it. I don't know when women's ordination would have come, legally, had they not done what they did. I'm not arguing with what they did. At the time, I just felt I couldn't support them that way."

Nancy says that she doesn't remember very much about the specifics of their conversation. "I guess my sense was that I was very fond of him; we'd been in some sort of deacon training together and saw each other fairly frequently. I think when he said no, I understood the possibility of our destroying any future ordination or ministry for ourselves in the Episcopal Church—because that was what we were putting on the line. I said over and over I was glad they didn't still burn women at the stake." She gave a brittle laugh. "So my sense is that I understood his decision. It would have been very dangerous for Gene. There was probably some initial disappointment, but there was also an understanding that he had more to lose than I did at that point. He was at a big church in Ridgewood, and my sense is that I felt he had probably made the right decision. It would have been very easy for those in power to chop off the heads right away of any of the young men who might be involved—and eventually, you know, it was the ordaining bishops who got the shellacking, because we women were invisible, or so they said—although it's amazing how many problems 'invisibility' ended up causing them."

On the evening of July 29, 1974, in Philadelphia, eleven women deacons were ordained to the priesthood by a resigned bishop and two retired bishops of the Episcopal Church. Nancy Wittig, who is not given to hyperbole, says simply, "It was wonderful. It was powerful. It was the right thing for the church to do."

The ordination took place at the Church of the Advocate, an Episcopal church in north Philadelphia that was a symbol for the African American community. Encouraged by their dynamic activist priest, the Rev. Paul Washington, parishioners had been regular participants in civil rights marches in the South, traveling there in buses provided by the church. "The choice of that church as the place for the ordination was all part of the idealism of those days," Nancy said. "We were still dealing with racism in its ugly form: Martin Luther King, Jr. had been assassinated not that many years before, and there was a sense that certainly I had, and I think most of us had, that engaging in these issues of social justice was where the church needed to be, because that's where the Gospel could be heard."

A young black woman named Barbara Harris was an active parishioner at the Church of the Advocate. She had been at the Selma March in 1965; in the coming years she would study for the priesthood and be ordained—and would eventually become the first female bishop in Christendom in 1989. On the night of the Philadelphia ordination, Barbara Harris carried the cross in the procession, followed by a delegation of supportive parish women and several dozen Episcopal clergy.

In her book *A Priest Forever,* written after the ordinations, Carter Heyward described that entrance into the cathedral:

> We began to move slowly in toward the nave. Smiling, we nodded in salutation to several scores of our brother and sister clergy, vested and ready to fall in with us . . . . Approaching the door to the nave, my eyes began to pop. There was no aisle, no room to walk. Well over a thousand, maybe two thousand people were pressed in close to participate. The path to the chancel cleared itself as we moved steadily, if timidly, on through jubilant hellos, waves, hugs, flash bulbs and television cameras moving with us . . . . When Bishops Corrigan, DeWitt, Ramos, and Welles stepped through the door, applause burst forth so resoundingly as to fill the space around and within us. The foundations of the Church seemed to tremble. I myself began to tremble. Tears ran down my cheeks as I turned to Betty Mosley, "Incredible!"[2]

That evening, at the prescribed moment during the formal ordination liturgy, people who objected were asked to come forward and speak. Five male priests rose to express their objections, naming impediments ranging from the canonical restrictions to the "perversion" implicit in attempting to ordain a woman. "The explosive nature of the objections that took place during the ordination brought to the surface, and let everybody know, the sort of stuff women had been hearing for years," Nancy said. "The guys got up and said it on camera. It wasn't just symbolic, it was real."

Carter Heyward described the moment of ordination as climactic, the culmination of everything that had happened in her life so far. Everyone was moved, perhaps most especially the older women who had lived their entire lives as unequal members of the church while serving it so faithfully. During the Communion that followed the ordinations, many people came to the altar rail to ask the new women priests for a blessing.

Nancy Wittig said, "We had begun to have an increasing sense of what the cost could be: we had figured we might get excommunicated, although that didn't often happen in the Episcopal Church. But mostly there was this sense of it being the right thing to do, and that we had been in tune with what the Spirit was doing, both in the church and in the world. So there was a sense of 'we did it': disbelief and joy. And afterwards we dispersed fairly quickly, because we knew there would be all kinds of reaction and the swarming by the media."

Following the ordination, reaction was immediate: criticism from conservative clergy, dismay and outrage among many bishops, joy among advocates for women's rights in the Episcopal Church and other denominations, and in the secular world. Although they hoped that their ordinations would be accepted and formally "regularized" by the bishops in their home dioceses, the "Philadelphia Eleven" realized that they might be barred from performing priestly duties, particularly from celebrating the Eucharist, and that is exactly what happened. Some of the women priests were prohibited from exercising any sacramental functions at all, others were asked to voluntarily refrain, and some were even prohibited from performing in their former roles as deacons.

"That was the summer we were impeaching Nixon, after all," Nancy Wittig noted. "My father, when I told him about this, said, 'Well, don't be disappointed, there's a lot of other things going on that may take center stage.' I said I wasn't anticipating being disappointed one way or the other, but that I thought this was something that was going to grab the headlines, and that turned out to be true. Various articles were being written all around the country, not just about those of us who were in Philadelphia, but about other women wanting to be ordained in the Episcopal Church, and in the other denominations."

Nancy recalled that there were a number of ex-Roman Catholics working as journalists in various venues, and that they sought out the women who had been ordained and spent hours talking to them. "Most were people who had thrown over the traces of stuff they felt they didn't believe any more, claiming they were Roman Catholics but didn't go to church. Their fascination with this whole story raised it up to a level we could never have reached on our own. It was a story that somehow caught people's interest and it was the journalists who took it up and kept bouncing it. I mean, every week, some big churchman-type with a lot of power had to open his newspaper and there was another interview with those damn women! So the story didn't die."

At an emergency meeting in Chicago in mid-August, the House of Bishops rejected the validity of the ordinations and filed ecclesiastical charges against the bishops who had performed them. In October, the House of Bishops reaffirmed its endorsement of ordaining women but voted almost unanimously not to act until the next General Convention.

"All of this was another lesson for me," Nancy Wittig said. "What I found so appalling at the time was that these were priests and bishops in the church . . . and *this* was what they thought of women? Who was in their congregation? Women! The blatant misogyny was devastating, because I realized, finally, that the word 'men' in the prayers and liturgy did not include me, and so it was important to say, 'men and women.' And I think that awakening was something that was happening around the world at that time as well."

The women and their supporters continued their activism and acts of disobedience. At the end of October, three of the women celebrated the Eucharist at New York City's Riverside Church (not an Episcopal Church) in defiance of Bishop Paul Moore's request that they not exercise their priestly functions within the Diocese of New York. Carter Heyward and Bishop Paul Moore, who had been good friends, were unable to reconcile their positions and became estranged. In November, Alison Cheek celebrated the Eucharist at St. Stephen's and the Incarnation in Washington, D.C., and in December, she and Carter Heyward celebrated at Christ Church in Oberlin, Ohio. The priests who had invited the women to Washington and Oberlin were the Rev. William Wendt and the Rev. Peter Beebe, who were later charged and tried for violating the canons of the church. The five-person ecclesiastical court voted 3 to 2 in finding Wendt guilty of "disobeying his bishop" and recommended that he be forbidden "to permit any person whose ordination is not in conformity with the canons of the Church to exercise his or her ministry in his parish." Beebe was also found guilty, but neither man was removed from his position.

It was both a difficult and exciting time because it forced many progressive people to confront the tension between their loyalty to the institution of the church and its rules on the one hand, and on the other, the progress toward full equality for women that they believed was right. Bishop Paul Moore wrote later:

> I thought to myself . . . that perhaps those errant friends of mine were right in ordaining the women. God knows, if it was these bishops against the former Bishop of Mississippi, the Bishop of the Central Gulf Coast, and the Bishop of Western New York, I would be on the side of the offending bishops. And yet they had made a mess. My own job would be harder; trying to avoid a trial in my own diocese and also trying to keep the "irregular" women priests from having illegal services in New

York. But this is the way progress comes, not smoothly through the system, but by disruption, reflection, and compromise. History moves in jerks, like an old steam engine pulling out of a station. Occasionally, I thought to myself, people fall down.[3]

But those who fell down continued to get up, and the struggle for women's rights in the church accelerated. At the beginning of 1975, Carter Heyward and Suzanne Hiatt were asked to become faculty members at Episcopal Divinity School in Cambridge, Massachusetts. In June of that year, the Anglican Church of Canada approved the ordination of women, and in July, the Church of England Synod approved women's ordination "in principle." In September, at the same Washington, D.C. church where Alison Cheek had celebrated the controversial Eucharist, four more women deacons were ordained priests by another retired bishop, causing the House of Bishops to censure all bishops who participated in the ordination of women.

The continual activism wore down some of the opponents, and inspired moderates with the courage to take a stand. At the General Convention of the Episcopal Church in 1976, a majority of both Houses finally voted to allow the ordination of women to the priesthood and episcopate (bishops). At the time, many detractors warned that this action would split the church. In addition to threats of general schism, some parishes withdrew from the Episcopal Church and formed "alternative" Anglican churches with a traditionalist view; other parishes withheld funds. Certain priests and bishops who remained within the Episcopal Church have fought against women's ordination to this day. Internationally, bishops in conservative parts of the world, such as Africa, declared themselves "out of communion" with the American church—a difference that has never been reconciled. However, over the past thirty years, the ordination of women has been widely accepted and supported throughout the Episcopal Church, as well as serving as an example for progress in other parts of the Anglican Communion and in other denominations. Once it voted to accept women's ordination, the church moved steadily forward in support of their ministries—which is not to say that the issue has gone away entirely, or that opposing forces have not continued to protest and attempt to block women serving as priests and bishops, contrary to official church policy. When Barbara Harris was ordained the first female bishop in the Anglican Communion, the same vicious rhetoric that was heard at the first ordinations of women priests surfaced again. But with each subsequent ordination, with the rapid increase of female students to 50 percent of the total in Episcopal seminaries, and with the growing recognition for the faithful and successful ministries of female clergy all over America, the protests lost more and more of their bite.

Geralyn Wolf, the present bishop of Rhode Island, who was also the first female dean of an Anglican cathedral, summed up those early years of women's priesthood very well when she remarked, "I've often thought of my ministry as a wedge plowing a field that is hard, leaving behind something softer that's ready for new life."

Dedicating the fireplace at The Sign of the Dove.

Chapter 4
Moving Toward Wholeness

The issue of women's ordination and the emerging consciousness about homosexuality in the church formed the general context of Gene's life in the church in the mid-1970s, but at the center were his new marriage and his work as a young priest. He served the Ridgewood parish for two years, from June 1, 1973 to June 1, 1975, as assistant to Rector Marshall Rice, and for the most part, he loved the experience of parish ministry and learned a great deal. A situation arose there, however, that proved to be very difficult for him.

About six months after his arrival in Ridgewood, Gene began to suspect, and then became convinced, that the rector was having an affair with the treasurer's wife. There were seven children involved between the two families. Gene finally confronted the rector, who admitted to the affair, but instead of having any resolving effect, this confession seemed to, as Gene said, "take some of the pressure off him." Having someone to talk to seemed somehow to enable the behavior.

"I was just out of seminary," Gene said, "and still wet behind the ears. You have to remember, this is long before we ever talked about clergy misconduct." He became so disturbed about the situation that eventually he went to George Rath, the bishop.

"I told him about the affair and that I needed some help, I didn't know how to handle this. I asked him to tell me what I needed to know or do. At which point he stood up, walked around to my chair, stood me up, walked me to the door, patted me on the back, and said, 'Don't worry, it happens all the time'— and showed me out of his office. I was a young priest, and this was the first time I'd ever gone to the bishop for anything!"

Gene was shocked and dumbfounded. "It just shows how behind we were on all those sexuality issues. He literally showed me the door. So I went back and just lived with it."

By the time he had been at the New Jersey parish a full year, he and his wife Boo began to talk about what they wanted to do next, and they made a decision to go back to New Hampshire, where Boo had grown up. "We'd both grown up on farms," Gene explained, "and we got this idea of buying part of her parents' farm and started to discuss how could make a living up there."

In September of 1974, Gene told the rector that he was going to leave. "It was as if up until then he had had someone to talk to—me—and when I said I was leaving he felt abandoned. Consequently he made life hell for me from that time until I left. It was just terrible. Fortunately, though, the parish was great. I think some people suspected what was going on—and then the whole thing blew up when the next assistant came in."

When Gene is asked if that early experience in Ridgewood soured him on parish ministry, the answer is an emphatic no. He says that while many people who are involved in non-parochial ministry have had bad experiences and feel negatively about parish ministry, that was not his feeling at all. He had particularly loved the parish and the people in it, and says he has nothing but fond memories of them. (In fact, one of the first things he did after his consecration as bishop was to return to Ridgewood for a reunion.) He and Boo had simply wanted to do something creative with the farm in New Hampshire so they could be there, in the country, and raise a family—and that meant leaving parish ministry, at least for a time.

So the couple moved north and established a horse farm and conference/retreat center, which they ran together. In the wintertime, it was called The Sign of the Dove Retreat Center, and in the summertime it was (and still is) called The Pony Farm, which Gene's wife ran as a horse camp for children.

"I think I had led one retreat in my life before coming to New Hampshire," Gene said, grinning sheepishly. "It was true that I was very interested in education, youth ministry, and pretty good at programming and designing things. I'd had some specialized training in leading workshops and had some skills, but no experience. None. But never mind—we incorporated The Sign of the Dove over Christmas vacation, 1974–75. My subsequent retreat work was always very much focused on congregations. I'd go into a congregation, work with them, set goals for a retreat, custom design it, do follow up—I always felt my ministry was in the service of congregations."

At first, the couple had to run both the riding camp and the retreat center out of their house. The retreat participants would arrive on a Friday night and the retreat would run until Sunday. Gene and Boo did all the cooking and all the programming. At that time, the hills of northern New England were still filled with hippies tucked away on their small plots of lands, "doing their own thing," which could be anything from "living off the land" to carpentry and weaving. Many years later, their daughter Ella said that her parents had been "little hippies—they did everything themselves, they had built this big beautiful log cabin, with trees from the forest."

"We were young and crazy and committed," Gene said, "and we sort of made up the difference with our sweat labor. I remember being in the lawyer's office incorporating the riding center and the retreat center. And the lawyer asked, 'How many years do you think it will take before you turn a profit?' And we were dumbfounded and said, 'What do you mean, how many years? We have to turn a profit this year, right now!' And he was like, 'Ohmigod—sign here.' The things we didn't know!"

So they ran the retreat center in their home while Gene raised money to build a building. The diocese was supportive, but not with money: at the time, Gene said, conference centers were going out of business right and left. "To my credit, I did do some checking as to why, so I made some pretty good choices about how big this should be and so forth."

In retrospect, he thinks that people who had money saw an idealistic kid who had a dream, and got a kick out of seeing if he could do it. Ultimately, half of the money, over a period of time, was contributed by Ned Johnson of Fidelity Investments. Johnson's daughter had come to the riding camp, and he thought what it had done for her was spectacular and he wanted to help.

The Sign of the Dove Retreat Center (Temple, New Hampshire).

Suddenly, however, the project ran into a huge problem.

"Around the first Friday in May, 1977—we were a month away from having the building finished and moving into it for the first time, I'll never forget it—one of my contractors came to me with a $15,000 overrun. That was a huge amount of money in 1977, and amounted to roughly 10 percent of the project. So I was just stunned. We had figured this down to the last dollar. We didn't have $15,000, and if we didn't get this work done, we couldn't open the camp."

That Sunday, Gene was scheduled to preach at the Church of the Good Shepherd in Nashua, New Hampshire. "One of lessons that day was 'consider the lilies of the field': how they 'toil not,' but God takes care of them. So I kind of preached to myself, and got myself calmed down, told myself to trust in God and so forth. And then, that Monday, the other contractors heard what had happened and it turned out that they were experiencing overruns too, and so they came to me—and suddenly the $15,000 went to $45,000. So it was just huge. I was just in a dither."

Leading a discussion during a retreat at The Sign of the Dove.

Gene couldn't figure out what to do, so he finally called Ned Johnson—their relationship was close enough that he could call him up at Fidelity—and said, "Ned, I'm not calling to ask you for more money, but you obviously know more about money than I do because you have a lot of it, and you manage other people's money, and I'm just looking for some advice. What do I do?"

So Ned asked, "What are you doing for lunch tomorrow?" Gene says he was thinking, "Umm, going hungry?" but instead said he wasn't doing anything in particular.

"Okay," Ned said, "I'd like to come up. I want to bring my financial person, and look over your books, and also bring my building guy and make sure you're getting what you're paying for."

Gene said, "So the building guy crawled into every nook and cranny and talked to the workmen and looked at everything, and the finance guy went over all the books while Ned and I chatted and had a little lunch, and then he said to the guys, 'So, what do you think?' And the building guy said, 'This is an incredible building. I've never seen such quality workmanship, I can't believe he's getting it for this amount of money, even with the overruns,' and the finance guy said, 'I wish clergy everywhere could have this kind of business sense . . .'"

Ned shook his head and thanked Gene and Boo for a lovely lunch, and walked off toward his car. Gene didn't know what to think. He followed him and said, "Uhh, Ned, what am I to take from this . . . ?"

And Ned said, "Oh, we'll finish the building. I know you'll need $10,000 by Friday to make payroll, and we'll take care of the rest of the $45,000."

Gene sat up the entire night. "I was so excited," he said. "I'd just preached on this idea that you have to just keep going, that God is with us and so on—and over the next few days I'd had this profound experience of it. It was just an amazing thing. Although I must say, that whole operation was graced in those kinds of ways."

Before that time, Ned Johnson had already contributed $30,000. Gene said he is such a shy and self-effacing person that he wouldn't even come to the building dedication because he was afraid Gene would single him out to thank him.

Randy Dales, the most senior priest currently active in the Diocese of New Hampshire, recalled that he had met Gene Robinson fairly early in the time he was in New Hampshire, after he and Boo had opened The Sign of the Dove. Dales was the chaplain at the Holderness School, an Episcopal prep school in central New Hampshire, when Gene moved into the diocese, and the two quickly became friends. In the 1970s, the Rev. Dales took youth groups to The Sign of the Dove for retreats.

"The retreats were fun and appropriate for youth," he recalled, "with some serious talking about faith and what it means in your life, and Gene was very skilled as a facilitator of these things. It was a wonderful addition to the diocese, and many, many congregations utilized it."

While the ordination of women was the big issue in the Episcopal Church in the 1970s, early in that decade the church had also begun talking about homosexuality. In his book of reflections on that time, Bishop Paul Moore summed up the connection between the two movements in a succinct and prescient statement:

> The women's movement, as so often happens with movements indirectly nurtured by Christian thought and experience, had come back fresh and vigorous to challenge the very church from whose teaching it was born. This movement for women's identity had encouraged an even more complicated struggle, that of gay liberation. Nor can these movements be separated from the current conflict over abortion, or indeed, from our whole understanding of human sexuality.[1]

In October 1974, four months after the "irregular" ordinations of the eleven women in Philadelphia, a gay Episcopalian English professor named Louie Crew started a newsletter called *Integrity: Gay Episcopal Forum* out of the small town of Fort Valley, Georgia. Very soon thereafter, he was contacted by two men from Chicago, one a priest named Tyndale and the other a lay person named Wickliff—an interesting coincidence for Louie, since both were historic names from the British Reformation. It was known that there were a lot of gay clergy in the Diocese of Chicago, and as it turned out there were enough to organize and start a movement, together with their lay colleagues. (Louie Crew quotes a popular joke from that time: "How many straight priests in the Diocese of Chicago does it take to put in a light bulb? Answer: Both of them.") The Chicago chapter of Integrity became the first in the country.

Ellen Barrett, a candidate for priesthood in New York City, and James Wickliff served as Integrity's first co-presidents. Before the first national meeting, Louie Crew drafted Integrity's first constitution "to ensure that we moved towards gender justice."

In 1975, members of the young organization met with the Standing Commission on Human Affairs of the Episcopal Church and proposed wording for a resolution about the church's responsibility toward homosexuals, stating that "homosexual persons are children of God who have a full and equal claim with all other persons upon the love, acceptance, and pastoral concern and care of the Church."[2] The next year, 1976, at General Convention, a resolution bearing that phrasing was passed. That same General Convention also finally approved the ordination of women, to begin in January 1977, and it retroactively "regularized" the ordinations of women which had taken place in Philadelphia and Washington, D.C.

In January 1977, Bishop Paul Moore ordained Ellen Barrett to the priesthood. Barrett was an avowed, non-celibate lesbian whom Moore had ordained as a deacon in 1975. Although her ordination to the diaconate had drawn some notice, it hadn't been a major media event. Once women won the right to be legally ordained as priests, her rector, the Rev. Bob Weeks, began pressing Moore to ordain her. Moore was worried about potential repercussions, and he stalled for time. He later wrote about his conversations with the Rev. Weeks. "Bishop," Weeks had said, "I never thought I would hear you, of all people, sounding like those white Southerners, sounding like a . . . a . . . a gradualist!" Moore noted that this had been the worst epithet you could earn in the sixties, when the rallying call of the civil rights movement was "Justice delayed is justice denied."[3]

Everyone knew that there had always been closeted homosexuals in the clergy. What was different about Ellen Barrett was that she admitted her orientation openly and did not claim to be celibate. When she had been a candidate for the diaconate, the Rev. Weeks had asked, pointedly, "Bishop Moore, are you going to keep someone from being a deacon just because she is honest?" Moore admitted that even after he ordained Ellen a deacon, he was haunted for the next three years by that question, knowing he'd someday have to confront it in its next form: "Are you going to keep someone from being a priest just because she is honest?"

The question finally did come up, as Moore had predicted, around the ordination of Ellen Barrett to the priesthood. Moore later wrote that both he and all the involved organizations who needed to give their assent to a proposed ordination— the Commission on Ministry in the Diocese of New York, the diocesan Standing Committee, and General Theological Seminary—found Ellen's life to be "spiritually, emotionally and morally blameless" and felt that she was qualified for ordination. At one point, he asked the Standing Committee whether or not he should withdraw from this ordination. "No," they said, and urged him to continue.[4]

During Barrett's ordination, Episcopal priest James Wattley objected verbally, calling it "a travesty and a scandal." Letters of reaction from bishops and other clergy, quoted in the *Integrity: Gay Episcopal Forum* in 1977 following the ordination, are eerily similar to what would be said about Gene Robinson's ordination as bishop nearly thirty years later. For example, the Rt. Rev. William C. Frey, bishop of Colorado, referred to Bishop Moore's action as "totally irresponsible" and said, "You cannot imagine the tremendous harm it will do to the rest of the church. At the very least, please show consideration for those homosexuals who are seeking more positive solutions to their difficulties, and who will be hurt by the inevitable reaction to this ordination." The Rt. Rev. James Brown of Louisiana wrote, "Insofar as ministers of the church are to be examples in personal as well as in public life, I cannot condone clerical lifestyles and sexual mores repugnant to Holy Scripture." Two Texas bishops called the ordination "a denial of Christian morality," and the Rt. Rev. William Evan Sanders, Bishop of Tennessee, said "I am in support of the ordination of women to the priesthood and the episcopate as they qualify. But I am opposed to the acceptance of homosexuals and I do not feel that a person who is dealing with that problem is a person who has the maturity and the stability to serve in the priesthood of the church."[5]

The Rev. Ellen Barrett responded later that month, saying, "If the church is to be a house of prayer for all people, then gay people belong in it, too. And if love is what the church is all about—and it says it is—then indisputably I belong in there, too, because my way of living is a way of loving . . . . It's important I was ordained as a lesbian. Gay people should have a place in the ministry as they should in the rest of the world. But I have a hard time grasping that, to a lot of the world, it's the only important thing about me—it's not! I'm a lot more than that. The changes in the church have always been to broaden and include—not cut off and turn away . . . . I care less about the church as a structure than as a community of Christians. I think that community is founded on love, and I think that love belongs in everyone—including women and lesbians."[6]

The reaction was not confined to discussion within Episcopal Church circles. In May, the Rev. James Brown, Vicar of St. John the Evangelist in San Francisco, and a seminary student named Douglas McKinney were attacked and beaten by angry youths yelling "f***ing faggots" in the Castro gay village section of the city.[7]

When the House of Bishops met in Port St. Lucie, Florida nine months later, a majority of the bishops remained against the ordination of lesbians and gays. They passed a resolution condemning homosexuality as unbiblical and asserted that the church "is right to confine its nuptial blessing exclusively to heterosexual marriage."

Even so, the bishops decided not to censure Bishop Moore for ordaining an avowed lesbian. As time went on, Moore became emboldened by the controversy. He eventually became a well-known champion of gay and lesbian rights, speaking out often and testifying for more governmental and city help for homosexual citizens of New York City, especially as the AIDS crisis worsened in the 1980s.[8]

At the Florida meeting, one of the bishops' other actions was to adopt a "conscience clause" permitting bishops to refuse to ordain women. That same conscience clause was used, ironically, in subsequent years, as progressive bishops quietly began to ordain people who were admitted lesbians and gays.

In the fall of 1977, Ellen Barrett moved to California from New York in order to continue her doctoral studies at Berkeley. Bishop C. Kilmer Myers stated that he wished to license her as a priest in his diocese. Myers was warned that he would be forced to resign or retire if he went ahead, but he persisted, and the license became official on October 19, 1977.

Tension and violence over homosexuality continued to increase in San Francisco. Another priest was attacked in October 1977; there were fire bombings in gay sections of the city; and a city gardener, Robert Hillsborough, was called "faggot" and murdered. His funeral took place at the city cathedral and was attended by 3,000 people.

On November 27, 1978, gay San Francisco City Supervisor Harvey Milk was assassinated, along with Mayor George Moscone, shortly after the enactment of a gay rights bill that Milk had sponsored. The murderer was Dan White, another city supervisor who had just resigned in opposition to that bill. White, who had clearly planned the murders and had viciously fired a second round of ammunition, pointblank, into Milk's head after shooting him in the chest, was convicted of voluntary manslaughter on the grounds of "diminished responsibility." His defense included the argument that White had eaten a large quantity of junk food on the day of the murders. In May 1979, he received a sentence of seven years and eight months, touching off the White Nights Riots through which the out-raged gay community protested the leniency of the sentence. (White only served one year of his parole and then committed suicide.) Harvey Milk is considered a martyr of the gay rights movement; over 100,000 gay civil rights activists marched on Washington, D.C. later that year, chanting, "Harvey Milk lives!" He had foreseen the possibility of assassination and stated, on an audio tape he had recorded in case of his unnatural death, "If a bullet should enter my brain, let that bullet destroy every closet door in the country."

At the General Convention of the Episcopal Church in Denver in 1979, a res-olution was passed stating: "We reaffirm the traditional teaching of the Church on marriage, marital fidelity, and sexual chastity as the standard of Christian sexual morality. Candidates for ordination are expected to conform to this standard. Therefore, we believe it is not appropriate for this Church to ordain a practicing homosexual, or any person who is engaged in heterosexual relations outside of mar-riage." But more than twenty bishops signed a statement disassociating themselves with that resolution, saying, "To do so would be to abrogate our responsibility of apostolic leadership and prophetic witness to the flock of Christ committed in our charge; and it would involve a repudiation of our ordination vows as bishops, in the words of the new prayer book, 'boldly [to] proclaim and interpret the Gospel of Christ, enlightening the minds and stirring up the conscience of [our] people, and to encourage and support all baptized persons in their gifts and ministries . . . and to celebrate with them the sacraments of our redemption'; or in the words of the old [Prayer Book], 'to be to the flock of Christ a shepherd, not a wolf.' Our appeal is to the conscience and to God. Amen."

"It seems to me," Louie Crew said later, "that 1979 was the high water mark of homophobia. But the tide almost immediately started to ebb. The General Convention had said that gay and lesbian ordinations shouldn't proceed. 'We will do it anyway,' two dozen conscientious bishops said in reply. The House knew it could not muster enough votes to prevent the dissent. Lesbians and gays and many straights who recognized our spiritual gifts then took risks to try to ensure the tide never again turned against us."

During these years, Gene Robinson was also working in the area of human sexu-ality and the church. In 1977 he worked with a committee in the New Hampshire Diocese to study human sexuality and co-authored a small manual on the subject. Gene said that he was doing this work at the time "not as a gay man, not as a spokesman, but as a priest, as a Christian." But it was around that time when Gene began to connect the church's responsibility toward gay and lesbian people with his own, as yet not-openly-confronted orientation. He himself was reading a lot, and still feels that some of the best things written about Christianity and homosexuality came from that period, such as *The New Testament and Homosexuality* by Paul Scroggs, a professor at Trinity College in Hartford, which Gene says he still gives to people.

At the time we had this conversation, I was in Gene's office in the headquarters of the Diocese of New Hampshire. He jumped out of his chair and scanned the bookshelves, and came back carrying a thin book with a purple cover, which he handed to me.

"Well, you know, the book that changed my life—is this one." The jovial mood in the room suddenly changed; Gene became very serious as he handed me the book. It was John Fortunato's *Embracing the Exile: Healing Journeys for Gay Christians*, written in 1982. "I think it's out of print now," Gene said. "I read that book when I was still married and living at the farm, and I knew after reading it . . . " He shook his head. "This unlocked the world for me."

I opened the book and looked through. "It's all underlined," I remarked, before handing it back to him.

"Oh, I'm sure it is," he said as he thumbed through the pages with a poignant, somewhat faraway smile. He looked up: "This is a guy who, twenty years before any of the rest of us, was in a same-sex relationship, had it blessed at a church in Washington, D.C., the press went nuts, it was a big media event. He was a therapist, and also a deeply religious man. I got to meet him—I brought him here to speak to our Provincial Convocation in 1987. But later he almost became a recluse. After all the media attention their relationship came apart; the experience almost destroyed him." (After the breakup, John Fortunato entered a monastic community for a number of years. He later received a doctorate and several graduate degrees in pastoral psychology and divinity, and has had a long career as a psychologist in the Midwest, now working primarily with the poor.[9])

"This book came out of his work as a therapist with many gay people," Gene continued. "It's an incredible sort of double-helix that's the best weaving-together of spirituality and psychology I've ever seen."

Fortunato's book speaks of "exile" as the place where so many gay Christians find themselves. To be both gay and Christian, accepting and rejoicing in both one's homosexuality and Christianity as gifts from God, "is to place ourselves on the outskirts of the community we most care about," he wrote. He said that "embracing the exile" demands not only the belief that living on the fringes of the spiritual community can be *endured* by gay Christians, but that "being banished can be viewed as an incredible spiritual opportunity" to learn to "love anyway":[10]

> For gay Christians to be able to love, give, and find meaning in a world that rejects and isolates them, the cruel gash separating their sexuality from their spirituality must be healed. Their freedom to love and give in a hostile world hinges upon their coming to believe in their wholeness and in their having a rightful place in God's universe.[11]

"Here," Gene said, finding the section he had been looking for. "Let me read this to you." He read, and I listened, with growing emotion. The passage was John Fortunato's description of his own, intensely powerful mystical vision of a conversation with God: the moment when he had finally realized that, as a gay man, he was acceptable to the God he loved and whose love he desperately wanted to know, feel, and believe in.

In this vision, Fortunato expresses to God his doubts and fears that the Christians who call homosexuality an abomination might be right. God gently answers, "How can love be wrong? It all comes from Me," and goes on to dispel Fortunato's fears about his own wholeness and worthiness as a person capable of giving and receiving love. Fortunato is overwhelmed, and asks, "But what am I supposed to do about 'them'—the people who hate and vilify me?" And God answers, "I have given you my gifts; I've given you my light; love them anyway."

Gene then turned to the book's epilogue, titled "Into the Lion's Den," in which Fortunato revisits this vision and asks, "How? How do I 'love them anyway'?"

> "You begin by just being who you are," God said, "a loving, caring, whole person, created in my image, whose special light of love happens to shine on men, as I intended for you."
>
> "Is that all?" I asked, fearfully.
>
> God shook his head. "No. You must also speak your pain and affirm the wholeness I have made you to be when they assail it. You must protest when you are treated as less than a child of mine."
>
> "Is there more?" I asked.
>
> "Yes," God said gently. "And this is the hardest part of all. You must go out and teach them. Help them to know of their dependence on me for all that they really are, and of their helplessness without me. Teach them that their ways are not my ways, and that the world of their imagining is not the world I have made. Help them to see that all Creation is One, as I am One, and that all I create, I redeem. And assure them by word, and work, and example, that my love is boundless, and that I am with them always."

Fortunato protests, saying, "They won't listen to me, they'll laugh at me and persecute me." And God's "radiant face" becomes very sad, and he answers, "I know. How well I know."

That was the breakthrough. Fortunato writes:

> Now I knew. Now I understood. And it was as though large chunks of who I had been, began falling away, tumbling through time and space and eternity. I just let them all fall. No fear now, no resistance, no sense of loss. All that was dropping away. It was unnecessary now, extraneous.
>
> I began to feel light and warm. Energy began to surge through my whole being, and widen me as though I were a rusty old turbine that had been charged up and was starting to hum.
>
> Then two strong, motherly arms reached out and drew me close to the bosom of all that is, and I was just there, just being, enveloped in being.
>
> And we wept.
>
> For joy.

When Gene finished reading, I wiped my eyes, and looked at him in silence. He nodded, solemnly. "That was it; this was the pivotal point in my journey," he said. "That unlocked the rest of my life. Pure and simple. Literally, my life changed upon finishing that book."

Up until that point, Gene had wanted to believe the Good News—that he was actually loved by God, just as he was—but after reading the book, he actually did believe it. He finally had the courage and faith necessary to accept his orientation, to reconcile it with his spirituality, and move forward with those two truths at the center of his identity.

Gene describes his marriage to Boo as "wonderful in almost every way," with the couple's two daughters, born in 1977 and 1981, at the heart of their relationship. Gene had always wanted to be a parent. "I used to babysit all the time," he said. "I love infants; I always have. They probably just bring out my maternal instincts." When asked why he loves babies so much, he laughed and joked, "I don't know—they don't talk back to you!" Then he grew more reflective. "One of the things I love about the Episcopal Church is that we baptize babies. I had grown up in a church where you had to come of age first—though how anyone who's twelve has 'come of age,' I don't know. The reason infant baptism is such a wonderful model is that baptism is a way of affirming that God offers this love without our doing anything in return, and with an infant, they are clearly incapable of doing anything to deserve this love. The same is true for those of us who are fifty-eight as well, but it's very clear that an infant can't know enough, do enough, say enough to deserve this. That's part of why I love babies. They're just there, and they're so open and everything."

Gene said that Jamee and Ella were very easy children. He took to being a parent instantly, and did most of the younger child care. "Boo is absolutely unbelievable with middle school and teenagers," he said. "She's just astounding. She's never been much of a baby person, though, so I did more of the early stuff."

But in spite of the happiness of their family and the success of the retreat center, problems began to surface after about thirteen years of marriage. Gene's growing acceptance of his orientation began to make it clear to him and to his wife that he couldn't suppress who he really was much longer. They entered therapy around 1982 or 1983 and made the decision to separate in 1986.

"We felt that Boo deserved a relationship with a man who could love her in a heterosexual way," he said, "and I deserved to see if I could make my life with another man as well. There was no one else involved for either one of us: we just wanted to do the right thing for each other."

Letting people know was difficult because Gene and Boo knew there would be shock and sadness. "The fact of the matter was," Gene explained, "our marriage was thought to be the model, so we couldn't get away with, 'Oh, we just drifted apart,' or, 'We had irreconcilable differences,' or something like that. Nothing short of the truth would work, not that we were considering anything else. But the reason had to be something big. So we were open with our friends, but I guess I just sort of told people on a need-to-know basis. I didn't take out a full page ad in the local papers—it was sort of a gradual process." When they were going to divorce, it became clear that they were going to have to separate themselves from their joint business, so Gene sold out to Boo.

Among Gene's old friends, both Deane Root and Marge Christie were surprised by the news. "The possibility never entered my head," Marge admitted. "But I think there are a lot of people around like me: my daughter is a lesbian and I didn't catch on to that for a lot longer than I should have. Those kinds of questions weren't on my radar."

Gene and Boo had married in the sight of God, and they decided to end their marriage in the same way. Whenever Gene tells the story, which he has often done, it is with obvious emotion. "We did something that was one of the most healing things in my whole life: we went back to church to end our marriage. We had taken those vows in front of God, and we didn't want to sneak away as if they had just melted or something. So we took a priest with us—a priest here in the diocese—to the judge's chambers for the final divorce decree, and then we went immediately back to his church, in Manchester, and celebrated the Eucharist together. In the context of that we asked forgiveness for whatever ways in which we had hurt one another, and we pledged ourselves to the joint raising of our children. We gave each other our wedding rings back, that symbol of the wedding vows that we no longer held each other to, and we cried a lot, and then we had Communion. It was just an—astounding moment."

Gene's former wife remarried about a year and a half later, and she continues to be his friend. (Many years later, their daughter Ella read a statement of support written by her mother at the Minneapolis General Convention of the Episcopal Church, which voted whether or not to approve Gene's election in New Hampshire. Boo was also one of the presenters—the lay witnesses chosen from among a new bishop's closest friends and family—at his consecration as bishop.)

When Gene moved out of the New Hampshire farmhouse, his daughters were four and eight. One of his greatest sadnesses is that Ella, the younger child, can't remember him living in the same house with her at the farm. "Given the fact that I did 70 to 80 percent of her care, it's just so sad. I know it became part of her, but there was a time when it really bothered her that she couldn't remember it."

Gene says he decided early on to be completely honest with his family. "One of the things that makes families crazy, and hurtful, and dysfunctional is when secrets are kept, and I was done with secrets," he said. He was also determined to let his children know that the break-up of the marriage was not their fault, as children sometimes believe. Taking Jamee, the older of the two, aside, he asked her if she knew what gay and lesbian people were. "She answered, 'Oh, yeah, most boys like girls, and most girls like boys, but some boys like boys and some girls like girls.'" Gene felt he couldn't improve on that. So he explained, "That's right. And Daddy's learned that I'm one of those boys that like boys."

At the time, he couldn't find any children's books that showed gay couples in family situations. Finally he got a book from Denmark, called something like *Jim and Joe Love Sally*, which depicted a gay man and his partner and a daughter living as a family, where the mother would come to visit. He read that book to his daughter Jamee one evening before her bedtime. "That night she called in to me from her bedroom, as we were going to sleep, 'Daddy, I hope you can find a Joe someday.'" Together, Gene and Jamee later explained the situation to her sister, Ella, who was four.

Gene says that one of the strangest questions he gets asked is when people sometimes wonder if he regrets having gotten married. "That is inextricably tied up with having children," he says. "And since I cannot imagine my life without Jamee and Ella, it's just a completely irrelevant question for me. And I don't regret having been married to Boo, either, even if there had not been children. It's just a part of my journey, and why would I possibly regret that?"

"On the other hand, for some seventeen-year-old kid who is coming to know himself as gay, I would like for him to be relieved of the pressure and the societal pressure of having to get married because, while I don't regret it, there was a self-alienating pain about all that as well. But I could no more wish that I didn't know Jamee and Ella than fly to the moon."

Still, the period following the divorce was fraught with huge uncertainties, loneliness, and difficulty. "I'd go to bed feeling that the two things I had left were my integrity and God," Gene says. "I thought my ordained life in the church might be over. But I knew that my integrity was worth that risk. What I learned in the dark days following my separation was that if you've got your integrity and you've got God, it's just enough. It's nice to have more. But if you've only got that much, it's enough. And nobody can take that away from you."

"I've never feared losing God since then," he says, simply. "It makes all the difference in the world."

The Rt. Rev. Douglas Theuner, the eighth bishop of New Hampshire.

Chapter 5
Preparation and Call

In one of our first interviews, shortly after his election, I asked Gene, "Why you, why now, why New Hampshire?" He immediately responded, "There are three answers to those questions: Doug Theuner, Doug Theuner, Doug Theuner."

"Gene seems to think that he placed his life in my hands," said Bishop Theuner, Gene's boss for seventeen years and his predecessor as bishop of New Hampshire. "He's said that publicly, he said that at his institution as bishop. I never really felt that way. I never thought it was that big a deal, but it was for him."

It's typical of Doug, as he is affectionately called by nearly everyone in the diocese, to be offhand about his own role in the events that led to the consecration of the first openly gay bishop in a small state known both for its conservatism and fierce sense of individual privacy. "I just did what felt like the right thing," is a response one hears from him quite often, accompanied by a little shrug. Yet anyone who has known Bishop Douglas Theuner, heard him preach or celebrate Communion, felt the force of his personality, watched him fearlessly take a vanguard position on issues others refused to touch, would recognize the essential truth in his successor's assessment.

"Douglas, our Bishop," named in the prayers for the clergy repeated in New Hampshire Episcopal churches each Sunday, became loved and respected by diocesan parishioners through the context of regular bishop's visitations to each of the forty-nine parishes scattered throughout the mostly rural and rugged state. It was always immediately apparent that the bishop had arrived: his booming voice usually preceded the appearance of his luxuriant head of hair (the retired Suffragan Bishop of Massachusetts, Barbara Harris, at a celebration of Bishop Theuner's ministry, quipped: "He has a better hair-do than I do!"). He's a tall, handsome man with a charismatic presence, distinguished and personable, authoritative and energetic, with a prodigious intellect matched in size by his enormous sense of humor.

Gene Robinson was right when he remarked, "Doug takes the office of bishop seriously, but not himself." I was astounded to hear some close associates greet him with a jocular "Hello, Your Eminence!" when he walked into a meeting. The bishop didn't miss a beat but came back with a big laugh and fast rejoinder of his own. By the same token, throughout his eighteen-year episcopate, he commanded enormous respect from clergy and lay people as well as policy-makers in the state, and became a senior figure among his bishop colleagues.

On this particular morning, six months after his retirement, we awaited Doug not in a sanctuary before a special service, but in a dockside café on Lake Sunapee in central New Hampshire, where the Theuners have a summer residence. It was strange to see him stride through the café door, ducking a little, in a brown t-shirt, shorts and sandals rather than ecclesiastical robes and mitre, crook in hand, or at least the usual dark suit, purple shirt and gold cross he'd wear to a vestry meeting, but the resonant voice and cheerful face were absolutely familiar.

"Hello! Been waiting long?" He went over to the counter, greeted the proprietor familiarly, and poured himself a cup of coffee from the waiting carafes. "Help yourselves! Want a muffin? They're good here." He gestured to us with a sweeping hand. "Come on, we can sit outside." We followed him out to a roofed platform behind the café where there were a number of empty picnic tables. A gentle breeze blew off the water, where boats were coming into Sunapee Harbor on an early run to fetch a bottle of milk or a newspaper.

"I think what Gene means," Doug said, settling down with his coffee and fixing us with his direct gaze, "is that he put a lot of trust in me. Now you can't avoid learning from somebody—anybody—who puts their trust in you. You may not learn facts, or skills, but you *grow* through that sense of people putting their faith in you."

Douglas Theuner and Gene Robinson worked together for a long, fruitful time, and certainly both learned from each other. Gene jokes about it, often repeating, "Nobody has a right to have as much fun at work as we've had," but he is absolutely serious when he says that without Doug's help he would not be where he is today, starting at the crucial point when he wondered if his life as an ordained priest in the church was over.

Douglas Theuner had become bishop of New Hampshire in April of 1986. He had very little staff, and the diocese was operating on a shoestring. Soon after he assumed office, he was visited by Gene Robinson and his wife Boo.

"They told me they were separating and were going to get a divorce because he was gay and had wrestled with that all his adult life, all his married life . . . and he wanted his bishop to know." Bishop Theuner wasn't really acquainted with Gene at that time. He recalls that he may have met him first at a clergy event, since Gene and Boo had been in this diocese since 1975, and had both been quite active and well-known, attending all of the diocesan-wide clergy events and running retreats at The Sign of the Dove. But for Doug, being so new to the diocese, this meeting was the first time they had talked.

"At the time he was not involved with anybody else, nor was she, nor were they actively looking—they just decided they needed to separate. So the first thing he wanted to find out was what this was going to do to his status with the new bishop. Now, this was 1986, so I could have said, 'Well, fella, you're out altogether.' But that never occurred to me to do, frankly. Here was someone coming to me; he had a situation I didn't completely understand, to be honest, but that didn't make it bad, or wrong. I wanted to be helpful; that was my responsibility as pastor to my clergy, to be helpful and help them work this thing through as best they could. They were being very honest and straightforward with me, and there was no acrimony between them or anything else. It was a positive thing. So I said, 'Let's work on it and see.'"

Gene had already been serving as secretary of Province I, the New England region of Episcopal dioceses. One of the first things he brought up was the question of continuing in that position, whether the people in charge would consider him acceptable under these new circumstances. And as he was leaving the bishop's office, he also said, "I'm going to be out of a job, at least three-quarters of a job, and if you can think of anything for me to do in the diocese, I need work!"

The visitor had made an impression on the bishop. "It was immediately apparent to me—and I would say immediate is the right word—that Gene was a very capable, bright, committed person. I mean, here was a guy, he needed help. Maybe I could get him on the cheap!" Doug laughed heartily. "I needed help too! But I didn't have any money. I couldn't go out and hire somebody full-time, I wasn't advertising for a position, but the next time we talked I asked him if he'd be willing to work for me on a per-diem basis as a consultant. And that was great, that was something for him, and it could keep him involved in the life of the church."

Theuner also wrote to his friend Arthur Walmsley, Bishop of Connecticut and the current president of Province I, explaining the situation and asking him to keep Gene on as secretary. Bishop Walmsley agreed on the strength of Theuner's recommendation and the fact that the people involved with provincial management all knew Gene already.

"I've never met anybody yet who didn't recognize his competence," Doug remarked. "And being competent gives you entrée into all kinds of things. People are inclined to at least give you a chance for that reason alone." Eventually the job of provincial secretary became half-time, so that Gene's time was technically split between the province and the diocese—although he always worked more than half-time for the diocese.

And at the end of the year, there were sufficient funds in the diocesan budget, so Theuner hired Gene Robinson to be his canon to the ordinary, essentially the bishop's executive assistant. He was the first openly gay priest to be serving in such a position anywhere in the Episcopal Church in the United States.

Doug sat back on the picnic bench and reflectively pursed his lips when I asked him if he'd felt like he was going out on a limb when he hired Gene to be canon. "No, I really didn't. That's just my personality I guess: you see something you think is right and you do it. It's not that I'm not concerned about what people think—I am. I pay a lot of attention to it. It's important; that's part of being sensitive to people. If you say, 'Who the hell cares,' then you're really not being very sensitive to people! But I really didn't have any big concerns about this being the right thing, and I wasn't concerned about being out on a limb."

But while Doug Theuner may downplay the significance of his actions, Gene Robinson does not. "I worship the ground he walks on," he says. "I love him."

Doug is almost completely inner-directed, says Gene. "He decides what he is going to do, and he does it. He is not deterred by criticism, nor is he motivated by praise. He really determines which way he is going to go mostly from the inside out, and then does it. Now, that inner direction can be both his greatest strength and his greatest weakness. It means he's not always the best listener in the world, but I owe my life to him. Absolutely owe my life to him."

"Think of it," Gene said. "In Doug's first month here, Boo and I came to see him and tell him we were getting divorced, and why, and two months later I came back and had the audacity to say, 'You have this great vision for the diocese and I'm just the guy to help you get there.'" Gene rolled his eyes and put his hands on his hips, with a struck-dumb expression on his face. "I mean, who died and made *me* God? Can you believe it? But I left with a job! And it's not like there was an existing job that I said I was the right person for. I was talking about him *creating* a job for me, and he *did!* At that time, back in 1986, there was not another openly gay person serving on any diocesan staff anywhere in the country. No openly gay deans of cathedrals, no openly gay cardinal rectors—so it was just astounding that he would do that. And then he took on a big gay issue right up front."

That issue—"the first gay issue I got him embroiled in," said Gene, grinning—was the question of gay and lesbian couples being denied foster children. Both the adoption of children by gay couples and the rights of gays to act as foster parents have been hot-button issues for many state legislatures, with opponents often insisting that such parenting arrangements are a cover for pedophilia. As of 2005, California, Massachusetts, New Mexico, New Jersey, New York, Ohio, Vermont, Washington, Wisconsin, and the District of Columbia allowed adoption by same-sex couples, with a greater number of states allowing foster-parenting by gays.[1] New Hampshire prohibited gay adoption and foster parenting until 1998, when the laws were repealed to allow adoption by a "single unmarried adult."[2]

The issue was first debated in New Hampshire back in the late 1980s. Prohibiting gays and lesbians from being foster parents seemed wrong to Theuner, and he said so publicly. That attracted the attention of the most conservative newspaper in the state, the Manchester *Union Leader*. During the 1970s, when arch-conservative Meldrim Thompson was governor, the *Union Leader* gained a national reputation for its reactionary "anti-communist" conservatism and biting, oft-quoted editorials from the pen of publisher William Loeb. The paper was largely responsible for defeating Edmund Muskie's bid for president in 1972, when it attacked Muskie's wife in an editorial and the senator subsequently broke down in tears as he defended her to the press, destroying his own image in the upcoming New Hampshire presidential primaries. Although the state of New Hampshire has become somewhat more moderate since that era, the paper remains conservative and outspoken today.

"The debate over gays and foster children was Doug's first big battle with the *Union Leader*," Gene explained. "They took him on in an editorial. Well, anytime the *Union Leader* takes you on, it's a red badge of courage. And I don't remember why, but the title of the editorial was 'The Bishop's Red Herring.' People were telling Doug," (Gene mimed a whisper, with one hand covering his mouth) "'Oh, you have to be careful, the *Union Leader* has power, they'll go after you . . .' and so on, but of course that just piqued his interest. So the morning after the editorial appeared, with that title on it, Doug decided he'd send the editors a case of herring, and with the fish he included a note that said something like, 'Since you seem to see Communist plots everywhere you turn, I'm sure you'll assume this is *red* herring.'"

Gene laughed uproariously. "It was just outrageous, and only the first of many times Doug tangled with the *Union Leader* over justice issues."

In 1988, the General Convention of the Episcopal Church was held in Detroit. The Presiding Bishop of the national church at the time, Ed Browning, who is still lauded for his courage in insisting that the church take a stand on many social justice issues, brought AIDS before the convention for the first time. The Convention authorized a Standing Commission on AIDS.

"After the convention Ed Browning called me," Doug recalled, "and asked if I would serve as the convener of the commission. Then I was elected as the first chairperson, so immediately I became immersed in AIDS, and with the gay community, because at that time AIDS was understood to be a primarily gay phenomenon. A number of people on the Commission, and the people we interfaced with, were gay, and up to that time I had had very little experience with gay people."

There were a lot of detractors, he remembered: people who didn't want to deal with AIDS or who were homophobic. Some of those people transferred their feelings to him. "A lot of people thought I was gay, because I was hanging around with gay people, which is what you did if you were involved with AIDS ministry at the time, and it never bothered me. It really never did. I didn't think, 'Oh no, people are going to think I'm gay.' I can't say that I struggled with it or thought, 'Oh God, I did the courageous thing.' It was just my job and I did it, and it was the right thing to do, but it wasn't a big deal."

"It wasn't like Doug had an agenda about gay rights to start with," Gene reflected. "I think he grew into that." He smiled, amused at something he was remembering. "I don't know if I have ever met anyone as ignorant about gay and lesbian stuff as he was when I first knew him. I can't tell you the number of times in those early years I'd be walking by and he'd come to the door and say, 'Can you come in for a second?'" Gene got up and went out, shutting his office door, and then came back in and sat down, leaning forward in imitation of what Doug used to do. "'Now tell me again about . . . now when two men . . . .'" He sat back and laughed, but with obvious and great affection.

"And then we grew into this language where he'd always say 'your people.' He started doing the AIDS work and he'd say, 'I'm with your people all of the time, and they're critiquing the décor in the restaurants we go to . . .'" Gene laughed again. "I just don't think there was ever a more heterosexual man anywhere. The man has not one gay bone in his body, and he just learned all this stuff because he thought it was the justice issue of the time, and he wasn't shy about hanging out there."

"He had a remarkable career around AIDS and the church. He didn't come to this with any notion at all that this would be an issue in New Hampshire. I think what happened to him happens to a lot of people, when they get involved with it: they suddenly get a lot of hatred coming *their* way, and they say, 'Well, if this is what gay and lesbian people have to put up with, then no wonder they want to be out from under this.'"

Gene explained that this was what had happened in Vermont, where same-sex civil unions have been legal since July 1, 2000. The Episcopal Church had an active role promoting that legislation: the lead plaintiff in the case that led to the creation of civil unions in Vermont is now active in the lay leadership at the diocesan cathedral; the committee in the Vermont legislature that wrote the civil union bill was headed by an Episcopalian who is now the chancellor of the Vermont Diocese; and the bishop of Vermont testified in the legislature in favor of civil unions.[3]

But when the right wing launched a vicious campaign against the proposed legislation, a lot of the old conservative local politicians—"who wouldn't know a gay or lesbian person if they'd landed on one," Gene said—were shocked by the vehemence and the hatred and changed their minds: they now saw it as a fairness issue. "'My God,' they were saying, 'we've only had to put up with this for a month or two, but if gay and lesbian people have to put up with this all the time . . .'" (It's worth noting that while a civil union grants equal legal and economic rights to same-sex couples under state law, those couples still lack a great many rights that are available to heterosexual married couples through *federal* law.) The state of Massachusetts became the first state to make same-sex *marriage* legal, on May 17, 2004. While many denominations are lenient in their attitude toward secular civil unions, the bulk of the religious controversy comes from disagreement over the definition of the institution and sacrament of marriage.

In the Diocese of New Hampshire, Doug Theuner established written guidelines for the blessing of same-sex unions in 1996. He left it up to individual clergy to decide whether or not to perform blessings, making it clear that these were blessings, not liturgies for same-sex unions, which are not sanctioned by the national church. "Maryland got in trouble for issuing guidelines in 2002," Gene recalled, "while we had already had them for a number of years. Now part of that was that Doug is so inner-directed that people knew that they could make a big stink and it just wouldn't matter: he was going to do it anyway. The people who couldn't live with that left early on. And the people who figured they *could* live with that grew to believe—and it was true—that Doug didn't mind at all if they disagreed with him. He's perfectly fine for you to be in a different place than he is. He's not going to write you off, and he's probably not going to change his mind either. But you're welcome to be a part of the family here."

So, far from being thrown out of the church, Gene Robinson became canon to the ordinary in the Diocese of New Hampshire. Episco-speak can certianly be daunting, if not downright incomprehensible. The word "canon" comes from the Greek *kanon*, which means "rule" or "measuring rod." In the Anglican world, the *canons* are the rules of the church, as in the term *canon law*. But canons can also be people. "Canon to the ordinary," this job with the strange name, is made clearer if one realizes that the Anglican name for a bishop is "the ordinary." Canons generally carry out the work of bishops, either in dioceses or at cathedrals, and "executive assistant" or "chief of staff" is probably the closest equivalent title in secular terms.

Gene Robinson and Jean Mulligan, also a member of the New Hampshire diocesan staff, on the day they were both made canons.

The Rev. Tim Rich, recently appointed to be Gene's own canon to the ordinary, laughs and says the job is "whatever the bishop wants it to be!" In general, as a canon, Gene worked on issues that were already dear to his heart: clergy wellness, helping new clergy get established in their parishes and in the diocese, creating a safe church, helping congregations and clergy deal with stress or conflict, and facilitating communication between the parishes and Diocesan House in the state capital, Concord. He also became, as Tim Rich is for him, the bishop's close assistant and advisor, helping with everything from letter-writing to strategizing about how to handle difficult situations. And in the bishop's absence, he became the person in charge of the diocese.

"The trust he placed in me worked both ways," said Bishop Theuner. "When I would go away on vacation, for example, and leave the running of the diocese essentially in Gene's hands, I never had any question about him making the right decision. Suppose some crisis came up, which it sometimes did: would he go off and do something that I'd then have to go and undo? I knew if anything ever came up that he had serious questions about, he'd call me. I don't recall ever having a serious argument or disagreement as to how to handle a situation. Maybe sometimes Gene just gave in because I was the bishop and I was going to do it my way! But I felt like we always listened to each other. So it was a very, very good relationship."

Gene had a few different recollections. "Our relationship was tested a few times," he said, and started to laugh before telling the story of one of those occasions. It was around Christmas time, three days after Doug Theuner's first carotid artery surgery in 2001. Gene had gotten a call from Doug's wife, Sue, who was very upset because the bishop had been previously scheduled to go to a meeting in New York and now seemed to have every intention of going. She hoped maybe Gene would be able to talk some sense into him. Gene had already told Doug that if he went to New York he might have to look for a new canon to the ordinary, but he agreed to come out to their house and try.

When he arrived at the door, Sue met him, and silently rolled her eyes before leading him into the kitchen, where Doug was sitting, having a glass of wine. Gene tried to talk to him about the need to take it easy and recuperate, and that maybe going to New York wasn't the best idea, but the bishop was having none of it. "Eventually I said something that pushed him over the edge. The wine glass went flying across the room and crashed into the sink, and he got up and strode across the room, plucked me out of my chair," (Gene is considerably smaller than his former boss) "and was depositing me out the door just when his wife appeared from a side room and I managed to say, 'Oh, I'm leaving now!'"

The next day Gene went into work at Diocesan House, and there was Doug in his office. He stuck his head in, and the bishop looked up sheepishly and said, "I was a bad boy yesterday, wasn't I?"

Gene said, "Yes you were! But I'm really glad you're here, and not in New York!"

When he finished telling the story, Gene grinned and shook his head in affectionate incredulity. "He's amazing," he said. "I'd walk across hot coals for that guy."

Doug Theuner, with his quite different, more formal style, wouldn't put it quite the same way, but in truth, he *has* walked across hot coals for Gene, and for gay and lesbian rights. He also returns the respect and admiration his former assistant gives him: "Gene is very bright, and that's important. And he's very personable. He's genuinely interested in people, and he really *likes* interaction with people. Those are his two principal characteristics. His organizational skills are far superior to my own. He's also a person of very great faith, which is helpful in this profession! His faith sustains him, and motivates him. I could go on with lots of adjectives, but that sums it up pretty well."

Had his assistant changed over the years they'd worked together? Bishop Theuner sat back and looked out over the small harbor. "'Blossom' might be a better way to put it," he said, "even though it's a corny word." He felt that he'd seen Gene "come into his own" and become more comfortable with his sexuality in reference to the world. "I think that after he came out," he said, "once he and Boo decided to separate, he was comfortable personally with his sexuality. But when you're marching to the tune of a different drummer and the world knows it, and you've got to constantly adjust to the fact that people are looking at you this way or the other way, and doors are opening or closing, it can be very difficult. I think he has become more comfortable with being an openly gay person, and that would be inevitable, that you'd have to become either more comfortable or less. He's become more comfortable."

Most of the congregations in New Hampshire ended up working directly with Gene Robinson on one matter or another. He was well known and respected by the clergy and almost universally liked. I worked with him for the first time when he came to my parish to facilitate difficult discussions about unresolved issues between the lay leadership of the parish and the priest, who was returning from a long sabbatical. By that time, a few years before Gene's election as bishop, he was a well-known fixture in the diocese and highly respected for the work he had done with our congregation during another difficult situation some years prior. Although matters of clergy/lay authority, attitudes toward homosexuality, and conservative/liberal values were central issues underlying the current problems in our parish, Gene's own views and orientation never came up in these meetings. He acted as a skilled, non-partisan, objective facilitator, encouraging us to develop a fair and workable process and to take responsibility for recognizing our own patterns and difficulties rather than expecting the bishop's office to step in and "fix" them. Other parishes, with their own unique and challenging situations, also came to respect Gene Robinson highly over the years he served as canon to the ordinary.

The Rev. Randy Dales, who was president of the Standing Committee during the early years of Doug Theuner's episcopate, feels that both liberal and conservative parishes in the diocese had similar impressions of Gene Robinson. Soon after Doug took office, a conflict developed with the Church of the Redeemer in Rochester, New Hampshire. The leadership of the parish objected to what they thought was a liberal rector who broke a promise not to change worship practices at the church. Several years after he arrived, he brought girl acolytes in to serve at the Saturday afternoon Eucharist. This was a radically disruptive move in the eyes of the congregation, and they also felt he had lied to them about his intentions.

"Gene Robinson was the one who went and dealt with that congregation," the Rev. Dales related, "and he tried to help them through the divide, because the bishop would be the person of last resort: he would be the one on whom a decision would finally fall, and it was not for him to be doing the negotiating. And Gene was magnificent in that. I watched him, as a member of the Standing Committee, and he did a marvelous job with a very conservative bunch. So it doesn't matter what arena he was in. People recognized his pastoral skills."

In order to facilitate communication, cooperation, and democratic decision-making, the Episcopal Church in the United States is organized into units. The smallest is the local parish, with a rector (priest), sometimes a curate or assistant rector, and an elected "board" of lay leaders, known as a vestry. Parishes are collected together into state or regional groups called dioceses, under the leadership of an elected bishop and a governing board, known as the Standing Committee, made up of half lay and half clergy leaders, chosen by the parish delegates to the annual Diocesan Convention. Nationally, the dioceses are grouped into ten regions, known as provinces. Except for those dioceses that are not part of the continental United States, these groupings correspond to logical geographical divisions. Provinces are less a unit of authority than a grouping for communication and cooperative work, and while provinces have officers, the authority for representing the parishes of individual Episcopalians rests with the diocese.

The Diocese of New Hampshire is part of Province I—New England—which is the smallest province geographically. Randy Dales laughed about that, saying that within the New England province people can actually drive to a meeting without having to stay overnight, which is impossible almost anywhere else in the country.

"More than fifteen years ago," he said, "we were in a process of rethinking how we could function together as a province, and Gene Robinson came in and assisted in the reorganization of the province by networks of common concern: network

Bishop Arthur Walmsley of Connecticut and Gene Robinson (Secretary of Province I) listen to Presiding Bishop Ed Browning.

on youth, on education, various ways of getting people together. He became the provincial coordinator, organizing the education gathering as part of the Provincial Convocation that takes place each fall, and he sort of established connections between people who were doing similar sorts of things in different dioceses, so he became a model for the kind of leadership within provinces for the national church. At the last convention there were funds set aside to assist in paying the salary of that kind of a person to work in other provinces around the church, just based on the model of the work he did."

The Rev. Hank Junkin recalled that Gene brought a legacy to Province I of getting the different dioceses together over social justice issues. "He made the fall convocation of Province I an annual event of fellowship between clergy and laity in the province. That convocation has dealt with issues of the environment, issues of racism, education of clergy and laity, and it's been absolutely wonderful, and a lasting legacy Gene has brought."

Randy Dales, Gene and a few others also got together with people at the Episcopal Church Foundation, an independent Episcopal foundation that tries to assist clergy by providing grants for programs such as continuing education. Bill Craddock, who now directs Clergy Reflection, Education, Discernment Opportunity (CREDO), a program of clergy refreshment, and was part of a group interested in developing a clergy wellness program. Gene already had a reputation for his work in that area, so the group approached him, and together they tried to design wellness guidelines and initiatives for clergy. A small book, *Being Well in Christ*, came out of that process, and Gene provided almost all the leadership for that project. Randy Dales described it as "a guidebook for clergy in terms of self-care, preserving one's integrity, continuing to study, to be refreshed, to concern oneself about health and wellness as well as effective ministry." Using the booklet as a tool, Gene was asked to run clergy conferences on wellness all across the church. Largely because of this national work, many dioceses already knew of Gene Robinson before he was nominated as bishop. Dales commented, "I don't think his sexuality ever came up in any of those discussions, and this was in upper South Carolina, in San Diego—places where his sexuality may have become an issue later in terms of consenting to his election. But they just knew him as a very talented priest, and an effective communicator, and one who can run a meeting in a conference better than anyone I know."

Louie Crew is an emeritus professor at Rutgers and the founder of Integrity, a non-profit organization of lesbian, gay, bisexual, and transgender [LGBT] Episcopalians and their straight friends. He's one of the best-known leaders on gay and lesbian justice issues in the Episcopal Church and has been a consistent voice for patience, love, and continuing dialogue. The "Anglican Pages of Louie Crew" are an indispensable internet resource of historical information about the Episcopal Church, especially on the political side of justice issues affecting women and gay and lesbian people. Louie has served on national committees of the Episcopal Church since the early 1990s, and in that capacity he soon became aware that everyone seemed to know "this guy Gene Robinson." People in the national church circles spoke of Gene as one of the most sought-after "blue book" report-writers in the church—the final report of national commissions—a task which requires a person who can study and quickly synthesize and articulate the complex work of such groups.

The first time Louie saw Gene in operation was right after the 2000 General Convention, at the origin of Claiming the Blessing, a collaborative effort of Episcopal justice organizations dedicated to promoting wholeness in human relationships, decreasing prejudice, and "helping to heal the rift between sexuality and spirituality" that John Fortunato had described so vividly in his writings. This took place at the College of Preachers, a center for study and ministry development and renewal next to the National Cathedral in Washington.

"It was just absolutely amazing to me," Louie said, "and I'm used to people being very good in that kind of a setting. But he was in a class all by himself— not in drawing attention to himself, but in group process, in getting people to understand what conflicts we needed to resolve, what vision we needed to shape, and all the while never dropping a stitch from the tapestry we were trying to weave together, because he kept track of all of them. He's brilliant, and extremely sensitive to people's needs without being maudlin about it: this wonderful sense of inspiring the best that you can do in working together. He does it in a brilliant way that only a few leaders can do. And it's not Gene Robinson's project when you get done with it, it's a collective thing."

He added, "Even before I met Gene I knew about his pastoral skills. He was already acting in a pastoral role to many bishops while he was canon to the ordinary in New Hampshire, and serving in a leadership role in Province I."

Ella, Jamee, and Gene on Mount Major.

During the same period, Gene's personal life underwent major changes. The first step was huge: coming out not only to his bishop, but to other people who knew him and his wife. Then he had to deal with a new living situation.

His most difficult adjustment was to not living in the same house with his children. "This was just not anything that I ever expected," he said, the sadness of the memory registering across his face. "They were with me every weekend, from Friday after school until Sunday night, but I still was feeling lousy about that." Gene and Boo had a friend who was a child psychologist, and he talked to her. She told him that the important thing was for the girls to know he'd be there when they needed him, but that they didn't need him all the time. "You may *want* to be there all the time," she said, "but they don't *need* you all the time. What they need to know is that when they *do* need you, you'll be there." Gene saw the wisdom in her words, and knew he could do that.

The psychologist also gave him another piece of advice: "Every decision you make with the girls, always do it light of, in the context of, wanting to have a relationship with them when they're adults. Do everything you do, say everything you say, make every decision you'll make, according to, 'Is this going to build up our relationship over the long haul?'"

At one point early in their separation, Boo had said, "You're the better parent, you should have custody of the kids," but then she broached that topic with her parents, who were extremely upset, so she backed down. "Boo and I had a pretty hard time that first year after the divorce, and I really seriously considered wanting the girls to live with me," Gene admitted. "As I was thinking about whether I should press for custody, I asked myself that question: 'What does this do for us all in the long haul?'"

"To this day, I believe the greatest gift I've ever given the girls was not pressing for custody because it would have wrecked Boo's and my relationship. And I think one of the reasons that our daughters have done so well is that Boo and I have continued to have a really good relationship, and they have never experienced us using the other parent, or using them, the kids, to work out whatever issues were going on." Gene says that he and Boo were both able to set aside whatever was going on between them in order to be able to co-parent the kids. "Boo would have lost a lot, and I saved myself from doing something that I think would have been stupid, and ultimately hurtful to all of us. But it was a little bit in the context of that, 'Okay, so when we're all grown up, how do we all want to feel about this? Oh. Well, this is actually not going to help that, this is going to undermine that.' So it became kind of a good mantra, all the way through, from how do I react to particular grades that they bring home, or the college they want to go to, or how late they stay up on Saturday night, I mean, whatever. It's a pretty good mantra."

Now, he said, he has "an unbelievable reward": a close, sustaining relationship with each of his daughters. "They've gone completely off in other directions, and I can't imagine being any closer to them. Not in a sick, icky, dependent way—just like, I'd want to know these people even if they weren't my daughters." He shook his head, thinking back on what else could have happened. "Yeah," he added. "It's probably the best piece of advice I've ever gotten."

Gene then faced the prospect of slowly re-entering the social world as an openly gay man. After a while, he started to date. He knew a few gay people in New Hampshire, but eventually he decided to join Gay Fathers of Boston. At that time, the late 1980s, very few gay and lesbian couples were intentionally having or adopting children. Those who did have children tended to be people like Gene who had been, or were still, married. He recalled that within the gay community at the time, "if you were serious about being parents and had children you were thought to be rather odd." He was very serious about his children, however, and his own parenting, and was sure that he would only be interested in meeting someone who was also interested in that. The Boston group turned out to be an excellent fit for Gene: it sponsored fun events that included kids and some that didn't; it was supportive, and he met a number of people who remain his close friends to this day. Gene also helped the group by leading spirituality workshops and an occasional interfaith service.

In the fall of 1986, he met a man who lived in New Hampshire, and they dated for a year. This person lived in an intentional, supportive community of other gay and lesbian people who shared a house in Canterbury, New Hampshire. He and Gene didn't live together, but Gene bought a piece of land in Canterbury, thinking that he wanted to be close to that community so that he and that person could share their lives in whatever way turned out to be best.

The following November, two months after his former wife remarried, Gene went on vacation by himself. He had some frequent-flyer miles that were going to expire, and he decided to go to New Mexico, where he had some good friends. He'd been there once before and loved it, and was looking forward to some warm weather before the New Hampshire winter set in with a vengeance.

"I was all excited," he recalled. "I called my friends in New Mexico and said, 'I have my shorts all packed, can't wait,' and my friends said, 'Wrong! It's cold out here!' And I said, 'Well then, I'm not coming, I need to go someplace warm.'" So he looked in *The Advocate*, the American gay magazine which he remembers was more of a tabloid then than the glossy publication it is now, and in the back, in the travel section, saw an ad for St. Croix. "Okay," he decided, "I'll go there."

"So I flew to St. Croix, and walked out to the pool, and met a guy named Jim Kelly who was there with his old boyfriend, Mark Andrew. They had dated when Mark had lived in Chicago, and Jim had called him and said he was going on vacation, would he like to come? Jim took me into town to get groceries (these were all little efficiency apartments that we were staying in), and then I came back and went out on the beach and met Mark . . . and we just fell totally head over heels in love with each other. It was like a travel brochure fantasy: 'Walk out on the beach, meet the love of your life.'"

Gene came home and broke up with the person he had been dating, which he described as difficult and painful, and then on the second weekend in December, he went to Washington to visit Mark, who was working for the national office of the Peace Corps. Mark wasn't out to anyone at work, or to his family—just to a few gay friends. He and Gene dated for about a year and a half, one or the other of them traveling between Washington and New Hampshire about every other weekend. Then they made a decision that Mark would move north as soon as he got a job, which he did, with the HIV/AIDS program at the State of New Hampshire. Gene flew to Washington and came back up with Mark and a U-Haul on February 20, 1988.

"Mark left this perfectly fine and wonderful career with the Peace Corps to be with me and Jamee and Ella, here in New Hampshire," Gene said. "I was very clear with him, as I was with anybody that I dated, that I would never move away from the kids. So if we were going to have a relationship, as unfair as I knew that was, if we were going to have a relationship, it was going to be here." He laughed. "I think he was ready to come here before I was ready to let him come! Then I got nervous, that if he made this great sacrifice—which, by the way, I was asking him to make—that somehow I would be forever in his debt, and we would not be on the same footing, and I'm like, 'Okay, well, not so fast!' We took a long time to get to that decision, but, like I said, he was ready to move here before I was ready to believe it would be okay. I had to be convinced that he was doing this for him and not just for me, because I thought being beholden was not a great footing for a relationship."

Jamee, Mark, Ella and Gene at home in New Hampshire.

Throughout that period Gene had been planning to build the house that he and Mark live in now. "I had had the architectural plans for this house—the beginnings of them—with me in my briefcase when I went to St. Croix," Gene said. "I was going to sit on the beach and plan my house. Well, I didn't get a lot of planning done that week, but subsequently Mark was able to be a part of all of that."

The following summer, on July 2, Mark and Gene invited all their closest friends and family to witness their house blessing, presided over by Douglas Theuner, an event which they considered to be the formal recognition of their life together.

"It was actually a very difficult day," Gene recalled. "By then, Mark had come out to his family. It's a big Catholic family, three boys and three girls. All but one of his brothers and sisters were just terrific about it, and ultimately the other brother came around as well, but his parents just totally flipped out. His mother wrote and said, 'Oh, they've recruited you!!' And Mark's father flatly refused to ever be anywhere we were, or to have us be anywhere where he was." Gene never met Mark's father before his death, a fact which he describes as "awful" and "so sad."

"Mark's father was very controlling. The Andrew family always gathered for a big annual Fourth of July picnic. We had picked Sunday, the second, for our house blessing. The Fourth was on a Tuesday—and the family moved their picnic back to Sunday. So on this biggest day of our lives, the blessing of our home, which was really going to act as our blessing ceremony, Mark's father let the other kids know that if they went to our house blessing rather than the picnic, they would never be invited back—and unfortunately, they all gave in to it."

The house blessing was scheduled for four o'clock, and Gene and Mark waited until five-thirty, hoping that his brothers and sisters would show up. "At one point Mark took me down into our basement so that we could be alone (we had eighty people there) and just burst into tears, which is not his normal mode of operation. He was just crushed. And they all showed up about eight-thirty, after leaving the picnic. Mark was furious, and in pain, and met them at the end of the sidewalk out front and said, 'I'm glad you're here, I want you to come in, but I need you to know that this was the most important day of my life and you weren't here for it.' So it was really hard."

The only family possession Mark's parents had ever given him was a clock. That night Gene found Mark in the bedroom wrapping it up to send back with one of his sisters. Gene said to him, "Please don't do that, this is way too fresh, way too painful. Let's give it a little time. Let's wrap it up, but let's put it in the basement and let a little time go by." Now the clock is on their piano, and they're very glad to have it.

Even though Gene was not welcome, Mark kept up the relationship with his parents—"to his credit," Gene adds. By the time his father died, his mother had come around, and was always "pumping the other brothers and sisters for information: 'What's the house like, how are they doing?'" Not long before Mark's father became ill and died, there was a family wedding, of one of Mark's cousins

who lived nearby, in Hopkinton, New Hampshire. Mark and Gene were invited, as were Mark's parents. Apparently his mother and father had a conversation, in which she said, "Gene and Mark are going to be at the wedding, so you can either come and behave yourself, or not come." His father stayed away. But after the wedding, Gene and Mark invited Mark's mother to their house, and she came and stayed for a short while. "By the time Mark's father died, his mother was so ready to mend this relationship that Jamee and Ella and I were invited to the funeral, and of course we went. Mark's mother died about a year ago, but we felt so fortunate to have had those years in which we had a great relationship with her."

In front of White House at the time of the AIDS Memorial Quilt (1996).

In coming north to live with Gene, Mark had joined a tightly knit family that was, and remains, the core of his partner's life. Boo had remarried and continued to run the horse camp for girls in the summer. Gene and Boo's two daughters, Jamee and Ella, lived with their mother during the school week and spent weekends with Gene and Mark.

When Ella was asked what it was like to grow up with her father, her answer was immediate: "He was so fun." She described him as always having a very strong presence in her life, even though she and her sister only spent the weekends with him. "He was just very dedicated to it," she said. "He'd drive an hour down to my mother's every Friday to get us, drive us back every Sunday and was always there on time and excited, and we had fun things to do at their house—we'd go ice skating, and we were a big game family, we played a lot of board games. He was very involved, he'd be there at school plays . . ."

Trekking the Inca Trail up to Machu Picchu (1997).

Ella went to a private middle school in Dublin, New Hampshire, which she describes as "kind of an alternative school," with its classroom in an old barn. "They were very welcoming and embracing of the fact that I had three fathers and one mother," she said. "There was no question of hiding or ignoring it by any means. I'd have my parent-teacher conferences with all four of my parents there, and I think that made a big difference at my age, when I was just figuring out that it wasn't the norm to have two fathers. And they were there at the school plays and May Day celebrations and all the things we all did, and Mark was very involved too, as a very positive force. They were both so strong and present and loving that it wasn't a big deal for me, and never has been. I think it's very commendable to them, that they were able to raise me that way, and to have just a normal family life. We lived a really normal life, we played Monopoly and Risk (Risk was our game) and had people over. It wasn't this 'alternative world' by any means."

As the girls grew older, they would invite friends to their father's house. Ella said sometimes friends would come up for the weekend who might not have spent a lot of time around gay people, and after a few hours they'd be caught up in the comfortable, welcoming atmosphere of Gene and Mark's home. "My friends would get there and go, 'Hey, it was great, they're great cooks, the place was really clean.'" She laughed. "All those clichés about gay people. They loved it, people coming up there. And the reason it is that way is that my father and Mark are so comfortable with themselves."

When Ella graduated from college, the whole family was there to celebrate with her. "This was my big day, and I had my mom there, and my dad and both families, and I felt so lucky that I had both of them there to support me. So many kids of divorce don't have that. My parents still fight over us for the holidays, but it was just very special to have us all gathered around one table together for that event. And at Jamee's wedding, Doug Theuner did the wedding because Dad wanted to play Dad, so he walked Jamee down the aisle, and Mark walked my mom down the aisle! How's that for a picturesque twenty-first-century family!"

Gene and Boo dancing at Jamee's wedding reception (2002).

Ten or eleven years ago, Gene says, God began to "niggle" at him. "It was sort of like, you know, when you were little, and you used to poke your brother or sister in the ribs, just to be irritating. It was a little like that. God began to poke me about a call to the episcopate."

When people ask him, as they often do when he talks about his prayer life, "Well, how do you know God is talking to you?" he cocks his head to one side, smiles, and tries hard to explain.

"Part of it is that you begin to feel touched in a way, and then out of the blue, people you have known for years begin to say things like, 'Have you ever thought about the episcopate? You'd make a really good bishop.' People began saying that

Jamee, Gene, and Ella cooking for a visiting delegation when Gene was a candidate for bishop of Rochester, New York, in 1998. Jamee's apron says, "Our Dad's The Greatest . . . Bishop."

who had never said anything before, and people from lots of different places are saying it to you, so you know it wasn't a conspiracy, they didn't all get together and decide to say it. And then you pray a lot, and agonize a lot . . . "

Part of sensing a genuine call is often a feeling of resistance, because responding to call often means change, conflict and upheaval in one's life. Gene said that he resisted for quite a long time, partly because he thought "this might get a little attention." But he freely admits he had no idea how much.

The first person Gene talked to when he began to sense his calling was Doug Theuner. "He was totally supportive of me," he said. "The best thing Doug ever said to me was, 'Sometimes I feel like your father, and sometimes I feel like your son, and most of the time I feel like your friend,' which was about the greatest compliment ever."

Ella Robinson remembers her father having conversations with the family about his calling. She remembers him saying he was talking to God a lot about it, that he felt he was really being called to this, and speculating on what it would mean. "He'd say that it's a long shot, this would be the first time for an openly gay person to be elected, and that the newspapers might be a little interested— that this is kind of a big journey and it could have some consequences for the whole family, not just for him. But he clearly felt that he was being called to do it, and if it was meant to happen, it would happen at the right time and in the right place."

When Gene actually decided to go forward, he was in five election processes before ever being nominated, and in all of those, he came down to the very last cut. "Then the dioceses, most of them, said to me straight out, 'You ought to be on the list, but in the end we just couldn't do it, because we just couldn't bear the kind of controversy that this is going to bring down on our heads.'" But finally the Diocese of Newark nominated him in 1998, and then the Diocese of Rochester, New York, in 1999.

Louie Crew, who had been a member of the nominating committee in the Diocese of Newark, remembers the "walkabouts" during the selection process—question and answer sessions where parishioners were able to meet the final candidates. "In every session, when it was Gene's turn, I said, 'The Diocese of Newark doesn't need a gay bishop, we need the best bishop for our diocese' and asked Gene to comment on that. As a gay man, I could ask that question, as opposed to many other people who would have been accused of being anti-gay. And Gene loved the question."

The first bishop race, in Newark, had happened when Ella was just beginning high school. The Rochester vote took place on the day of her graduation. "Dad was there, in the audience, and I think he had a cell phone set on 'vibrate' so he could find out how the vote was going!"

Ella says she remembers thinking, "Well, this is such a long process. Are you *still* running for bishop?" She laughed with the warm, amused-at-life delight she shares with her father. But his calling really stuck with her. "I haven't had a calling to do anything in my life! I'm still waiting for that. But to have that strong a sense of being called—you know, that's kind of a big deal, that's pretty cool!" Gene came very close to being elected bishop in Rochester, losing by only a few votes.

Although he was not elected in either Newark or Rochester, he had become a major and frequent contender for the episcopate. But would he ever be elected? Would a diocese be able to elect him because he was the best person for the job, rather than focusing on his orientation as either a positive or negative issue?

"There's a pattern in the Episcopal Church," explained Doug Theuner. "Frequently people run for bishop two or three times before they get elected. Part of it is name recognition. Maybe it takes a while to get known. But after a person has run four times and not made it, then they are sometimes perceived as not being a winner. Gene was getting old to be a bishop. He was fifty-seven, which is not real old, but . . . he came so close in both Newark and Rochester. It's not as though he finished last and got a handful of votes. A number of people wanted to put his name in for bishop of Vermont, but Gene had felt it just wasn't the right place for him. If it hadn't been for New Hampshire, I think he would have been elected somewhere, but time might have been against him."

In spite of the rise of the religious right as a political force in both church and secular life in the United States, the decades of the 1980s and 1990s had seen slow but incremental progress toward equality for gays and lesbians in the

Episcopal Church. As Bishop Theuner described, progressive bishops were ordaining homosexuals, and by the late 1990s, allowing priests to perform same-sex blessings (not marriages, but blessings). Some priests were living in open, committed relationships with their partners, known and accepted by their parishes. Most of those ordinations and blessings took place quietly and did not receive much attention in the media after the first few "test cases" which had been highly publicized.

A good deal of the progress was attributable to the election of the Rev. Edmond L. Browning, Presiding Bishop of the Episcopal Church from 1986-1997. In 1982, the bishop of Louisiana had denied Integrity permission to use any Episcopal Church during General Convention in New Orleans. But in 1986, at his installation as Presiding Bishop, Ed Browning made his now-famous statement that the Episcopal Church was open to all, and that "there will be no outcasts in this church." After being left out of churchwide discussion initially, Integrity complained, and then began to meet regularly with Presiding Bishop Browning. The organization gradually developed its organizing and networking skills to become much more effective on the national level, while attracting more members and supporting them in their parishes and dioceses. By 1995, Integrity membership was larger than all other Protestant LGBT caucuses combined.[4]

On the flipside, in 1984, a group of conservative bishops, adamantly opposed to the ordination of lesbians and gays and to same-sex blessings, which they saw as threatening the institution of heterosexual marriage, had met to discuss how they might organize a so-called "revitalization" within the Episcopal Church. In 1985, this group became known as Episcopalians United for Revelation, Renewal, and Reformation. The conservatives organized carefully and quietly, remaining for the most part "under the radar" of the majority of Episcopalians, including even the bishops.

Two significant events took place in 1989. That year, Barbara Harris, a black woman priest, was elected and consecrated bishop suffragan of the Diocese of Massachusetts, making her the first female bishop in Anglican history. (A *suffragan* bishop is a full-time assistant to the diocesan bishop, but, unlike a bishop *coadjutor*, does not have automatic right of succession if that bishop should die or retire.) When Harris was consecrated bishop, her race was not an issue, since there were already twenty-eight black bishops at that time. What caused the firestorm of controversy was the fact that she was female, and, worse than that, liberal, having directed a coalition of progressive Episcopal organizations including Integrity, the Union of Black Episcopalians, the Episcopal Peace Fellowship, the Episcopal Women's Caucus, and the Urban Bishops' Coalition. The episcopate, that final bastion of male power within the church, had been breached. The formal objections made during the liturgy at Harris's consecration were numerous and vicious, citing the same arguments that had been made in Philadelphia fifteen years before when women became ordained as priests for the first time. Then, at the end of 1989, the Rt. Rev. John Spong, Bishop of Newark, ordained the Rev. Robert Williams, a gay man, and commissioned him to head Oasis, a ministry of the Diocese of Newark for lesbians and gays. This ordination was immediately attacked by Episcopalians United, who said that sin was taking over the church. For years conservatives had wanted to go after Bishop Spong, arguably the most liberal and outspoken bishop in the church, and they saw this action as an opening, although their attempt would not be made for several years more.

The following year, Bishop Walter Righter, Bishop Spong's assistant, ordained an openly non-celibate gay man who was involved in a committed relationship. The House of Bishops disassociated itself from the actions of Bishop Spong and Bishop Righter. By that time, 1990, opponents of gay and lesbian ordination had realized that closeted homosexuals had been, and were being ordained and serving as priests. As in England, there was a grudging acceptance of admitted homosexuals who said they were celibate. What incited the greatest anger and revulsion were *non-celibate* homosexual ordinations, which the conservatives insisted went not only against Scripture, but against the church's position on the sanctity of marriage and the prohibition of sexual relations outside it. Of course, it was also true that heterosexual clergy, like Gene Robinson's rector in New Jersey, had been having extramarital affairs forever, and in most cases the church had simply pretended not to notice. The hypocrisy of this double standard for heterosexuals and homosexuals was not lost on either progressives or the media; neither was the hypocrisy of condemning openly gay persons for their honesty while turning a blind eye to gay clergy who were in the closet.

At the General Convention in 1991, the conservatives proposed a resolution that "All members of the clergy of this church . . . shall be under the obligation to abstain from sexual relations outside holy matrimony." That resolution failed. Progressive bishops continued to quietly ordain known gays and lesbians to the priesthood, and more gay and lesbian clergy felt free to come out publicly. In 1993, the Rt. Rev. Otis Charles, retired bishop of Utah and former dean of the Episcopal Divinity School, admitted his homosexuality.

The opposition continued, however, to pursue Bishops Spong and Righter, and in 1996, in a highly-publicized ecclesiastical trial, the conservatives were able to push the Episcopal Church to try Bishop Righter for heresy. Although they would have preferred to attack Spong directly, he was perhaps seen as too strong and too popular; he was a best-selling religious author, widely read by non-Episcopalians as well. Righter, who was older and had ordained a non-celibate gay man, was a more vulnerable target. The trial, taken with deadly seriousness by all levels of the church, was viewed by the media and many outside observers as a medieval farce. Seven of the nine bishops on the ecclesiastical court, one of whom was Bishop Theuner of New Hampshire, voted to dismiss the charges against Bishop Righter, writing that "neither the doctrine nor the discipline of the Church currently prohibit the ordination of a non-celibate homosexual person living in a committed relationship."

Clearly, the center of opposition to the full inclusion of gays and lesbians in the life of the church was not holding. But just as Barbara Harris's election as bishop had reignited vehement opposition to women's ordination, the church did not seem ready to accept an openly gay bishop.

In New Hampshire, Randy Dales was also watching Gene's progress through the various diocesan elections and the struggles of the national church with homosexuality, and he was concerned. "It was no secret," he said, "that many people were upset that he was considered for bishop by the Dioceses of Newark and Rochester. I thought he would be elected in Newark, a very liberal diocese electing someone to succeed John Shelby Spong. And he did very well in the election in Rochester. So I thought several times he'd be elected in other dioceses, and I worried about it—because he's my friend. I worried about what kind of personal attacks would come his way, and toward Mark as well."

He voiced some of his concerns to a diocesan search committee from Vermont that came to New Hampshire to interview some of the leadership when they were considering whether or not to put Gene on their ballot.

"I said to them at the time, 'I hope you're willing to stick with him all the way through to the end about this, because I am not sure that he would be confirmed by the national church, and you have to be prepared for the possibility that your choice might be rejected, and then you will have to care for your diocese, and care for him, and go back and redo the process to select someone else.' I've always been aware that the first openly gay person living in a committed relationship who gets elected bishop would face the slings and arrows of whatever fortune was out there."

Furthermore, the last thing either Gene or the church needed, as Louie Crew pointed out, was for a diocese to elect him and say, "This is a wonderful service you're doing to the world, then when it's all over we can get a real bishop."

"Gene needed to become a bishop in the right way," Louie stated emphatically. "Not as a gay bishop, but as a bishop of the whole church."

Judith Esmay at a meeting of the New Hampshire Election and Transition Committee, for which she served as chairperson. Her husband, Robert Strauss, is at her left.

Chapter 6
The New Hampshire Election

In January 2001, Bishop Theuner came to the Standing Committee—the small group of elected clergy and lay people who serve as a "board" for the diocese and are responsible for running it in the event of the incapacity or death of the bishop—and told them, privately and quietly, that he planned to formally call for the election of a new bishop at the Diocesan Convention that coming fall. A bishop search is a long process, and Bishop Theuner was firm about his timetable: he wanted to retire by January 2004, when he would be sixty-five years old.

The Standing Committee did some initial preparation, and at the Diocesan Convention the following fall, when the bishop formally charged them with the responsibility of holding a search and election for a new bishop, he also told them he was going to stay completely out of it. "I knew that I had to stay out of the election altogether," he recalls. "Now, I would have done that anyway: I would not have wanted to influence the election of my successor. But especially because Gene would probably be a candidate, people could say that I was kind of manipulating things for him. So I told the Standing Committee I didn't want to know anything. And I didn't know anything. I was *scrupulous* about distancing myself from it."

As it turned out, the Standing Committee soon had other issues on their hands. In 2001, Bishop Theuner developed serious health problems. During that summer and the year afterwards, he had two major surgeries: he had carotid artery surgery twice. And during the preparation for the second surgery, the doctors discovered he had an aortic aneurysm. As Randy Dales recalled, the bishop's health in that second summer "looked tenuous."

"He's a workaholic: he thrives on work," said Dales. "That's who he is. We chose him because we wanted an energetic leader, and we got it! And happily so. But it took a toll on him. You could see it in the later years, especially the periods of recovery after his surgeries. We were quite mindful of the fact that those surgeries had taken a lot out of him, and we wanted to honor his desire to retire on time."

Shortly after Doug Theuner returned to parish visitations after the second of two heart operations, I remember being close to him as he celebrated the Eucharist at my church and watching with great concern as he, already visibly weak, became ashen as the service progressed.

The Rev. Hays Junkin, president of the Standing Committee in the Diocese of New Hampshire, had observed the same thing, with consternation. "Part of what I don't think the rest of the world saw, as we developed a timeline for this election, was that we had a bishop who was not well, and did not look well. He had served the diocese for seventeen years and almost given his life for us. He and Sue had been clear about wanting to be done by 2004, and all of us on the Standing Committee felt that we owed it to Doug to relieve him of this as soon as we could."

The prayers of a grateful and loving diocese and Bishop Theuner's own determination helped him return to his full capacity, and during the last two years of his episcopate he was vintage "Doug": vigorous and healthy. The transition process had begun, however, and it had a clear endpoint: a new bishop in place by Doug Theuner's sixty-fifth birthday, at the end of 2003.

It had been seventeen years since the last election in New Hampshire. The formal process was set in motion when the Rev. Junkin called the national Episcopal Church office and made an appointment with Bishop Clay Matthews, who works on pastoral matters for Presiding Bishop Frank Griswold, to talk about a schedule and procedures for the transition. Matthews visited the diocese and laid out the timeline suggested by the national church as a guideline for a transition. Such work includes defining what sort of person the diocese wants as its new bishop, developing communication materials, the search and nominating process to identify candidates and narrow the field to a workable number, and finally the election process itself, giving diocesan-wide exposure to the final candidates and planning and conducting a fair election.

"The timeline he laid out covered about eighteen months, and there wasn't much room in it for maneuvering," Randy Dales remembered. "When we overlaid it on our own requirements for our bishop's retirement, it was clear that our election would have to take place in June 2003."

The Standing Committee immediately began the work of finding people in the diocese to chair and serve on the crucial committees that would lead the search for a new bishop and handle the detailed process of the election. The central figure in that process was Hays Junkin himself.

Hopkinton, New Hampshire, is a quintessential New England town that appears unexpectedly after a long stretch of woods and upland fields. The historic central street is lined with nearly-identical, original colonial homes clad in narrow white clapboards, most labeled with modest signs revealing the dates the houses were built, "1806," for example, or "1810," next to the front door. There are two churches in the center of Hopkinton: the Congregational Church, better known as "First Church" (established in 1790) and St. Andrew's Episcopal. On the day we visited, I could hear cows somewhere behind the church, where an old stone wall adorned with forsythia and daffodils separated the graveyard from the pasture and woods.

The Rev. Hays Junkin, known to everyone as "Hank," came to Hopkinton seventeen years ago. He and his wife, Anne, raised their children there. He knows everyone, parishioner or not, and everybody in Hopkinton knows Hank. While we were talking, his beeper went off, and we waited while he listened intently to a police scanner report of an accident nearby. "Excuse me," he said, "I just needed to make sure I heard that."

At lunchtime, he led us a few miles out of town to a favorite little café where he knew we could get a good sandwich and cup of soup. "Take good care of these folks," he told the proprietor, who then enter-tained us with her favorite "Hank" stories and retellings of his best jokes while we ate her home-made chicken salad on rye. If she ever managed to find time for church, between running the café and taking care of her kids, she said, she'd like to go to Hank's: "He doesn't seem like the priests I've known."

There's nothing of the ethereal, otherworldly cleric in Hank Junkin, nor does he seem like a man with sin and judgment on his mind. Jovial, personable, and down to earth, he'd be as com-fortable mowing his lawn or shooting the breeze with other parents at a softball game as in the pulpit or counseling parishioners. A solid man with a near-crewcut and a thick neck rising from his clerical collar, his directness, immediate

Rev. Hays Junkin, president of the New Hampshire Standing Committee (2003).

smile, and affable sociability have undoubtedly contributed to his popularity and longevity in Hopkinton. After you've been with Hank awhile, another quality comes across: his calmness. He's not somebody who's going to get ruffled easily or lose his temper.

Small-town rectors like Hank Junkin have constant everyday responsibilities dealing with individual parishioners and parish life, but it becomes quickly apparent when talking to him that he also thinks a great deal about the church at large, and what it means to live his faith responsibly and dynamically, adapting continually to societal change. He was also a political science major in college, has always been fascinated by history, and says he loves "the polity of the Episcopal Church."

"I think those of us who have been around for a while and have a bit of the history of the place should take our turn at some of the diocesan responsibilities," he said. As of 2003, Hank had been a member of the Standing Committee of the diocese for five years and was in his second year as president.

"I ran for Standing Committee assuming, some years ago, that we might be in a transition. Otherwise, being on the Standing Committee is a pretty boring job. It's somewhat unique in that we act, in some issues, as a check-and-balance to the bishop, on matters of property sales, for instance, or use of resources in the dio-cese. Ordination is a place where we would get involved. If there's an allegation of misconduct by clergy, or even by the bishop, we would have to, by canon, be involved in resolving that. If the bishop dies in office, or becomes incapacitated for a time, then the Standing Committee becomes the ecclesiastical authority."

"We're a political body. Every diocese must have a Standing Committee, and we're elected from diocesan convention, we're not appointed. There are three clergy and three lay members, so in that sense I think we represent the wider diocese on some of these decisions—not just having a bishop decide on some of them, but we have a constituency to represent as well. And I think we are pretty unique in the Anglican polity. It goes way back to the American church's unease with lords and bishops and all of that stuff. So the Standing Committee does act as a check on bishops' authority, as well as a council of advice, if the bishop wants to use us that way."

When he ran for Standing Committee, Hank had asked his congregation to sign his nomination form, saying he "didn't want to go off half-cocked" but wanted to have the support of the parish, since they would in effect be sharing some of his time with the diocese. "If I had really known!" he said, shaking his head.

The election in New Hampshire, like all elections of bishops in the Episcopal Church of the United States, was democratic. In most other parts of the Anglican Communion, bishops are appointed. Not so in the United States. Dr. John Westerhoff, in his book *A People Called Episcopalians*,[1] describes the Episcopal Church as a representative democracy. Each parish has an elected vestry of lay people, and elected delegates who represent the parish at the yearly diocesan conventions. In turn, each diocesan convention elects delegates, both clergy and lay, to the triennial General Convention. Thorny issues such as the ordination of women to the priesthood and episcopate and the church's official position on homosexuality are taken up, openly discussed, and ultimately voted upon by lay, clergy, and bishops at General Convention.

Reflecting back on the election process, Hank Junkin was effusive in his praise of the Standing Committee, saying that although the six members didn't always agree, they worked closely together to find common ground. They had all quickly realized that the circumstances surrounding this election were unique, and that they owed it not only to the diocese but to potential candidates to make the process open, fair, and transparent.

"It wasn't long after this began," he said, "that we became aware that Gene could be a potential candidate, and if he was going to be a candidate, that he would more than likely run as a very strong candidate, and if that were the case, then, well, this might attract some attention."

Hank furrowed his eyebrows. "There's a whole spiritual element of this that's still a little mysterious to me," he said. "How could you find better people than the chairs we found for the two crucial, central committees: Search and Nominating, and Election and Transition? The Standing Committee decided to open up the process of finding people to serve on these committees by allowing convocations to elect them rather than us appointing them. And a wonderful collaboration of people came together who put in hundreds and hundreds of hours of work. I was humbled by it, and I couldn't be more proud to be a part of anything."

Early in the process, a questionnaire was sent out to all parishioners in the diocese, asking what qualities were most important to them to have in a new bishop. Based on that feedback, the Search and Nominating Committee began to develop a diocesan profile and to prepare the package of materials they would need to attract and inform potential candidates.

One of Hank Junkin's parishioners in Hopkinton was a man named Michael Barwell, then the communications director at St. Paul's School, a highly-regarded Episcopal prep school located in Concord, New Hampshire. Mike was also a friend of the Rev. Scott Erikson, a St. Paul's faculty member who was serving on the Search and Nominating Committee. Mike was an expert on public relations and marketing, and he had a lot of knowledge of the Episcopal Church. Through Scott, the Search and Nominating Committee asked Mike to do a workshop to help them focus their marketing materials for the bishop search.

Working with Mike, the committee was able to better define the type of person they were seeking. They eventually decided to develop a video portrait of the diocese rather than an elaborate printed brochure. They also used the internet and sent out postcards instead of letters to bishops, seeking nominations.

"In this process," Mike said, "there's a sort of formula that the national church suggests. No one, so far as we know, had ever done a video for their bishop search, and it was an expensive project, but it engaged people here in a different way, because it gave them an opportunity to be, and to show, who they were."

Mike Barwell, media consultant (2003).

On a summer morning, slightly more than a year after the election, I drove to Concord to speak to the Rev. David Jones, who, along with Cathie Talbert, was co-chair of the Search and Nominating Committee. His church, St. Paul's, is around the corner from the gold-domed New Hampshire state capitol, built around 1818, and Rev. Jones serves as chaplain to the New Hampshire senate. A statue of the state's most famous native son, Daniel Webster, stands in front of the building. Itis the oldest state house in the country where the legislature still meets in its original chambers.

Rev. David Jones, rector of St. Paul's Church, Concord, New Hampshire (2003).

Concord's main street is pretty low-key for a state capital, lined with small locally-owned cafés, bagel delis, clothing boutiques, a bank or two. Cars stop obediently for pedestrians, and even the local cop was standing outside the capitol building, talking and joking with friends. St. Paul's itself is a lovely modern facility that was rebuilt in the late 1980s after a disastrous fire. A new banner outside the church reads, "Welcome to St. Paul's—A Place to Belong, Whoever You Are, Just as You Are."

Rev. Jones is a small man, bearded, with greying temples and intense eyes that crinkle at the corners during his frequent smiles. He welcomed me into his bright, book-filled corner office, where Gregorian chants were playing softly on the CD player, and took his shoes off. After making sure I was comfortable, he curled one foot, clad in a navy blue sock woven with red chili peppers, underneath himself, and settled into an upholstered chair. There was a cheerful stuffed "Jesus" doll sleeping on one corner of the sofa, and a number of framed pictures, including one of a younger, darker-haired David Jones with Fred "Mr." Rogers.

On the phone David had described himself to me as an evangelical from a conservative theological background, and he had sounded eager to tell me his story. "You might find it kind of unique and interesting," he had said, "because I didn't really come to this from the same point of view as many of the progressives." As we began talking, he told me he had come to New Hampshire from Pittsburgh, where he grew up and was ordained. For sixteen years, he had served as the rector of a midsized Pittsburgh parish and then as archdeacon/canon to the ordinary of the Diocese of Pittsburgh.

The Diocese of Pittsburgh is currently headed by Bishop Robert Duncan, former fellow seminarian of Gene Robinson and an outspoken leader of the American Anglican Council, a well-organized and well-funded coalition of conservative Episcopalians who have urged parishes and dioceses not to accept the election of Gene Robinson.

"Pittsburgh now represents everything that's opposed to what we've done here," David said. "It wasn't quite like back that then, although it's a theologically conservative place. I've always been an Episcopalian, but my faith actually began to be important to me during my teens, through Billy Graham. The 'personal relationship with Christ' part of our tradition has been what has nurtured me and my ministry all the way along. For me, that relationship has to be the platform on which everything else rests: outreach and service, all the rest. My theology, certainly by the standards of the rest of New Hampshire, would be seen as conservative. And this parish, which called me—and that's a reflection of them—tends to be a bit more conservative, I think, than the diocese as a whole."

David shook his head, and smiled in wonderment. "This whole adventure, the search process and its outcome, has really been an interesting spiritual journey for me. It's not that I've changed my basic theological position at all, but it's forced me to think about how, if you consistently and accurately apply what you say you believe, you might come out in a place you didn't expect. And having had the experience of going through what happened over these more than two years, I realize, from my perspective, that the hand of God and the power of the Spirit is so clearly in charge of that, that I can't say, 'God, you're not allowed to do that, that doesn't fit in with my understanding, stop that!' So I had the privilege of seeing it unfold from the inside, through the Search Committee, because I know what it was and how it worked—and I know what it wasn't, which is a set-up."

The Standing Committee, wanting both a lay/clergy and male/female team, had picked the co-chairs for the Search and Nominating Committee. David represented the parish clergy view. He was experienced and mature, and he had also worked for the bishop in Pittsburgh, so he was familiar with the episcopate.

"It was a cohesive group right out of the chute," he said. "It required a lot of face-to-face time, people driving from all over the place to do this over a New Hampshire winter. Commitment was very high. But unlike a lot of groups, we had one clear task: to come up with four to six names. We also knew when our work would be over."

Speculation about Gene Robinson's possible nomination and election—some coming from the Presiding Bishop's office itself—had begun as soon as Doug Theuner announced his upcoming retirement. David Jones and others circumspectly mentioned that there had been "some external pressure" at the very beginning of the process to avoid having the consent process happen at General Convention. "They seemed to think it would highjack the convention, which of course it did. But at the time that made us think, 'Okay, somebody at the top of the food chain thinks they know what's going to happen,' and we found that kind of insulting, as if we were just going through the motions." In fact, it wasn't clear until the last cut that Gene would even be one of the candidates.

Nevertheless, the people in New Hampshire began to realize that there was more than a casual interest in the process that was unfolding in their small diocese.

At that early point in the process, Mike Barwell couldn't have known the crucial role he would later play as media coordinator for the diocese and its new bishop. But as a journalist who had been involved in Episcopal Church media for years, he anticipated the potential firestorm to come and helped walk the committee through various potential scenarios for the election.

"There was every possibility that Gene would be nominated," he said, "and if he were nominated, he would possibly be elected. It was never *assumed*, but we knew it was a possibility, and if it *did* happen, the entire process would be scrutinized by any opposition."

"When it got down to the last few weeks before the nominees were to be announced, I was called in again, along with another consultant who had worked with Gene in one other election. We met with the committee, and we talked about what might happen if Gene were elected. We had a Plan A and a Plan B. Plan A was that it was just 'every other election': it's one of the smallest dioceses in the country, basically nobody would notice if he were nominated. Plan B was, all hell would break loose."

Being so small, the diocese had no ongoing communications function or staff except for a part-time editor who handled the monthly newspaper. "Before, if Doug wanted to say something, he just said it," Mike explained. "If he wanted to call a press conference, he called it, but there was never any planning about it. So I said to the committee, 'If Gene is nominated, what are your preparations for anything from nasty phone calls to bomb threats? What are you going to say to people? How are you going to answer the phone? What do you do if someone does make a threat? Have you notified the police? What statement does the diocese have about why it would nominate Gene?' All those things had to be developed from scratch. No one had thought about it, and we were two weeks away from the nominations."

The Search and Nominating Committee eventually narrowed the original field of several hundred candidates down to about a dozen, each of whom were visited in person in their own parishes all over the country. David Jones described the consensus process the committee adopted: "At the very beginning we agreed we would never, ever take a vote on anything, so until we reached consensus we weren't going to do anything. And since we couldn't vote on it, we had to talk. There were tears, there was shouting, because someone or a couple of people would lobby for someone, but we had to keep going, keep talking, even when everybody but one was opposed, because we realized that sometimes that one voice was the voice of the Spirit."

He described the final meeting of the committee as "wonderfully brutal" and "beautifully uncomfortable." But at the end of it, he said, "Everybody knew we had heard the Spirit." When pressed to explain *how* they knew, Rev. Jones was nonplussed. "The group had formed such a bond by this time that there was no b.s. at all, and we knew if someone was holding back, we'd hear about it. But secondly, there were several what I would call 'Pentecostal experiences,' including that last meeting. If you read the Book of Acts, Chapter 2, you'll read how the disciples were struggling for words: 'Well, it was sort of like *wind*, it was sort of like *fire*, it was sort of like *jabberwocky* . . .'" He smiled. "I don't know how to tell you. But nobody doubted it."

When the nominations were announced, Gene Robinson's name was among them. The list also included the Rev. Ruth Lawson Kirk, rector of St. Peter's Church in Glenside, Pennsylvania; the Rev. Pamela Mott, pastor at Trinity Cathedral in Portland, Oregon; and the Rev. Robert Tate, rector of St. Martin-in-the-Fields parish in Philadelphia, Pennsylvania. A fifth nominee, the Rev. Joe Goodwin Burnett, eventually withdrew after being elected bishop of Nebraska.

The Standing Committee had listened to Mike Barwell's concerns, and the diocese was prepared to deal with a reaction, if it came. It did. There was hand-wringing among conservative Episcopalians both locally and nationally, what Mike Barwell described as a "how could you do this?" outcry, and there was concern within the church hierarchy. It was also becoming clear that if Gene were elected, the fight at General Convention, as well as the reaction of the Anglican Communion at large, could be enormous and very divisive.

The Standing Committee wasn't overly concerned. Hank Junkin echoed Mike Barwell's characterization of the diocese's strongly-principled position: that if they were going to do it, they were going to do it "publicly, right out in the open, in front of everybody, at General Convention."

Mike speculated that the Presiding Bishop probably "didn't want it that way, because it's messy." Then, grinning, he added, "But messiness is sort of the way we operate, as Episcopalians."

He and Hank both explained that the diocese's intention and strategy, as soon as the nominations were announced, was to say, "We're nominating the best people for the job. These are our best nominees. Gene is among them. And, oh, he happens to be gay." The Standing Committee absolutely didn't want to make the gay issue a platform or a focus for the election, and that was undoubtedly driven by the feelings of New Hampshire Episcopalians, who neither wanted to become the focus of wide media attention or to make homosexuality a "cause." In fact just the opposite was true: they had had a beloved bishop for seventeen years, and now they wanted to elect the best possible person to replace him.

Hank Junkin was very pleased with the final slate of candidates, all of whom, he predicts, will eventually serve as bishops in the church. "It was a great concern of ours," Hank said, "that because Gene was so well known, he would be known as a favorite son of the diocese. I felt that it was unfair both to Gene and to the rest of the church not to trust us to run an open process where all clergy of good standing were welcomed. And I have to say a major concern of mine was that a lot of good candidates would not bother to go through all the nonsense of running in an Episcopal election because they'd think, 'Oh, Gene's a shoe-in.' That fear left me after I met these candidates. They were all people of integrity, and each one brought particular gifts. I would have been happy with any of them as my bishop."

With the announcement of the final nominees, the work of the Search and Nominating Committee was finished, and the reins of responsibility were passed to the Election and Transition Committee. This committee was in charge of making sure the nominees and their positions on various issues were widely visible and known to New Hampshire parishioners and the delegates who had been chosen by each parish to vote on their behalf. They were responsible for planning and conducting the election itself, and for planning the consecration ceremony for the new bishop.

The chairperson of Election and Transition was a woman named Judith Esmay, from St. Thomas Church in Hanover, New Hampshire—a large, wealthy parish that serves the Dartmouth University community. Judith is a striking woman of indeterminate age, with beautiful white hair and dancing blue eyes that immediately betray her keen intelligence and quickness. Energy animates her small frame as she listens intently or speaks, and one immediately discovers that she is passionate about many things—family, knitting, politics, reading—but none more so than the church, which has occupied a major part of her life as a lay person. Her professional career has been spent as a lawyer. Since moving to the Diocese of New Hampshire from New Jersey in the early 1990s, she has been the first female senior warden in Hanover, run countless adult education programs, become a certified spiritual director, and served on diocesan committees.

Before the election, she was well-acquainted with, and greatly respected by, Douglas Theuner, but she didn't know Hank Junkin particularly well—and she certainly didn't expect the phone call that came in January 2001.

"Hank Junkin called me, out of the blue," Judith recalled, sitting in her bright study on an early spring day a year after the election. Her computer and phone sat on an orderly desk beneath walls hung with many framed photographs and certificates and drawings. On the wall to the left were floor-to-ceiling bookshelves, filled with books on religion, spirituality, and church history, and beyond the desk was a built-in daybed covered with a handmade quilt and piled with pillows, bright with light spilling in from the windows overlooking the garden outside. "He asked me if I would be Election and Transition Chair, and briefly explained what the job was. I said, 'I'll need to sit on that, Hank,' but within fifteen minutes of hanging up the phone I knew I couldn't say no. But I did let it sink in for a couple of days, and talked to my husband, and then I called him back."

Hank Junkin said later that when he called Judith he didn't know that he had found the perfect person, not only to chair this committee, but to handle the consecration of a new bishop under circumstances none of the participants could have anticipated back in January of 2001. He hadn't gotten her name through the bishop. "I went talkin'," he said, in his folksy way. "I talked quietly to people in the diocese: 'Who's good?' And 'Judith Esmay' kept coming up over and over again."

During that first phone call, Hank described the job to Judith, based on materials from the national church.

"Apparently this duality of the process—bifurcating Search and Nominating and Election and Transition—is fairly recent," she explained. "And it does make sense to do it that way, because the first committee works under wraps, and the second committee works utterly out in the open. And it really makes sense for there to be a moment when Search and Nominating hands the process off to Election and Transition and says, 'Here you are, you take it.'" Her eyes sparkled, a little mischievously. "It's very hard for them to do that. One of the strains in all this was getting them to do that—kind of 'unwrapping their fingers' from the candidates. I remember telling the co-chairman, 'You have to let us see them with our own eyes, not through your eyes.'"

Judith didn't meet her own committee members until a weekend retreat on the 19th of May, 2001. Nearly all of the members were people she hadn't known previously. Their names had come from the six convocations, or geographical regions, into which the Diocese of New Hampshire is divided.

The Election and Transition Committee began meeting regularly, even though they knew they wouldn't be receiving the final slate of names until much later. Looking back, Judith says that was very important, because the committee got to know each other well and laid a firm foundation for the work they'd be doing together—which of course became far more complicated than they had anticipated. "For example," she said, "the rules for the electing convention had to go before the annual convention in October of 2002, even though they wouldn't be applied until June of the following year. Those rules were really carefully worked over in anticipation of the electing convention."

Judith herself was not a delegate and did not have a vote at the election, which she felt was both right and "very important," but nearly all the members of her committee were either clergy, who automatically had a vote, or lay delegates who had been chosen by their convocations.

"Our committee had no part in choosing the slate of candidates," she reflected, "but we were in a position where we could have been potentially favoring one or another or being accused of that. Now I, personally, knew Gene, had watched him at work, had seen how good he is working with people. I did not know any of the other three. I personally would have welcomed his election, and I *did* welcome his election. But to the extent I could, I tried to keep myself in a place where I could welcome the election of any one of the four. To let the diocese make its choices. My job was to make sure that the choice was done absolutely according to the books, absolutely fairly."

She told her committee that she felt it was very important that as committee members, despite the fact that some were going to be voting, they must *never* discuss the candidates. "This hit them hard," she said, "because some of them, especially once it became known that Gene was going to be a candidate, really wanted to talk about Gene and wanted to talk about the candidates. But they abided by it. I thought it was essential that there could not be a whisper of feeling that anyone on the committee had a bias, or was pushing the fortunes of one candidate over another."

Judith's eyes were resolute, and her lips fixed with utter seriousness. "From the beginning I knew it had to be absolutely unassailable. I promised that to Hank: this will be an election that no one can touch. It's going to be rock solid."

The New Hampshire diocesan leadership knew that if their election broke a major precedent, the election results would be subject to intense scrutiny by those seeking an excuse for annulling or overturning the results. Actually, there was also another reason why the process needed to be handled extremely carefully and well documented: most other parts of the Anglican Communion do not elect their bishops in the same way as the American church, as was glaringly apparent in press reports and international commentary following the election, suggesting that Gene Robinson should voluntarily step down or be asked to do so—which would have constituted a complete break with the rules of the Episcopal Church and its historical tradition.

Although the national church gives guidelines and suggestions for how a diocese might approach its search for a new bishop, very little of the election process is actually dictated by canon law, the legal, democratically-adopted operating laws of the Episcopal Church.

"The vote has to be a simple majority of both orders—lay and clergy—voting separately, but at the same time, on the same ballot. That's in canon law," Judith explained. "But the election is according to the rules of the diocese. The amount of notice you give to delegates, the manner in which you cast ballots, the rules around the election (as to whether you have it in the context of a Eucharistic service, which we did, and as is conventionally done), the number of ballots you'll permit before you adjourn to another day, *how* you'll adjourn to another day—all this is by local rule. Whether you'll permit people to speak to the merit of one candidate or another or not, how you'll handle that kind of discussion if you permit it—that's all left to the diocese. There is, however, a lot that's specified about the matter of consent to the election by the General Convention of the church."

Judith pulled out a well-thumbed, heavily-underlined blue book—her copy of *Constitutions and Canons*—and read a few lines out loud. She laughed when I asked her if she considered herself an expert on canon law. "Oh no, no," she said. "I mess around with it—I like it—I love it—being a lawyer, it's something that I love doing, like I love being on the planning board in town. It gives me a chance to practice this stuff. I love being on the Constitution and Canons Committee for the diocese." She shook her head, laughing at herself. "This committee is such a joke to other people, who just say, 'Ugghh! What do you want to be on *that* for?' Doug Theuner used to walk into our little room and here would be these people struggling over, 'Do we want to use *this* word or *that* word?' and I'd say to him, 'Oh! This is so much fun! Thank you so much for putting me on this committee!'"

After the nominees were finally announced, the Election and Transition Committee held "meet-and-greets," informal "walkabouts" in six central locations around the state, where all the parishioners in the diocese had a chance to meet, hear, question, and talk to all the final candidates. There was also a series of six forums for the election convention delegates, one in each convocation, before the open session walkabouts, and a series of six afterwards.

The committee had prepared carefully, motivated by the goal of making the process as sound and fair as they possibly could. Months before the nominations, they had talked to people living close by who had been through the process of a bishop search—people like Don and Elizabeth Hart (Don had been bishop of Hawaii and later served as assistant bishop of Southern Virginia), Stew and Kristin Wood (he is the retired bishop of Michigan), and Gene Robinson himself, before they knew he would put his hat in the ring, since he had already been a candidate in several elections.

Judith said that this input had been invaluable. "By the time we got to the meet-and-greets, to the nitty-gritty planning of them, we had hard and fast rules that all the candidates would stay in a hotel, no matter where they lived; that everybody would be conveyed in a van, all together, to the meeting place; that they would be left alone and left to their own desires to get together or be separate after hours, as they each wished; that all our moderators would have to be trained before they could moderate; and on and on."

The meet-and-greets were well received. Randy Dales, who attended the meeting in Littleton, New Hampshire, said that the general reaction was very positive. Questions centered on areas of small parish ministry and common concern; people asked things like 'How are we going to be more effective in small congregations at working with young people?" he recalled. As for questions directed at

Gene Robinson, people wanted to know if he was just going to be an extension of Doug Theuner, since they had worked side by side for so long: was this going to be a fresh start for the diocese or not? "It's somehow more comfortable to elect someone from the outside," he said, wryly. "Someone who you believe is going to come riding in on a white horse and lead you from victory unto victory!"

As the election neared, Mike Barwell began to get nervous. He went back and talked to the Standing Committee, the bishop and the diocesan staff. "Do you have any idea what's going to happen if Gene's elected?" he asked. They said no. Mike replied, "It's going to be an absolute zoo! Do you realize how many people are going to show up?"

They hadn't thought much beyond local television Channel 9 and the *Concord Monitor*. "What's going to happen?" they asked.

"All hell's going to break loose," Mike told them. "It's going to be pretty intense. And you can't handle it yourselves, you have no one here who can do it. I'll volunteer."

Mike Barwell is in his forties, a tall, thin man with narrow features and short dark hair who favors white shirts and blue blazers. He has the taut, wired energy of someone running on caffeine; he's a dedicated tea drinker. Like the best of the security guards we'd all come to know later, Mike's dark eyes are constantly roaming. He notices everything and is ready to react to whatever change he observes in his environment. He is prepared, efficient and dedicated under pressure, even when exhausted; he can be brusque and tough when necessary, but also charming and personable. Mike's career has included years of experience not only in journalism, public relations, and media, but within Episcopal Church circles.

"No other Episcopal election since Barbara Harris had garnered so much attention," Mike said. "And I had been at Barbara Harris's consecration, so I knew what I was talking about. I wrote the story for the *Episcopal News Service* and the *Church Times of London* that went around the world on that one, and I'd been at her consecration at Hines Auditorium, back in '89, and in fact sat with the photographers, hundreds of photographers, in the balcony, first row, and said, 'Okay guys, it's going to happen, so if you need to change your film do it now! You're going to miss it otherwise!' when the bishops were about to lay their hands on her head in that dramatic moment of consecration. It was a very fun process."

Mike had never talked to Gene Robinson directly until a few days before the announcement of the final candidates. "We'd met once, at our parish, but I had no idea who he was or what he was like, had never met his partner Mark or anything like that, knew very little about his story other than what I'd read. So I was coming at it totally fresh, from a totally professional and objective point of view: 'Here's what needs to happen.' My work in the Episcopal Church dated back to the mid-seventies. I had been the news editor at four General Conventions, so I knew the issues, I knew a lot of the legislation, I knew almost all the players, I knew where the polar opposites were on the issue of homosexuality in the church, I knew a lot of the people who were heading the polar opposites—retired conservative bishops and Louie Crew, for example. Plus, I had a newspaper background, so I knew how newspaper editors and TV people think and what they were after."

Shortly before the election, calls began to come into New Hampshire from the national press, just as Mike had predicted. He began registering and credentialing the media, letting them know what would be happening and what kind of access they could have on the day of the election.

Meanwhile, Judith Esmay and her committee were preparing to hold the election at St. Paul's Church in Concord, New Hampshire. On Saturday June 7, each delegate would be registered and would receive a package with a set of ballots designated for that person alone. It's not uncommon for the election of a bishop to require many ballots: it had taken eight ballots to elect Douglas Theuner in the last diocesan election, seventeen years before. "I think there were six or eight already printed up and packaged that went into each pack," Judith remembered later. "You have to be rigorously careful with ballots, make sure each person who is to vote gets one set and one set only. That has to be done with great care. The registration and certification around any election is hard work."

To eliminate any possibility of duplication or fraud, the committee prepared numbered ballots with the four candidates' names on them in alphabetical order. The ballots were also color-coded: one color for lay and another for clergy so that tellers could keep them separate, since a majority election must be achieved among both lay and clergy. The committee also established a set process by which the ballot box must be taken back to a teller's room and a special set of procedures for the tellers so that they could sort and count the ballots efficiently.

"I still have the ballots!" Judith said, getting up and rummaging around under her desk. She pulled out two large cardboard boxes and handed me two sealed Tyvek envelopes, the seal over the flap signed by Frank Phillips, chief teller. "I haven't opened them again, but I felt it was important to keep them, at least past Convention. So these are the two—I guess I'll make a present to Gene of them some day. And here are the registration papers for all the delegates. I could reconstruct the entire election from this."

The day before the election, the committee was at the church setting up their registration tables, which required moving the large altar back so that a table could be put in its place. They had some extra helpers, people not on the committee, and when the work was done, one of them suggested, "I think we should protect this building, before we leave, by walking around it in prayer."

Judith said, "Wonderful. You lead us."

And so a group walked around the perimeter of the building, "not in procession, or even in prayer," Judith recalled, "but talking with each other and stopping from time to time. Before we began, and when we ended, we said, 'Lord, protect this place.'"

St. Paul's is located right in the city and it's not easy to walk all the way around the various fences, parking lots and outbuildings, but they did, "asking angels to guard the building with what was going to happen on the next day." Judith said she arrived the next morning feeling absolutely secure and calm. "There was a feeling that this was a joyous place, and that stuck with me all day. The *irony* was that the woman who suggested that we walk around the building and pray for protection was one of the people who opposed Gene's election, and has since allied herself with Rochester, the parish that has refused to accept his oversight. So I don't know what her protection was intended to do. It may be that she was protecting it against the people who wanted Gene, and of course, if that's so, she failed, but I don't know that."

The election for a new bishop of New Hampshire took place on June 7, 2003. The electing convention was presided over by the Bishop Theuner, wearing a *rochet* and *chimere*, the garments bishops wear when they're participating in a worship service but not celebrating. The *rochet* is a long white garment with ruffled sleeves, and the *chimere* is the long, sleeveless red vest that goes over it.

"He looked just wonderful," Judith recalled, "and he conducted with his usual mix of being very formal so that it was done exactly right, and being very informal so that you'd know his stomach was rumbling or whatever. Doug has a way of combining the two, of giving you the comfort of knowing that everything is being done exactly right, 'jot and tittle,' according to the book, and at the same time, we're all folks here together, and we're family, and we love one another, and anything can come up and we'll be able to deal with it because we're being honest about who we are."

She remembered "a kind of orderliness—that it was proceeding in orderly fashion, in spite of great numbers of people, because people wanted it to," and a sense of enormous responsibility: that it was her duty to ensure that the election was fair, and that she had to stop anything that might impede that. At one point, she said, Mike Barwell asked if some of his press people could cross the sanctuary to the other side, and she said they could not.

When the first vote had been taken, Judith escorted the tellers out and stood at the door while they were counting. A question came up, and the tellers asked her to go get Hank Junkin, so she went back into the church, and saw that all the people were absolutely silent, sitting there in prayer.

David Jones had gone into the election convention not knowing who he was going to vote for and with little certainty about who he thought would win. (In Episcopal elections, being the "hometown" candidate is not always an advantage. It certainly hadn't been in the previous New Hampshire election, when Douglas Theuner had prevailed over Hart, on the seventh ballot.) "The one person I had thought wasn't a good match had gotten no traction in the recent meet-and-greets," David said, "so I didn't think that person would win, but among the others, I really didn't know."

After the first ballot was counted, David said he was somewhat stunned because it was so clear where it was going. Gene was way over the top on the clergy ballot, and within six on the lay side.

"We voted the second time, and it was during that half hour, while the votes were counted, when my heart began to get adjusted to what was about to happen. And I saw the east transept begin to fill up with television people, because they had gotten the word that something was about to happen, and you could feel this thing rising. And when Doug read off the count—it was just amazing. And I was swept up in that like everyone else. It was so clearly of the Spirit."

"People now still talk about that moment," Judith Esmay recalled. "That moment of exultation on the second ballot, when Doug read the number of votes that Gene had, and it was instantly clear that he had a majority in both orders, and the sound just went up, like the sound at the end of *Gotterdammerung*, when the audience just goes 'Ahhhhhhhhh!'"

Gene speaks to the diocesan delegates immediately following his election as bishop; St. Paul's Church, Concord, June 7, 2003.

Thirty-nine clergy votes and 83 from the laity were needed to elect. On the first ballot, Gene Robinson's tally had been 51 clergy votes and 77 lay votes. On the second ballot, he received 58 votes from the clergy and 96 from the laity.

Paula Bibber, Bishop Theuner's executive secretary, was seated near him on the altar during the afternoon. "I have never felt, in a church, the way I did that day," she said. "In the very beginning, everything was pretty normal: it was a full house; there was excitement, because we were there for a very special reason; but when the final vote was announced the feeling in that church was just amazing. I think everybody felt it; the place was charged. I know that it stayed with people, it stayed with me. Later I could not unwind, I felt so energized by all that had happened that day. I think everybody felt it a little differently, and of course we had a ton of reporters there with cameras and everything, but even that didn't take away from the feeling in the room. Even they must have felt what was going on, it was so powerful. I don't see how anyone could not have felt it."

Bishop Theuner is not given to hyperbole, but he, too, remembers the moment of election as something unique and remarkable. "I've been in Episcopal elections before," he said, "though not where I was sitting up in front and moderating. But when I announced Gene's election there was a palpable feeling of joy, a spontaneous outpouring of ecstasy—I don't think it's too strong a word." He shrugged and opened his hands, as if to say, "Who knows?"

"Because we're religious people, we talk about the 'Holy Spirit'—we do that when we're very happy. But I don't remember anything like this before. It was a great thing, a very powerful thing. I had assumed Gene would be elected, so I wasn't surprised, or even relieved. But I was very happy. My visual memory is of seeing Gene's kids and their joy, because they were right there in the front of me."

"I had two other feelings," he continued. "Number one was that I was ready to get out, to retire. Some people have to retire and they're not ready; I was ready. Number two, I wanted to leave the diocese in the hands of someone who was capable and competent and I could feel good about."

Rev. Randy Dales, who had now been involved in two election processes in New Hampshire and had known even Doug Theuner's predecessor personally, felt elated. "There were good candidates nominated," he said. "One was so good he had been in two processes at once, and he was elected in Nebraska before our own election took place. So I wasn't worried about the outcome at all, but my sense was that Gene had what it took to be the bishop, and while there had been talk about his sexuality, that was such a small part of conversations, but it was never because it was an issue for us, it was always, 'How will other people respond? What will other people say about that?' And he was elected on the second ballot."

Obviously struggling with emotion, the new bishop-elect stood next to Bishop Theuner and made a few brief remarks after the vote was announced. David Jones recalled, "The things Gene said when he got up were just so in line with what he's like. No pumping the air, even though that's what some people were doing. His message was, 'This is about God, not about me talking to you. Don't forget about the people who are heartbroken because of what you've just done . . .' That's what people resonate with—his authenticity."

After the vote, the delegates were given box lunches and they spread out over the church to eat. Judith remembered, "There were knots of people comforting one another and being sought out by the press, too, because of course the press would hone right in on that and report in the papers their interviews with some of those people who were very, very disappointed."

Rev. Jones had come out of the intense atmosphere of the church and immediately run into four reporters, one of whom was from the *New York Times*. "The reporter asked, 'What do you think?' and I said, 'Ten years ago I would not have been happy with this outcome, but today I'm thrilled.' And then I sat down on the steps right out here with a lady from the Church of the Redeemer in Rochester who was sobbing and saying, 'This is the end of the life of the church,' and that's when I realized that this has a huge downside for a lot of people . . . and that was all within fifteen minutes on that day."

The rugged, remote White Mountain setting of the paper mill town of Berlin, New Hampshire is typical of many of the settlements in the "Granite State," where individualism and privacy are prized and commemorated in the state motto, "Live Free or Die."

Chapter 7
A Swift and Sharp Reaction

Even with all their preparations, the leaders of the Diocese of New Hampshire were not ready for the intensity of the reaction to Gene Robinson's election or the descent of satellite trucks and swarming international media on the small capital city of Concord.

Rev. David Jones said that Gene once told him that while he had expected "a big attention thing," he had not anticipated the huge extremes of those who were ecstatic and those who were horrified. David recalled that at one of the Search Committee meetings, the group had talked about "what if," because they had considered some other "non-traditional" candidates. At the time, he had said he thought Gene's election could split the Anglican Communion into pieces, but no one else in the room had agreed with him. "So I guess I did have a sense of it," he said. "But all the media, the film crews from ABC News showing up Sunday morning in church and asking if they could interview people—I wasn't prepared for that part. I did think that in the life of the Anglican Communion it would be a big deal. It never occurred to me that anybody would leave this parish as a result. I don't know why. Only one guy had said to me, a few Sundays ahead of the election, 'If Gene Robinson is elected bishop, I can't stay here.'"

Judith Esmay, whose face had glowed with the wonder of that "Spirit-filled" moment as she described the election to a group of fellow parishioners the day afterward, said later, in a much more sober mood, "I think I was pre-pared for some people feeling that an openly gay bishop should not have been elected. I was *not* prepared for the depth of feeling around that, and the vigor with which that feeling was made known."

Over the next days and weeks, she saw the volume of mail that flooded into the diocesan website from all over the world and read much of it. All of the pertinent messages came into her computer and two others, and they were approximately split between those in support and those opposed. She remarked that she had been surprised at how important the election was to so many people. "There were those who felt that it was the worst *possible* thing that could happen to the church and those who saw it as *salvation*, the most redeeming thing the church could have done, as proof that God loves them and invites them into the community of the faithful. The span was so wide."

"I don't think any of us could have been prepared for that," she concluded. "I think maybe Gene had some inkling. But the press interest . . . just kind of staggered me. And I was very, very grateful that there was a professional running that. Without Mike Barwell we would have been in the deepest trouble."

Within minutes of the election, Gene was swamped by reporters clamoring for interviews. That day and afterwards, Mike Barwell screened all the requests. Early on, there was a decision not to do group press conferences; almost all the interviews that were accepted were one-on-one. "It's a more intimate, higher-quality way of transacting the information," Mike explained. "It's less confrontational, because the press can't feed off each other—there's just you and the reporter."

"We were more responsive than proactive," he said, "and that was intentional. We didn't want to turn it into a media circus. That has been the case all the way through. We didn't necessarily seek the media attention. We responded appropriately and accommodated them, but we didn't 'market' Gene. And we said 'no' to more interviews than we ever granted, and we've continued to do that. That was because we wanted to say that Gene was the bishop-elect of New Hampshire, who happens to be gay, and we're just not going to get involved in it. Well, of course, you can control a story like that just so far."

Overnight, "Gene Robinson" became a celebrity and a household word. His extroverted, people-loving personality, natural optimism, and deep faith helped him make the transition quickly and enthusiastically, seeing the media attention as a chance to, as he often repeated, "use the opportunity for God." While the negative reactions were often shockingly vehement and hateful, they were balanced by the outpouring of positive reaction both from within and outside the church: the gay and lesbian community, for example, turned to Gene as a new hero, and people started showing up at Episcopal churches just because they had heard about what happened on television.

For the people close to the bishop-elect, there were both joy and consternation. They were worried about how he could maintain his energy level, concerned about the extent of the attention and the fact that, despite all attempts to the contrary, the story was not controllable—and that it was very much about Gene's gayness.

Mike Barwell had had the experience of working with other celebrities. Earlier in his life, for example, he had been in charge of media planning and some event planning during two trips to Ohio by South African Archbishop Desmond Tutu, and he had learned how essential it was to set up firm boundaries with the media. He had also learned that while the media would always push for an edge or a special entrée, they respected good communication and fairness.

"It's a question of balancing and trying to treat everyone fairly while protecting the interests of the person you are working with," he said. "I was with Desmond just about every waking moment. We tried to be very open, accommodating every request if we could do it, and saying 'no' when we couldn't.

We also said to the media, 'Look guys, he's going to be in a church, there's no extra room, you pool the cameras, you figure it out, I'm not going to do it for you, if you want anything you're going to have to cooperate with each other and you're going to do it on our terms, not yours'—and everyone did. They loved it. They had unlimited access, almost, because we planned it so well that they got everything they wanted and more. They couldn't use all the material they had. And that's what we started doing with Gene."

Even within the diocese, clergy and parishes had to deal with opposition to the election. In nearly every congregation, some conservative members left or threatened to leave or to refuse to pay their pledges, while the clergy and a clear majority of parishioners remained supportive.

Gene decided to meet any opposition directly, trusting in the established relationships he had with parishioners and clergy, his own faith, strength, and directness, and in his ability to communicate. Starting immediately after the election, he began a series of Sunday visits to New Hampshire parishes, accompanied by his partner, Mark Andrew. They came as visitors, worshiped in the pews with the congregations, and then stayed for the coffee hour or an informal parish forum of questions and answers afterwards.

Gene's warmth is perhaps his most engaging character trait. When he walks into a room, he can be heard saying, "Hi! How *are* you?" to one familiar face after another, turning to look at them with his beaming smile. He is disarming, even to detractors, and few people fail to give him enormous personal credit once they've met him face-to-face.

The states of New Hampshire and Vermont together form a tall rectangle in northern New England, running between the Canadian border on the north and Massachusetts on the south. The main dividing line between them is the Connecticut River, which cuts the rectangle into two roughly triangular shapes, upside-down mirror images of one another. In other parts of the country, people think of the two states as twins, but not so in New England, where they are often seen as alter egos of each other.

The geological differences between the states have something to do with it. The Connecticut River actually follows an old rift valley. Vermont, the "Green Mountain State," is verdant and pastoral. Despite the influx of tourists and new residents—"flatlanders"—from the south, it still has the red barns, covered bridges, white-steepled churches and enough sheep and black-and-white dairy cows to give Ben and Jerry's and many other Vermont-made products their wholesome image and rural cachet. The Green Mountains are tall, beautiful, weathered and, except for a few rocky outcrops on the highest peaks, rounded and almost soft in appearance. Vermont, while sharing with its neighbor a typical New England reserve, fiscal conservatism, and respect for the individual, is unabashedly progressive in its social and environmental policies; historically even its Republican

Party has been liberal by national standards. No one was surprised when this state, one of the first to pass a "bottle bill" back in the 1970s, also was the first to pass a law allowing civil unions between couples of the same sex, granting them the same civil rights and privileges as heterosexual married couples, or when, in 2004, the Episcopal Diocese of Vermont led by Bishop Thomas Ely became the first to publish a set of liturgies for the blessings of same-sex civil unions.

By contrast, the "Granite State" of New Hampshire is much more developed and urban in the south, where it is becoming a virtual suburb of Boston, and wilder and more rugged in the north. Its White Mountains are also aptly named, because they are bare and snow-capped much of the year, and inhospitable year-round to inexperienced climbers. Locally, residents say that land with many granite outcrops is "bony": a description that fits most of the land in the state. That bony orneriness seems to extend from the land to state politics. New Hampshire has gained a reputation for its refusal to pass an income tax, for its bellwether presidential primary, and for the "Live Free or Die" motto emblazoned on every license plate. Until very recently, the state has been staunchly Republican and fiercely tight-fisted about funding everything from schools to prisons and mental health facilities.

Under the long governorship of Meldrim Thompson, who embodied many of these New Hampshire values, a state paper, the Manchester *Union Leader*, gained a notorious national reputation for its conservative editorials.

"The joke for a new bishop was, how long does it take for a criticism of you to appear in the Manchester *Union Leader*?" said Hank Junkin. "Probably Doug Theuner got the quickest reaction, but we had a history of that with other bishops as well. This Episcopal diocese has never been afraid of speaking up for issues of social justice or matters of segregation and integrity. Doug is clearly a spokesman for social justice, and he's unabashed about it, and God bless him for it. I don't always agree with him, but I've always admired his courage at just standing up and—here we go! 'Let's let 'er rip!'"

Hank spoke about how his own parish had come to terms with homosexual parishioners and same-sex couples, with some initial, theoretical negativity giving way to love and support for the individuals themselves. "If someone were to ask, 'Would you vote for civil unions?' I think most people here would say no. But if I asked, 'What about Susan and Emily?' they'd say, 'Oh! Well, that's *Susan* and *Emily*! I mean, we *know* them!'" Hank mimicked a perfect New Hampshire accent. "So I do think there's a 'Live Free or Die' kind of thing that does create an opportunity for people that know each other and care for each other—it enables them to look past stereotypes and prejudices for the most part. Skin color is maybe another issue here, and maybe religion, but on sexuality, we seem to be almost libertarian about that in a way."

"New Hampshire was just the perfect place to have the first openly gay bishop," said Doug Theuner, many months later. "There's just no question about the fact that people knew who they were voting for! By and large the people *knew* him. Gene has been a high-profile person in the diocese for years, and nearly everyone, not just those who went to Convention, had had some experience with him personally. So they were voting for someone they knew."

He smiled. "The thing about the election that I really don't expect anyone outside New Hampshire to understand is that Gene was not elected because he was gay and because he was going to be the first elected openly gay bishop." Doug rubbed his hands together gleefully, faking a malicious grin, and leaned closer, whispering conspiratorially, "It's not like the people here were just salivating, wanting to elect the first gay bishop." Then he waved his hand back over his shoulder in a dismissive gesture. "First of all, New Hampshire people aren't that way, for the most part. They're—unpretentious. They have their quirks and idiosyncrasies that they love—the 'Live Free or Die' thing, no income taxes—but they're not out there to win the world to their point of view. That's part of the 'Live Free or Die' thing: I'll do my thing, you do yours. There might have been a few people who were all excited"—he rubbed his hands together again—"about the idea that we might elect the first gay bishop, but most people never even thought about that." The former bishop sat back and straightened up, and his voice boomed out, large enough to fill any cathedral. "They elected someone they knew and trusted! And knew was competent! And, oh yeah, he happened to be gay."

Gene Robinson himself has said that New Hampshire is the only place in the world where he could simply be "the bishop," and not "the gay bishop." Hank Junkin agreed. "I think there are other places that would welcome him," he said, "but here he has that legacy of having been in the diocese for twenty-eight years and people knowing him and coming to see him as a human being and not an issue."

Hank saw Doug and Gene as often being complementary. "Doug would be, 'Damn the torpedoes, full speed ahead!' and then Gene would quietly go in and smooth the ruffled feathers," he said. "They had a wonderful marriage as bishop and canon together, and the diocese prospered because of that. And over those years Gene quietly did his ministry—helping new clergy, developing safe church procedures and training, on and on—with an integrity and a skill that just endears him to people. He's pretty authentic. You sit with him for a while: he's the real deal. There's not a whole lot that's hidden there. And I think people here have come to love him deeply."

But with the New Hampshire election, the larger Episcopal Church found itself reeling. An already-controversial issue that had been simmering below the surface in most congregations had suddenly been pushed into the open. Within the pews, individual people and parishes were suddenly forced to consider how they felt, while clergy, often reluctantly, felt compelled to preach on the issue and state their position.

Some disaffected parishioners had acted immediately, withdrawing their pledges from their parishes or leaving the community. Nationally, the controversy split into two camps: those who wanted the election approved, and those who desperately wanted to have it overturned. Some parishes refused to send their annual pledges to the national church and threatened to withdraw altogether. Most decided to wait until the General Convention of the Episcopal Church, to be held in Minneapolis in August 2003, to see what decisions would be taken. And it was on General Convention that the organized opposition set its sights.

Hank Junkin and the Standing Committee in New Hampshire had already done some groundwork to find out what sort of opposition the diocese might be facing if Gene were elected. Hank said he had begun to get "an inkling that this could be bigger than we'd thought" well in advance of the announcement of the final nominees. The person who had an ear to the ground was the Rev. Randy Dales.

"Randy was here when Jesus set up the church," said Hank, "so he's been on and off the Standing Committee before. He's kind of the Dick Clark of Episcopal clergy." He grinned. "He doesn't look a day older than when I met him, either. So when we knew there was going to be a transition, we went out and kind of recruited him for the Standing Committee."

Randy Dales has been the rector of All Saints' Church in Wolfeboro, New Hampshire, on the eastern side of Lake Winnepesauke, for twenty-six years. He grew up in Los Angeles and came east to attend Virginia Seminary, where he met a chaplain named Phil Smith. Later, Rev. Smith was asked by the rector in Exeter, New Hampshire if he had any suggestions for possible curates, a few years out of seminary, who might fit in, and Phil suggested Randy. He came to New Hampshire in 1969 and served as curate (assistant rector) in Exeter for two years. Later he had a small congregation in Meredith and was a teacher and chaplain at the Holderness School, an Episcopal prep school located in the heavily wooded hills near Squam Lake, the pristine sanctuary of loons and the well-heeled, Eastern-establishment WASPs that became famous in the film *On Golden Pond*.

"So I was around in 1973 when we elected Phil Smith our bishop, before Doug," Randy said. As a young priest, he had quickly become involved in both the diocese and the national church. He was president of the Standing Committee during the next transition, in 1986, when Doug Theuner was elected, and has been elected repeatedly as a New Hampshire delegate to General Convention. Dales has attended the last ten General Conventions, twice chaired national church standing commissions, and been elected to represent New England on the Executive Council of the national church.

"Not everybody is interested in working beyond their parish boundaries," he explained. "Many clergy are more comfortable at home. But having been in this same community for twenty-six years, the parishioners see my involvement in the national church as an extension of their stewardship: they are giving back to the national church."

When the diocese began to think about the ramifications of nominating—or possibly electing—Gene Robinson as bishop, Hank Junkin said that Randy "did some poking around and found out that there was already a lot of discussion out in the wider church about this."

"I wasn't out there scouting in front of the wagon train," Randy said, "but I've been very involved in the national church, and I've been in touch with a lot of people—so I think they recognized that I might have some sense of their responses."

Rev. Dales had been very frank with the Diocese of Vermont when they were considering their neighbor, Gene Robinson, as a potential candidate. "I always thought that it might be a possibility that the national church would not consent to the election of an openly gay bishop in a committed relationship. So, I admit, we did call friends that we knew around the dioceses, asking what the feeling was among their clergy and lay deputies to General Convention, and what the feeling was among the bishops."

However, Rev. Dales said he didn't worry too much about the House of Bishops. "My sense was always that bishops in the Episcopal Church have always strongly supported the concept of allowing a diocese to choose their own bishop. And even in places where people have been elected who appear controversial, people on the opposite side of those controversies have quite often stood up and said, 'We may not agree, but it is this diocese's right to choose their own bishop.'" He recalled a time when the *other* side might have tried to block an election but did not: a very conservative priest who, as well as being an Episcopalian, belonged to a Roman Catholic order, had been elected by the diocese of San Joachin in California. During the consent proceedings in the House of Bishops, John Spong, the very controversial and liberal former bishop of Newark, stood up and said, "This diocese chose that person, and we need to respect their choice."

Randy Dales decided that although it was clear that there would be strong opposition among the bishops, there was also plenty of reason to believe that they would support the diocese, as long as they thought the diocese had had an honest, fair, and open election. "It was hard to know about laity and clergy delegates in the House of Deputies," he said. "There are just so many, over 800—how could we know where they would come down? So we simply thought about presenting our best case when we got there."

The Episcopal Church in the United States meets, as a body of elected representatives, once every three years. Some of the reasons for meeting are collegial: it's a chance for church leaders and friends who rarely see one another to get together informally for conversation and socializing. There are presentations focusing on specific aspects of church life, such as youth ministry, and there are many opportunities to worship together as a body. There are displays by vendors who sell everything from church furniture to bishop's shirts. There are meetings of specific groups within the church. But most importantly, General Convention is the place where the most pressing issues facing the church are debated, prayed about, and voted upon. It is the only place where changes may be made to the *Constitutions and Canons*, the written collection of binding, legal rules under which all parishes in the national Episcopal Church operate.

The location for General Convention varies, but its legal structure is always the same. There are two representative, voting bodies: the House of Deputies, made up of elected clergy and lay delegates from each diocese across the country, and the House of Bishops, comprised of all the sitting bishops of the Episcopal Church in the United States. Furthermore, the entity known as the Episcopal Church in the United States is not confined to the fifty states: Province IX includes the dioceses of Colombia, the Dominican Republic, Ecuador, Honduras, Puerto Rico, and Haiti, all of which are full members of the Episcopal Church of the United States, governed by the same *Constitutions and Canons*, and have exactly the same voting rights at the triennial convention as the Diocese of Kansas, or Maine.

Canon 16, in the blue book known as *Constitutions and Canons*, contains the detailed rules for the election and ordination of bishops. New Hampshire, like all other dioceses in the Episcopal Church, had to follow these rules in its bishop search and subsequent election. Both the election procedure and the candidate who is elected are subject to review and must be consented to by the national church. However, the rules governing that consent process are different, depending on how close in time the election is to an actual meeting of General Convention.

If the election takes place more than 120 days before a General Convention, as most do, the Standing Committee of the diocese is required to formally notify the Presiding Bishop of the election results, providing evidence that the candidate has been previously ordained a deacon and a priest of the church, and including certificates from professional medical, psychological and psychiatric examinations of the bishop-elect stating that he or she is fit to undertake the work for which he or she has been elected. At that point, the Standing Committees (elected clergy and laity) of all the dioceses in the national church are notified, as well as all current bishops. A majority of both groups—Standing Committees and bishops—is required to respond affirmatively within the next 120 days for the election to stand.

If the election occurs *within* three months of General Convention, the same proofs of lawful election must be presented, but the vote to consent to the election, or not, occurs at the Convention itself: first in the House of Deputies, and then in the House of Bishops.

Although there were certainly people in New Hampshire who objected to Gene Robinson's election, no one raised any objections to the legality of the election itself. There was a procedure for doing so: if objections about election irregularities had been filed in writing within ten days by no less than 10 percent of the voting delegates—in this case that would have meant 10 percent of the New Hampshire delegates to the electing convention—the Presiding Bishop would have requested that the Court of Review in the specific province governing the diocese (in this case, New England) investigate the alleged irregularities and present a report within thirty days.

Because the procedure had been followed to the letter, none of the objectors, at either the diocesan or national level, were able to take the tactic of suggesting that the election process was illegal or irregular. Instead, they had to address the question of acceptability of the bishop-elect himself.

The formal statement, required to be signed by the Standing Committee of a diocese when submitting an election for consent, states that the bishop-elect has been, to the best of their knowledge, "duly and lawfully elected," and that the Committee knows of no impediment on account of which the bishop-elect should not be ordained. It concludes with a statement that the bishop-elect is

> *of such sufficiency in learning, of such soundness in the Faith, and of such godly character as to be able to exercise the Office of a Bishop to the honor of God and the edifying of the Church, and to be a wholesome example to the flock of Christ.*

In the absence of a written rule prohibiting homosexuals from ordination in the church, that final statement was the real question that now would come before the Convention of the whole Episcopal Church. Was Gene Robinson, as an openly gay man in a committed relationship, of "godly character" and "a wholesome example to the flock of Christ"? Was he, as an openly gay man, suitable to be elected bishop?

Every ten years, Anglican bishops from the entire world meet at Lambeth Palace in London, home of the Archbishop of Canterbury. This worldwide gathering is known as the Lambeth Conference, or in Anglican shorthand, simply "Lambeth." Although the "hub" of Anglicanism may still be located in England, since that is where the Archbishop of Canterbury lives and works, Anglican church membership is declining in numbers in the West, and rising in the Third World, particularly in the Global South, where a more evangelical form of Anglicanism, rooted in Biblical literalism and opposed to Western progressive liberalism, holds sway. The 1998 Lambeth Conference was the first where a coalition of conservative bishops from the Global South dominated the discussion, and this was particularly evident in the debate that took place over the church's proper response to homosexuality. A report, "Human Sexuality," reflecting the wide range of views held by the various participants, had been issued at the end of that conference, but it was overshadowed by a controversial "Resolution on Homosexuality," which was quite conservative, more in line with the views of the Global South majority. The resolutions taken at Lambeth are not binding on any of the member churches—the Anglican Communion is not like the Roman Catholic church in that way, nor does the Archbishop of Canterbury issue opinions on doctrine as the Pope does—but the resolutions can be seen to reflect "the mind of the Communion" at a particular point in time and are intended to be used, in good will, as a guideline.

In March 2003, at one of the twice-yearly meetings of the House of Bishops of the Episcopal Church, the Theology Committee wrestled with the same issues. During that gathering, they wrote and issued a statement on human sexuality. The long document, entitled "The Gift of Human Sexuality: A Theological Perspective," considered varying views and theological interpretations. Toward the end, the authors referred to the 1998 Lambeth Conference Report, "Human Sexuality." They quoted its statement that "promiscuity, prostitution, incest, pornography, pedophilia, predatory sexual behavior, and sadomasochism (all of which may be heterosexual and homosexual), adultery, violence against women and in families, rape and female circumcision" are clearly sinful and contrary to Christianity, and agreed that churches should be encouraged to teach "the virtue of abstinence" to young people who are under pressure to become sexually active. But beyond these points of agreement, the Episcopal bishops of the Theology Committee again quoted the Lambeth report, admitting:

> We must confess that we are not of one mind about homosexuality. Our variety of understanding encompasses:
>
> i) Those who believe homosexual orientation is a disorder, but that through the grace of Christ people can be changed, although not without pain and struggle.
>
> ii) Those who believe that relationships between people of the same gender should not include genital expression, that this is the clear teaching of the Bible and of the Church universal, and that such activity (if unrepented of) is a barrier to the Kingdom of God.
>
> iii) Those who believe that committed homosexual relationships fall short of the biblical norm, but are to be preferred to relationships that are anonymous and transient.
>
> iv) Those who believe that the Church should accept and support or bless monogamous covenant relationships between homosexual people and that they may be ordained.

We have prayed, studied and discussed these issues, and we are unable to reach a common mind on the scriptural, theological, historical, and scientific questions that are raised. There is much that we do not understand.[1]

But now, with the election of Gene Robinson in New Hampshire, a "yes" or "no" vote would be required at the General Convention in August. More so than for the lay and clergy representatives sent by each diocese to the House of Delegates, each Episcopal Bishop knew that his or her vote would be public, and that it would have consequences.

Shortly after his election, Gene answers questions from parishioners at St. Luke's Church, Woodsville, New Hampshire.

Chapter 8
The Opposition

The vehemence of the opposition to Gene Robinson's election as a bishop came as a shock to many, especially those young enough not to remember the threats of schism that had been made over the ordination of women back in the mid 1970s. On the issue of homosexuality, members of the Episcopal Church in general tend to be more liberal than the population as a whole, but certainly the range of opinion that surfaced reflected that of the entire country. While some parishioners were appalled that their church would even consider consecrating an openly gay, non-celibate priest as a bishop, many others were equally dismayed at the vitriolic rhetoric and the hate mail received by the bishop-elect. And people across the spectrum of opinion were dismayed by the threats of schism which seemed, as General Convention neared, to be more and more serious. Among people outside the church (and this was the source of much of the hate mail), negative reaction ranged from visceral disgust to the more political view that the election of an openly gay bishop was one more example of the breakdown of American morality. For others, especially gay and lesbian Christians and their supporters who had struggled for years for full acceptance within churches and society, the prospect of this barrier being crossed was deeply symbolic and filled with hope. As had happened after the ordination of the first women bishops, the controversy was watched with particular interest by liberal Roman Catholics and gays and lesbians who had been rejected by the Catholic Church for admitting their homosexuality openly, while sexual abuse by closeted priests—which some of them had experienced personally—had been systematically covered up by the institution. And, of course, for many people of a more secular bent, the religious debate over homosexuality was viewed as a soap opera.

The well-organized and strident opposition to Gene Robinson's consecration, led by a group of conservative Episcopal bishops mostly grouped under the banner of the American Anglican Council, or AAC, took many people by surprise. In the extraordinarily mixed-message sexual climate of United States—where sex is used to sell everything from beer to provocative clothing for nine-year-old girls, and yet the sight of a rock star's bare breast can spark national outrage—there is a ready audience for any story with a sexual edge. Within the general climate of George Bush's presidency and the emboldened Christian Right, the objections and warnings of the AAC, carefully orchestrated for maximum effect, played effectively to the American media, making it seem as though the church was evenly split.

To most observers, it appeared that the driving force behind this intense opposition was the issue of homosexuality alone. Certainly that was what got talked about, and it is an emotional and difficult issue for many people. But in actuality, the current debate reflects a number of theological differences that have led to a power struggle over who should control the church—including the seminaries and the property—and where and how the resulting influence is going to be exerted.

Historically, Anglicans (especially in the United States and Canada) have been very tolerant of a wide variety of opinion. But it's exactly that tradition of moderation and tolerance that has come under attack. The organized opposition seized a moment when American conservatism was on an upswing. And they latched onto homosexuality because they knew it would be a wedge issue, capable of creating polarization rather than moderation, and one that could ultimately cause the split long hoped for by the most dedicated conservatives, shifting the balance of power and influence in their direction—both in terms of the Episcopal Church and the Anglican Communion at large. One might expect this white-hot conservatism from the Southern Baptists. But from Episcopalians?

Heated debates over theology are actually nothing new within Anglicanism. In October 2003, between Gene's election and his consecration, I went up to Woodsville, New Hampshire where the bishop-elect had been asked to lead the service and preach at the church's 125th anniversary celebration. The Woodsville service, held in the tiny but lovely Episcopal church in this small northern New Hampshire community, used an historic liturgy, and hymns appropriate to that period were played on their antique tracker organ. In his sermon, Gene pointed out that his election was not a singular event in Anglican Church history, but one point in a continuum of debate and change.

Back in 1878, he told us, there obviously wouldn't have been a woman priest such as St. Luke's now had, nor girl acolytes. He also pointed out how the older liturgy created a much greater sense of distance between the clergy and the congregation; there was a markedly different sense then about the roles of clergy and laity, and who had authority in the church. For present-day traditionalists, this question of patriarchal authority remains as strong in defining the roles of the church and the priest as it does in defining the "traditional" family.

People walking into an Episcopal Church today, even a small one like this church in Woodsville, will see trappings—vestments, altar cloths, perpetually-burning sanctuary lamps that symbolize the presence of Jesus in the consecrated bread and wine and therefore in the sanctuary itself, even crucifixes and occasionally incense—and they will experience a liturgy that is very close to a Catholic Mass. That's both ironic and somewhat deceptive. As Gene explained in his sermon, back in the 1800s the great debate in the Church of England was whether to hold to a strict Protestantism or to move back closer to Anglicanism's Roman Catholic roots, perhaps even reintegrating with Rome, undoing the original schism that created King Henry VIII's church.

This move toward Catholicism, known in England as the Oxford Movement, had a profound effect on the British and American churches. Back in 1878, as Gene pointed out, people in the small parish of Woodsville would have been arguing over whether there should even be candles on the altar, let alone a sanctuary candle. But over time, the Episcopal Church as a whole has moved much closer to "high church" (Catholic) traditions, which are now taken for granted in many parishes and reflected in the liturgy. While some of the theology behind those symbols has also changed, such as the emphasis on the centrality of the Eucharist and the reestablishment of monastic orders, the Episcopal church has nevertheless distanced itself politically from the Roman church, moving—haltingly at times, but moving—to embrace issues of social justice and equality and reflecting them both in outward statements and inward changes. This movement can be seen in the church's involvement in the civil rights movement, opposition to the nuclear arms race and strong stand on subsequent foreign policy issues, acceptance of divorce and remarriage, greater acceptance of the ordination of women and admitted, non-celibate homosexuals in congregations and behind the altar, liberal views on birth control and a woman's right to choose, and the change to inclusive, non-patriarchal language in the prayer book. Opposition to all of the above has continued within the church as well, but so far not to the point of splitting it. Episcopalians—especially in their home parishes—have, for the most part, "agreed to disagree."

The tension experienced in the Episcopal Church has been, of course, a reflection of the changes in family life and the debates over morality, sexuality and the role of religion in the culture at large that unfolded after World War II. Many mainline churches took an active and leading role in the labor movement, the struggle for civil rights and women's rights, the protest against the nuclear arms race, and in issues of international social justice. As the sense of an interconnected world became greater, progressives in the churches also became more interested in ecumenical and interfaith dialogue.

This tension began to come to a head in the 1960s and 70s. There were two U.S. government decisions that galvanized conservative religious opinion: the decision to abolish school prayer in 1962, and *Roe v. Wade*, legalizing a woman's right to abortion, in 1973. Both were seen by conservative religious people as governmental overreach, and they began to clamor for more involvement in the shaping of government policy. Before that, evangelical religious leaders like Billy Graham who were interested in politics certainly had friends (like Richard Nixon) in high places, but their influence was mostly spiritual and not an organized attempt to influence policy or election results directly through the creation of voting blocs in their denominations. But these landmark decisions prompted religious leaders to start moving out of the churches and into Washington think tanks and lobbying groups, where they fought for a more conservative political agenda. At the same time, conservative factions began to make organized efforts to take control of all the mainline American denominations from the ground up.

The first big denomination where this struggle played out was the Southern Baptist Convention. A theological split began in the Southern Baptist Convention in the 1970s. The SBC is the largest American religious affiliation[1] outside of Roman Catholicism, with 16.2 million members in 42,775 churches. Most of these churches are located in the south-central and southeastern parts of the country. Billy Graham and Jerry Falwell are the best known Southern Baptist preachers; both Jimmy Carter and Bill Clinton were members as well.

The split began with a widening gap between moderates, who felt the Southern Baptist Convention should adapt its positions according to a changing society (where, for example, women had greater equality and new roles), and conservatives, who pushed for a strictly fundamentalist interpretation of the Bible and the maintenance of traditional values with regard to the sexes, the family, homosexuality, abortion, and social behaviors such as alcohol and drug use, premarital sex, and sexually-explicit images in the media. The conservatives were alarmed by the possibility of liberalization, and they launched an organized and successful effort to regain control of every aspect of the Southern Baptist Convention, from the seminaries to the administrative leadership of the denomination. These slow but relentless and highly organized efforts started in the seminaries, which the leadership felt had been infiltrated with liberal ideas in the 1960s.

In 1998, the Convention adopted an amendment to the Baptist Faith and Message doctrinal statement that called for women to submit to their husbands. In 2000, an additional amendment stated that women were not allowed to be pastors in local congregations. The justification given by the leadership was that these values were consistent with the views of most Southern Baptists. With their new consolidated base, Southern Baptist leaders began to tell local members how they should vote, and they began to lobby in Washington and to seek greater access to all branches of government, as well as becoming highly skilled at media relations.

Former U.S. President Jimmy Carter and his wife disassociated themselves from the denomination in October of 2003. In his press release, Carter said that he and his wife wanted to associate with "other traditional Baptists who continue to share such beliefs as separation of church and state, servanthood and not domination of pastors, local church autonomy, a free religious press and equality of women." Carter also mentioned the SBC's stance on homosexuality, saying, "Homosexuals have a perfect right to profess to be Christians, accept Christ as Savior, and I wouldn't have a problem if they worshiped side by side with me . . . Jesus never singled out homosexuals to be condemned. When the Southern Baptist Convention started singling out homosexuals as a special form or degree of sinfulness, I didn't agree with it. Now, that target has shifted to the subjugation of women."[2] The new amendment to the doctrinal statement also caused the largest state contingent, the Texas Baptist Convention, to split away from the Southern Baptists.

Religious conservatives in other denominations watched what happened in the SBC very carefully. Surfacing later, and with less fanfare, similar efforts to further a conservative agenda and dismantle "sixties-style liberalism" were organized in the Methodist, Lutheran, and Presbyterian churches. These self-titled "renewal movements" were billed as efforts to "return" the churches to their "traditional roots," but they were also intended, as in the Southern Baptist Convention, to place control of the denominations—all of which have lived with considerable theological differences for many years—into the hands of the conservatives.

The Episcopal Church has always had a reputation as the most progressive of all the mainline denominations, and the most tolerant of diversity. So it was perhaps perceived by the right wing as the toughest nut to crack.

Up until the election of Gene Robinson, it had been entirely possible to be an Episcopalian and not hear much of this. While progressive activism has often tended to spring from the grassroots—from laity and sympathetic priests, eventually finding courageous champions among the bishops—much of the most strident opposition to gay and lesbian priests has been top-down, from the bishops and priests, for whom theological debates and the struggle for power in the institution have always been more of a life-and-death matter than they have for the people in the pews. But as it does in all organizations, outspoken opposition tends to gather as it rolls along. Therefore hotbeds of conservatism grew up in particular dioceses, some in conservative southern areas, but also in places such as the Diocese of Pittsburgh and the Diocese of Albany, New York, where outspoken and tenacious conservative bishops held sway. Likewise, dioceses such as that of Newark, led for many years by the ultra-liberal bishop John Shelby Spong, became centers of progressive activism, first for the ordination of women and soon afterwards for the full inclusion of gay and lesbian people in the life of the church. Doug Theuner of New Hampshire, partly because of his AIDS work and his opposition to gambling, has always been perceived as a progressive bishop, and there are many others.

But some of the most strident rhetoric was coming not from American conservatives, but from Africa, where the Anglican Church has the largest number of members and was experiencing the greatest growth. Suddenly, African bishops such as Peter Akinola of Nigeria appeared in the British and American press, quoting Scripture, denouncing homosexuality, and threatening schism. More alarmingly, Akinola and his colleagues were coming to America as invited guests of some conservative American bishops, evidence of alliances that had been all but unknown to most Episcopalians.

On the 15th of July, 2003, following Gene Robinson's election, twenty-four Episcopal Church bishops joined with a group of worldwide Anglican leaders in declaring a state of "impaired communion," or broken relationship, with the Diocese of New Hampshire and the Canadian Diocese of New Westminster, which had approved the blessing of same-sex unions. Discussion of liturgies for same-sex blessings was also on the agenda for the upcoming General Convention of the United States church. The concerned primates wrote that the election of a non-celibate homosexual as bishop, and the planned discussion of the blessing of same-sex unions at the upcoming General Convention, were "symbols of a desperately confused, errant and disintegrating Anglican province."

On July 22, there was a meeting of worldwide conservative Anglican leaders in Fairfax, Virginia. They issued another statement, saying that approval of these two actions "would shatter the church, separate it from historic Christian faith and teaching, alienate it from the fellowship and accountability of the worldwide Anglican family, and confuse the witness of the church to the love and joy of Christian marriage." The statement was signed by the Anglican primates (provincial leaders of the rank of Archbishop or Presiding Bishop) of Nigeria, the West Indies, Rwanda, Central Africa, the Southern Cone, Southeast Asia, and Sydney. It was also signed by fifteen American bishops, thirty-three other American priests and lay leaders, and seven other international priests and church representatives. The group vowed to meet again after General Convention to respond to whatever decisions were made there.

It was hard to tell from across the Atlantic how much of the hand-wringing coming from Anglican church leaders in England was due to Lambeth's difficult position, trying to hold the Anglican Communion together in spite of marked theological differences, and how much was anger and frustration at those "upstart colonies" who had once again rushed forward and taken action without considering how much it would upset "the family." The Americans and the Canadians, they felt, had gone forward too far and too fast without considering the consequences: how could the Archbishop of Canterbury be expected to keep the evangelical African churches, the fastest growing segment of Anglicanism in the world, in the fold?

In actuality, the ties between the African churches and English-speaking evangelicals go back very far. The Very Rev. Michael Pitts, Dean of Christ Church Cathedral in Montréal, an Oxford-educated theologian who spent his earlier career as an Anglican chaplain attached to the British diplomatic corps, explained that Anglicanism had come to Africa as a result of British colonialism and was today, in many respects, a last vestige of the British Empire. The original British missionaries who went to Africa represented two quite different approaches. The United Society for Promulgation of the Gospel represented the "high church," more Catholic tradition of Anglicanism, while the Church Missionary Society was more "low church" and evangelical. The places where the latter group established its missionary efforts are today the places where African Anglicanism is the most evangelical and conservative, based on a strictly literal interpretation of scripture.

There are also cultural roots for African attitudes toward homosexuality. Most African cultures are strongly patriarchal, with a tradition of polygamy, wide acceptance of extramarital sexual relations for men, and a strict taboo against homosexuality. A Nigerian friend told me that in his native language of Yoruba, he knew of no word for "homosexual," and it wasn't until he was in his twenties that he heard homosexuals referred to at all—and then with a slang, derogatory, descriptive term. President Robert Mugabe has been widely reported to have said that homosexuals are worse than pigs, and Archbishop Akinola has compared them to dogs—terms that didn't go down well in the West but are especially inflammatory within cultures influenced by Islam, where both pigs and dogs are absolutely *haram*, unclean and forbidden not only as food but even to touch, and to be compared to them is the worst possible insult. Sam Nujoma, President of Namibia, is also known to have used publicly unpalatable terms to describe homosexuality. In fact, he is reported to have ordered the arrest and deportation of homosexuals from the country.[3]

The use of those linguistic metaphors is quite deliberate, combining cultural values with the already strict religious prohibition against homosexuality that exists in Islam, with which Christianity in Africa is often in competition and, at times, in deadly conflict. Gene Robinson and other Western church leaders have also suggested that the vocal preoccupation with homosexuality as an issue among African conservative religious leaders is a smokescreen to detract attention from the AIDS epidemic and the failure of the church to successfully address the sexual issues that contribute to it.

Another factor in the aggressiveness of the African demands to Lambeth is certainly deep resentment for the years of colonialism, slavery, and exploitation of Africa by the West. Representing the region of the Anglican Communion with the greatest number of members and where the most growth is occurring, the African churches feel they should have more power. Strengthened and aided by Western religious allies, they are now in a position to demand it.

The English evangelicals maintained ties with the conservative African churches long after the British Empire declined. In recent decades, a scholarship program was developed to bring Anglican ministers from the developing world to England for theological training. When the Western-educated ministers returned to Africa and Asia, they started evangelical revival movements. The English evangelicals also began to develop deliberate connections to American seminaries and to establish close relationships with conservative American bishops, some of whom came from an evangelical position, and others who were more Anglo-Catholic and therefore opposed to the ordination of women and changes in patterns of church authority and hierarchy. In the 1970s, Trinity Episcopal School for Ministry in Pennsylvania became the first significant institutional base for the Episcopal right under the leadership of John Guest, a Church of England evangelical transplant. His assistant was John Howe, who is now bishop of Central Florida. Virginia Seminary also underwent a period of significant influence by English evangelicals.

Anglo-Catholic traditionalists and evangelical conservatives seem, at first, like quite unlikely bedfellows. For the former, the crucial dividing issue with progressives was women's ordination. For the evangelicals, homosexuality probably loomed larger—but evangelicals have, for the most part, always stressed the prime authority of men in church leadership and in the home, so there was shared concern over authority and hierarchy in the church as women began to play a larger role. While approaching the issue of marriage from similar Biblical interpretations but from somewhat different cultural perspectives, both these groups make adamant pronouncements about protecting "the sanctity of marriage" and its definition as being "between one man and one woman." Anglo-Catholics and evangelicals alike now use that definition as a catch-22 argument: if all sexual relations outside of Holy Matrimony are sinful, then not only are homosexual relations just as sinful as those between unmarried heterosexuals, but same-sex unions cannot provide a solution, because marriage can only be between a man and a woman. The only option for a homosexual person, therefore, is to remain celibate (as the large number of homosexual Catholic priests are supposed to do).

Episcopal Bishop Edward Salmon, Jr. and Bishop Suffragan William Skilton, both of South Carolina, expressed this view in a statement following Gene Robinson's election. They said that what General Convention faced was not simply church approval of "a person or a diocesan election process" but "a radical change in church doctrine":

> The union in which Canon Robinson participates is not Holy Matrimony but an intimate relationship outside the bounds of marriage. This would be true whether he were cohabiting with a man or with a woman. For the church implicitly to sanction such a partnership will be a clear repudiation of the teaching of Holy Scripture and the tradition of the church; it also would signify a massive overhaul of the Christian theology of marriage by the Episcopal Church.[4]

Evangelicals have generally been much more vocal than Anglo-Catholics in expressing visceral disgust at homosexuality, which may explain some of their attraction to the African position and rhetoric. Within American evangelical circles, as in Gene Robinson's own background, the "solution" for homosexuals has not been focused as much on a lifetime of celibacy, but on "loving the sinner and hating the sin." This has led to evangelicals advocating "changing" or "overcoming" homosexuality through prayer. Psychological therapy used to be used in this way, but based on emerging scientific evidence about a genetic origin for homosexual orientation—as opposed to it being a lifestyle choice or sinful failure of will—the majority of the American psychiatric community now feels this sort of therapy can be extremely damaging and no longer engages in it. Undeterred, "rescue" ministries have sprung up among evangelicals, aimed at intervening in the lives of homosexuals and "healing" them of their "disorder" through prayer. Exodus International, for example, is a worldwide network of over 150 interdenominational Christian ministries that promote "freedom from homosexuality through the power of Jesus Christ." Their website says that neither reacting to homosexuality with "ignorance and fear" nor accepting it as a valid orientation can "convey the fullness of redemption found in Jesus Christ, a gift which is available to all who commit their life and their sexuality to Him." A number of conservative Episcopal priests still subscribe to this view and participate in attempts to heal homosexuals and return them to their "natural state" of heterosexuality.

The 1998 Lambeth Conference of Anglican bishops was the main target of the efforts of the conservative coalition Episcopalians United for Reformation, Renewal and Revelation, Inc. (EURRR). During the decade between that group's founding and the 1998 Lambeth Conference, relationships were nurtured and alliances built between conservative evangelical bishops from developing nations, especially in Africa and Asia, and a small faction of conservative American bishops. These conservatives were well prepared when 1998 came around, and they dominated and controlled the discussion at Lambeth, to the almost complete surprise and great consternation of progressive Anglicans.

During those years, EURRR also had an increasingly strong presence at the General Conventions of the Episcopal Church in America, where it lobbied against the ordination of non-celibate homosexuals. In 1992 the group started a newspaper, *United Voice*, and in 1993, a publishing arm, Latimer Press, both dedicated to disseminating the work of conservative authors. After the 1998 Lambeth Conference, the newspaper changed its name to *Anglican Voice*, and, in 2003, Episcopalians United became Anglicans United.[5]

After the 1994 General Convention, a new group, the American Anglican Council (AAC), was formed as a separate entity from EURRR. The latter continued their publishing ministries and their lobbying efforts within the international Anglican Communion.

In January, 2000, yet another organization was formed, called the Anglican Mission in America. Two American priests were consecrated as bishops of the AMiA by Rwandan Anglican bishops Emmanuel Kolini and John Rucyahana. Four other bishops of the AMiA were consecrated in Denver in June 2001. This action—of international bishops coming, uninvited and unannounced, into another province and consecrating new bishops—is illegal under the canons of the Episcopal church and was immediately denounced by the House of Bishops. For many, these actions were the first inkling of the ultimate intentions of their conservative colleagues.[6] The AMiA's focus was different from that of the AAC, who were still organizing from within; the AMiA encouraged parishes to leave the Episcopal Church altogether, and it also established new churches in the United States under the oversight of the Rwandan bishops. For the AMiA, acceptance of homosexuality was merely one of many indications of how far the Episcopal Church had strayed from its "Biblical roots"; their response was to establish a new structure and a new home for dissenting congregations, although conversation between all these opposition groups was ongoing.

The AAC took the lead in opposing progressive Episcopalianism in the United States from *within* the church. It attracted a diverse group of Episcopal conservatives, from evangelicals and charismatics to Anglo-Catholics. Six conservative Episcopal bishops were on the founding board of the AAC, which began an aggressive networking, organizing, and publicity effort targeting conservative priests and their parishes, aimed ostensibly at changing the policies of the Episcopal Church. The AAC also became increasingly skillful at getting its message into the national media.

It is doubtful that this coalition of conservative Episcopalians ever really believed that the Episcopal Church would change and conform to the theology and political direction espoused by the AAC. Although not stated overtly at the time of its founding, the AAC had two goals. One was a schism that would result in the formation of an alternative Anglican province in the United States, recognized by the Archbishop of Canterbury—a province which, they believed, would maintain an "orthodox" form of Anglicanism, free of the tainting influence of progressives, whom they called "revisionists." (The goal of schism and establishment of an alternative province was shared—and acted upon—by the AMiA as well, although it is unclear how the AAC and AMiA intend to share power and authority if that should happen.)

The second goal of the AAC was to exert greater influence in Washington. To that end, Episcopalians have played a leading role in the Institute of Religion and Democracy (IRD), arguably the most important Washington think tank working to influence the agendas and leadership structures of mainline Protestant churches. Funded by right-wing foundations, including the Sara Scaife Foundation (a major funder of political/legal attacks on President Bill Clinton), the Bradley Foundation, and, most notably, Howard Ahmanson's Fieldstead & Company, the strategy of the IRD has been to attack the mainline churches' public positions on foreign policy and domestic issues and weaken their influence. Ahmanson, a major Republican donor, has been a funder and trustee of the Chalcedon Foundation, an organization devoted to the extreme right-wing religious ideology known as Christian Reconstructionism. This movement advocates the establishment of a worldwide Christian theocracy, with power in the hands of Christians and organized according to Biblical teaching and law. It is perhaps not surprising that the IRD also supports Christian evangelical foreign policy initiatives in historically Muslim countries. Ahmanson's wife, Roberta Green Ahmanson, is currently on the board of directors of the IRD.

As the millennium began, the IRD set aside a budget in the neighborhood of $3.6 million for a four-year project called "Reforming America's Churches," aimed at affecting future policies of the major mainline churches by targeting their national general conventions. Until her untimely death in 2005, the president of the IRD was Diane Knippers, a highly talented and dedicated strategist of the religious right who was one of the founders, and a board member, of the AAC.

The following quote from Dr. John Rodgers, a bishop in the Anglican Mission in America and former dean of the Trinity Episcopal School for Ministry, illustrates the shared philosophies and leadership ties between these various conservative organizations:

> It was my honor to serve on the Board of the IRD before and during Diane's service as its Director. She came to that position at a time when IRD was in need of a fresh focus since the Iron Curtain had fallen and the anti-godly forces were no longer led by the Communist threat. It was Diane that helped us see that the Culture wars were even more dangerous and that we needed to assist the Churches to become conscious of their need to speak up and out concerning what was happening in the mainline Churches. Her leadership in this was superb. In addition she was a leader within the Episcopal Church in its attempts to stem the secularist tide. She was instrumental in forming the AAC, and a superb tactician for the forces of light at General Convention. She continued in giving leadership to the AAC right up until the end of her far too brief life.[7]

Diane Knippers was a member (along with Oliver North and Clarence Thomas) of Truro Episcopal Church in Fairfax, Virginia, a highly influential and historically evangelical parish near Washington, D.C. The Rt. Rev. John Howe, the highly conservative current bishop of Central Florida, was rector there from 1976-89. Truro's current rector, the Rev. Canon Martyn Minns, is a current board member of the AAC . . . the connections between these organizations continue.[8]

Although the ties between the AAC and the IRD nevertheless remain unknown to most observers, their well-planned, generously-funded strategy to promote division and a conservative agenda has gradually become more and more obvious, in spite of repeated assurances that their intention is to encourage dialogue and reconciliation. As American liberals have learned to their chagrin, the Republican right wing has become far more organized and skilled at presenting its message to the public, playing on personal anxiety, fear of change, and making minority opinions appear to be widely held. It is undoubtedly true that the AAC has been aided greatly by the organizational, lobbying, and public-relations experience of the IRD.

As the Minneapolis General Convention of 2003 approached, many bishops issued statements indicating how they would vote and why. Some of those opposed to Gene Robinson's election cited theological reasons based on scriptural literalism. Others seemed primarily concerned with the threat to unity and the potential for "tearing the fabric" of both the Anglican Communion and the Episcopal Church in the United States.

The Rt. Rev. Robert Duncan, Bishop of Pittsburgh and a leader of the AAC, wrote:

> The election of a man partnered to another man, a man who years ago left his wife and children because of his understanding of his own sexual orientation, a man who is an otherwise good and able man, is a grievous wound to the Episcopal Church as we have known her. It is a grievous wound to the worldwide Anglican Communion. It is a wound to Christians everywhere, though some wholeheartedly rejoice, and many others are uncertain. Whether this election will prove a mortal wound to the Episcopal Church is a determination that cannot now be made, but this revolutionary decision most assuredly has that possibility.

The Rt. Rev. Keith Ackerman, Bishop of Quincy, said:

> Indeed, this has been a very difficult week for the Anglican Communion. The alleged marriage of a homosexual couple in New Westminster by a woman priest with the consent of the Bishop sent shockwaves throughout the Anglican Communion. Not only was this action contrary to Resolutions passed at Lambeth Conference, but was in direct contradiction to the actions taken by the Primates of the Anglican Communion at their recent meeting in Brazil. Quite obviously this is also contrary to Holy Scripture and the Ecumenical Councils of the Church. Even if the Anglican Church in Canada were to approve such "marriages" it would do so without the authority of the One, Holy, Catholic, and Apostolic Church of which the Anglican Communion is but one small part. In fact unilateral actions of this type only serve to reinforce a denominational style that has rapidly overtaken provinces of the Communion.
>
> Just days later we received word that the Rev. Canon Gene Robinson was elected Bishop Coadjutor of the Diocese of New Hampshire. Canon Robinson who divorced his wife and is living in a homosexual relationship is the first person in such circumstances to be elected Bishop. I know Canon Robinson to be a talented, winsome, and energetic priest. These wonderful attributes, however, are not qualifications alone for inclusion as a Successor to the Apostles. . . . Even an approval by General Convention cannot legitimize the circumstances related to this election, nor alter the divinely inspired Word of God.[9]

The head of EURRR, the Rev. Todd H. Wetzel, had once called Gene Robinson "the most dangerous man in the Episcopal Church." He now elaborated on that, saying that he had said so not because of any lack of ability or compassion on Robinson's part, but that on the contrary he was "one of the most talented clergy in the church and a powerful candidate for Bishop in any diocese . . . Were it not for the fact that he is engaged in an immoral lifestyle and openly displays his commitment to another man, he would in all other areas be qualified . . . [but] exemplary capabilities do not warrant an exception to 2000 years of the teaching of Scripture . . . Clearly, Canon Robinson's behavior is a scandal, not only to the overwhelming majority of Christians in the world, but to Moslems as well."[10]

Edward L. Salmon, Jr., Bishop of South Carolina, put it bluntly: "If Gene Robinson's election is confirmed by General Convention, it would bring through the back door a practice that the Episcopal Church has never agreed to approve through the front door."

A number of other bishops spoke in favor of Gene's election, and expressed the hope that he would be confirmed at the Convention.

Bishop Leo Frade of Southeast Florida disagreed with many of his southern colleagues, saying that there was no need to be afraid of controversy, because "our Anglican heritage has been strengthened by diversity and dissent." He reminded others that "the church has always found a way to discover and follow God's will, as long as we do not allow the differences that divide us to distract us from what unites us—our vision and mission as God's people."

The Rt. Rev. Jack M. McKelvey, who narrowly defeated Gene Robinson in the vote for bishop of Rochester, New York in 2000, matter-of-factly stated the same basic position as New Hampshire—that Gene had been elected because he will be "the best person to lead the diocese as a bishop, not because he is gay."

Another issue was respect for the rules of election. As Randy Dales had foreseen, many bishops felt that overturning a legal election would establish a dangerous precedent. William D. Persell, Bishop of Chicago, stated firmly that "it would be a shame to deny the right of the clergy and people of New Hampshire to have Gene Robinson, their overwhelming choice, to serve as their bishop."

Persell, like a number of other bishops, went on to praise Robinson as an outstanding priest and pastor and to mention the "special gifts" he would bring to the office of bishop in the areas of "spiritual development, administration, anti-racism training, clergy wellness, peace and justice, and conflict resolution." He wrote that he and his fellow leaders in the Diocese of Chicago were all aware that the election would cause pain in some areas—locally, nationally, and within the Anglican Communion. "At the same time," he wrote, "we are aware of how discrimination and exclusion have weakened our church's witness to the Gospel and have hurt many persons over the years. We pray that Gene Robinson's election will be ratified by General Convention."

And Bishop Thomas Ely of neighboring Vermont, the first state to have enacted legislation allowing civil unions between couples of the same sex, expressed a perspective that perhaps reflected his familiarity with the intersection between religious views and the civil struggle over the issues of fairness and sexuality: "In some ways, Gene is a reluctant symbol of the church's need to reach out to those who have often experienced themselves on the margins of the church."

Ely was right. While the Episcopal Church turned itself inside out over theological disagreements and the threat of schism, many people who were not Episcopalians, and not even churchgoers, watched the growing controversy with avid interest because it *was* symbolic of the struggle, rejection, exclusion and occasional victory that they themselves had experienced. An openly gay person had *never* reached a top leadership position in a mainline church. Would Gene Robinson be the first to do so? And what would his election say to the thousands, perhaps millions, of gay and lesbian people who had felt shamed and rejected by their churches, and perhaps by God himself?

Back in New Hampshire, as the time for departure to Minneapolis grew near, some of the concern was much more personal than talk of schism. The bishop-elect had begun receiving death threats, and the Standing Committee was alarmed. How seriously should these threats be taken? What security measures were needed? How was the diocese going to pay for them? Would Gene be in particular danger at General Convention, especially if his election was approved?

The Rev. Tim Rich was the rector at St. John's Church, Portsmouth, New Hampshire, a beautiful, historical church that is the oldest in the diocese. He and his wife and family had become close friends with Gene and Mark. In the summer, after the election, Gene asked Tim to become his canon to the ordinary if he was approved—the position Gene had filled for seventeen years for Bishop Theuner. Tim said he considered it a great privilege to go to General Convention and stand beside Gene, and had been taken aback when some people had said, "Aren't you worried that this is going to taint your career, to be so close to him?" Others had expressed concern about his safety.

On the night before his flight to Minneapolis, Tim sat talking with his wife at their dining room table. "She was a little concerned for my safety," he said, "and I told her, 'You know, I don't think the people who were marching alongside Martin Luther King Jr. thought what they were doing was that big a deal. It was more, "I believe in what he's marching for," or, "I've known him for all these years, so of course I'm going to be here," or, "because it's the right thing to do.""'"

Tim's response reflected the feelings of many of the people who had known and worked with Gene. "I don't think many of us really thought what we were doing was that big a deal," he said later. "It was what fit, because it was a natural extension of the relationship we've shared with him for years. When people said those things to me, my response was always, 'It's the natural place to be. I know this guy, I love this guy, I want this guy to be my bishop, so of course I'm going to stand next to him. And this is a dear friend, so of course I'm going to support him.' There wasn't this big agenda that had us thinking big thoughts, it was just sort of simple, little steps that seemed as natural as could be, even when the media was making it very clear that it was a pretty major event." He remembered, "Someone asked me how it feels to be in the eye of the storm. And I thought it was actually a pretty good metaphor, because the eyes of hurricanes are pretty calm."

Hank Junkin, the president of the New Hampshire Standing Committee, had been the first to say that New Hampshire "had the benefit of incarnation." For people around the country, ordaining a "gay bishop" was an issue. He may have had "a name and a face and maybe some quotes and a video," as Tim Rich put it, but to strangers who encountered his name in the press, he was merely the symbol of a political and moral issue. However, to the people who knew Gene personally, he was a human being and a friend, and they were ready to stand with him at General Convention.

Gene, Mark, and Ella rejoice as the results of the final vote are announced at the 2003 General Convention.

Chapter 9
General Convention

"I still have this romantic view of General Convention," said Hank Junkin, "that it's *the* place where the Episcopal Church speaks. You could spend a lot of time talking to the average Episcopalian in this diocese, though, and ask them to name one thing that comes out of General Convention—and if you can find an Episcopalian who has anything more to say than 'the prayer book' and 'women's ordination,' I'll give you five bucks." He grinned. "So in that sense, it's a big political convention that's necessary for our polity, but it doesn't really hit people in the pews where life and ministry are really lived." His face then became very serious. "But, boy, the issue of homosexuality does."

Hank Junkin had been a political science major in college, before he decided to go to seminary. "I love the process of the body politic," he says, and from the way he lights up when talking about political systems, he clearly means it. "All the preparations for General Convention—counting the votes, talking to people who are going—that's how a system works: talking, relating, sharing stories, cajoling, listening. There was lot of that prior to General Convention, and I loved every minute of it."

He had been elected an alternate member of the New Hampshire delegation for the first time back in 1997 and had seen firsthand the excitement and pride of diocesan delegations when they introduced their new bishops-elect to the assembled church representatives. He had hoped that someday he might be part of a New Hampshire delegation doing exactly that. When the New Hampshire election did come around, Hank had been prepared, and would have been honored, he said, to bring *any* of the final candidates before the convention for its consent. "But I also knew that with Gene we had the real deal," he said. "The best thing that we could do was put him in front of people. They would come to know, in a very short time, what we'd known for twenty-eight years—and I saw that happen over, and over, and over again. Having the honor to sit in those delegation meetings with Gene early in the morning, late at night, was really amazing."

Like many people, clergy included, Rev. Junkin himself had gone through a process of coming to terms with homosexuality. For him, as for many, the transition from a more negative, set theoretical position to one of acceptance and flexibility had a great deal to do with knowing, working with, and caring about real people who were open about their orientation or in the process of coming out. "When I realize I'm still feeling surprise at why this issue is so volatile," he said, "it's because I have forgotten my own visceral reactions when I was suddenly dealing with the issue face-to-face, with the first real parishioner who came to me. Once I remember that, I can say, 'Okay, I've got it now. Others have to have the time to grow, to go through it.' In the case of introducing Gene at General Convention, I felt that we just needed to be non-anxious and allow people to meet a human being who is a superb pastor, and not an 'issue'—and let the Spirit take it from there."

Students of political systems will find much that is fascinating about the polity of the Episcopal Church and the intentional differences between it and its predecessors. Hank said bluntly that the founding fathers of the American church, in the sixteenth century, wanted to break away from the idea of a small group of appointed bishops speaking authoritatively for the entire church. "Hmm, what church does that sound like? Oh, yeah, now I remember!" he said, laughing. "We wanted to reform Catholicism in a way that brought the laity much more forward in the authority of the church. It's still a lesson the Roman Catholic Church hasn't learned."

The Episcopal Church in the United States, not surprisingly perhaps, reflects many of the same decisions that were made, at about the same time in history, in establishing the American democratic form of national government with its separate branches and systems of checks and balances. Hank Junkin calls the church's version "an ordered structure of hierarchy" based upon a kind of "Jeffersonian and Hamiltonian, American give-and-take." There are two "orders" or recognized types of ministry: the laity and the clergy. The laity, not the ordained clergy, are considered the prime ministry of the church; the clergy are *supporters* of that ministry. "It's really a wonderful part of the American Anglican experience, that we're all involved," said Hank. "The church only speaks with authority when all the orders of ministry are speaking. And when we speak in union—in this diverse community—I think that's a pretty significant thing."

The involvement of the laity is an aspect of the United States Episcopal Church that Gene Robinson is particularly proud of, too. Speaking to an audience at Dartmouth College, he mentioned that the controversial appointment earlier in the summer of Jeffrey John, an openly gay priest living in a long-standing celibate relationship, as a bishop in England, was the result of a decision by a single person, the bishop of Oxford, who had the authority to make John the bishop suffragan of Reading. The Archbishop of Canterbury also had sufficient clout to trump the Bishop of Oxford, and pressure John to step down—and in none of this were the laity involved. "That's a very different thing than having the people of New Hampshire call me to be their bishop," Gene said. "In most provinces of the Anglican Communion, what the bishops say is what goes. I think it would shock most people, either coming out of the Catholic tradition, or Anglicans overseas, to know that there was not a single bishop involved in the choosing of me to be bishop of New Hampshire. It was the laity and clergy of the Diocese of New Hampshire who decided that."

Episcopal bishops are elected to serve their diocese until retirement (mandatory at age seventy-two) or death. Retired bishops often continue to work in the church in other capacities, and they retain a seat in the House of Bishops, which gathers twice each year for discussion and fellowship. Because of their long tenure, bishops have the opportunity to take on larger issues affecting both religious and secular society and to reach out to a constituency beyond the confines of the church. In his office, Doug Theuner had a picture of a minister holding the church so tightly that he could not reach out to touch a poor man who came for help—a reminder not only to himself but to the clergy and lay people who came to meet with him. "Doug's ministry was exactly the opposite of that picture," Hank reflected. "When you have a bishop who's an outrider—someone who's out there provoking, standing up for those who can't stand up for themselves—it's kind of like the Supreme Court. You have a life appointment, so—go for it. Go big or go home!"

Another unique aspect of the American Episcopal Church is its transparency. Gene Robinson told about a conversation he had with the journalist Michael Paulson, religion reporter for the *Boston Globe*, who won the Pulitzer Prize for his coverage of clergy sexual abuse scandals in the Roman Catholic Church. Gene asked him what it was like to be working on the Episcopal Church after all the work he had done with the Roman Catholic Church. "He had the most fascinating observation," Gene said. "Paulson said that when the bishops met for the Roman Catholics' national meeting, they would meet behind closed doors to do all their business and then open up the doors and come out and pray. And in the Episcopal Church, the House of Bishops closed its doors so the bishops could do Bible study and pray with one another, and then they opened up their doors so the world could see how they did their business."

That transparency was about to be put to the test when the world turned its eyes toward Minneapolis to see how the General Convention would debate and vote on the election of the first openly gay bishop in the Anglican Communion.

"Engage God's Mission" was the theme of the 2003 General Convention, certainly chosen well before the controversy over Gene Robinson's election. The four key words chosen to illuminate that theme were "Receive, Repent, Reconcile, and Restore"—an apt description of the steps that would seem so vitally necessary afterwards. There had been fears that controversy and the media attention might hijack the convention and its focus on other pressing issues facing the church. And since the church gathers as a representative body to seriously consider a whole range of issues only once every three years, that was a legitimate fear. On the other hand, Convention is a time for conviviality and fellowship, too.

It's a big deal for a diocese to host one of the triennial conventions, and the host has a chance to infuse the convention with some local color. In this case, Minnesota, the first diocese to ordain a Native American priest, Enmegahbowh, added some appropriate touches to the already-eclectic Episcopalian mix of worship styles and diverse music that had been strongly requested by the Presiding Bishop. There was a circular altar reminiscent of the Native American sacred circle; some Native American music and drumming, and a special Eucharist on August 5 commemorating Enmegahbowh, who was ordained in the late 1800s. For all the services at the convention, the worship leaflets were printed in two languages, Spanish and English, and prior to each morning's Eucharist, or Communion, a "visual prelude" of images appeared on a screen above the altar.

Part of the "mission" focus at the convention stemmed from a recent thrust in the national church known as "20/20," which has as its stated goal the doubling of national church membership by the year 2020. The 20/20 program has, at its center, a focus on young people and the future. There is an emphasis on defining a wider church than the "typical" Episcopal church of the past, with talk of the revitalization of worship, church messages, and outreach to reflect the growing acceptance of diversity. The program also advocates a broader range of styles in music and liturgy and awareness of technology, all of which tend to interest younger spiritual seekers and church members.

While the central, shared concerns of the national church (which, like all mainline denominations, has undergone a steady decline in membership since the mid-1960s) were represented by these efforts to focus on mission and young people, the poles of political opinion around issues of sexuality were equally present from the first day of the convention. In the first issue of the *Convention Daily* newspaper, published by *Episcopal Life*, were articles about two organizations, Claiming the Blessing and the American Anglican Council, which had come to the convention with opposite goals.

Claiming the Blessing is a ministry collaborative based in Pasadena, California and supported by various organizations within the church. The collaborative's executive director, the Rev. Susan Russell, summed up their goal as "working to abolish prejudice and oppression, to promote wholeness in human relationships, and to heal the rift between sexuality and spirituality in the church." They had made progress at the previous General Convention, in Denver, toward gaining approval of liturgies for the blessing of same-sex relationships. The group hoped that liturgies for same-sex blessings would be approved in Minneapolis and included in the Book of Occasional Services to be used, on an optional basis, by those parishes that wished to do so.

On the opposite side of these issues, the American Anglican Council came to Minneapolis with what it called "a comprehensive mainstream presence," including daily noontime legislative briefings and late afternoon breaks. Calling the council's presence "A Place to Stand" for "traditional views," the AAC's media officer and program director Bruce E. Mason said that the AAC would "work diligently to ward off, on theological and practical grounds, any attempt by General Convention to affirm homosexuality through the development of liturgies for same-sex unions or the giving of consent to the election of Canon Gene Robinson, the openly homosexual bishop-elect of New Hampshire." In fact, the AAC's efforts would also include separate celebrations of the Eucharist so that delegates and attendees opposing those elections and unions could worship separately and be assured that no openly homosexual clergy were involved in the consecration of the bread and wine.[1]

The convention officially began on Wednesday, July 30. There were ten bishop elections to be brought before the legislative sessions in 2003, with hearings scheduled according to the order in which they had occurred. Consent by the House of Deputies and House of Bishops is generally a formality; in fact, no bishops-elect have been denied approval at General Convention since the 1870s.[2]

As in the American political system, any piece of legislation in the Episcopal Church has to go through a legislative committee first. Then it goes to one House and if it passes, it goes to the other House. The requests for consent to bishop elections are presented by the Standing Committees of the dioceses to the Committee on the Consecration of Bishops, which hears testimony, asks questions, and then sends a resolution to the House of Deputies, asking for its vote.

Early on Friday morning, in the ballroom of the Hyatt Hotel, the Committee on the Consecration of Bishops held a two-hour hearing on Gene Robinson's election. The New Hampshire delegation made a ten-minute presentation, and then both supporters and opponents of Gene Robinson's election were allowed time to speak. The room was packed with over 300 delegates, bishops, and members of the media. The crowd overflowed outside, and the proceedings were broadcast on closed-circuit television.

Randy Dales had been asked by Gene to organize those who wanted to speak on his behalf. He had been approached, over the previous two days, by many people, most of whom he barely know, who had said they would like to make a particular point; it was up to him to choose the speakers since there would be limited time.

Speakers for the New Hampshire delegation were the Rev. Dales, the Rev. Hank Junkin, Bishop Doug Theuner, Jenny Lombardo (a young woman from St. Paul's, Concord, who spoke about Gene's commitment to youth ministry), and Gene's daughter, Ella Robinson, who read a letter from her mother, Gene's former wife, Isabella McDaniel.

Ella began by saying that although theirs was an "unusual family, it's one filled with love." Her mother's letter explained the couple's divorce, and how it was undertaken prayerfully and in a private church service that concluded with the Eucharist. "During this religious service," Gene's former wife wrote, "we promised to protect and cherish each other while continuing to co-parent our two daughters."[3] This statement by Gene Robinson's ex-wife stood in stark opposition to stories published in British tabloids implying that the bishop-elect had abandoned his wife and children for another man. Ella said that her family wanted to dispel those rumors.[4]

When the floor was opened for other comments, one of the speakers was the Rev. Ruth Kirk, a finalist in the New Hampshire election, who spoke about the fairness of the process, saying, "From the moment I opened the first mailings to the calls and letters I received after Gene's vote, my experience is that the search committee fulfilled its charge from the diocese to be open, fair, transparent and Spirit-driven."

Those who spoke in support of Gene's election focused on his character and qualifications; the right of dioceses to choose their own bishops; the parallels between the ordination of women and the ordination of homosexuals; honesty, openness, and integrity; and the positive changes they expected to see in the Episcopal Church as a result of taking this action.

Bishop Thomas Shaw of Massachusetts spoke about the consecration of the first woman bishop, Barbara Harris, in 1989, which took place despite dire warnings of schism. "Instead it has made us stronger and a more vibrant church with the full inclusion of women in ministry," he said, going on to argue that the consecration of Gene Robinson could hold the same promise for the inclusion and participation of gays and lesbians. The Rev. Mariann Budde of Minneapolis spoke about her experience as a woman priest, the mixed reception she had initially received, and how it had eventually changed to acceptance.

In its broadest sense, "catholic" means any member of the universal Christian church. Speaking about what the confirmation of Gene Robinson would mean to other people, the Rev. Howard Anderson of Minnesota pointed out the fact that a unique quality of the Episcopal Church, unlike the Roman Catholic Church, *is* its inclusivity. "The committee needs to think hard about that," he said, "and decide whether we will be the last catholics—big 'C' or little 'c'—or whether we will be watered down Roman Catholics trying to defend some moral like the Pharisees, or dressed up Presbyterians."[5]

The opposition, too, was both civil and impassioned, centered on the speakers' interpretation of Scripture; the church's position on marriage and on celibacy outside of marriage; and on the speakers' sense of the departure from historical precedent and church teaching, which the election of an openly gay bishop in the Anglican Communion would represent. ("It's not that there aren't gay bishops in the Anglican Communion and Episcopal Church," Randy Dales remarked, "but there aren't *openly* gay bishops out there.") The speakers were particularly concerned about the division this election would cause, both nationally and worldwide.

Bishop John Howe of Central Florida, Bishop David Bena, suffragan of Albany, Bishop Robert Duncan of Pittsburgh and Bishop Edward Little of

Northern Indiana all warned about the consequences of confirming Robinson's election. Disagreeing with Presiding Bishop Frank Griswold, Bishop Howe insisted that the church had always taught that sexual relations must take place only within the context of heterosexual marriage, and that to affirm as "a wholesome example" a person who is engaging in sexual relations outside of holy matrimony would be "a massive repudiation of that teaching."

Bishop David Bena warned that consent "[threatened] to shatter the Episcopal Church as we know it." He predicted that the church stood to lose "vast numbers of congregations, members and revenue" and that the church would be seen "not as the prophets of the Anglican Communion but American mavericks going our own way."

After the long, intense testimony, during which eighteen people spoke in opposition and nineteen spoke in favor of the election, the legislative committee deliberated in private for fifteen minutes and then voted by secret ballot. They then announced that they would send a resolution for consent to the House of Deputies. In keeping with the request made at the beginning of the hearing by the committee's co-chair, the Rev. Carolyn Keil-Kuhr, the crowd refrained from any demonstration of agreement or displeasure. [6]

On Sunday, another debate session was held in the House of Deputies. Randy Dales recalled that prior to the House of Deputies debate, one delegate had said, "I know that only a certain number of people will be able to speak, but I think it would be great if our line-up of people waiting at the microphones could stretch all the way around the hall." Some of Gene's supporters who were listening thought that would be a wonderful image, so they got the word out that people who wanted to stand in support should line up at the microphones, saving space at the head of the line for the people who had been chosen to speak. When the time came, there were twenty or thirty people in opposition, while the line formed by those in support of Gene stretched two-thirds of the way around a very large hall. As Randy said, "It was a visual show of support that wasn't missed by anybody."

Following the debate, a vote was taken after the delegates were again cautioned by the chairperson, the Very Rev. George Warner, to refrain from expressions of joy or disappointment. The House of Deputies voted in the affirmative, giving consent to Gene Robinson's election. The breakdown of the votes among the lay deputations was as follows: 63 yes, 32 no, and 13 divided. Among the clergy, the deputations voted 65 yes, 31 no, and 12 divided. The announcement of the vote was again received without demonstrative reaction, and the president immediately asked Chaplain Brian Prior to lead the House in prayer.

At a press conference after the vote, George Warner said, "What you saw out there today was the church when it is at its very best. You saw the demeanor of that House; you saw the restraint and the discipline."

Warner, who is from the Diocese of Pittsburgh, one of the centers of opposition to homosexual ordinations and same-sex blessings, said he had made the final decision to vote in favor of consent after listening to the debate and testimony and talking to other delegates. He acknowledged that his vote would create some problems for him back home, saying, "For many it is going to be a time of hope, and for many it is going to be a time of great despair. But that is why we turn at moments like this to prayer, silence, discernment." Warner may have been reflecting on the difficulty of his own decision when he remarked, "You saw something today that you are not going to see again for a long time in your life. You saw something today about people really trying to find their souls."

Gene Robinson spoke to the press briefly after Rev. Warner and said he felt peaceful and very humbled by what had just happened. A vote by the House of Bishops was expected the following day, Monday.

Hank Junkin had been moved to the point of tears by some of the speeches made on Gene's behalf, and that night, after the vote, he and the rest of the delegation allowed themselves to feel a little optimistic. The next morning, Monday, Hank had gotten up and gone out to get some coffee when his cell phone went off. It was a consultant from Ohio who was working with the New Hampshire delegation. She told Hank that he needed to come right away to the lobby of the Hilton: several allegations had been made against the New Hampshire bishop-elect.

That same morning, Doug Theuner was in his assigned seat on the floor waiting for the morning communion service to start when the consultant suddenly appeared. "She told me I needed to come with her immediately," he said. "It was clear there was some kind of great crisis, but she wasn't going to tell me what it was. So I said, 'Shall I leave my stuff here?' and she said, 'No, bring your stuff with you, we've got a terrible problem.'" Both Doug and Hank hurried to the Hilton lobby, where Gene and Bishop Tom Ely of Vermont were waiting for them.

Late Sunday evening, Bishop Ely had received an email from David Lewis, a parishioner at an Episcopal church in Manchester Center, a town in southern Vermont. The email had said, "I am a straight man reporting homosexual harassment by a gay male priest from another diocese," and stated that he had been touched "inappropriately" by Canon Gene Robinson during a convocation of Province I in 1999, in Holyoke, Massachusetts.

A second allegation involved an adult-content website that could be reached through links from Concord Outright, an organization in Concord, New Hampshire, which provided support and counseling to gay, lesbian, and bisexual teenagers. Gene Robinson had helped found Concord Outright in 1995. The question was the extent of his current knowledge or involvement with the organization, its website, and the pornographic site that could supposedly be reached from it. Two bishops had notified the parliamentarian of the House of Deputies about this issue, and this person had then contacted the chancellor to the Presiding Bishop.[7]

Bishop Ely had called Mr. Lewis on Sunday night to talk about his email and assured him that the church took these matters very seriously. Mr. Lewis told Bishop Ely that he had sent the same email to a number of bishops. In the morning, Bishop Ely notified the Presiding Bishop, Bishop Theuner, and the New Hampshire Standing Committee about the allegations that were made in the email.

Doug Theuner turned to Gene and asked him, "Do you know this guy?" and Gene said, "Not really . . . I think I may have met him at some provincial convocations but I can't place him."

"Well, that's all that I needed to ask," Bishop Theuner recalled later. "I didn't need to ask any more."

Thanks to the work done many years earlier by Gene Robinson himself—a leader in the Episcopal church on matters of addressing sexual misconduct—and others, the Episcopal Church already had a policy and detailed procedures in place describing exactly how to deal with allegations of this sort. There would have to be an immediate and thorough investigation. During the emergency meeting that morning, Doug Theuner suggested Bishop Gordon Scruton from western Massachusetts as the person to lead the investigation into the charges.

"In addition to the fact that the alleged offense had taken place in his diocese, my reasons for suggesting him were, number one, because he is a person of absolute integrity; number two, he's very supportive personally of Gene, he likes Gene, but he just could not vote for him because of his [Bishop Scruton's] principles; and finally because he's a neighbor, a guy in the province. So I thought he was absolutely the perfect person to do that. So probably the biggest contribution I made was suggesting Gordon, because his integrity was known not only by me, but by everybody else. Nobody really questioned his integrity, and that was good; that was an important thing."

At the end of the meeting, Gene asked Doug to call his parents in Kentucky and assure them that he was all right, knowing that the story would be all over the media that day. His greatest concern was having his mother learn the news while watching CNN.

The Presiding Bishop issued a short statement which said that "questions" had been raised regarding the bishop-elect of the Diocese of New Hampshire, and that the Standing Committee and bishop of New Hampshire and the bishop-elect, Canon Robinson, had asked that "a thorough investigation be undertaken before we proceed with seeking the consent of the bishops with jurisdiction." He named Bishop Scruton as the overseer of the investigation and said he would advise "the bishops with jurisdiction" as to the timetable for proceeding.

"That was the start of two days of some very interesting time," Hank Junkin recalled. "It wasn't fun, but the allegations turned out to be what I thought they were in the very beginning: absolute nonsense and spurious." Like many others, he was skeptical and surprised about the eleventh-hour timing.

"I had thought if we were going to get that kind of reaction that we would have already gotten it. And the *press* . . . my goodness. I had members of the national press coming over to me and going . . ." Hank stuck out his nose and sniffed the air. "I told them, 'Yeah, it does smell a little bit. There's somethin' wrong here. Why didn't this come two months, three months ago?'"

But as the president of the Standing Committee in the diocese, which would have to weigh the results of the investigation, Hank Junkin suddenly had to distance himself from Gene and to become part of the investigative arm. "So all of a sudden I was cut off from my deputation, in a way," he said. "I was cut off from the bishop-elect; I had to ask some very uncomfortable questions. That wasn't fun. I wasn't sure where all that was going to go and whether all these months of very hard work were going to be flushed by this information."

He described the sudden turn of events as a kick in the stomach. "I was not hungry at all that day," he said. But in spite of the sickening feeling, Hank remembered something else about that day that reminded him how wonderful the church can be. "Tom Ely of Vermont was very helpful to us, but I remember that his primary concern was the gentleman back home in his state. Did he have pastoral care? Did this person understand that CNN was going to be rolling up on his lawn in about five minutes? I learned a lot by observing Tom and Bishop Chilton Knudsen of Maine. They were really concerned about that individual: would he be okay, and did he have pastoral care?"

It became clear within hours on Monday morning that the charges probably did not amount to anything serious. The investigators talked directly by phone to Mr. Lewis, who declined to press sexual harassment charges and said he regretted using those words in his original email. The other allegation, about Concord Outright, took a little more time to investigate. But within a day, Hank was starting to feel better. He tried to remain calm and to help other people as much as he could, reassuring them that the people investigating the charges were doing all the right things.

For security reasons, the hotel room shared by Gene and Mark was registered under Mike Barwell's name; Mike was staying in another, smaller room on the corner of the same floor. Twenty-four hour security protected Gene in the hotel. Since he had been with the bishop-elect nearly all the time during the convention, Mike had taken it upon himself to care for him, getting him water when he needed it, monitoring his energy level and trying to move him out of the crowds when he was fading. "Of course, he's an extrovert," Mike said, "so he just winds and winds and then crashes and burns."

On the day that they later dubbed "Dark Monday," when the allegations surfaced and a crowd was gathering in the lobby of the Hilton, Mike had insisted: "Get him into a room, get him out of here, now, GO." His most immediate concern had been for Gene's safety, and he also realized that public exposure and making statements that could—and would—be quoted were the last things they needed right then. They got Gene back to his room, got the security in place, and he remained there quietly with Mark and Ella, not answering the phones, not talking to anyone but his family and close associates.

"I checked in on him periodically and took Bishop Scruton in to see him," Mike said. "The one thing I think I brought to the process, right from the beginning, was the ability to stay calm—not to panic, to have a plan, to stay calm in the midst of chaos, and to be non-anxious. Whether we won or lost the day, to be non-anxious. And Gene and I kind of fed each other on that."

Ironically, Mike Barwell had written a booklet for the Episcopal Church, back in 1993, called *Communications in Crisis*: it was about how to deal with clergy misconduct. The booklet had compiled the best plans for handling such problems, gleaned from around the national church. "We became the first national denomination to deal with those issues openly," he said. "As we've seen in the Catholic Church scandals in Boston and elsewhere, ultimately these things can't be hidden. But at Minneapolis, the depth-charge that exploded between the votes by the House of Deputies and the House of Bishops was a major test of crisis communications."

Because of his prior work on these issues, Mike had been aware how important it was to reach out to the man in Vermont. "The more you reach out, the less likely he is to push far," he had told Bishop Ely. Mike also realized how important it was not to make comments to the press while the investigation was proceeding, but as the crisis unfolded he was "very torn." He had put a huge amount of effort into building up good relationships with the media, relationships based on transparency, access, and fair play, and now, suddenly, those lines of communication were cut. "I really did want to make a statement. I really did want to say something to the media, simply explaining why we couldn't comment," he said, "but I was wisely counseled against it." Instead, he ended up being able to speak one-on-one, and not for attribution, with various media outlets, as opposed to making an official statement.

"It was clear to me that I was not a spokesman for the diocese: I was a media coordinator. And of course I couldn't speak for the national church: that was the responsibility of the Episcopal News Service. What I *could* do was to provide enough background information for the media to ask intelligent questions, but I would not be quoted directly. This helped people and made them look good when they went into a press conference or went in to ask a question. And we built friendships that way. There was a lot of trust that evolved, and that trust was returned."

On Monday evening, Mike Barwell went back to Gene's room to say good night. "It was about 10:30 at night and we were all just totally fried. There was a small group of people there: Tim Rich and Gene's daughter Ella, Mark, obviously, and a few other people. I took Gene aside and put my arm around him, and I just said, quietly, 'How're ya doing,' and he just *slumped*. It had really hurt him: he had no defense against this. He couldn't understand how anyone could be so *mean*, because in many ways I think he's really an innocent person: he's very trusting. I think it hurt him that someone would be so unfair, because I think he has a general sense of fairness, as most of us do, but he is really—I wouldn't want to say childlike—but there's an innocence about him that's very refreshing, very similar to Bishop Tutu. Tutu knows evil. He's stared at it. But he still has this wonderful sort of openness: 'Everyone loves me, because I'm one of God's creatures, and I'm going to love you!'"

"So anyway, I put my arm around him and said, 'How are you doing,' and he kind of slumped, and shook his head, and I was almost in tears. I am even now, thinking about it!" Mike blinked, and shook his head. "And Gene said to me, 'I feel like a very little man in a very small boat, in a very big storm.' And then he straightened up and said, 'But, you know, that's okay! Because I know who's in the boat with me.'"

The Gospel on Sunday, the day before, had been the story of Jesus in the boat with the disciples in the storm. "In that moment I realized," Mike explained, "this guy is going to prevail! There was no question about it. In the midst of this terrible, visceral anger and ugliness that these people felt toward him, he knew that Jesus was in the boat, and it was okay."

Ella Robinson had lived with her father and Mark that summer, right after she graduated from college. Because she was interested in public relations, she worked with Mike Barwell in Minneapolis, helping with the communications and public relations efforts.

"At General Convention we had a hospitality room where people could come by and meet my father, and we had a lot of people visit who were, if not blatantly confrontational, certainly in opposition and wanted to voice that and see how he would react. And then during the debates people said some awful things. So I think Mark and I had a very different experience there, along with his other supporters from New Hampshire who knew him so well, because we were so close to him: this was my *dad* they were talking about! And that's something we had talked about going into it, that there would be some pretty ugly things said, so we definitely prepared—but you're still standing there hearing some pretty awful things. At the convention we'd all talk about it each night, kind of finding it hard to believe this was all going on around us."

Ella said that she felt her father took it really well. "Some of it certainly hurt him, but he kept his eye on the goal that the right things would happen in the end, and feeling like God was there in his corner and right by his side, and that he needed to help people understand that this wasn't such a big scary thing. I think he understands the hardships that come along with all of this, how it is scary for people, and tries to takes an understanding perspective rather than putting a 'they're out to get me; they're wrong, I'm right' kind of twist on it."

She was unequivocal in asserting that what hurt her father the most was the widespread story that he had abandoned his wife and children. That falsehood had been printed right in the beginning, when Gene was first a candidate in Newark and Rochester. Ella quoted the headlines, the hurt very much palpable in her throaty voice: "'Left Wife to Live with Gay Lover!' 'Abandoned Kids.' Anyone who knew him would have known that wasn't right, but among all the other things that were said, that definitely hurt him the most. My father is such a family man. That's his inner core. That this was being said about him struck right to his core, although that might not have been obvious, even to the people in New Hampshire."

The lowest point, Ella agrees, was when the allegations came out. "We were so close [to having the election approved] and had gone through so much, and then to have this happen! It wasn't that he was shaken, really, or even close to defeat, but it was this sense of *one more thing*, having to keep crawling, one hand after the next. I think he really relied on God that day, and on Mark and me—on his family. That's one reason I wanted to be there, in case of things like that. So I think that that was pretty hard. But he wasn't really *shaken*, it was more that he was exhausted. There was just kind of constant pressure from all angles."

In spite of all the intense attention from the media during the time of the allegations, Ella says that many of the reporters were quietly supportive. "One woman even pulled my father aside and said, 'This is bull crap.' And Mike Barwell had done such an amazing job . . . there was a trusting relationship with the press, both ways. But there we were in our hotel room ordering room service so we didn't have to go out and talk to anyone. It was pretty surreal."

Ella was glad that she and Mark were there and felt, "Hey, we've made it this far, we can make it through." And it was both ironic and fortuitous that Gene himself had done so much of the work to make sure that rules and procedures were in place for handling allegations of sexual harassment. "Dad wrote the book!" Ella exclaimed. "And good thing that he did, because there was a very clear process for it all, and that helped get him through."

The New Hampshire Standing Committee had agreed that they would with-hold their consent if there were any question at all that the bishop-elect had engaged in sexual misconduct. As soon as Hank Junkin and Randy Dales received Bishop Scruton's report on Tuesday, they got all the Standing Committee members on the phone in a conference call together with Bishop Scruton.

Scruton's report was detailed, clear, and direct with regard to both areas of concern, the Lewis email and the questions about the Concord Outright web-site. In the report, he described the entire timetable of events beginning with the receipt of the email by Bishop Ely, discussed the allegations, and detailed his personal conversation with David Lewis:

> The individual then described to me the feelings he had during these two exchanges. He said that in his opinion, Canon Robinson's placement of his hands seemed inappropriate to him, given that they did not know each other, and presumed a far greater familiarity or intimacy than was the case. The individual said these incidents made him feel uncomfortable. He said he has never said anything to anyone about this, but did mention it to his wife but not at the time. He acknowledged that other people could have seen the exchange as natural and normal.
>
> He said he had not thought that the House of Deputies was going to consent to Canon Robinson's election, and when he learned consent had been given, he found himself late Sunday night needing to tell someone of his experience. He observed that when he wrote the e-mail, he was feeling upset, in part because he expected his concern to be brushed under the rug. He thought the Church would close ranks and not listen to him. I asked him whether he wanted to bring a formal charge of harassment. He said very clearly, no. He regretted having used the word "harassment" in his e-mail.
>
> The Title IV disciplinary process for priests was then explained to the individual, and I asked him again if he wished to proceed to file a written complaint. Again, he indicated that he had no desire to pursue the matter any further. He said he was thankful the Church has taken this seriously, and that he felt "listened to." He also indicated that he was not seeking any personal attention or notoriety, and regrets that it has been taken this way by some.[8]

Bishop Scruton's report then went on to describe the investigation into the Concord Outright website and his findings:

> What appears to be beyond dispute is that Canon Robinson helped to found Concord Outright in 1995. Investigation shows that the organization was founded to provide support and counseling for young people concerned about their sexuality. Canon Robinson's role in the Concord Chapter of Outright was primarily to provide training to insure that appropriate boundaries were observed for the protection of both young people and those working with them. Canon Robinson ended his involvement in Outright in 1998 and has not been associated with Outright since that time.[9]

The report ends with his conclusion that there was "no necessity to pursue further investigation" and no reason for the House of Bishops not to go forward with the vote of whether or not to consent to Canon Robinson's consecration.

The Presiding Bishop had requested that the New Hampshire Standing Committee review the report, and if they agreed with its conclusions, to send a formal proposal to the House of Bishops requesting consent.

Hank Junkin explained, "I wanted the Committee to hear what had been found directly from Bishop Scruton, so that they could say with one voice, 'We've investigated this, we've thought about it, we've prayed about it, we find no reason not to go ahead.' That's why we couldn't talk to the press earlier than we did, because we were trying to get all of these things in line. I didn't want anybody who had a decision to make about this saying, 'Nobody called me.' So we were of one voice, and it was wonderful. In the end, I think it came out *better* than all right. I think we showed the world how seriously the Episcopal Church takes allegations of sexual misconduct."

Gene Robinson agreed, as he later remarked publicly: "When the allegations of sexual misconduct were brought forward, it was a great day for the Episcopal Church, because we knew what to do. We've had those procedures in place for well over a decade. They didn't get shoved under the carpet, and we knew exactly what needed to be done and how to do it. So I've come out of the process feeling that it's really a very positive one and one that every congregation in the diocese is involved in, one that is completely led and carried out by clergy and laity and not by some centralized governmental body or magisterium, but in fact by the people themselves."

The long-awaited vote took place in the House of Bishops on Tuesday afternoon, following Bishop Scruton's report. After the report, the Presiding Bishop requested that the bishops partake in a process of "communal discernment." He asked them to pray for their "interior spirit" and then to share, in private conversation with their colleagues, reasons why Canon Robinson should *not* be elected. The bishops then prayed again and shared reasons why he *should* be elected. After this, the bishops voted by paper ballot.[10] A simple majority was required, with only currently-sitting diocesan bishops permitted to cast ballots (retired bishops and suffragans could not vote). Sixty-two bishops voted in favor and forty-three were opposed, with two bishops abstaining.[11]

At the convention in Minneapolis, there were 360 media representatives to deal with, and that meant temporarily shelving Mike Barwell's rules and consenting to a few press conferences, as part of the national church's press operation. Gene also continued to do many one-on-one interviews immediately following the vote for consent, particularly with the BBC and other organizations identified as "key" media, such as the *Boston Globe*, the *New York Times*, and the Associated Press.

Gene appeared on the *Today* show, CBS, ABC, CNN, and FOX, back-to-back. Mike recalled, "We had one video crew with Gene in one room, starting at 4:00 a.m. on the morning after the final vote, and we just rolled over to the next crew—and he did marvelously."

Back home in New Hampshire, the media also descended on Concord, looking for any quotable phrase or reaction. Rev. David Jones showed me two pictures taken on the morning after the decisive vote. One shows the street outside St. Paul's Church, Concord, filled with sound trucks and satellite dishes. The other shows a carpeted room crammed with media: photographers, reporters, and sound technicians with boom microphones are circled around David, who is speaking. "That's my own living room," he explained, still incredulous.

How had Gene reacted to all of this attention? Most people become celebrities gradually, but this unassuming priest had become world news literally overnight, and had entered the history books.

Mike Barwell sat back in his chair, his thin face pensive. "I think at first—and there's no judgment here—he was naïve. I think he really believed—he had no idea what would happen, or how quickly celebrity status would be thrust upon him. And he had no defense against it: he's such a nice guy, he would have said 'yes' to everything. So I had to play the cop and be the bad guy and say 'no.' And at all times what was being weighed, on his behalf, was what benefit was there for him, or for us as the diocese, to do that interview? What do we gain from it?" He leaned forward and snapped his fingers. "And these were sometimes snap decisions. We were getting bombarded, I was getting literally hundreds of requests at a time." He sat back. "And the second consideration was, what was his energy level like? What was it doing to him?"

As Gene's family, friends, and the people who had elected him already knew, the bishop-elect loved people, loved the chance to connect, and was a person who saw every encounter in his life as an opportunity to communicate something about the faith that sustained him.

"When I get asked questions, I want to find a way of pointing to God, rather than pointing to me," he told Michelle Gabriel of *Episcopal Life*. "It seems to me that whatever it means to be Christ-like, that is part of it. The sexual orientation piece of my story is secondary to what I'm interested in: my call from God and my call from the people of New Hampshire. That's really what I want to do: while the focus is on me, on the sexuality issue, I want to use that to tell my story about God."[12]

He also happily showed pictures of his first granddaughter, Morgan Isabella, who had been born to his daughter Jamee and her husband on July 20, a week before General Convention—a great gift and solace in the midst of the dramatic drum-rolls heralding the upcoming convention. Before coming to Minneapolis, he had had a chance to hold her when she was four hours old and said the memory of having her in his arms reminded him that the most important thing was to "stay grounded."

The partnership and trust that developed between Gene and Mike Barwell during those tense days in August was a help to both of them. "I could joke with him," Mike said, "and I think that was a relief for both of us: we could say what we really wanted to say in response to a reporter's dumb question, or say what we thought the other side should hear. That time during General Convention was very intense, very compressed, very uncertain in some ways—and very dangerous. I don't think I really had a full understanding of how dangerous it was or could have been because we always felt that nothing wrong was going to happen. Maybe having that kind of faith or confidence is childlike, but we had done our homework, we knew we had security, we knew what the game plan was, we knew what the message was—and we prevailed. And that was great."

Questions will always remain about the timing of David Lewis's email and whether or not the organized opposition to Gene's election had a hand in it. Mike Barwell did discover how the allegation about Concord Outright and its website had come about. On the last day of the convention, a young woman reporter from Reuters came up to him and said she needed to speak to him. Mike demurred, saying he was really tired and that it had been a long day, but she persisted, saying it was really important. "I wanted to apologize to you," she said. "It's about the website thing. I'm afraid I was responsible for that." Mike was astonished and asked her to explain.

It went back to the first public presentation Gene had made in Minneapolis, the young woman told him. There had been a talk in a church, focused on a youth group that Gene was meeting with, and it wasn't officially open to the press, although the media had been allowed in to take pictures and write quotes but not to ask questions. This was the first time Gene had talked about the work he had done with Outright New Hampshire—his ministry to high school kids who were dealing with sexual issues. He had explained that this was an organization for kids who wanted a safe place to talk honestly and openly and that he had been one of the advisors, serving on the board, but that he had eventually given up that commitment because he didn't have enough time for his responsibilities as a board member. This particular reporter had had a few questions she wanted to ask about this but she wasn't recognized because she was part of the press. Mike said later that he certainly wished she had come to him afterwards because he would have made sure she had a chance to ask her questions, since the New Hampshire delegation was being very open about everything.

But instead, the reporter went from there to an event hosted by the AAC, and she happened to bump into some people, including Bishop Howe of Central Florida. "Did you even know he had done this?" she asked, telling them about Gene's connection with Concord Outright. They went to the website, and two clicks away, found pornography.

So that was how the story originated, and soon it got around to CNN and the BBC. A couple of newspapers had approached Mike the next day asking, "What's this about a website Gene has that's related to pornography?" and he had said, "What are you talking about?" They replied, "Well, if you go to this website where Gene's an advisor, and you do two clicks, you get to a pornography site."

As Mike eventually found out, Concord Outright had listed some affiliated organizations where teens could go, and it turned out that you could access pornography from one of them in a few clicks—"like just about everything else on the web," he added. So he had dismissed the speculation, telling the reporters, "This is the most ridiculous thing I've ever heard. Of course he's not going to endorse this kind of stuff, or if it's there, it's without his knowledge. He hasn't been affiliated with the group for years. In fact, he didn't even know they *had* a website—*No!*" So the story had died for about three days because the conservatives couldn't convince anyone to run with it, and every time the press approached Mike he had said, "That's nonsense, go away."

"Well," he said, "finally someone took the story up. They found out about the letter from Lewis, and then they had a package deal, and away they went with it. I think the timing of it was very specific, between the House of Bishops and House of Deputies votes, because the conservatives had hoped they would prevail in the House of Deputies but they had not. Everyone was counting votes, and it was very scary, because they knew we had a good chance of prevailing instead."

Even after Convention, many people continued to speculate about Doug Theuner's role in Gene's election and about New Hampshire's timing, causing the consent vote to take place in this most public way, at the once-every-three-years General Convention. If the election had taken place during an off-year, some people wondered, when General Convention approval was not required, and the media had not been in such a frenzy, would the event have had the same impact?

"My retirement was not a matter of speculation," said Doug Theuner, a year later. "I had said for years that I was going to retire when I was sixty-five, and then I went to the Diocesan Convention at least two conventions before the electing convention, and announced my retirement and the actual date. So there shouldn't have been any question in anybody's mind about my desire to retire at the age of sixty-five. So that was the first thing."

He continued. "Everybody knew I was in favor of Gene's election. And Gene is my *friend!*" he exclaimed, his big voice starting to project as if he were back in the pulpit. "Gene is very *capable*. I can't think of anyone who would make a better bishop of New Hampshire! So did I want him? I voted for him! Afterwards, I *told* people I voted for him. I was very straightforward about that. But I didn't say a word beforehand to anybody about what I was going to do or my feelings."

Doug relaxed, laughed, and raised his eyebrows. "Even at the national level, more than the diocese, people might be more likely to say it had been a set-up, that Doug Theuner had engineered this thing—because I have been known to engineer some things in the past. I'm not beyond that! And people may have assumed . . . I'm noted as a person who has had a pro-gay stance in the church, back from the AIDS time and other things after that. So I'm sure some people would say, 'This was his agenda,' but no, it wasn't at all. This thing was going to carry itself, I didn't need to do anything. Anything I would have done would probably have been counterproductive! And General Convention itself was strange, kind of otherworldly, because I stayed out of it pretty much. I felt on the edge, a little distant from what was going on. I felt already it was time for me to step back and let things happen."

In retrospect, it is certain that even without the unprecedented media attention at General Convention and the soap-opera drama of the eleventh-hour allegations of sexual misconduct, the election of the first openly gay bishop would still have rocked the foundations of the Anglican Communion, both nationally and abroad. From the moment that Gene Robinson's nomination was announced in New Hampshire, it became an international story that simply gathered momentum as time went on.

At the conclusion of General Convention, although consent had been given and he had been seated in the House of Bishops, Gene was still a bishop-elect. Now the stage was set for the final, formal ritual through which he would become a bishop, taking his place in the line of ordained apostles stretching back to the original twelve, in the indelible moment of consecration. He and his small diocese would have three short months to prepare.

An informal conversation with Dartmouth College students, Hanover, New Hampshire.

Chapter 10

Centering

"I knew what it was right away," said Paula Bibber. "I was the only one who handled the letter: I opened it, and I bagged it—and then I only let the bishop look at it, because I didn't want to let anyone else get their fingerprints on it. So I had a little experience with the police department. They were kind enough to come here to fingerprint me, as opposed to having me go down to their office."

As the bishop's executive assistant, Paula opened all the mail for Bishop Doug Theuner and for Bishop-elect Gene Robinson. There had been some hate mail after the New Hampshire election, but it increased dramatically after all the media coverage at General Convention made it clear that the consecration would go forward. The date for the consecration was set for November 2, immediately following the annual New Hampshire Diocesan Convention.

The hate mail was taken seriously from the beginning but, perhaps because this was New Hampshire, unused to hate crime and still a little slow to grasp just how big a tidal wave was being created by the ripple in their small pond, the idea that anyone would truly want to harm, or even kill, their bishop-elect to prevent his consecration seemed astounding. But when this particular piece of mail arrived— a clear death threat to Gene—the Concord police contacted the FBI, and the New Hampshire Standing Committee and bishop's staff realized they had a serious situation that must be addressed. The envelope contained a picture of Gene and Mark from an article in an out-of-state newspaper. Gene's head was circled in red and an arrow led from the circle to the margin, where words indicated that he was either dead or would be killed. "The threat was more visual than verbal," said Paula, "but its intent was very clear."

"At first I felt that both Gene and Doug were somewhat cavalier," said Hank Junkin. "I was getting scared. These were nasty, hurtful, personal letters. We also had a budget that we were responsible for, and that's a place where Doug played a critical role. When I went to him and said, 'We've got problems here, for security,' he found a way, along with the diocesan trustees, to open up accounts that we hadn't been planning even to touch. And he said, 'Whatever we need to do in terms of security, we need to do it.' So we put a security system in at Gene's house, and we hired bodyguards from time to time." Hank said he made some mistakes because this was such a new area for him: at one point he signed up a security service and Gene called him soon after and said, "I think I need to protect these people—they're not going to protect me!" But the coordination improved, and Gene and Mark began to feel more comfortable with this radical change in their lives.

The professionals recommended that Gene move from his first-floor office, which had a large window, to a less accessible place in the building. The entrance to the building was permanently locked, a buzzer was installed, and mandatory visual recognition by the receptionist was necessary before any visitor was allowed entry; when Gene was in the building, his bodyguard was there also, aware of everyone who entered or exited. As had been the case for Barbara Harris, the first woman bishop, who had also received death threats before her consecration, Gene and his family were told they would need to wear bulletproof vests at his consecration.

The diocese was quiet about both the threats and the security efforts, heeding the advice that media coverage only tended to give fanatics more attention and make them believe their behavior was legitimate. Gene himself was calm and pragmatic; he remained confident but agreed to the precautions.

Both Gene Robinson and Doug Theuner were acutely aware that in spite of the large majority of supporters in the diocese, there were a few unhappy parishioners in nearly every parish who, like vocal opponents in the Episcopal Church at large, were threatening to withdraw their pledges or leave because of the election. Both recognized the worry and difficulty this created for diocesan clergy and lay leaders, as well as the increase in financial pressure on some already-struggling parishes.

On a bright New England fall morning, the diocesan clergy assembled in Concord for a special private meeting, called by both the bishop and bishop-elect, to give the clergy a chance to share information about what was happening in their congregations, express their concerns and need for support, and ask questions. After coffee and muffins, the group prayed, and both Gene and Doug addressed them and then opened the floor to comments.

The New Hampshire diocesan clergy are fairly representative of the state at large, both demographically and culturally. On this day, many of the clerical collars were peeking out of plaid flannel shirts, and more than one female priest wore a long flowing skirt and Birkenstocks. There is only one black priest in the diocese, but there are many women and several openly gay clergy. Perhaps because of its rugged beauty, many lakes, and proximity to a number of colleges and universities, the state has also become the place of retirement for a number of priests and bishops, many of whom take an active role in diocesan affairs and act as occasional "supply" priests (substitutes) for nearby parishes; quite a few of them were in attendance that day in Concord as well.

Several of the priests spoke openly about difficult circumstances back home—longtime parishioners who had left or threatened to leave and precarious financial situations. Since every parish is expected to pay a diocesan assessment as well as maintain its own budget, several priests asked what relief they could expect from the diocese and received satisfactory answers from the bishop. But there were no recriminations; not one priest said, "How could you have done this to us?" or anything similar. The faces in the room were composed and thoughtful, and the tone of the conversation was concerned, prayerful, collegial, determined. The room erupted easily and often into laughter. It was a congenial and successful gathering, with the enormous affection and support of the clergy for their bishop and bishop-elect palpably evident.

I spoke to one of those priests a while later, over breakfast, on a blustery day. Like everyone in northern New England, we spent ten minutes moaning about the weather, but that seemed to justify the plates of eggs, sausage, biscuits, cheese, and home fries we ordered and happily wolfed down while talking over Episcopalian affairs.

I asked how things were going in this priest's small parish. "I think we're going to be okay in the long run," she said. "We have a budget of under $50,000, and this year we're going to have a deficit of $20,000, so that's not great. And we also need to replace the roof on the church. We lost some parishioners due to Gene's election, and unfortunately some of them were conservative members who

Following Gene's election, members of the New Hampshire clergy met with Gene and Doug Theuner to discuss the situations in their home parishes.

made large pledges. We've also gained some families, but they're still new, and it doesn't seem like the right time to visit them and say, 'Could I talk to you about proportional giving?'" She made a funny face, and grinned, looking up from her eggs. "Some people who left have also come back; it's a pretty small town, and they realized they missed the community here and maybe they couldn't find another congregation that fit as well, in spite of these differences. And that's good. They were welcomed back with open arms."

"I keep getting surprised," she said. "We had a meeting of the Episcopal Church Women recently, and if you looked around you'd think, wow, northern New England, elderly—they're going to be conservative. But some of the women started talking about politics, and I couldn't believe how upset they were about the current administration's policies. *Really* upset. And it has been the same way on the issue of the bishop and gay rights."

She laughed and told me a story about a woman who is elderly and a typical pillar of the congregation, who acts as a greeter at the door for most services. "It was during the Minneapolis convention, that weekend when all the allegations had been brought forward. Another couple was coming up the church steps, grumbling about Gene Robinson and the damage this was doing to the church. This woman who was the greeter overheard them, and when they reached her she drew herself up, looked them in the eyes with a steely glance and said, 'It's 2003! Get over it!' And it's true, a lot of people had to do their grumbling and venting— we had forums especially for that—but to a large extent they're getting over it."

She said she had also been surprised, during these forums, by the people who had come because they were frustrated with the opposition and wanted to talk to other people about why they held a different view. "One man spoke up and said, 'The current situation with gays is just like when I was in the military, and it became integrated. I'd grown up in the South and had never had to mix with black people. Suddenly the guy in the bunk above mine was black. I didn't have a lot of choice about it; I had to examine my attitudes and discover that most of the notions I'd held about this whole group of people were wrong; they were people very much like me.'"

The priest raised her eyebrows. "That's pretty powerful, when it comes from an unexpected place: somebody in the congregation who nobody expects to articulate that view. People listen when that happens." She laughed, remembering another incident. "And when Gene actually came to the parish and people had a chance to meet him and talk to him, of course he won a lot of them over. This same elderly woman who had said, 'Get over it!' was there the night Gene came to visit. He greeted her, maybe even by name, since she's been there such a long time I think he knew it, and as he was going on up the aisle she said, 'That Gene Robinson, he's a hot ticket!'"

We paid our bill, bought a sugared cruller to go, and went out onto the street, where we were instantly shivering from the wind.

"So I think it will work out over time," she said. "And it helps, too, that the bishop and the diocese have listened to our financial problems. The diocese is helping us with a partial grant for the new roof, and we should be able to raise the rest of the money locally. It said to the people, 'We may be a small parish and we may have a famous bishop-elect, but he cares about us.'"

Immediately after returning from Minneapolis, Gene, accompanied by his partner Mark Andrew, started a series of Sunday visits to the parishes in the dioceses, hoping to visit all of them before his consecration. Gene's round, smiling face and bubbly "Helloooo!" began to enliven parish coffee hours as the couple drove to the far reaches of the rural state in order to see and be seen, and to give parishioners a chance to voice their concerns and ask questions face-to-face. Gene hoped that these visits would take some of the heat off the local clergy and help calm the waters that had been stirred by the media storm, the strident anti-gay rhetoric from opponents, and the talk of schism.

In some cases Gene and Mark attended a regular Sunday morning service, staying for informal conversation at the coffee hour. In other places, where the clergy knew some parishioners were upset and needed a chance to ask difficult questions or even to be confrontational, he made himself available for a more formal question-and-answer session on an afternoon or evening. He also found himself inundated with more speaking invitations—from secular organizations, other denominations, and the media—than he could possibly accept, and wherever he went he always tried to include time for questions. During these few months before the consecration, you could see Gene working out his own answers to the questions he had pondered mostly in private before his election. While he was remarkably good on his feet from the very beginning, quickly establishing a charismatic and disarming personal rapport even with opponents, he rapidly became more and more comfortable with a variety of audiences and situations and with being put on the spot. He noted that only twice before, in the entire sixteen years he had worked in the Diocese of New Hampshire, had he talked about homosexuality, and then only because two congregations specifically requested him to.

As the news of the death threats, the bulletproof vest, and the bodyguards filtered out through the New Hampshire diocese, parishioners were deeply worried. It would be hard to overstate the affection of the diocese for their bishop-elect, and the quiet, hard-working, rural and private people of New Hampshire were incredulous that anyone would resort to violence to prevent his consecration. People understood disagreement and lived with it: New Hampshire is a state of stark contrasts in its landscape and in its politics. Although historically conservative, close to a majority in the state had become more liberal in recent years, probably as a result of an influx of new residents from the Democratic states of Massachusetts, Connecticut, New York and New Jersey. Although the lack of both a personal income tax and sales taxes were part of the New Hampshire's attractiveness, some of those voters even favored "breaking the pledge"—the promise never to vote for a state income tax that had been required of successful political candidates in the past. And as its "Live Free or Die" motto indicates, a high premium is placed on personal privacy and the right of law-abiding individuals to live as they choose.

So Gene was one of their own, and the majority of parishioners felt protective and concerned for him and for his family. "How is Mark?" they would ask. "How are your children?"

Ella Robinson lived with her father and Mark during the months following the election. "That summer that I lived with them we had a full security system put in," she said. "It had a key that I wasn't very good at—it was very loud when that alarm sounded! Before we had barely locked the doors at night, and now . . . Dad got some pretty nasty emails and letters, pretty serious death threats throughout the whole thing. That's a lot to handle if it's your significant other or your parent. But because Dad was so . . . kind of strong, it put the rest of us at ease. If he had been freaking out, unwilling to leave the house without a bodyguard or something, I think it would have affected the rest of us a lot, but still, that was scary."

"The protesters go away," she added, "but at the end of the day the threats are still there, they stay with you. 'A bullet with your name on it'—that's pretty awful. But even with those negative things, Dad had a faithful kind of assurance that it was all going to be okay. He believed in this so much, as we all did, that we all just felt we were in this together. Of course we'd take the proper precautions, but we were going to be able to do this, it was important enough."

Ella said that it wasn't at all that Gene had talked his family into accepting the risk to him, and potentially, to them. "It wasn't like, 'I'm going to do this whether you want me to or not'—it never got like that," she said. "He's a really strong person, with a core of strength, but that's not enough. That's like doing it with your will. It comes

Gene, Ella, and Mark at a pond near their home in New Hampshire.

from faith, and his faith is simple, and trusting, and very loving. And he had Hank and Doug and Tim and all these amazing people in the diocese supporting him and willing to put their own necks out on the line."

Ella feels that one reason her father is such a good priest is his ability to convey his faith so palpably to others. "He really believed in this and was willing to go through these hard times, and I think we each respectively saw that faith and understood that that was where he was coming from, and believed in him and what he was doing, and that he was the right person for it, and that this really *was* God calling. We *wanted* to be supportive, and wanted to see it happen, because he believed so strongly in it. But even with the setbacks, he and the people supporting him were strong enough to make it to the next step. It was like each step up prepared you for the next one. We were all such firm believers that we felt that this really was meant to happen, and if we just kept thinking along those lines, it was going to be okay, and that God was kind of looking out for *all* of us. And He did."

Without ever betraying the privacy of his family, Gene always acknowledged the role they played in his life. He spoke lovingly and appreciatively of his daughters, the closeness of their family, and the joy and peace he found when holding his new infant granddaughter—"which puts just about everything else in perspective." And he always spoke of the enormous support he received from his partner Mark and expressed his amazement that this man, an intensely private person, was willing to accompany him on all his parish visitations and to be in the public eye. He said that they'd both been surprised and very grateful for the support and friendship extended to Mark by the other "bishops' spouses" in the weeks after General Convention. "They call up and want to talk to him," Gene said. "They have no interest in talking to me!"

Primarily, people in the diocese wanted to know how Gene could possibly handle the constant pressure and anxiety of being at the center of a storm that showed no signs of letting up. Gene often repeated the story of a gift he was given during the period when the allegations of sexual misconduct were made against him at General Convention. It was a piece of calligraphy given to him by the Rev. Tim Rich, who had recently accepted Gene's request that he become *his* canon to the ordinary. It read: "Sometimes God calms the storm. And sometimes God lets the storm rage, and calms his child." The image and verse meant so much to Gene that he had the calligraphy framed and placed it on the wall of his office.

Talking to a parish audience at a small rural church in northern New Hampshire, Gene told that story and then elaborated: "In spite of all the difficulties—the death threats, the hate mail—it has been a time when I've felt God very close to me. And I feel that God has been with us in this process. During the electing convention, something was going on that made the hair stand up on the back of your neck. It was a very powerful experience for most of the people who attended, and we had the same experience this summer at General Convention."

He said someone had sent him an email asking what it felt like to be at the center of this thing and to have caused so much pain and confusion and anger, and that he had answered that he didn't like it, but that it had actually been helpful to realize he worshipped a Jesus who had also caused a great deal of pain and confusion and anger.

"And it was among the churchy types!" he elaborated, raising his eyebrows and peering over the rim of his glasses. "It was the Pharisees and Sadducees who were infuriated by him. And the same statements that infuriated *them* sounded like *good news* to the people on the fringes. For example, Jesus treated women differently from anyone in the religious establishment of that day, but let me tell you, the woman at the well knew that she had been touched in her soul."

"I don't mean to equate myself to those events in any way," he went on. "But I think sometimes that God calls us to do things that some people won't understand and will resist, but God means for us to move ahead anyway, so long as we keep saying our prayers and trying to discern what He really would have us do." He said that, short of God making known to him that he should not move forward, he intended to be consecrated on November 2, but that he would do that as humbly as he could, because he was greatly humbled by it. He expected the consecration to be a joyous event without being a triumphal one, and was careful to point out the distinction.

He told people he had been working very hard with his spiritual director to try to make sure that it was God's voice that he was hearing "and not my own ego doing a fabulous rendition of God's voice," cautioning that we can all make that mistake. But he was firm in his belief that God was calling us to move forward. "And when we do," he said, "we're going to be as welcoming and kind and patient and pastoral as we can be with those for whom this is a confusing or troubling development."

Gene said that he'd be very glad when "all these cameras and things aren't on me" and he would be old news. He said he was really, really looking forward to November 3. But, he said, he realized that you couldn't buy this kind of attention in the religious world: there had been an unprecedented 390 credentialed members of the press at General Convention, including representatives of the major media and newspapers who had sent their best writers.

"What I've decided," he said, over and over, at every venue, "is that if I'm going to get all this attention, I'm going to use it for God and for telling people about the Episcopal Church." He joked that evangelism, Episcopal style, is like going out in a boat and waiting for the fish to jump in—but that he recognized that he'd been given a rare opportunity.

"It's not a bad thing to get Episcopalians reaching for their Bibles!" he said. "And every congregation in this diocese, and every diocese I've talked to, is saying, 'What makes us a church? What do we really believe? What holds us together? What are the limits of community? What kind of mutual responsibility do we have?' To have that kind of substantive discussion going on in every congregation is not exactly to be lamented. We have those big red, white, and blue signs that say, 'The Episcopal Church Welcomes You.' And unless we're going to put an asterisk after that and in fine print list the people we don't really mean it about, then we better start acting that way. I think one reason why this is as exciting to some people as it is painful to others is that the church is beginning to really act as if it really means that."

Gene always told his audiences about the positive results of his election. After doing four interviews with Matt Lauer on the *Today* show, he had quickly received a number of emails from priests around the country telling him that people had showed up at their churches asking, "Is this the church of that guy who was on TV?" When a woman told him she had sat in a supermarket parking lot for an hour listening to him being interviewed by Terry Gross of NPR's *Fresh Air*, he replied that after that broadcast he was contacted by over a thousand people. "Those people don't make up for people who've walked away, but it's undeniable that there is also some very good news coming out of this," he said. "At one church a woman came up to me and said she hadn't been in church in thirty years and was coming back because of this." Then he laughed and said that when the *Daily Show* devoted half a program to his election, his own kids had finally decided he had arrived!

At that early date, Gene seemed, to some extent, like a kid in a candy store— surprised by, but enjoying the limelight. "I'm just having so much *fun!*" he'd say, over and over, and it was clearly true. He was genuinely glad to have the oppor- tunity to talk about his faith and the Episcopal Church he loved, still surprised to be treated as an icon, and hopeful that the controversy—and the attention— would blow over after the consecration. He was convinced that reconciliation with the dissenting parties was possible and willing to work very hard to try to make that happen. His naturally optimistic personality, his historic success in meeting people and establishing a quick rapport, and the deep faith that had carried him through the time of the allegations at General Convention continued to support him during the long days of traveling, speaking, and preparing for his consecration. "Once people see that the walls don't cave in, and it feels pretty much like church always was, I think this will die down and hopefully be okay," he often repeated.

People continued to ask about the personal threats, amazed that he seemed so calm. "I try not to think about it too much but I'm having to think about it more," he admitted. "We're trying to strike a balance between being 'wise as serpents, innocent as doves'—between being prudent and going overboard." In late September, the diocese stopped hiring bodyguards for a while because it was so expensive, and Gene was uncomfortable with special funds, at Bishop Theuner's discretion, being used in that way. But starting two weeks before the consecration, he said, they would be "getting some serious coverage in."

"I just want to be the bishop, not a martyr," he said, "and there are a lot of crazy people out there. And if something should happen—well, I'm doing what I'm called to do, and I'll be all right."

Invariably, Gene would be asked about Scripture and homosexuality. He has come to where he is, theologically, through a lifetime of questioning, prayer, studying theology, and considering the world as it is. And while he has moved, over the course of his life, from a literalist tradition (the Disciples of Christ is a "Bible" church where Scripture is taken more or less literally) to a much more open one, he knows where fundamentalists are coming from.

In one forum, Gene was asked, "In your mind and in your journey, what would you say is the role of Biblical texts in modern theology? Can modern theological writings be considered with equal weight as Biblical writings, or is there something more essential to the Bible?"

He responded by saying that the Holy Scriptures were absolutely primary. "I don't hesitate about that," he said. "It is the quintessential description of God's love affair with humankind, as told through the eyes of many, many different witnesses. And it always needs to be primary. And then it needs to be weighed against how, over time, the church has understood those Scriptures, and understood itself theologically, and then, we need to add in what has been our experience as human beings, and as human beings with one another, and then we need to have that mix of Scripture, tradition, and reason discussed and examined in a community because any one of us can twist things to make it sound like what we want it to sound like. So you always need to be doing that kind of discernment in community to at least lessen the risk that you are fooling yourself about what it says. That's always a fallible process, and one that we always need to be working on, because it's not easy."

The questioner continued, "Is there anything in particular that makes you turn toward that earlier witness, as opposed to modern witness about God's relationship to humanity?"

"Yes," Gene said, "because I believe that it is the word of God, and it has supported and nourished and educated countless Christians before me, and I honor that. It's where I found Jesus. I mean, despite some of the things that my church was saying, and doing, the good news came through to me. *It saved my life.* If I had not believed the good news that I read in the Scripture, rather than some of the vile stuff that was being said in my parish when I was growing up, I wouldn't be here today. So I owe my life to the Scripture, because I believe God speaks through it, in spite of us."

Richard Hooker, the "father" of Anglican theology who wrote at the time of Elizabeth I, is credited with a description of Anglicanism as a faith supported by Scripture, tradition, and reason—what came to be called the "three legged stool." This strong heritage, which Gene often mentions, of recognizing the value and interaction of all three sources of knowledge, is now under assault by conservative Anglicans who adamantly insist on the primacy of literal Biblical interpretation. In almost every audience, someone rose to ask Gene about how he interpreted the Biblical passages that seem to clearly denounce homosexual behavior. Gene often said his answer would be "the Cliffs Notes version" and that if the discussion could go on for two days, "we could really do it right." He usually began his answer by saying that, as Christians, we take Scripture very seriously—and then adding that Episcopalians have always taken Scripture *seriously*, and never *literally.* "Some of the critics are calling themselves traditionalists," he said, "and yet are trying to take us to a place that has *never been our tradition.* Ever. We've never been a denomination that literally read and believed every word of the Bible. On the other hand, we take it all seriously. But what I'm going to end up telling you is that I don't believe the Bible addresses what we are addressing today, which are faithful, life-long, monogamous relationships between people of the same gender. The Bible doesn't talk about this."

The Bible contains seven brief passages that seem to speak to homosexuality. Gene divides them into several different categories. The Old Testament contains the Book of Leviticus, a part of the Hebrew Bible which contains the "Law." Leviticus spells out rules about how the Jews were to live, and much of this is a so-called "purity code," detailing how the people were to keep themselves pure and untainted by the pagan cultures around them. That involved keeping kosher, not wearing cloth and leather at the same time, and a number of other rules. To his audiences, Gene explained his view that the Levitical code also included instructions for survival, as a race. At the time, all that was thought to be necessary for continuation of the race was contained in a man's sperm, and the woman "sort of just provided a nest in which it could grow up." The woman didn't contribute anything; what was precious was the sperm. So to "spill one's seed on the ground" was sinful, and therefore masturbation, sex between two men, and other acts that didn't preserve the sperm for procreation were excluded. "That doesn't seem to be about faithful, committed relationships between people of the same sex," he said.

The often-quoted Sodom and Gomorrah[1] story, in the Book of Genesis, is an example of the wide difference between literal interpretation and the interpretation of scholars who examine ancient texts according to linguistic, cultural, historical, and archaeological evidence. The ancient cities of Sodom and Gomorrah were located in Palestine, near the Dead Sea. According to the Biblical story, because of the unacceptable behavior of the inhabitants—their specific sin is not spelled out—God tells Abraham that he intends to destroy Sodom. Abraham asks God what would happen if he found there were any righteous people in Sodom. God promises Abraham that he will spare the city if it contains ten righteous people, and sends two angels to investigate. Near the city gates, the angels find a man named Lot, who invites them to his house for a meal and shelter:

> But before they lay down, the men of the city, the men of Sodom, both young and old, all the people to the last man, surrounded the house; and they called to Lot, "Where are the men who came to you tonight? Bring them out to us, so that we may know them."[2]

Lot refuses to give the visiting angels to the men of Sodom and instead offers them his two virgin daughters. The crowd refuses to accept this compromise. The angels then save Lot from the crowd; Lot and his family are told to leave the city, and God destroys Sodom and Gomorrah with fire and brimstone.[3]

In speaking about this story, Gene explained that showing hospitality to guests is, and always was, of great value in the Middle East. Travel was difficult; not to offer strangers shelter and food put them in grave danger. "But," he continued, "even if you want to look at the homosexual part of Sodom and Gomorrah, it's about homosexual *rape*, not faithful, loving relationships. And, when the two angels do not offer to be raped by the townspeople, Lot offers his *daughter*s, his virgin daughters, instead. I mean, *hello*? Are these the kinds of Biblical values we want to espouse? Even Ezekiel,[4] and even Jesus, mention that inhospitality was the sin of Sodom, and its failure to take care of the poor, the fact that it lacked justice, and so on. Neither mentions homosexuality. So even within the context of the Bible itself, homosexuality was not thought to be the point of the story."

Paul mentions homosexuality in the New Testament, but those passages also strike Gene as murky. He uses an interesting analogy when explaining this difficulty: "I think the passages written by Paul are very difficult to be certain about, because no one knows exactly what those words mean. There are a number of theories. But the fact is, we've lost the primary knowledge. Let's say the game of baseball were lost to us, and a thousand years from now, someone discovered a novel, and it said, "Erik is a little out in left field." Well, you could claim to know what that meant, because you know what left is, and you know what a field is: you would know what each of the words meant, but if you didn't know anything about the game of baseball, you wouldn't get the meaning of the text. You wouldn't know that most people are right-handed batters, and that if you're playing left field you have to back way up. The term 'being in left field' came to mean a person who's a little out of touch, a little bit isolated and so forth. It's the same here: some of these texts are pretty difficult to understand unless we can figure out what they meant to those who wrote them and what they meant to the people who heard them at that time."

Jesus never mentions homosexuality at all. In Gene's view, in the New Testament passages most often cited, Paul may have been speaking against the common Greek practice by which an older man took a younger boy sexually, as well as intellectually, into manhood. "Today we would call that child abuse, and no one's arguing for that," Gene said.

He continued: "It's very difficult to take a modern psychological understanding, like homosexual orientation, and plug it back into an ancient text, in which it was unknown. Those texts were written at a time when everyone was presumed to be heterosexual. So to act in any other way was to be against one's nature. The whole psychological construct of sexual orientation is a little better than 100 years old. So we can't take something that we know now, and plug it back into a text that's several millennia old, and think that *they* meant what *we* mean."

Gene agrees that the seven passages are all negative. But, he says, "they are not talking about what we are talking about today." Likewise, he says he values being in a church in which different interpretations of the same passages can and do coexist.

"It's pretty easy to say that everything in the Bible is literally true, or none of it is true. But the way we have traditionally done Scripture in our denomination is that any one verse must be seen in the context of the whole. In other words, you can't take one verse and raise it to a position of importance if it flies in the face of the whole of the Scriptures. Conversely, just because we decide that one part of Scripture is not eternally binding on us, it doesn't mean that the whole thing comes tumbling down."

Gene says he likes to think of the Episcopal Church as "advanced placement religion" and explains, "It's hard work if you start saying, 'We have to use our minds and prayerfully engage one another as a community of people, using the best scholarship we have among us, to figure out what those writings meant to the person who wrote them, what they meant to the person who heard them, and then ask the question, "Are they eternally binding?" But that's what we, as Episcopalians, try to do.'"

In one of these question-and-answer sessions, a young woman came to the microphone. She was obviously distressed and spoke in a pleading voice: "But how do you know for sure that what you're doing is right or what you're doing is wrong? If you don't believe that all Scripture is God-given, then how do you know how to live your life?"

Gene looked at her with a great deal of compassion, and answered, "So—you live your life not being sure of any particular verse. But I'll tell you what I'm sure of. I am absolutely sure that I'm going to heaven. I'm absolutely certain of it. I'm also absolutely certain that I'll do a lot of bad stuff between now and the day I die, that I will fall far short of what God has in mind for me, but I believe without any shadow of a doubt that I'm going to heaven."

"I feel like the Prodigal Son, you know. God has given me all these gifts, and I have, I'm sure, squandered many of them in a far-off realm. But I'm trying to get back home. I'm probably not going to get there before I'm dead and gone, but what I can be assured of is that God will come running toward me with his arms outstretched, and before I can utter, 'I'm sorry,' God will be putting a robe on me and a ring on my finger and ordering up a party. That's what I really believe. So I don't have to be sure about any one verse or any one story. I could be wrong. But I don't believe that my salvation depends on it, because my salvation has already been won. All I have to do is accept it, and then do my very best to be God's hands and feet in the world."

"In the context of all of Scripture, the question we need to ask is: with the ideas of loving God with heart, soul, mind, and strength, and loving your neighbor as yourself, which are the two great commandments, what does it make sense to discern that God is trying to say to us? And we'll perhaps disagree on that."

When listening to Gene's certainty about going to heaven, one wonders: what about the people who are equally convinced that he—and everyone like him—is going straight to hell? Gene's answer to that is usually a quiet, short statement: "Time will tell." But on a more subtle level, what does he think will happen to the people who wish him harm?

"I don't know what's going to happen to them," he says. "I worry for them, in the sense that they don't strike me as very happy people. If they have heard the good news, it hasn't made them very joyful. So I wouldn't begin to judge them, but I do worry for them. And most of the time I am able to feel sorry for them." He's quite aware that there are people who are convinced he's going straight to hell or some version of it; he gets letters and postcards from them all the time, saying precisely that. One questioner mentioned talking to someone who insisted Gene could not be a spiritual person—that he was being deceived by the devil because of his sexual orientation.

"I don't have to satisfy those people," Gene replied. "All I have to satisfy is my own heart and my own conscience, and my reading of Scripture. I don't have to convince the person who thinks I'm damned. I'm the one who's taking the risk that I'm wrong. But, frankly, that part doesn't feel risky to me at all. My experience is of a living God. Right here, right now. Especially in this time: God feels so close that prayers seem redundant. I really feel surrounded by God's presence. Now, I could be delusional, but I don't think so, because over time, that same God has stuck with me in lots of situations that were Good Friday moments."[5]

"And as for the part about whether I am a spiritual leader or not—when folks were trying to figure out whether John the Baptist or Jesus was the Messiah, some people came to Jesus and asked him if he was the Messiah, and instead of saying yes or no, Jesus just said, 'What do you see?' The lame are walking, the blind are seeing—he named some of the other things very reminiscent of prophesies in Isaiah about things that the Messiah would accomplish."

"I wouldn't want to arm-wrestle a person like that," Gene said. "I would just say, 'What do you see?' Am I a spiritual leader? I don't know. Ask the people I work with, minister with, and so on, and then judge."

Gene read every negative letter that came in to him until General Convention. He finally decided that he couldn't let that much negativity come his way without allowing a little of it to seep in. "It's toxic," he stated flatly.

He described receiving a postcard that showed a beautiful photograph of the *reredos* and high altar at Durham cathedral in England. There was a beautiful rose window above the altar, the card was stunning—and then he turned it over and read the salutation: "You fornicating lecherous pig." He thought to himself, "What is the state of the soul of the person who first of all would write such a thing, but on the back of a card of a beautiful altar of God?" Gene is a person so much in touch with his own integrity, so completely used to examining his own conscience and considering his words and actions, that he was floored by a disconnect of that degree. While being a mature, experienced professional who has seen and handled a great deal, at his core he has a childlike, simple goodness, and on that basic level he couldn't conceive of how certain people could be so cruel, or so misguided, or so twisted that they could say the things or take the actions against homosexuals that they did, while still insisting they were faithful Christians. His instinct and his desire, honed by years of experience, was to listen, to face the opposition and confusion, and to try to understand—all this as a prelude to positive engagement and, hopefully, reconciliation. Not to hear or read what each voice was saying went against his grain, but he realized the need for self-preservation as well.

Gene's witness about his faith and the strength he derived from it was particularly poignant for other gay people, and increasingly he attracted a large, admiring audience, some religious and some not, who saw him both as an icon for gay rights and a symbol of spiritual hope. Perhaps even before Gene recognized the fact in himself, gays and lesbians saw that he embodied the love that John Fortunato had so poignantly written about, and they wanted to hear it and be close to it.

A woman in an audience at a New England university identified herself as a lesbian and said she was considering returning to the faith community that she hadn't been part of for years because of her sexual orientation. She said it meant a tremendous amount to her to hear about the kind of commitment he had. "It seems like, in your personal life, you return to a source of love in order to face the kind of antagonism that you constantly are a magnet for," she said. "And I'm thinking about how, in my struggles here in the community and other places in my life, how faith-based communities seem like such an important part of not being reactive—is faith central to approaching difference from a place of love?"

When Gene answers questions like that, he listens with his whole body. He was quiet for a moment, and thanked the questioner. "Yes," he said, "I think it's all about faith and finding a quiet place. It's that thing about finding the calm place in the center of the storm. And that's the kind of place of faith that lets you not be so reactive. I'm also interested—and I'm not in any way comparing myself to Jesus—I'm reading the Gospels completely differently now. I've always been interested in how, in at least two of the three synoptic Gospels, Jesus is depicted as saying nothing at his trial. And I've always wondered about this. How could all this awful stuff be coming his way, and he just doesn't say anything? But now I'm

162

beginning to see that sometimes the only way to stop evil is to just not engage it. But it takes a toll. It's really hard, and if you're absorbing that kind of evil coming your way, you'd better be in good touch with God, because God is the only one who can take it away. I can only absorb so much until I just have to hand it over. But sometimes the best way to play that evil game is not to play. And then hold onto the knowledge that, when all is said and done, I'm going to heaven. And if I screw up, and I get snagged by somebody's comment or anger or whatever, and I'm not able to do it, and I do it wrong, and I come back and am hateful or something— okay, I'm going to heaven." The woman returned to her seat with tears in her eyes.

Like many gay people, Gene found it both difficult and annoying to have his sexual orientation treated and discussed as an abstract idea, rather than a fact about the way he lives. In a very short amount of time, he had gone from being a well-known and well-liked priest and administrator in a small diocese, where his sexuality was a complete non-issue, to having what felt like the entire world focused on that issue alone. But there was a flipside to that: Gene, who had been a supporter but never an outspoken activist for gay rights, either within or out- side the church, found himself regarded as a hero by gays and lesbians, regardless of their religious beliefs. He had begun by saying he just wanted to do the job for which he'd been elected—being the bishop of New Hampshire—but suddenly, here was this other role, and this other constituency, and it felt important. It felt like an additional calling. As that reality began to sink in, he seemed to be feeling his way into it reluctantly, probably because of his basic humility. He had simply felt called to be a bishop, not to prove a point, not to be "first," and certainly not because he wanted to be famous or regarded as an icon.

Between the time of General Convention and the consecration, Gene was receiving thirty to fifty emails and ten to twenty letters a day from gay people or their relatives, telling him what his election meant to them and how important it was. Many of those people lived in places and situations where they still couldn't come out of the closet because it was too dangerous. "Those letters," he said, a shadow passing across his face, "are something I can't let slide off me. And they're troubling because I'm neither the devil that one side makes me out to be nor the angel that the other side makes me out to be. I'm just me. But I *do* feel the weight of those letters that talk about what this means to people, and so if I can shoulder that somehow, then I'm going to try to do that. It seems like the least I can do. I can't be responsible for their liberation; they're the only ones responsible for that. But I can cheer them."

At first, the burden of the dual roles and the pressure of being a celebrity were too new and too surreal, to use Gene's own word, for him to take them seriously. He didn't see them continuing indefinitely. He was focused on the consecration and on doing the job he had been elected to do: becoming the bishop of New Hampshire. One parishioner put it succinctly: "Gene, we elected you knowing you would be a good bishop. How can we best help you be a great bishop?"

Gene laughed and answered that the way people could help him the most was to believe with him that we're going to heaven—and that because we're going to heaven we can take a whole bunch of risks. By that, he said, he meant an ability "to think outside the box about what this church is, and what we want it to be, and who we can reach out to." He said that the church sometimes loses its imagination or becomes so fearful that people are going to be angry and cut off their pledges that they don't try to do the right thing.

Gene said he'd heard that the bishop of Wyoming had recently said, "You know, only once or twice in my whole life have I seen the church risk its life for anything."

"Let's figure out what's worth risking our life for, and then do it," Gene told his audiences. "Join me in that adventure, and let's have fun and not be so worried about survival, and be far more worried about mission."

When asked about the international effect of his election, Gene said he was *deeply* aware of the confusion and anger and difficulty it was causing, but at that relatively early date, he still seemed optimistic that the Anglican Communion would hold together, a position he would continue to articulate throughout the next two years.

"I have great hope for the church, the Episcopal Church in this country and the Anglican Communion worldwide," he said. "First of all, some of us are already in 'impaired communion,' where some of us who have been ordained here are not recognized as legitimate priests in other parts of the Anglican Communion. If, as some of the archbishops say, I will not be recognized in their provinces as a bishop, I just joined all the ordained women in this church who are not recognized by most of the Anglican Communion. Now I don't like that one bit, that they are not recognized, but you know what? The Communion didn't come apart over that, and it need not come apart over this either. And the thing that concerns me, from those who want to leave this church in America, or leave it worldwide, is that they're saying that this one thing that divides us is more important than all the other things that hold us together. *This one thing.* It's more important than the creeds that we've held up for, what, 1,700 or 1,800 years; it is more important than our baptismal covenant; it's more important than the doctrine of the Trinity—the list goes on forever, of the things that hold us together. And these people are saying this one thing trumps all of that. And I just don't believe that for a minute. I really don't. I think it's important. I think we have to figure it out. But I think that as Christians we can continue coming to the altar of God, and receiving the Body and Blood during Holy Communion, and be brothers and sisters in Christ—and then fight like cats and dogs over some of these things. If you lined up Episcopalians and asked them what they thought about capital punishment, genetic engineering, abortion, who should be president, whether or not we should be in Iraq—you would find the entire spectrum. And then they all go up to the altar rail and receive the Body and Blood of Christ. I don't see why we can't do that with this."

Of course, as he himself pointed out with great sadness, this 'impaired communion' wasn't confined to his relationship with conservative African bishops: there were bishops within the Episcopal Church in the United States who refused to take communion with him or to participate when a woman priest was the celebrant, and who held separate Eucharists whenever the House of Bishops gathered.

Still, he hoped for the best. He said that several bishops who had been very much on the other side of this issue were now saying, "Okay, it's done, let's get on with it." "I was seated in the House of Bishops right before the end of Convention," he said, "and at the first break, one of the bishops who had voted against me and had stood up with the group who said, 'This is the worst thing that's ever happened in the history of the church,' came over and knelt down beside my chair and said, 'Hello, I'm Bishop So-and-So from the diocese of So-and-So.' He said to me, 'When you were introduced to the House today, I neither stood nor applauded like the others did, and two minutes later I was thinking, "What a lousy way to begin a relationship." So I hope you'll forgive me. And this is going to be really hard for me, but I'm going to work as hard as I can.'"

"And I said, 'I couldn't ask for anything more.'" Gene told him that he was moved and humbled by what he had said and that he was going to work really hard too. "That's all we need to do," Gene insisted. "God will do the rest."

Deep down, he felt that the controversy was out of proportion to the issue of homosexuality alone. "When something gathers more energy than it ought to have, when it's attracting more attention than it deserves, it means that something else is going on," he said. He had been thinking about the possible reasons, and, though he said he'd probably live to regret saying so, he began to attribute the hostility to resentment over the end of patriarchy. "I think that in the last thirty or forty or fifty years, people of color are coming into their own, women are coming into their own, and now gay and lesbian people are coming into their own. And what that means is that straight white males are not going to get to run the world any more. And that's got to be painful. I mean, I've at least reaped the benefits of being at least two out of those three! It's painful. But I think that's why this is gathering so much steam. It shouldn't be getting this much attention, but it is. I think that's because it's challenging patriarchy all over the world, even in some cultures that haven't even gone through some of those other gate-breakers."

At the time, he said this was just a hunch on his part, and that certainly it was only one piece of a complicated set of reasons. Another was the general disregard in which Americans were held, worldwide. The invasion of Iraq had begun six months earlier, and foreign criticism of U.S. arrogance and militarism was rising rapidly. "Whether that's justified or not, I think some of this reaction is happening because the reason for the controversy is coming from America, and people in other parts of the world are tired of being pushed around by America and Western ideas."

Gene had two stories that he repeated at the end of nearly every public appearance. One was a tale of four soldiers in Europe during the Second World War.

One of them is killed, and the other three find a church and a priest and ask them to bury their friend. The priest does so, but the cemetery in the churchyard is consecrated ground, only for baptized Christians. He asks the others about their friend's religious background, whether he was baptized, but they don't know the answer. So the priest tells them he can't bury the soldier in the churchyard, but that they can bury him just outside the fence.

After the war, the three friends are on their way home, and they decide to stop by the church and pay their respects to their friend. They find the church and go to where they remember burying him, but they can't find the grave. Disturbed, they seek out the priest.

"Yes," he says. "I remember you. After you left to go back to the war, I started thinking about what I had told you, and it seemed so wrong. I couldn't change where he was buried, but I did what I could: I moved the fence." Gene told this story endlessly. Each time it was a little different, depending on his mood and the tone of the audience, but he would get to the end and repeat, "He moved the fence."

"It seems to me that the God who loves us beyond our wildest imaginings," he said, "is a God who wants us to move the fence ever broader and broader, to include all of God's children. It certainly seems to me that this is what Jesus did. Jesus was always hanging out, not with the churchy types, but with those on the fringes, on the margins. And if we as Christians are really trying to be Christ-like, it seems to me that we need to be always moving the fence, moving the fence, so as to include all of God's children. It seems to me that this is what God is up to in this, and we haven't seen the end of it yet."

His other story was a related but personal one that came out of his ongoing relationship with the inmates at the New Hampshire State Women's Prison. Three days after the election, he received a letter from a woman at the prison. And it said, "I am neither gay nor particularly Christian, but your election makes me think that maybe there is a community out there that could love me despite what I've done." He went down to the prison to see her.

"She's eighteen years old," he said. "She looks maybe fifteen, quiet, shy, demure, soft-spoken, you'd think maybe she'd be a wallflower. And she had killed her mother when she was fourteen. I'm getting to know her."

Gene stayed at the prison to play a game of softball, which he described as "a near-death experience." He had fallen over his own feet twice, gotten "completely wrecked up, bloody here and here, just a mess," he said, grinning. Working with the Rev. Alice Roberts, a remarkable woman and Episcopal priest who is the chaplain at the prison, he went back during the first week of September to baptize one of the other women. This woman was about thirty years old; she told him that she had gotten into drugs, and in order to support her drug habit had gotten into prostitution. She invited everyone at the prison to come to her baptism, and over half of them did—about forty-eight women. "They had followed the story of my election and the General Convention absolutely, every minute of every day," he related. "After the baptism I stayed and talked to them for a couple of hours, and they were—they were amazing. We talked about Scripture, we talked about life. Some of them openly identified as being lesbian and we talked about what that meant for them, and at the end they made me promise that I would come back and bring all of my fancy duds from the consecration, and that I would put them all on and do a communion service for them. So after the consecration I'm going back."

Gene said he had been paying particular attention to the Scripture lessons that had been appointed for Sundays throughout the summer and fall, and that it had really struck him how Jesus could do or say a thing, and to one group of people— the Sadducees and Pharisees—it didn't sound like good news at all. In fact, they were angered by it and sought to do him in. But the very same statement or action sounded like fabulous news to those who were disenfranchised, or marginalized, or dispossessed.

"There is something in that about the real calling of the church," he mused. "It's very difficult when you're an institution, and especially one that owns as many buildings as we do, and all that kind of stuff, but I think unless we move in that direction—toward the people on the margins—we are just going to become hopelessly irrelevant."

"And the only way to move in that direction is to do the other side of it as well—that is, to assist people in their personal journeys toward God. Otherwise, in the simple social action stuff, you just run out of steam. But if you're talking to God all the time, and then you're being silent and letting God talk to you, you can stay at full steam. So those are the two sides of it. We've got to be companions to people in their journey to God, and we've got to get out onto the streets, because there are people desperate to hear the good news. Over half of the people in the state of New Hampshire claim no religious affiliation whatsoever. Never mind those who claim a religious affiliation and never go to church. I'm not talking about them. But no affiliation whatsoever? Half."

"We don't need to go across the ocean to be missionaries. We just have to go next door and borrow a cup of sugar, and stay a while."

Inside the Whittemore Center (University of New Hampshire, Durham) as preparations start for the consecration (November 1, 2003).

Chapter II

Preparations

The safety of their bishop-elect was not the only issue facing the New Hampshire diocese as the November consecration drew nearer. Judith Esmay, whose job as chair of the Election and Transition Committee had morphed into chairperson for the consecration itself, said that the potential magnitude of the event first became clear to her when she received a call from the bishop's office. "They told me that the original site (a local convention center) wasn't going to be adequate because it would only hold 2,000 people. My husband Bob said it looked like a parking garage. We really needed to nail down another place and knew we'd better do it *tout de suite.*"

New Hampshire simply doesn't have a lot of large venues. The biggest—and most convenient to the Diocesan Convention—was the Verizon hockey rink in Manchester, but it was unavailable. The second largest was the Whittemore Center, another large hockey rink on the campus of the University of New Hampshire in Durham. Fortunately the Whittemore had a number of dates that were open, and Judith began a series of phone calls with the Center director, Bob LeBaron, to nail down the necessary dates.

"That was when I began to feel this was going to be a big event," she said, "when we changed the venue so that we'd have up to 6,000 seats, and we began thinking about invitations, and liturgy, and the number of people involved. It was a slow-growing thing."

Judith said that the New Hampshire delegation had come back from Minneapolis "wiped out," and it took a while to get the planning process in gear. She and her committee had known that they could have done a lot of planning before General Convention, but neither they nor the Standing Committee had wanted to presume that the vote would be in their favor. She said it was very important to go to General Convention with the attitude, "We are putting the issue before you, here is our election, solid as a rock; what is your decision?"

Judith herself had decided months before not to go to General Convention. She wasn't a deputy, but she could have gone as a visitor or found work on the floor, as some of the New Hampshire young people did. "I was urged to do that by a number of people," she said. "But I decided, no, it's better for me to stay home and pray. My job is not to try to get the election through the convention. That's for the deputies and the Standing Committee to work on. My job is to do whatever the convention decides." She admitted that it had been agonizing to sit home and pray, but said that throughout most of the process she had felt an interior calm. "That was true all through the election, through the convention, and beyond. I felt a kind of surprise sometimes, and sometimes some worry and anxiety, but inside there was a deep calm, and a feeling that all would be well."

The Rev. Scott Erickson and Judith Esmay discuss consecration details with the bishop-elect.

On a morning in mid-September, 2003, the Liturgy Committee for the consecration convened at Diocesan House in Concord. Their rather daunting job was to figure out how to hold a solemn worship service for several thousand people—with the possibility of worldwide television coverage—in a hockey rink. And they were going to have to do it on a shoestring.

The big oak conference table in front of the fireplace was covered with several dozen cobalt blue, hand-thrown ceramic dishes, and Judith Esmay, Gene Robinson, and the Rev. Scott Erickson, a young Episcopal priest, teacher, and liturgical expert from nearby St. Paul's School in Concord, stood behind the table, surveying the array of blue islands. "This reminds me of one of those carnival games where you toss the pennies . . ." Gene said.

In Episcopal parlance, these were "patens," the dishes that hold the communion wafers or bread as the priest gives it to the communicants. The patens had been commissioned from a New Hampshire potter, according to specific instructions, along with matching hand-thrown chalices for the wine. The idea was that after the consecration, a set would be given to each parish in the diocese. This was the only "special" item the Consecration Committee had purchased. The large pitchers for the communion wine had been a serendipitous find at IKEA, along with baskets for the bread; nearly all the other liturgical items were being lent or donated. The finished patens were beautiful, but there was just one problem: they were too flat. One jiggle of the hands or one jostle by a milling crowd, and the bread or wafers would fall off. "People really go nuts when the bread falls on the floor," Gene said, finally. "There's no way you could do communion for a regular-size parish using these."

"All right," Judith said, with a resigned look, as she considered the phone call she would have to make. She glanced toward the doorway and asked, "Is Peter coming?" The Rev. Peter Faass, the fourth member of the Liturgy Committee, was driving from the eastern side of the state.

"There may be a lot of traffic on Route 4," Scott said, citing a notorious state thoroughfare.

Gene added, "You know, there's a bumper sticker that says, 'Pray for me, I drive Route 4.'"

Just then, Peter, a very tall, jovial priest with intensely black hair and sparkling eyes, came through the door, apologizing: "Sorry! I was on Route 4," and everyone broke into laughter.

Scott, efficient and precise, chaired the meeting. He reported that he'd recently heard from Krister Stendahl,[1] Bishop Emeritus of Stockholm, who said he planned to come to the consecration. "We want to try to get a prelate of the Church of England, but the one I had hoped we could get is having surgery."

Gene suggested someone else, saying he didn't think the Archbishop of Canterbury would allow it in any case; it was very unlikely that he would want to be seen as endorsing the consecration in any way.

The group talked about the ticketing procedure for the event. It would be open to all, but, for planning and security reasons, everyone attending would be required to present a "ticket" that had to be requested in advance. Scott asked if school kids from the diocesan schools would get tickets to attend, and suggested that each school could have a banner in procession with the parishes.

"Wonderful idea," Judith said. "I'm ashamed not to have thought of it."

"I was just mobbed by young people at General Convention, just mobbed," Gene said. "We might want to seat all the kids from the schools together."

Scott concurred, and then said, "Gene, we want to tell you what we want to do, hear your thoughts and what you want, and then I think you're going to have to just let us do it, otherwise you aren't going to survive . . ."

"I am planning to survive," said Gene firmly. "I plan to be there. In every way possible, I am going to be there."

Scott smiled and picked up the stapled pages of his agenda. "Episcopal vestments," he said, "Page one."

An hour later, the group had discussed what the clergy would be asked to wear, the training procedures for acolytes and the teams from each parish who would be helping to distribute communion, which church in the diocese might have a suitable altar that could be used for the event, sources for processional torches and large rugs, and whether or not to have flower arrangements. They reviewed a floor plan showing where everyone involved in the service—the "altar party"—would sit, including a list of bishops that was already over twenty in number. Close to fifty bishops were expected, a number that would have been even greater if the consecration were on a Saturday rather than a Sunday.

The efficient distribution of communion to a congregation of several thousand people, of all ages and mobilities, in a steeply-banked hockey rink, was one of their biggest challenges. They decided that the bread and wine would have to be consecrated near the altar and moved quickly to the people, rather than moving the people themselves. The arena would be divided into sections, with communion "stations" on the concourse level above, and Eucharistic teams bringing communion down to those who could not walk up and down the stairs. All the other people would walk up to the concourse, receive communion, and return to their seats. It would be a bit chaotic, but it was a solution. The consumption of the remaining bread and wine and the cleaning of the vessels would take place at the normal concession-stand sites on the concourse, with the usual signs for soft drinks and hot dogs carefully draped.

The discussion then turned to the likelihood that protesters would ask to speak during the formal, required part of all ordination and consecration rites in which objections are invited. The Presiding Bishop, Frank Griswold, would be leading the consecration, and the objections would be addressed to him. Scott said, with a worried look, "I don't want to be an apocalyptic person but I think maybe we need to get on top of this *now*." Several suggestions were made, ranging from complete quiet on the audience's part during the objections to printing a series of hymns in the service leaflet that the congregation could sing while the Presiding Bishop heard the objections. In the end, it seemed that the final decision would have to be left to the Presiding Bishop himself.

As the meeting was winding down, Judith pulled out a sample ticket. "People will keep these, they'll put them in their scrapbooks," she said, reading a quotation from The Book of Common Prayer ordination service she had put on one side. "I thought perhaps there should be something on here besides just the name of the event and the date."

"I have an idea for the text," Gene said. "I think it's Augustine of Hippo. It's the one about, 'I count it a greater honor to be a servant with you than a bishop over you,' or something like that. I can get it for you right now, if you hold on a minute . . ." He jumped up and went out of the room, coming back in a few minutes with the quotation.

"I've got to go," he said, getting up again. "I'm off to do some premarital counseling and then I have three hours of Commission on Ministry tonight." He turned to leave, and then ran back into the room. "Oh! Quick!" he exclaimed. "Let me show you the sketches for my vestments." He pulled some drawings out of his briefcase, and all four heads bent over the table, oohing and ahhing at the depictions of gold satin with bright appliqués.

Gene, who is generally a conservative dresser—quite at home in a navy blue lambswool sweater and grey slacks, and, true to his simple Kentucky heritage, somewhat uncomfortable with these glorious trappings of office—seemed blown away by the designs. For him, the thought of being attired in such robes was one more astounding development in a trajectory that was becoming ever more surreal.

New clerical robes are one of several items traditionally presented to bishops at their consecrations. Bishops also wear rings, usually set with an amethyst that is carved as a signet in a design unique to the bishop's diocese, on the fourth finger of their right hand; the ring symbolizes the marriage between the bishop and the church. Like their medieval counterparts, modern bishops occasionally press their signet rings into sealing wax, as a sign of their approval, on official documents. After the election, the Rt. Rev. Philip A. Smith, retired seventh bishop of New Hampshire (Doug Theuner's predecessor), expressed his desire to give Gene the ring he had worn on his own finger for more than thirty years. When it was checked for size, it turned out to be a perfect fit.

Bishops also carry a crook, symbolic of their role as shepherd. Douglas Theuner gave his successor a Palestinian shepherd's crook from the Holy Land: it was hand-carved from olive wood, with the city of Jerusalem represented in a detailed, cast silver band around the handle.

But of these official trappings, it was Gene's pectoral cross—the large gold cross traditionally worn by bishops on their chest—that seemed to be writing a new story. The idea had occurred to him and to the committee that the people of the diocese might like to donate small pieces of gold jewelry to be melted down and recast into a cross. The cross, to be made by Mark Knipe, a local goldsmith, would not only symbolize but literally represent the people, and it would be worn daily next to the bishop's heart. The response to Gene's invitation was large and immediate, and along with most of the donated gold came a note or a letter explaining where the piece had come from and why the giver wanted to give it for this purpose. Those notes were collected by Judith, to be put into a scrapbook that would later be presented to Gene. At the time, he and the committee were deeply touched by the response and the outpouring of generosity. No one anticipated the drama that would eventually surround this particular object.

The raging remnants of Hurricane Isabel were gusting outside a week later, pelting the interstate with rain. Inside the warmth of Diocesan House conference room, the members of the Consecration Committee met to hammer out further details.

Peter Faass was there, representing the Liturgy Committee. Terry Knowles, a dark-haired woman in a blue suit, was in charge of the ushers. Dr. Jerry Weale, from St. Thomas Church in Hanover, New Hampshire—a large man with a large personality and tremendous knowledge about Anglican music and liturgy— would be the music director for the consecration. Mike Barwell was in charge of the media and was already busy handling applications for press credentials.

The Rev. Peter Faass at a meeting of the consecration committee. (Richard Daschbach, foreground.)

On one side of the table, Judith was engrossed in conversation with Bishop Doug Theuner. "Is there something I can do for you?" Doug asked.

"Well, you're in charge of this whole thing," Judith teased. Doug put his head down on table and mocked bursting into tears. "The canons say so!" Judith continued, laughing.

Doug lifted up his head up and told her about a call he'd received from the Presiding Bishop's "right hand man." "He was worrying about everything," he said. "I told him, 'Just call Judith Esmay, she's in charge of this entire project, she's marvelous, everything is completely organized.'"

He looked at Judith, whose eyebrows headed for the ceiling as she peered at the bishop over her reading glasses. "He did call. I think he must not be impressed with my ability to reassure him."

"Well, you see, the thing is, he knows *me*," Doug said. "He doesn't know *you*. He needs me to tell him everything is under control." Judith gave him an affectionate, wry smile that meant, "Like I said."

The group discussed the invitations, which were already a little late in being sent. They also discussed the color-coding of tickets and seating sections for particular groups of people: the choir, distinguished guests such as bishops' spouses, government representatives, clergy and wardens, and people "at large." There would be an information packet sent to everyone who requested a ticket, containing a map, parking advice, and clergy vestment information. They discussed how to handle special needs—people in wheelchairs and the hearing- and sight-impaired.

There were scheduling issues and various rehearsals to coordinate, all of which needed to share the same space on the day of the event; the need for box lunches for volunteers, since no one would be allowed to leave the building after presenting a ticket; the need for a place where the visiting bishops could congregate before the service. Mike Barwell tapped the table with his pen. He said he'd need access to the building early on Saturday for media registration and at least 300 reserved seats for the press, including 75 people in the press boxes; he said he already had 50 people registered. Mike mentioned that there were three people he wanted nowhere near the building because he considered them a hazard. The group asked if they were members of the press, and he said they were.

The committee members would have special badges giving them total access to all areas of the Whittemore Center. They discussed the need for headsets and who should have them. Jerry Weale said that the organ would be delivered to the rink's loading dock on Saturday; all the vendors would need to be on a list that would allow them to clear security.

With most of the set-up happening on Saturday, would they need to hire special security guards through the night, between Saturday and Sunday? What was the responsibility of the Whittemore Center itself, and how much would be on the shoulders (and budget) of the Diocesan Committee?

Could they use college students as volunteers? Mike said that a liability release would be needed for volunteers, in any case. "There is a risk associated with this event, even if it's somebody yelling 'bomb' and there's a crowd stampede: they rush down the stairs and there are these kids. If it were my kid I'd want to know who was responsible."

Terry said there was a liability policy at the college, but she would also need to advise the people volunteering to be ushers. She mused for a moment and then looked up. "Someone could be held hostage!" she said.

Jerry Weale's eyes became the size of LP records. Mike said, "I could see it in his eyes: 'Organist held hostage!'"

Someone else joked, "They did research. Who's the most entertaining person we can hold hostage for a week?" Everyone burst out laughing and relaxed again.

The Consecration Committee met for the last time a month later. Security changes had been implemented at Diocesan House: a sign saying "Please Ring Doorbell" was now on the exterior wall to the right of the entrance door, and the door remained locked until a receptionist, located in line-of-sight, confirmed the identity of the visitor and buzzed the person in.

On a table beside the reception desk was a new addition: a stuffed bear wearing a red bishop's robe and mitre, wire-rimmed glasses, and skis. But this bit of levity was in marked contrast to the mood behind the oak doors of the conference room.

The conference table was full, the feeling somber, tense, and worried. Judith began by asking for silence, and she offered a prayer that began, "Dear God, we hold up to you our fears." She reminded her assembled colleagues that while they were all worried about what might happen and about the tremendous pressure that had built up, the event was also about joy. Everyone closed his or her eyes and prayed and uttered audible "amens."

So far, about 3,000 people had confirmed that they would attend, and the number seemed unlikely to go above 4,000. 48 bishops had confirmed their participation. In a new wrinkle, the Presiding Bishop had asked the bishops of Province I to have a meeting with him on Sunday morning, before the consecration, and this would take several key people away from the rehearsal.

The greatest worry was security. In addition to the death threats the bishop-elect had received, which created great concern about security inside the consecration venue, Fred Phelps and members of his Kansas-based Westboro Baptist Church had applied for a permit to hold an exterior protest, as they regularly did whenever there was a large-scale pro-gay event with a media presence in the U.S. Because of the explicit and deliberately provocative style of the Westboro group, students at the University of New Hampshire (UNH) had announced they would stage a counter-protest, alarming both the campus police and the state police. The campus chaplain had become involved, and the American Friends Service Committee had also offered to train students at the college in non-violent tactics.

The stated position of the Westboro Baptist Church is blunt and inflammatory. Their homepage on the internet is located at the URL godhatesfags.com and that motto, rather than the name of the church, is the banner which greets visitors to the site. The homepage has a section entitled "Love Crusades," which is a schedule of upcoming planned picketing events under such headings as "Sodomite whorehouses masquerading as Ann Arbor churches, Sunday, Nov. 20." The "News" section contains clips from the press. There is a long list of featured links, such as "God hates America," "Thank God for Katrina," "PriestsRapeBoys.com," and "All nations must outlaw sodomy (homosexuality) and impose the death penalty." Yet another section is entitled "Memorials." It begins with, "Matthew Shepard has been in hell for 2596 days." Shepard, a twenty-one-year-old homosexual, was viciously beaten, tied to a fence, and left to die in Laramie, Wyoming, on October 7, 1998. He was discovered unconscious about a day later, and died of his injuries on October 12. Fred Phelps and his group picketed the funeral and the trials of his attackers, bearing signs reading "Matt Shepard rots in Hell," "AIDS Kills Fags Dead," and "God Hates Fags." Matthew Shepard's two assailants each received two consecutive life sentences for their crime; both have claimed that their actions were justified by the Bible. This, one of the most vicious and notorious hate crimes of recent times in America, prompted then-President Bill Clinton to try to extend federal hate crime coverage explicitly to gay and lesbians, women, and disabled people. In 1999, that proposal was rejected by the Republican majority in the House of Representatives. More recently, Fred Phelps has tried to obtain a permit to erect a large stone monument with a bronze plaque bearing Shepard's picture and the words, "Matthew Shepard, Entered Hell October 12, 1998, in Defiance of God's Warning: 'Thou shalt not lie with mankind as with womankind; it is abomination.' Leviticus 18:22."

The Westboro group had applied for a legal permit for their protest on the day of the consecration. The local police had received the application and decided they were going to put the protesters on the far edge of the volleyball courts that are right outside the Whittemore Center. When word of this decision reached the student senate, a number of students were horrified and went to the police. They said, "We paid, out of our student activities fees, for the surface on that volleyball court, and we don't want their feet on it." What came out of that meeting was a justifiable concern about the UNH students engaging with the Westboro group—professional picketers who were very cognizant of how their provocative message would be received—and starting a riot.

"The Westboro people survive on legal suits," Judith told the Consecration Committee. "We need to do everything we can to insure that they have no basis for one." A message had been sent to clergy and parishioners, asking the priests to prepare people attending the consecration for what they were likely to see and to explain that no purpose would be served by responding to the protesters or engaging them in any way.

"We have a contract with the Whittemore Center," someone said. "Is there a chance that the university will pull out on us?"

"We assume not," she answered. "We hope and pray not."

Mike Barwell had concerns about the relationship between inside and outside security: "Who will be assigned to get Gene out of there if something happens?" he asked. In confidence, the committee was told that a member of the state police who was a former altar boy would be robed to serve as one of the chaplains, walking and standing next to Gene throughout the entire ceremony. A special security meeting of all the responsible parties was scheduled for Wednesday at the Whittemore Center.

"How should we be better prepared?" someone asked.

"Be aware of what's going on around you. Call security if you see anything." Judith again impressed on the group the need for them to be leaders: "We need to convey a sense of fearlessness, taking as our example the bishop-elect. We should have a sense of confidence, and a sense of joy: it's part of our job as ministers," she said fervently.

The conversation turned to last-minute details: having a supply of rice-flour communion wafers for those with gluten allergies; the procedure for consuming any leftover consecrated bread and wine; details of the table coverings; who would pick up the huge Oriental rug; a decision on when to cut off the ticketing requests. The group ran through a schedule for the Saturday pre-event set-up, confirming who would be where. They heard a report on the post-consecration reception, which was in the capable hands of Lisa Scigliano.

The Rev. Hank Junkin of the Standing Committee arrived around 7:30 pm and took a seat against the wall, listening carefully to the discussion and breaking in once to say that the Presiding Bishop would decide how to handle any objections during the service.

Mike Barwell spoke about the press arrangements. The BBC would be covering the entire event and planned to do an interview with Gene on Saturday. He showed the special badges that would be given to the cleared media and technical crews. "There will be three cameras inside that we control, fed to a satellite truck outside," he reported. "All the external TV media will be outside. Audio feeds for NPR and other radio stations will be provided." Mike expected between 75 and 100 other journalists. "Once they're in place, they'll have to stay in place. Nobody will be allowed to roam around the arena. *60 Minutes* is going to be doing a documentary behind the scenes; I'll be accompanying them." Mike said he was giving special access to a couple of photographers but that there would be no pre-consecration interview with Gene. He hoped a few people, such as Hank and Judith, would be available to talk to the media. "Let's also think about people from outside the diocese who would be good spokespeople," he said.

"Will the whole consecration be on TV?" someone asked.

Mike grinned, if rather grimly, for the first time that evening. "Remember," he said, "we can't compete with the true God of Sunday afternoon: NFL football."

A final choir rehearsal took place later that week at St. Thomas Church in Hanover. Members of some other choirs had driven to Hanover in response to Jerry's invitation, coming from as far as two hours away, and extra chairs filled every inch of the floor. "Here's the game plan," he said. "We're going to work on notes for the first half of this rehearsal, until about eight o'clock, and then we'll take a break for coffee, and then come back and sing everything through. Now what you need to remember is, not your loudest. Frankly, none of us knows what the acoustics are going to be when we get into this hockey rink, and you're also going to have the brass to contend with. Everybody's tendency when they can't hear themselves very well is to oversing. So here's the point: *save the vocal gold.* Otherwise we're going to have tonsils on the ice."

After the 8:00 p.m. break, the Rev. Canon Henry Atkins, Jr., interim priest in Hanover, came in and asked if he could address the choir. Father Atkins, a tall, lanky man in his late sixties with a long career of progressive activism in the U.S. church and in Latin America, stood wearing his cap and winter coat, swaying slightly as he talked. "As many of you know," he said, "on Sunday, there are going to be various protesters who are going to be outside of the hockey rink. Since you will be entering early, it's been suggested that, number one, you do not get into debate with them. They are not there because they are interested in changing, okay? They may try to provoke you by what they say. We've also been informed that they will be handing out literature, some of which is sexually explicit. In the past it's shown such things as young boys and men engaged in explicit activities, and the message is, 'This is what you're encouraging.' And the material is designed to provoke you. You can just refuse to take it, or walk on by, or what-ever. Just don't get into a prolonged conversation with them. These are not Episcopalians. They are members of an evangelical church. They typically carry signs that say things like, 'All fags should be killed for Jesus.' I mean, it's not signs that say, 'We protest this,' okay?"

Shock registered on the faces of some of the choir members who hadn't heard about this group before; the room was silent and filled with consternation. One person mentioned that an evangelical church in Concord had offered their space so that dissenting Episcopalians and other folks could have a service at the same time as the consecration.

Jerry Weale added, "My advice would be, if you see these people, smile sweetly and look away, and walk right on. They're looking for a photo op with you in it, and they take their own pictures, by the way." Rev. Atkins nodded his agreement.

"Okay," Jerry said, sitting down at the keyboard. "Let's sing!" The group sang through all the pieces they had rehearsed in detail during the previous hour, and by 9:00 the concern that had been on a number of faces was replaced with hap-piness: the music sounded remarkably good.

"Remember," he said, "this is a marvelous, spectacular occasion, and also a worship service. It ought to be full of joy, and all the good stuff that comes with being a Christian, and especially an Episcopalian Christian. One of my colleagues at Boston University asked me last year, 'So, why are you an Episcopalian?' And I said, 'They're the only people who can have a celebration for the opening of an envelope!' And I love that about the church."

Meanwhile, other people were preparing for their own journeys to New Hampshire. Most of the non-diocesan participants would be supporters of progressive religious politics, both gay and straight, clergy and lay people, who realized the enormous significance of this event and simply wanted to be part of it. For some gays and lesbians it was even more personal, representing a watershed moment in the history of their own struggles to find acceptance and spiritual peace. Gene also received many messages of support. One that moved him particularly was from Judy Shepard, the mother of Matthew, who wrote, "I am sure Matthew is smiling down at you from heaven."

Another person planning the trip was the Rev. Earle Fox, an Episcopal priest who had for a number of years been a leader in "recovery" missions to "reform" homosexuals and lead them back to what he believed was their God-given heterosexual nature. The Rev. Fox is an Episcopal priest who graduated from Trinity College in Hartford, Connecticut and General Theological Seminary in New York City and then received a D. Phil. from Oxford University in 1964. Since 1989 he has been a lecturer for EXODUS and other ex-homosexual ministry meetings and, in the late 1990s, he was director of Transformation Christian Ministries, an Exodus referral ministry, in the Washington, D.C. metropolitan area, "helping persons out of the homosexual lifestyle to restore their God-given heterosexual nature." He is the author, with David Virtue, of a book entitled *Homosexuality: Good and Right in the Eyes of God?* Lately, Rev. Fox had felt himself called to speak in public, in detail, about the homosexual acts that clearly fill him with revulsion.

Rev. Fox later wrote that on the Monday preceding the consecration, the Lord told him that he should go to the New Hampshire consecration and speak publicly in front of the assembled congregation. At first he said he felt filled with fear, but he called his prayer partners to ask their advice, and they affirmed that they thought it was the Lord's will. "Someone needed to break the ice . . . on the very unpleasant subject of homosexual behavior," he wrote. "I also knew that few persons were trained for such a task. And I was. The homosexual agenda will not long survive such a discussion. And the Lord was calming my spirit."

"In the car on the way to the Whittemore Center, the Lord showed me the dark powers with a clarity I had never seen before: a picture of the arena with dark shadows swirling around inside the building. He said that was to be the target of my prayers."

Carrying out an ancient ritual, the bishops' signet rings are pressed into wax seals on the official document declaring a new bishop's election.

Chapter 12

Consecration

Outside the Whittemore Center at noon on a beautiful, bright, unseasonably warm autumn day, girls in shorts played field hockey on brilliantly green artificial turf. Inside, under the cool fluorescence, the university ice hockey rink was in the first steps of its transformation into a holy place.

The ice had been covered by a layer of crumbly grey Homasote, but when you stood on it, it was cold. When Judith Esmay entered the rink for the first time a month and half earlier, she saw a cloud hovering above the ice. Stepping onto the surface, she felt rain falling.

"They told me that the rink has its own atmosphere, its own weather," she recalled, "but it was more than that. There was something mystical about it. The rink was dark that day, deserted, but the ice seemed like a living, breathing thing. Every time I've come back, even when the ice was covered up, I've felt its presence."

On this first day of November, though, the air was dry, and the overall impression was of blue, the predominant color of the hard plastic seats, and, in the surrounding shadows, the grey of the concrete structure itself. Colored college banners hung from the ceiling struts—Boston University, Maine, Northeastern, Amherst, Providence—along with advertising banners for cell phone plans and banking institutions. There was a faint smell of locker room. It was hard to imagine a worship service here, let alone a grand ecclesiastical event with hundreds of priests and bishops, an audience of thousands, and a choir of 200.

Judith Esmay was down on the ice, wearing one of her signature hand-knit cardigans, a short grey skirt, and red clogs. She greeted us warmly and pointed out the Sky Lounge where the bishops would be gathering. Up in the rafters, the glass-windowed sky boxes had a private bird's-eye view of the ice, partially blocked from our vision by the big electronic scoreboard in the center of the arena. It was a bizarre combination of worlds.

At ice level, a crew of electricians worked on two huge banks of theatrical lights, readying them to be raised into position around the cubical scoreboard near the ceiling. Over in one corner, two technicians poked at the Rogers electronic organ that had just been specially delivered to the arena. The hymns for the consecration were printed in blue in the service programs, also just delivered and waiting in a big stack of printers' cartons out in the receiving area. Two carts of folding chairs, silver with blue cloth seats, were wheeled onto the ice: these were for the "altar party," as the contingent of celebrants, preachers, and readers is called, and for the attending bishops—around fifty at last count. A blue rug led in from one of the central, rink-level doorways from which a team in shoulder pads and helmets would normally emerge. The rug was there for the ecclesiastical procession, but the big Genie Bucket which was used to lift lights and adjust the scoreboard had been driving over it all morning, leaving folds, tire tracks and shredded bits of grey Homasote all over the blue surface. Organ, chairs, carpet: all seemed dwarfed by the size of the rink and the omnipresent sports atmosphere.

At 1:45 the lights were lifted into position. An Associated Press photographer who had been juggling hacky sack balls down on the ice for an hour waited nervously while his tripod and a remote-controlled camera were secured to the bank of lights. He had made special arrangements in hopes of getting a dramatic overhead shot of the moment of consecration, when the assembled bishops would lay their hands on Gene Robinson's head in the ancient ceremony conferring the apostolic succession. "I'm usually here for hockey games," he said. "This is . . . pretty different."

The other members of Judith's Consecration Committee soon returned from lunch. Dr. Jerry Weale walked down the stairs from the concourse level toward the organ just as the techies did the first sound check. "One, two, three, testing" quickly gave way to blasting rock music that reverberated off the concrete walls. Jerry just kept his head down and walked on, ignoring the nightmare of sound.

By 2:30 the crumpled, dark blue carpet had been moved and straightened, and a large Oriental rug had been delivered by forklift. The members of the Liturgy Committee unrolled the rug, checking to see that it was centered. From the press box, high up on the concourse, a carpet that would be far too large for most people's homes seemed like a postage stamp—a gloriously beautiful and intricate postage stamp, to be sure. But when the crew tested the lights, suddenly a "center" became apparent: a focal point for the pageant, the mystery, and the history that would be made the next day. Some of that would happen through theatrical effect: lighting, color, costume. Some would come from the ritual and emotion of the event itself. Much of it would come about through an unspoken compact with the congregation, most of whom would be willing to look beyond the venue, suspending their normal, wide-angled view of reality for a more inner and concentrated one. And some of it would simply happen by grace, what some would call the Holy Spirit working both through centuries of history, and through a particular moment in time.

By 3:00 pm it was clearly happening: a "church" was being created. The ornately carved bishop's chair from St. Paul's School now stood on the beautiful carpet, flanked by chairs for the co-consecrators. There were seats for the bishops and the other clergy; an altar table and side tables, still uncovered, awaited the bread and wine, the chalices and patens.

On one side of the rink stood trolleys brimming with lighting and sound equipment and anvil cases overflowing with electrical cords. Workers bustled back and forth accompanied by the noise of scraping metal and thudding drawers and latches, motors and squeaking wheels, pods of disconnected conversations. But behind the altar, the four tall processional crosses now rested in their stands, the shining brass glimmering against the blue rows of seats: calm, silent symbols of a different presence.

The techies wheeled the organ into its place directly across the ice in front of the penalty box. After a few sound checks, Jerry Weale sat down at the keyboard and suddenly the rink filled with "Take Me Out to the Ball Game," causing a burst of laughter. "We've always thought you'd sound great at Yankee Stadium," someone quipped.

"Oh, yeah," he said, grinning, his big voice easily heard over the din. "I missed my calling. Would've loved it." Then he segued into the hymn "For All the Saints," playing with obvious joy and authority, and the rink filled with a huge, majestic sound.

I walked down onto the ice and was willingly pressed into service cleaning the plexiglass diffusers for the huge consecration candles; unpacking the boxes of hand-thrown cobalt blue chalices and the re-made patens, the glass pitchers for the wine and baskets for the bread; and helping to set the communion tables. Embroidered brocade linens were placed on the altar and the lecterns, and in front of them, large, beautiful flower arrangements of bright gold and red blooms.

Mary Hamlin-Spencer from Christ Church in Exeter, New Hampshire, who would be playing the organ while Jerry directed the choir during the anthems, was rehearsing the accompaniment to Ralph Vaughn Williams's "O Clap Your Hands" when Gene and his partner Mark arrived, beaming, with a large entourage of security. Unlike the affable bodyguards who had been accompanying Gene during the past weeks, these were stone-faced Secret Service types from a Boston agency, with curly cords fastened behind their ears. Immediately they started scanning the arena for potential security loopholes. Everyone tried to ignore them; it was impossible. Gene, though, looked relaxed and happy and delighted with the set-up. He moved from person to person, hugging, laughing, praising their efforts. Judith stood back and watched him looking at the altar, touching the open Bible. He turned and saw her, and held out his arms.

By five, the preparations were nearly complete. One security man paced back and forth while another talked on his phone; others were up on the concourse and in the tunnels where the procession would assemble. Gene and Mark turned to leave, and immediately the security team regrouped. Judith, standing behind the altar, made a last scan of her list. The organ swelled toward the finish of the Vaughn Williams while the usher team put the last "reserved" signs on the rinkside seats. The organ fell silent, Mary rose and gathered her music, and the arena went dark. Walking backwards, Judith took a final look, and went out toward the light.

At dinner that evening in a seafood restaurant in nearby Portsmouth, on New Hampshire's Atlantic coast, Judith didn't seem worried, although her head must have been spinning with a thousand last-minute details. During the afternoon, she had been talking to Bob LeBaron, the director of the Whittemore Center, who had been watching the transformation of the rink as he sat back in a chair, hands on his head. She told him how amazing the transformation already seemed to her. "But you must know all about that," she said.

"Wait until tomorrow," he had replied. She raised her eyebrows, puzzled.

"It's the people," he said. "It's the people who make it happen. They make the rink come alive."

Judith had confidence in the security arrangements, and she had simply decided to believe that Gene would be safe and that the consecration would proceed without incident. She looked up with mischievous eyes and lifted a forkful of grilled salmon. "Did you see the ice today?" she asked. "There's that one spot when you come in where a little strip of it is uncovered." She was right; near the west entrance a piece of opaque white ice still peeked out beneath the plywood and Homasote. "I reached down and touched it for good luck," she said. "It's there. The ice is there."

After dinner, there was a private reception for Gene at St. John's Church in Portsmouth, one of the oldest parishes in the diocese. Outside the door of the reception hall, security guards in suits tried to be efficient and affable as a milling crowd of invitees, chattering and laughing, walked up the old stone steps and tumbled into the brightly-lit interior where tables laden with flowers and elegant hors d'oeuvres awaited them. The bishop-elect, beaming, his delighted laugh occasionally carrying above the din of the crowd, stood in the center of the room surrounded by friends and associates who buzzed around him, stopping now and then for a commemorative photograph. St. John's Church was hosting the reception, and it was lavish and lovely: beautiful cheeses, small sandwiches, imported chocolates, wine. Already tired, we headed for the coffee pots over in one corner and ran into Mike Barwell, who, like me, was trying to find a cup of tea. Mike looked like hell, but was smiling as he rubbed his upper sternum. "Acid reflux," he said, shrugging.

"You look like you could use about a week of sleep."

"Yeah, I'll get it eventually. But not until tomorrow is over." His dark eyes darted around the room and stopped on the clump of people surrounding Gene. "He's doing great, though. Look at him! Having a ball. He's loving this." He shook his head and his smile, still directed toward Gene, was full of affection. Then his gaze broke: "I've got to get out of here and go home," he announced, looking around for a place to put down his empty cup. "Everything will be fine," he said, to no one in particular. "Everything will be fine."

On Sunday morning, November 2, the playing fields near the Whittemore Center were deserted except for a few frisbee throwers and an overexcited dog. On the far side of the fields, a bevy of television broadcast trucks were parked side-to-side, their satellite dishes arranged like huge white plates in a rack. Orange traffic cones and wooden barricades had sprung up overnight, guarded by well-trained volunteers with neon vests and walkie-talkies. On the sidewalk, the security forces and media staked out their positions. In the distance, a pair of policemen escorted an elderly couple down the path through the woods from the hotel complex; we later discovered they were Gene's parents.

An officer gathered a milling group of state police troopers on the corner of the walkway, carefully positioning them just beyond earshot; the CNN and BBC crews, at a slight distance, were observing the proceedings just as intently. The uniformed troopers were armed, and beyond them was the startling sight of more police troops on horseback. Other police officers ominously paced back and forth

The press.

on the roof of the Whittemore Center. On the grass, CNN began setting up for a live report with the playing fields in the background. To their right, a large section of the grassy area above the fields was defined by an orange plastic snow fence; this was for the expected protesters and their permitted demonstration.

In the Whittemore lobby, a small crowd had already assembled by 10:00 am. The "credentials" table was busily processing arrivals. Every person who entered the hockey rink had to present a ticket as well as identification upon request, and the credentialing team had the authority to deny admission to anyone who seemed suspect. Once they had entered, people would not be allowed to leave and then return. Everyone, from the press to the visiting bishops, was required to pass through the security check, airport-like metal detectors and baggage-check counters run by security officers. Baggage that couldn't be inspected sufficiently by hand would be sniffed by a police dog.

The people arriving this early were committee members and special volunteers, including greeters who were to escort the bishops through the security procedure and whisk them up the private elevator to the Sky Lounge. Also among the early arrivals were the media and the people who had a part in the service itself and planned to attend the 11:00 am rehearsal. The people wandered back and forth in the lobby, talking to friends they recognized, waiting for the metal detectors to become operational. Finally the security guards announced they were ready, and people formed the first of

Some of the New Hampshire State Police outside the Whittemore Center on the morning of the consecration (note sniper on rooftop).

the long, slow-moving lines for admittance that would continue until four in the afternoon. Patiently resigned, dignified guests in suits and clerical garb moved through the metal detectors, dutifully emptying pockets of keys and change and taking off wristwatches when the equipment beeped, which it frequently did. Every case of equipment, every briefcase and purse was opened and cordially but thoroughly disassembled and hand-checked, and then sniffed by a large brown dog. "You can pat him," the officer said, holding the powerful dog's leash and encouraging him toward a reporter's open handbag, which had been placed on the floor.

"What exactly is he trained to detect?" she asked.

"Oh, all sorts of things," the officer replied pleasantly, motioning to her that she could pick up her laptop case and audio gear. "I wish my nose were worth half as much as his."

Down on the ice, Scott Erickson and Peter Faass, who were to act as Masters of Ceremonies during the consecration, silently leading each participant to his or her proper place and ensuring the flow of the service, began an efficient rehearsal. They addressed the co-consecrating bishops, all the people who would be reading testimonials during the formal "examination" or Scripture during the liturgy, the deacons and priests who were part of the altar party, and Bishop-elect Robinson and his family, including his parents and his newborn granddaughter, in the arms of his daughter Jamee and her husband. Absent were Presiding Bishop Frank Griswold and all the bishops of Province I (New England), who had been asked by Bishop Griswold to meet with him that morning. Meanwhile, on the edges of the worship space, wine was being poured into the vessels, communion bread placed in baskets, and Gene's vestments laid out on a table. The members of the committee paced anxiously around the periphery, and beyond them, Gene's bodyguards kept their watch. After an hour, the Presiding Bishop and other bishops joined the rehearsal, and the remaining details of the liturgy were worked out, with all the readers getting a chance to stand at the lectern and test the microphones.

By early afternoon, the rehearsal was over, the worship space deserted, the lights turned off. From the aerie of the press box, Gene's golden vestments, carefully draped over one of the communion tables, seemed to give off a light of their own. During a lull before the music rehearsal and the arrival of the first members of the congregation, the members of the Consecration Committee sat down for a few moments, eating box lunches of sandwiches, apples, and cookies, some keeping the chocolate bars and caffeine-laced sodas to keep them going through the long afternoon. Three of the security guards sat in an empty press box, smiling and joking in a rare relaxation of their stern professional demeanor. Across the rink, choir members, coming together from all over the diocese and wearing their own robes of bright blue, black, powder blue, and red, slowly filled their seats. Jerry Weale leaned against the organ, which was flanked by three copper-colored tympani and the seats for the rest of the brass section, and waited.

In half an hour, the 200 choir seats were nearly full. The trumpeters warmed up their lips with a few flourishes, and church delegations of clergy, wardens, and banner-bearers began to enter the arena and mill around. A flock of ushers-in-training made a slow, complete circuit of the arena. "This is the press area," said Thelma Hutton, the ushering organizer, walking backwards and waving one arm in our direction. "You don't need to worry about them!"

Still, it seemed incredible that a major religious event would happen here in a matter of hours. What were the BBC religion reporters thinking, looking down at the empty hockey rink, its floor so ugly and grey? These people were used to covering ceremonies in huge, ancient cathedrals and halls built especially to create a feeling of majestic solemnity and the weight of the ages, underscored by the tombs and crypts of kings and queens and the likes of Handel, Darwin, and Lord Nelson. "That's America," they probably figured, with a wry shake of the head at this latest example of seat-of-the-pants Yankee ingenuity. Here were people riding a wave of infectious human enthusiasm rather than standing on the rocks of history, buildings, and tradition. A hockey rink for a consecration? Why not?

As if in answer, the friendly BBC producer I'd met earlier in the day came by and visited for a few minutes. Earlier, there had been a major technical problem with their live television feed, and she said she was very relieved things seemed to be working now. "What do you think?" I asked, smiling and gesturing around the rink: clearly this was not Westminster Abbey. She smiled and ducked the question; she'd been based in America long enough to have a bemused appreciation of our general informality and ebullience. She allowed that in the past few months of working on this story, she had come to admire Gene, and that, as a non-church-going Anglican, a lot of what he said "made a great deal of sense" to her.

Up in the Sky Lounge, about thirty bishops had already gathered, with more arriving each time the spacious, private elevator opened. New Hampshire's Douglas Theuner was the charismatic host, greeting his colleagues with his booming voice and enveloping them in a warm embrace. Rather than a closed-club atmosphere, there was a sense of collegiality, camaraderie, and closeness that was generous and kind. The air was rarified, nevertheless: thick with purple shirts and gold pectoral crosses on heavy chains.

An acrid smell of hot wax burned in the air. Two sheepskins with elaborate calligraphy, one bordered by heavy purple grosgrain ribbon, were spread out on tables. Two pots of hot red wax melted in little burners, stirred by a monk. Informally, one by one, the bishops approached the table and signed the sheepskins that officially recorded the consecration of Gene Robinson "as a Bishop in the One True Church of God." Then they removed their gold signet rings, licked the surface, and pressed the signet seal into the glob of hot wax that the monk placed on the purple ribbon. With each signature, the fate of the Anglican Communion grew more uncertain. It was a strange and powerful moment, a medieval ritual that at the same time propelled the church into a future many did not want to acknowledge. Yet, in this room, there was no hesitation. The signatures were made, the signets pressed firmly, decisively, but not arrogantly. The mood was convivial but determined. The decisions had already been made; this day they were being set into history.

Again the elevator door opened, but instead of announcing the arrival of another bishop, dignified in black and purple with white and crimson robes folded over his or her arm, this time it released a teeming mass of security people and a television crew, armed with microphones on a tall boom and a large video camera. In the center was a small white-robed figure: the bishop-elect himself. The media crew scrambled to follow Gene as he enthusiastically greeted old friends among the four dozen bishops now gathered in the room. Emotionally, he acknowledged the colleagues who had come to support his consecration, at one moment showing his bulletproof vest to Barbara Harris (who herself had had to wear one at her own consecration), in the next turning to greet the retired bishop of New Hampshire, Philip Smith, who would be giving him his own ring to wear. Gene beamed when he saw the Rt. Rev. Otis Charles, and the two embraced: Charles is the former bishop of Utah and retired dean and president of the Episcopal Divinity School in Cambridge, Massachusetts. When he retired in 1993, he announced that he was homosexual, thereby becoming the first openly gay bishop in any Christian church. Subsequently, Bishop Charles co-founded Oasis/California, and he currently lives in San Francisco with his partner. He served as an assisting bishop in the Diocese of California until 2004. When he made his decision to come out, he wrote to the House of Bishops, saying, "I have promised myself that I will not remain silent, invisible, unknown. After all is said and done, the choice for me is not whether or not I am gay, but whether or not I am honest about who I am with myself and others. It is a choice to take down the wall of silence I have built around an important and vital part of my life, to end the separation and isolation I have imposed on myself all these years."

Finally, Gene separated himself from the media crew and went over to the table where the finished sheepskins lay, bearing the seals and long lists of signatures. He became silent and still, and, for a moment, was alone with his thoughts.

As I descended from the spacious atmosphere of the Sky Lounge, the crush of people in the lobby came as a shock. Long lines waited in front of the metal detectors outside, and, inside, a milling crowd of clergy, carrying their robes, looked for the place where the procession would be forming. Volunteer lay eucharistic ministers who would help administer communion headed for their training session. Young people carried church banners; late-arriving choir members rushed toward the music rehearsal that had already begun; vested acolytes carried crosses and torches through the crowd; bishops waited patiently to pass through security; and the first members of the general public, some wearing round blue, red, and white "Proud to be Episcopalian" stickers on their lapels, started to fill up the seats of the hockey arena.

Unlike our relatively calm walk into the Whittemore Center that morning, these visitors had entered through a gauntlet of protesters standing in the drizzling rain outside the building. On one side, a dozen shouting members of the Westboro Baptist Church, from Topeka, Kansas, held fluorescent green and yellow signs with slogans such as "Fag Priest," "Episcopal=Sin," and "AIDS is God's Curse." On the other, about 300 UNH students, many wearing t-shirts reading, "Gay? Fine by me!" tried to drown them out. News accounts later counted 14 satellite trucks and about 100 police officers. On the roof were two police snipers.

The press scrum. A CBS crew records Gene (in white) greeting arrivals. The three impassive bodyguards were part of the contingent protecting Gene at the consecration.

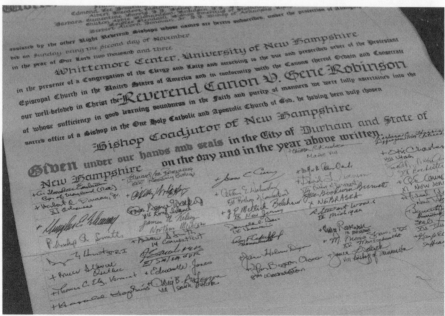

Top: Presiding Bishop Rev. Frank Griswold III signs the official document.

Above: The official document.

Top: Gene embraces the Rt. Rev. Otis Charles, retired bishop of Utah and former dean and president of Episcopal Divinity School, Cambridge. Upon his retirement in 1993, Charles publicly announced his homosexuality.

Above: The Rt. Rev. Douglas Theuner summons his fellow bishops to the consecration. Behind him are the Rt. Rev. Bennett Sims, retired bishop of Atlanta, and the Rt. Rev. Philip Smith, retired bishop of New Hampshire.

Inside, from the far side of the arena, the choir sounded magnificent, but from the choir seats themselves it was very difficult to hear the organ and the other singers. Jerry Weale was working very hard. He couldn't hear well either; there were about 200 singers, the organist, timpanist, and a contingent of brass players who had never rehearsed together, and an hour to get all the music together. He didn't know how wonderful it sounded from every other spot in the arena.

Scanning the steep banks of rapidly filling seats, one wondered if it was really possible to control or secure a crowd like this. No wonder stadium crowds and concerts could be so volatile. But along with the security nightmare came the excitement that only exists in a crowd of human beings united for a single purpose. Nearly everyone was smiling, joyful, excited, expectant, and proud.

By 3:45, almost all the seats were full. Shortly after 4:00, a group of young people from the Church of the Good Shepherd in Nashua filed onto the floor. They surrounded a white-draped table, and, with white-gloved hands, each picked up a pair of gleaming brass hand-bells. The crowd hushed, and the first peals of the bells split the silence. The mesmerizing ringing and swinging of arms was a perfect meditative prelude for the ears and the eyes. Then, after a hush, the organ and brass began the stirring fanfare of Richard Strauss's "Festival Entry." The crowd got to its feet, thinking this would be the first hymn, and then, laughing, sat down again. It was still difficult to gauge the tone of the event: in this bizarre mix of sensory stimuli, it felt more like a crowd waiting for a performance than for a worship service. Then the organ began the first hymn: "The Church's One Foundation."

The first acolytes entered the arena, carrying crosses and torches and wearing bright red robes with white cottas, followed by the procession of clergy and wardens behind the banners of each parish in the New Hampshire Diocese. Then another group of acolytes led in a huge contingent of non-diocesan clergy and interfaith guests, two by two, all in festival white robes: these were clergy who had come to show their support for what was happening. There were Jewish *yarmulkes*, the black hat of an Orthodox priest . . . the procession was so long that the organist had to improvise interludes between every verse of the hymn.

The Rev. Nancy Vogele, a priest from neighboring Vermont, said later that she had attended because of her personal experiences with Gene, who had helped her as a young priest in New Hampshire when she was having a difficult time after coming out as a lesbian. She had also witnessed what a great job he had done in other churches. "When Gene was elected, he had already established his relationship and his incredible competencies with so many people in New Hampshire, and he was prepared to continue that and take it to a new level. It's like when people start to date who've already been friends for a year: so much has already been taken care of in a non-charged setting that their relationship can just blossom quicker in so many ways."

The procession starts. Gene is in white, at the front of the group in the center.

What she hadn't expected on the day of his consecration was the powerful sense of camaraderie she felt with her clerical colleagues while vesting and preparing for the procession and then witnessing the consecration itself. She recalled the ordination of her best friend to the priesthood several years before: "When we laid hands on her, I think I understood for the first time how hard this is, what we're being called to. And how important it is to be colleagues and to surround this new priest. I think that was also so important for me to do for Gene: to be there together, and to be a witness."

She said she had had to brace herself for the demonstrators and objectors, but that as she walked in, the first thing she saw was a contingent of supportive University of New Hampshire students. She laughed and continued, "When we came in, it was so interesting because you know, it's this dignified procession, but all these people that I know were calling my name from the crowd, so I'm thinking, what do I do? Do I try to look dignified or do I wave back? So I waved back. What the heck. But it wasn't just the gay clergy, but there were so many people with tears running down their faces. I mean, we were singing the words to 'The Church's One Foundation':

> . . . *by schisms rent asunder, by heresies distressed;*
> *yet saints their watch are keeping, their cry goes up 'how long?'*
> *and soon the night of weeping shall be the morn of song.*

It was just so incredibly powerful."

The organist moved into the second hymn, and a huge roar went up from the crowd as the procession of bishops entered behind a third group of acolytes. The bishops were all wearing white albs with sleeveless red cassocks over them and individually chosen stoles, some embroidered, some appliquéd with ethnic designs, some woven, and the effect was stunning.

Another roar: this time for the entrance of the co-consecrators, the six bishops who would carry out the formal "examination" of the candidate during the liturgy, all in their most elaborate festival white vestments, including copes (floor-length capelike garments) and tall mitres (the pointed hats found on real bishops—and on ivory ones in chess sets) except for Barbara Harris, the diminutive black woman who was the first female bishop in Christendom, who was resplendent in bright blue satin. People were continuing to sing, but many were crying. The sight of so many clergy in courageous partnership with so many lay people, and the gravity and joy of the historic moment, were intensely moving, and no one, even the most seasoned Anglican groupies, had ever seen anything like this.

Finally Gene entered, in a simple white monk's cassock with a hood, followed by the Presiding Bishop. The participants all took their places, the hymn ended with a soaring descant by the choir sopranos, and the liturgy began.

Gene takes his place in front of the Presiding Bishop and co-consecrators.

Anglican services can seem strange at best—and intimidating and confusing at worst—to people who don't come from liturgical traditions. Those who did grow up in churches that use a liturgy (a written ritual and order of service such as is found in Catholic, Anglican, Lutheran and Orthodox churches) often find the repetitive recitation of the memorized words of the various services poetic and moving—and even comforting—during times of their lives when they are separated, by choice or circumstance, from the church and religion itself. On the other hand, certain parts of the liturgy, such as the creeds with their lists of "I believe" clauses, can turn people off and drive them right out of the church.

In spite of the fact that consecrations of bishops are relatively rare, the liturgy for that occasion can be found right in the Episcopal Book of Common Prayer. As in a baptism, confirmation, or the ordination of a priest, the special words and rituals for the consecration are folded into a fairly normal communion service, along with readings from the Old Testament, a psalm, the Gospel, a sermon, the passing of the peace, the opportunity to give an offering, and the administration of communion. The unique parts are the presentation of the candidate, certain prayers and litanies, the "examination," and the ritual of consecration.

The Presiding Bishop "presides" over the entire event, sitting in a high-backed, throne-like chair, faced by the candidate. Those who wish, or are required, to speak address the Presiding Bishop. In the first part of this service, half a dozen representatives of various commissions and official church bodies read testimonials certifying that Gene Robinson had completed the requirements that would allow him to qualify as a bishop and had been duly elected and approved. Gene was also accompanied by a group of "presenters," people of significance in his own life whom he wished to formally recognize and have with him on this day. They included his partner and immediate family (his parents, sister, daughters and their families, and his former wife, Boo), Dr. Louie Crew, Marge Christie, and several other close friends, both lay and clergy. Then, according to the prescribed form in The Book of Common Prayer, the Presiding Bishop said to the people that this candidate had been "duly and lawfully elected" and found suitable, but that "if any of you know any reason why we should not proceed, let it now be made known."

This was the moment for a collective intake of breath. After the congregation was asked to please refrain from any demonstrative response of approval or disapproval, three people approached the Presiding Bishop, and one by one, read statements, speaking into a microphone held by the Rev. Scott Erickson. The first to speak was the Rev. Earle Fox, who had indeed made his way to the Whittemore Center to give his testimony. In the most explicit language possible, he began to name and describe sexual acts that he accused homosexuals (and only homosexuals, one had to assume) of engaging in, from fellatio and anal intercourse to much more graphic examples. Some 3,000 lay people and hundreds of bishops and priests, including Gene Robinson himself and his daughters, partner, and parents, were forced to hear these sexual acts not only named but described in the middle of a worship service. Bishop Barbara Harris cradled the side of her head in her hand. A young woman below the press booth burst into tears and ran up the stairs. Gene Robinson simply sat and listened, with the rest of us, in silence.

The Presiding Bishop cut the recitation short as quickly as he could. He said, "I am sure we all know what you are saying. This is a worship service. Please spare us the details and come to your point." Rev. Erickson pointed at the next paragraph in Fox's prepared speech. Rev. Fox skipped the rest of his planned recitation, concluded his remarks, and yielded the floor to Meredith Harwood, a New Hampshire woman who spoke on behalf of disapproving families in the diocese. "This is the defiant and divisive act of a deaf church," she said. "The clear teaching of Holy Scripture in both testaments without exception is that sexual activity outside of marriage is wrong for the people of God, yet we are deaf to the Bible." Finally, the Rt. Rev. David Bena, Bishop of Albany, read a formal statement, signed by thirty-six dissenting bishops in the American church. In language similar to that which had been used against the ordination of women, he said that the consecration represented "a dramatic contradiction to the historic faith and discipline of the church" and that "it is impossible to affirm a candidate for bishop and symbol of unity whose very consecration is dividing the whole Anglican Communion." The Presiding Bishop paused to allow everyone time to reflect and then thanked those who had come forward to speak according to their consciences in what he acknowledged were painful and difficult circumstances for many.

"However," he said, "these objections are known to us, and I believe they have been carefully considered. Therefore, we will proceed."

Bishop Bena and Mrs. Harwood left the arena after giving their objections and went to the Durham Evangelical Church, where about 400 unhappy Episcopalians had gathered for an alternative Communion to be led by a number of conservative Episcopal priests, bishops, and lay leaders. A candlelight vigil in support of the protest was held by several hundred non-Episcopalians outside the church. The Rev. Kendall Harmon, canon theologian of the Diocese of South

Carolina, was scheduled to preach at the service, which he said was "part of a truthful witness" to Robinson's consecration. "This is a very, very decisive moment in the history of Christianity."

Meredith Harwood's husband, Terry, a member of the Marine Corps who had recently finished a tour of duty in Afghanistan, told reporters that the participants were grieving, that they felt they had been "dismissed by the Episcopal Church and the Diocese of New Hampshire," and that "he [Robinson] seems to delight in this." Unlike the strident Westboro protesters, most of the gathered opponents at the church spoke of "loving the sinner, hating the sin," stating bluntly that that they felt homosexuality was definitely a sin. Like his wife, Harwood said he could not accept what he saw as a redefinition of morality. "We're all sinners. It boils down to whether you fundamentally believe homosexuality is a sin or not. For me, it's a no-brainer. The only thing I can hold onto is the Bible and 2,000 years of teaching."[1]

After the objectors had been heard and acknowledged, the Presiding Bishop asked if it was the will of the people to ordain Gene as bishop and was answered with a resounding "That is our will!" He asked if they would uphold Gene as bishop, and again the people thundered, "We will." Then followed prayers, including the long Litany for Ordination and readings from Scripture. A passage from Isaiah was read in Hebrew. One of the lectors was Nicholas Anderson, a young boy from St. Paul's Church, Concord, who had become a particular friend of Gene's and had prayed for him throughout the election and consecration process.

Then Douglas Theuner came to the lectern for the sermon.

St. Francis of Assisi is supposed to have said, "Preach the Gospel at all times. If necessary, use words." In actuality, it's rare for priests, let alone bishops, to really preach the Gospel that Jesus taught and lived: a message of humility before God and one's fellow human beings, the equality of all persons, simplicity of spirit and living, compassion toward all beings and the world. Taking that Gospel seriously means a change of heart that can lead to transformation, not only of the individual, but of the church and the world. But to preach it, and to live it, takes great courage. When the Rev. Sarah Hague, an Episcopal priest, was once asked why we so seldom hear sermons about the church's responsibility for social justice, she retorted, "You know why! Because throughout history, *prophets keep getting offed.*" She was not implying that an American priest who today dared preach progressive sermons would be in physical danger, but her remark strikes to the heart of the fact that the Gospel is, and has always been, preached at considerable risk.

Bishop Theuner, though, has always preached and lived from that courageous center. The sermon for Gene's consecration was, uncharacteristically, delivered from a prepared text (he rarely even consults a set of notes), and it was an example not only of his preaching gifts but a declaration of his theology and vision for the church in the future. He knew he had a rare opportunity to speak to a wide audience about what the progressive church could and should be, and he took it, preaching a prophetic, moving, often funny, and inspiring sermon about what he saw as the true call of Christians.

He began by saying he had reread the four Gospels in preparation for this sermon. A bishop is charged to "boldly proclaim and interpret the Gospel of Christ," he said, and "to show compassion to the poor and strangers, and defend those who have no helper." That, Theuner said, was the entire focus of Jesus' ministry.

> Our Lord's attention was entirely directed to the outcast and the marginalized; the poor, the halt, the lame, the blind, lepers, women, people possessed with demons, prostitutes, tax collectors, Roman soldiers, Samaritans, Syro-Phoenicians, thieves . . . His wrath was reserved for the members of the religious establishment of his own faith community; Pharisees and Sadducees, scribes, elders and chief priests, money changers in the temple . . . and his own chosen disciples.
>
> And now we seek to incorporate a new member into the religious establishment of our time; to make him a bishop, a modern day chief priest. Oh to be sure, the Pharisees and Sadducees, scribes, elders and chief priests were generally "fine" people; believing themselves dedicated to God and the service of God's cult. They fasted, they tithed, they were, by their own proclamation, "not as other men are." And yet, we are told by our Lord, they went down from the temple condemned; condemned because they thought so much of themselves, condemned because they "bind heavy burdens, hard to bear, and lay them on men's shoulders." They were chastised by our Lord because they thought people were made for their religious establishment; not their religious establishment for people. They were condemned because they loved to go about in long robes, and loved salutations in the marketplaces and the best seats of honor in houses of worship and the places of honors at feasts . . . and for a pretense made long prayers . . .

The booming voice paused for dramatic effect, and then demanded:

> Who are we kidding? Look around us! Have we met the enemy and found out that they are us?

To their credit, the assembled bishops seated in the first rows in front of the pulpit, wearing their glorious robes, smiled and nodded knowingly. Theuner went on to speak about the great need, if we are serious about being welcoming and inclusive, for the "center" of privilege and comfort and power to move toward the "margins." Does unity mean excluding certain people for the sake of an institution, he implied, or does unity truly mean the equality and dignity of all people?

"Because of who you are, Gene," he said, looking closely and affectionately at his longtime friend, "you will stand as a symbol of unity in the church in a way none of us can."

And then he talked about what this consecration was really about: the "raising up one of our own . . . to lead us through this world of violence and anger and into God's coming reign of acceptance and forgiveness." He said:

> In this time when the culture of violence seems to be all-pervasive, the disagreement over your election and consecration has been labeled by one of your detractors as "the defining battle in the war for Anglicanism's soul." Well, guess what? IT ISN'T! I am quite sure that since the Holy Spirit came upon our apostolic forebears in an upper room in Jerusalem, no "defining" moment in the Christian life has ever taken place in a by-invitation-only gathering of ecclesiastical nabobs. Not in Concord, not in Minneapolis, not in Dallas, not in London, not in Rome, not even in Durham, New Hampshire!
>
> Let me share with you what I think are some "defining" moments in the Christian life.
>
> When an abused woman attends a Bible study in a local church and feels enough love and support there to realize that she is a child of God filled with worth and value and that God and God's people will give her the strength and help to stand up for herself and assert her own personhood, that's a "defining" moment in the Christian life.
>
> When a young man unsure of his sexual orientation reads "The Episcopal Church Welcomes You" on a sign outside a church and enters that church and finds out through the love and full acceptance of its members that the church really means what the sign says, that's a "defining" moment in the Christian life.
>
> When a slum landlord kneels next to one of his tenants at the altar rail and realizes through the witness of word and sacrament offered in his local parish that he is a sinner and repents of the evil he is doing to his fellows and determines to treat them fairly and to "respect the dignity of every human being," that's a "defining" moment in the Christian life.

Bishop Theuner then asked Gene to stand, and, as is customary at a consecration, gave him specific charges for his new ministry. The first was to be humble, despite the many gifts he had been given by God. And the second was the same charge Jesus made to his disciples: to "shake the dust off his sandals" whenever he came to a place where he, and his message, were not welcome.

The sermon was followed by a hymn and then the "examination," a formal series of questions and answers that are part of the consecration liturgy, not unlike the examinations of conscience and intention that are part of a marriage or baptism. These questions were asked of Gene by the six co-consecrating bishops, whom he had invited to serve in that capacity. The Rt. Rev. Edmond Browning, the retired twenty-fourth Presiding Bishop of the Episcopal Church, had been a lifelong champion of inclusivity and a ray of hope for gay and lesbian Episcopalians during previous decades; it was he who had said, "There will be no outcasts in this Church." He was joined by The Rt. Rev. Herbert Donovan, Jr., the retired bishop of Arkansas; the Rt. Rev. Thomas Eastman, the retired bishop of Maryland; the Rt. Rev. Barbara Harris, the retired bishop suffragan of Massachusetts; the Rt. Rev. Chilton Knudsen, the bishop of Maine and president of Province I; and the Rt. Rev. Krister Stendhal, Bishop Emeritus of Stockholm in the Lutheran Church of Sweden.

The bishop-elect stood in front of the co-consecrators, who recited the formal ways in which bishops, throughout the life of the church, have been called to serve God and the various tasks the new bishop would be asked to perform, in particular to "guard the faith, unity and discipline of the church," to administer the sacraments, and to ordain priests and deacons and join in the ordination of bishops. "Your heritage is the faith of patriarchs, prophets, apostles, and martyrs," they repeated, "and those of every generation who have looked to God in hope. Your joy will be to follow him who came, not to be served, but to serve, and to give his life as a ransom for many. Are you persuaded that God has called you to the office of bishop?"

Gene answered, "I am so persuaded."

Then, as in a marriage or a baptism, a series of other questions were asked, which the candidate answers by pledging his commitment. After the final question, "Will you be merciful to all, show compassion to the poor and strangers, and defend those who have no helper?" Gene answered, "I will, for the sake of Christ Jesus," and the Presiding Bishop proclaimed that the bishop-elect had committed himself to God and to the service of the church.

He asked Gene to lead the congregation in reciting the Nicene Creed. Then the most solemn part of the consecration liturgy began with the singing of the "*Veni Creator Spiritus*":

> *Come Holy Ghost, our souls inspire,*
> *And lighten with celestial fire,*
> *Thou the anointing Spirit art,*
> *Who dost thy sevenfold gifts impart.*
> *Thy blessed unction from above*
> *Is comfort, life, and fire of love.*
> *Enable with perpetual light*
> *The dullness of our blinded sight . . .*

The *"Veni Creator Spiritus"* ("Come, Holy Spirit") is an ancient hymn that dates from the ninth century and is sung at Pentecost and on other solemn occasions when the Holy Spirit is invoked, such as the consecration of bishops, the ordination of priests, the dedication of churches, and the opening and closing of the academic year in religious institutions of learning. Historically, it has also been used on state occasions such as the coronation of kings.

In the Roman Catholic Breviary, which gives the order of service for the daily offices to be sung or said in churches and in monasteries, the *"Veni Creator*

Spiritus" is assigned to Vespers, the service said or sung for evening, as the sun sets, and is used especially during Pentecost and the following week, when the gift of the Holy Spirit to humanity is especially celebrated. Eleventh-century manuscripts indicate that the hymn was used this way and also that it was sung at the Council at Reims in 1049.

How did Gene feel as the decisive moment approached? Did he feel as alone as he looked, standing down on the ice, a small bareheaded figure in a white robe? He had prayed for months about this very thing. "Of course I would turn aside if I heard Him tell me not to go forward," he had said a week before. "I know there are many people for whom these events cause great pain. I know that I am in danger. But . . ." he looked up, his expression somewhere between wonder and tears. "I have never felt God so close to me."

"Apostolic succession," the unbroken line of bishops ordained by bishops, stretching all the way back to the apostles chosen by Jesus, is a major defining concept of Catholicism, Orthodox Christianity, Anglicanism, and Lutheranism. There have been questions about "illegal ordinations" throughout history, causing ruptures and schisms, of which the formation of the Anglican Church by Henry VIII of England was the most dramatic. Roman Catholics and the Eastern Orthodox do not generally recognize Anglicans as having maintained the apostolic succession, and do not consider them part of the "true church" or believe that their bishops and priests have valid "holy orders" to administer the sacraments and ordain other priests and bishops. Of course, Anglicans *do* believe that they are part of the original succession. Anglicans are not usually welcome to receive communion in a Catholic church. Catholics are welcome to receive communion in an Anglican church, but many will not partake because they do not recognize that the bread and wine have been legitimately consecrated, since according to them, the priest falls outside the apostolic succession.

The political and ecclesiastical arguments about who is or who is not legitimate are, as one can well imagine, complicated. Interestingly, though, the Catholic Church *does* accept the apostolic succession as having been maintained in the Lutheran Church of Sweden. In 1994, an agreement was made between twelve European churches, such as the Church of England and the Lutheran Church of Sweden, recognizing "full communion" among them— which means, among other things, the right to mutually ordain bishops. Similar agreements to bring the Lutheran Church and the Episcopal Church into full Communion have been made in the United States. The participation at Gene Robinson's consecration of the Rt. Rev. Krister Stendahl, Bishop Emeritus of Stockholm in the Lutheran Church of Sweden, could therefore be seen as doubly significant.

Gene Robinson would become the 993rd bishop in the American succession. While Roman Catholics would not recognize his episcopate as legitimate any more than they would recognize that of any other Anglican bishop, there was no procedural basis for anyone *within* the Anglican Communion to deny the legitimacy of his ordination. Every rule had been followed to the letter.

After the singing of the "*Veni Creator Spiritus*," the assembled bishops moved to the center, in front of the altar, facing the Presiding Bishop. Gene knelt in front of him. The bishops who were closest laid their right hands on Gene's head, and, as the circle radiated further out, each bishop placed a hand on the shoulder of the bishop in front. There was silence, and then the Presiding Bishop recited the first consecration prayer, giving thanks to God for "gathering and preparing a people to be heirs of the covenant of Abraham," for raising up "prophets, kings and priests," and for accepting the ministry of those whom He had chosen.

Then all the bishops prayed together:

Therefore, Father, make Gene a bishop in your church. Pour out upon him the power of your princely spirit, whom you bestowed upon your beloved Son Jesus Christ, with whom he endowed the apostles, and by whom your church is built up in every place, to the glory and unceasing praise of your Name.

The Presiding Bishop prayed:

Fill, we pray, the heart of this your servant . . . with such love of you and of all people, that he may feed and tend the flock of Christ and exercise without reproach the high priesthood to which you have called him, serving before you day and night in the ministry of reconciliation, declaring pardon in your Name, offering the holy gifts, and wisely over-seeing the life and work of the church. In all things may he present before you the acceptable offering of a pure, and gentle, and holy life, through Jesus Christ your Son . . .

And, in accordance with the italicized instructions in The Book of Common Prayer, the people "responded in a loud voice": "Amen."

It was accomplished: Gene Robinson had become bishop. The solemnity, majesty, and relief of that moment became a fountain of tears springing from thousands of eyes. The gold satin stole and chasuble were placed over Gene's shoulders by his parents and sister; the mitre, a gift from his partner Mark Andrew and his family, placed on his head. Douglas Theuner put the Palestinian shepherd's crook into his hand, and Bishop Smith put his own ring on Gene's hand, symbolizing forty years of the episcopate in New Hampshire.

The Presiding Bishop presented the new bishop to the congregation. Gene was at first unable to speak. Then, still struggling to control his emotions, he said that the occasion was not about himself, but "about so many people at the margins." He told the listeners that their presence today was an invitation to the marginalized to move to the center. He also pleaded for reconciliation. "There are many faithful, wonderful Christian people for whom this is a time of great pain, confusion and anger. God is served by our being loving to them." And he reiter-ated his own wish that rather than concentrating on him and on this event,

Christians should take advantage of the media attention to use the moment for God. "So many people don't know the love of God. Let's tell them about how God has saved us by reaching out to all who are hungry for Him."

I glanced over at the press box and the photographer whose camera had (so he hoped) captured a bird's-eye view of the laying-on of hands. He was looking down at the bishops, now beginning to move back to their seats after congratulating Gene, the joyful, tearful embraces of his family and close friends, and the small figure, now in shining vestments, clutching a shepherd's crook, standing in the center. Sensing my glance, perhaps, the photographer looked toward me and our eyes met. "Ah," I thought, seeing that he, too, was moved, "Maybe it became more than an assignment."

"The peace of the Lord be always with you," said the new bishop.

"And also with you," the people responded.

I stretched out my hand across the laptop computers and telephone wires. "Peace be with you," I said. The photographer extended his hand, nodded, and smiled.

Several weeks later, as Gene looked at pictures of the consecration, he was asked if he had felt small with all the bishops around him, pressing on his head. "Very small," he replied. "Truth be known, the standard joke is that when the bishops gather around you, what they're doing is removing your spine, which is a comment on how wimpy some people get when they become bishop. So I immediately thought of that, because they were pushing so hard. It was all I could do to remain upright. So I thought, quite to the contrary of removing your spine, if you didn't have a spine, you couldn't withstand the pressure."

"Also," he said, "the two things that drew me into the Episcopal Church (because the church I had come from wasn't that different theologically) were first, the liturgy, because it is so beautiful, and second, the sense of history and the connection back to the early church. So this moment of having hands laid on me, by people who had hands laid on them, who had had hands laid on them, all the way back to the apostles, was just a mind-boggling kind of a thing."

In his gold robes, Gene celebrated the Eucharist for the first time as bishop. During the offertory hymn, the Eucharistic teams (three people from each parish who would distribute the bread and wine to the multitude) encircled the altar, and after the final consecration of the bread and wine, they moved out to distribute it to the crowd of worshippers.

After communion, the congregation prayed:

We pray that Gene may be to us an effective example in word and action, in love and patience, and in holiness of life. Grant that we, with him, may serve you now, and always rejoice in your glory.

Following the blessing, the service ended with the traditional dismissal: "Let us go forth into the world, rejoicing in the power of the Spirit." The people's loud response came: "Thanks be to God."

Gene celebrates his first Eucharist as bishop. The Rev. Canon Tim Rich and Presiding Bishop Frank Griswold look on.

The organ broke into the triumphal hymn "For All the Saints": it was indeed All Saint's Day. The bishops rose and began their procession out of the arena, accompanied by the joyful singing of all eight verses of that glorious Anglican hymn. Again, tears flowed freely as the bishops slowly filed out, and finally, the crowd erupted, arms waving, into spontaneous cheering when Gene, his crook in hand, took his place at the end of the procession. The cheering didn't stop until his figure disappeared and the final lines of the hymn died away:

> *From earth's wide bounds, from ocean's farthest coast,*
> *Through gates of pearl streams in the countless host—*
> *Singing to Father, Son, and Holy Ghost,*
> *Alleluia! Alleluia!*

Accompanied by the strains of Handel's *Water Music* played by the brass, a reception was quickly brought onto the ice, and the crowd finally left their seats. Friends met, embraced, shook their heads from side to side in happy wonder, trying as humans do to fit words around indescribable experiences and tumultuous emotions. The reception went on for a long time: a colorful flow of monks and bishops, parishioners and children, parish priests and visitors, some of whom had probably never attended an Anglican service before. And gradually, as the plates of cheese and fruit, cookies and cakes, began to disappear, people reluctantly took their leave, coats and robes and church banners over their arms.

Outside the main entrance, the protesters still remained. One, who identified himself as the pastor of a Massachusetts church, called, "You liar. You thief. You whore. . . . You liars with your white robes and your dark hearts," to one of the exiting priests. But the UNH students, who had sat outside for three and a half hours, continued to chant their support for the ordination and for homosexuals, with slogans like "Two, four, six, eight, Jesus loves you, gay or straight." One of the students said that she felt this was a major step forward for Christianity. Looking toward the protesters, she said, "I feel sorry for them. They don't believe that God is a just and loving God."[2]

We left through the back of the arena. Opening the heavy doors, we stepped out, for the first time in ten hours, into a waiting world. The sun had set; it was colder. Quietly, we walked with friends down the sidewalk that had been patrolled this morning by police on horseback. The orange snow fence was still in position, but there were no signs of the protesters or police. A small group of UNH students greeted us as we climbed the steps to the parking lot level, cheering and waving signs that said "Thank you." Beyond them, we passed a lone man with a sad, concerned face, holding a large sign that said "Repent," and made our way to our cars.

"Goodnight," said the priest who was walking with us. She had to drive back to her parish in the far north and had nearly the full length of the state ahead of her.

"Drive safely," we replied. "It's been an amazing day."

She nodded. "An amazing day."

Bishop Douglas Theuner greets his successor after Gene Robinson's installation as the ninth bishop of New Hampshire.

Chapter 13

Becoming a Bishop

To kneel before a bishop, to feel the weight of his hands upon your head, to hear the ancient words . . . is to be permanently changed. You feel the power of the Holy Spirit, so it seems, entering your nerves, entering your mind, filling the innermost crevices of your unconscious. At that moment body, mind, emotion, spirit, soul are open, vulnerable, alert. The moment of ordination is one over which you have prayed and prayed, whether kneeling before God in a monastery in the dead of night or at a crowded altar rail on a Sunday morning. Like marriage, it is an irrevocable act which can never be completely undone.

—Bishop Paul Moore[1]

What really happens when someone is ordained a priest or consecrated a bishop? Theologically, ordination is said to be "indelible," marking the person in a way that will always leave traces. Moore expresses it psychologically: "Ordination is a traumatic experience so deep and important that you can never be the same afterward." Recognition of that idea is also written into the canon law of the church, which states that no person can be ordained twice. If a person resigns or is removed from office and is later reinstated, there is no second ordination. Likewise, a Catholic priest who becomes an Anglican is not reordained.

Just as I can still recall the bishop's hands on my own head at confirmation, or the moment when my husband and I married, something irrevocable and grave happened when Gene Robinson was consecrated. Nearly everyone who attended agreed that it had been an extraordinary event, not only historically but spiritually. But when the day was over—the bishops' mitres folded, the torches extinguished, the festival music remaining only as a tune in people's heads, remembered absent-mindedly on the normal commute to work—did it *matter* that a new bishop had been created? To be sure, this consecration was already making political headlines, and its ramifications would continue for years. But why all the fuss, in this day and age? Do bishops matter? Or is the creation of a new bishop merely an ultimate sort of job promotion in an increasingly irrelevant institution—the "raising up of another peacock," as a bitter former Catholic commented to me? What sort of mantle was Gene Robinson inheriting?

In the days before the Church of England even existed, bishops wielded great power and were, along with feudal lords, often involved in the political intrigue that led, literally, to "king-making." Historical reality is reflected in the game of chess, where bishops are extremely powerful pieces, placed directly to the right and left of the king and queen. That heritage also remains in the makeup of the British House of Lords, which grew out of the council of earls, barons, and ecclesiastical advisors established under the Magna Carta in 1215. The two houses of Parliament were begun about a century later, during the time of Edward III. When Henry VIII abolished the monasteries (1536–1540) and established the Church of England, he diminished the power of the clergy by eliminating the parliamentary seats formerly held by abbots and priors. The House of Lords then included both the Lords Temporal—the hereditary peers, appointed peers and High Court judges—and the Lords Spiritual—two archbishops and twenty-four diocesan bishops. If all this sounds completely medieval, think again. There are *still* twenty-six bishops seated in the present-day House of Lords in Britain, including permanent seats for the Archbishops of Canterbury and York, and the bishops of London, Durham, and Winchester. The others are chosen by seniority from the current diocesan bishops. It is also no coincidence that Lambeth Palace, the seat of the Archbishop of Canterbury, is not in Canterbury at all, but right across the Thames from Westminster Abbey and the Houses of Parliament. And while the House of Lords no longer runs Britain, the power and influence seated in that chamber are more than symbolic.

This non-separation of church and state in Britain and the elevated political role of bishops seem not only strange but abhorrent to most Americans. Indeed, the founders of both the fledgling American government and the Episcopal Church were clear that they did not want to replicate that structure—and they didn't. As was discussed earlier in this book, bishops in the American Episcopal Church are not appointed, either by religious or political figures. In England, however, the lines of demarcation between cross and crown are much murkier. Bishops are chosen, not elected, and they can also be asked to step down—as the Archbishop of Canterbury asked gay cleric Jeffrey John to do after he was nominated to become bishop of Reading. But it was Tony Blair, the prime minister, who turned the tables when he appointed Dr. John to be dean of St. Albans Cathedral.

It's no wonder that some of the dominant emotions about Gene Robinson's election, expressed by Anglican traditionalists in England and elsewhere, were frustration and outrage at the "cheek" of the bloody Americans: those New Hampshire Yankees were at it again, bulling ahead without considering the ramifications for the institution at large. The decent thing for Gene Robinson to do, said one such commentator, was to consider his "duty" and simply step down. This commentator failed to understand that in America, duly elected people consider it their duty to *serve*, not step down. Ironically, though, by making such a fuss about him, the critics have given Gene Robinson far more notoriety and a much larger podium than he would ever have received simply by virtue of being a bishop in the American Episcopal church.

After his retirement, Douglas Theuner was reflecting on the importance of bishops, and he saw two sides to the question. Even within secular society, he pointed out, there is a cultural belief that bishops are important: "'Oh, God, you're a *bishop*,' someone will say—and that can be someone of no religious background or commitment. They think you're something special. And so there's that sense that if Gene had been anything else, it wouldn't have been so important." He mentioned Jeffrey John's two appointments as an example. The conservatives in England were still very upset that an avowed homosexual had been appointed dean of a cathedral, which is a very prestigious job in England, perhaps even more so than that of a bishop in some places. But they were placated to some degree because Dr. John did not receive the *title*—he's not a bishop.

On the other hand, Bishop Theuner said, "Bishops are not all that important." He told an amusing story from his early days as a bishop, when a group of bishops were invited to spend time with the American Management Association in New York over a period of several months. The AMA had never worked with a group of religious leaders before, and the man in charge finally told them, "We've tried to tailor a program specifically for you, and we've tried to match it up with our normal experience in the business world, and we've determined that the category you come closest to, in terms of what we've done before, is 'regional managers of a small corporation.'"

Doug laughed: "That's humbling! That's humbling to people who've just gotten their purple shirt!" He thumped his chest with both fists and grinned. "But," he said, "the guy was right. Bishops *are* regional managers of a small corporation. So bishops are important, but they're not terribly important either. And in terms of the effect they have on a diocese, I think bishops are like rectors, or probably anybody in a position of leadership: they can do more harm than they can do good. Leadership can only take you so far, but a lack of leadership can really take you backwards."

That comment, coming from a bishop who, during his tenure, tried to use whatever authority he had for the good of society and the world, is both measured and humble. Bishop Theuner admitted that if he got up and spoke out in the New Hampshire legislature—against legalized gambling, for example—he was more likely to be quoted in the media than, say, the conference minister of the United Church of Christ would be, even though conference minister is a job comparable to that of bishop. Some of the attention he received was due to his status as a bishop of the Episcopal Church. But some of it was also because he was Douglas Theuner.

Paul Moore wrote that bishops, as the successors of Christ's apostles, are called to be "prophets of truth prevailing over social injustice, and conservators of virtue against the licentiousness of secular society."[2] Bishops are also supposed to "preserve the unity, health, and growth of the Church." There have been bishops who took the former role very seriously and did become eloquent, public voices against injustice—Moore himself was a good example, having become a staunch gay rights advocate and a strong voice in demanding public attention and funds to combat the AIDS crisis. The eloquent moral leadership of someone like Archbishop Desmond Tutu of South Africa can spill over to influence society—

but so can negativity and divisiveness. As we have seen in recent years, bishops can also be effective instruments of division and discord.

All this stood before Gene Robinson as he assumed office. How would he use the authority and visibility of the job, as well as the celebrity that surrounded his election? Would he, as he had so often mentioned prior to the consecration, seek the quiet that comes with being bishop of a small rural diocese, or would he assume the larger role that people seemed to want to thrust upon him? Could he somehow manage both?

For several months after the consecration, Gene served as bishop coadjutor, the title given to an assistant bishop who has been duly elected to succeed the sitting bishop. Then, on March 7, 2004, at St. Paul's Church in Concord, Bishop Douglas Theuner officially retired, and Gene Robinson was installed as the ninth bishop of the Diocese of New Hampshire. The Rt. Rev. Chilton Knudsen, Bishop of Maine and president of Province I, presided over a service that was both an emotional farewell and outpouring of gratitude to Douglas Theuner as well as equally emotional welcome for Gene Robinson. The service of installation was intentionally kept small and low-key, meant for the diocese as a "family," with music by an adult choir and a children's choir, and with a very limited media presence.

Gene began his episcopate by calling a meeting of lay and clergy leaders from across the diocese. The delegations from each New Hampshire parish filled the ballroom of a hotel convention center in Concord on a snowy, mid-winter day. The project Gene inaugurated that day was called "Re-imagining the Diocese," and in his address he introduced a catch-phrase that became a kind of diocesan motto as well as an encapsulation of the Gospel he preached whenever he had a chance: "Infinite Respect, and Radical Hospitality." The new bishop spoke about the need for the center of the church to move toward the margins and for its boundaries to become wider and much more porous. He said he felt that New Hampshire had a chance to take that phrase as a calling and a challenge, and—as it seemed to be the only diocese where people *weren't* focused on the issue of homosexuality—to explore what "infinite respect and radical hospitality" might really mean, both in the parishes and in daily, individual lives. But in typical Gene Robinson-as-facilitator fashion, the bishop refused to give answers of his own, instead empowering and exhorting the delegations to first take the discussion back to their own parishes, and appointing a committee to lead a diocese-wide "re-imagining" process during the following year, which would consolidate the results of the parish discussions and make recommendations for action.

Gene had said, quite clearly, that he looked forward to the day after November 2, when he could start doing the work he had been elected to do: becoming that "regional manager of a small corporation"—the bishop of a small diocese in a rural, rocky, northern state. He commented that if he didn't love working with congregations so much and wasn't looking forward so much to doing that, he would have "fallen apart a long time ago." But as the months went by with no let-up in requests for interviews and appearances across the country and even internationally, he admitted that he was being thrust into another role as well.

"My model in all of this is Barbara Harris," he insisted during those first months. "She was the first woman to be consecrated bishop in all of Christendom, and she's always been very clear in her mind that her primary job is to be bishop suffragan of Massachusetts, and, oh yeah, also, she's the first woman. So I tend to follow her as my hero in that and always to remember that my first responsibility and role is to the people of New Hampshire, and then to pay attention to this other role that it is my privilege and humble honor to be called to."

Gene and Mark went on vacation in the Caribbean just before the investiture, in late February of 2004. The night before they left, Gene was taking off his new gold cross, which he had decided not to take with him on the trip. Even though their house had an alarm system and motion detectors, the thought occurred to Gene that if someone were to break in and steal the cross he'd be devastated, so he said to Mark, who was packing, "I'm going to go hide this somewhere," and left the room. "That was the cleverest place!" he said to himself as he returned and resumed packing. The next morning, they left.

When Gene and Mark returned to their house two weeks later, tan and rested, Gene went to the hiding place to retrieve the cross. It wasn't there. "Hmm," he thought, and looked in a different place. It wasn't there—or in the next place he tried. He called to Mark and the two of them began searching, growing increasingly panicked. When I saw him in his office, a few weeks later, he told the story, his shoulders slumped, eyes still wide with disbelief. "We've turned the house inside out," he said. "I've had two psychics in the house try-ing to find it. I'm now searching for some-one who can hypnotize me. I'm considering asking a dowser to come over and try. I'm completely freaked out over this. I don't

Mark Andrew and Gene Robinson at their "favorite place in the world," St. Barts, French West Indies.

remember doing anything dramatic when I hid it: I didn't go outside, didn't get out a ladder, I don't even think I went downstairs. Now we're going through the house room by room. Tonight we're doing the downstairs closet, all of my sweaters, all of my shirts; we've looked in every pocket, every pair of shoes, every pair of socks; we've cleaned out the attic over the garage, the entire guest room, every piece of clothing, every drawer, every book—you can't imagine. We haven't thrown away any trash since we got back! Mark even repotted all the orchids! It's driving me completely crazy."

Gene offered his children a free trip to St. Bart's if they could find the cross before his investiture, and they couldn't, though they spent an entire day looking. The fact that the cross not only symbolized his office but was actually made of gold contributed by people in the diocese made the loss even more devastating, the cross impossible to replace, and the story too painful to forget. Besides, every Sunday people came up to him and asked to see it. Even on a visit to his old parish in Ridgewood, New Jersey shortly after his formal investiture as bishop, Marge Christie said, "Show us your new cross and tell everyone about it!"

"I was just crestfallen," he said. "The cross is such a wonderful, meaningful thing." He shook his head and his eyes grew huge behind his glasses. "This is the worst story in the history of the world!" He was able to laugh at his own tragic tone—just barely.

But life, of course, went on. Back at Diocesan House, Gene's new staff took over. The Rev. Tim Rich, Gene's new canon to the ordinary, arrived in February to occupy Gene's old downstairs office and began his work of interfacing with the diocesan clergy and acting as Gene's advisor, confidant, and close assistant.

Paula Bibber, who had been hired by Doug Theuner in 2001 and continued on to work for Gene, is a quintessential executive assistant, managing the schedules of very busy people, handling appointments, telephone requests, and correspondence, and keeping track of innumerable details with apparent ease, intelligence, confidentiality, and efficiency. "My job is probably one of the more interesting things anyone could hope to do," she said. "There are numerous things I do regularly, but the bishop is always first, so as his schedule changes, so does mine." As the diocese became involved in the search for a new bishop, Paula was astounded by the volume of responses they received from interested priests. And in her typical, understated style, she said that since Gene's election, they had all learned to do things a little differently. "I've certainly learned how to deal with the press," she said, "and I've learned to be a little more patient with some people. I realize that not everybody agrees with what New Hampshire did, and as difficult as it is at times to read some of the things they write to us, or listen to their phone calls, I've learned to be very tolerant of that, and just keep in mind that their views are different and I certainly must respect them, even though they're yelling in my ear while they're expressing them."

Paula said that some people call repeatedly, feeling the need to vent, and will talk only to her. Other people call and say, "I just wanted to pick up the phone and say how proud I am to be an Episcopalian," or, "I just wanted to tell you that not everybody in Texas is against what New Hampshire has done. Many of us down here just love it."

After Gene's election, Paula began handling a huge number of requests for Gene to make personal appearances. These demands on his time had to be balanced with the regular business of parish visitations, ordinations, confirmations, and other special services, administrative work and planning, and his work as the primary pastor for the priests of the diocese. "I told him one day, 'If we could clone you we'd have it made: one of you could be on the road and we'd keep one here, and everybody would be happy.'" She said that after people saw or heard Gene at an event, the office would invariably receive a call or an email asking him to come and speak to other groups.

"That is such a juggling act, to go through and try to choose the ones that will give Gene the opportunity to reach the most people. He feels that if he's going to take time away from the diocese, he wants to try to reach a large number of people at one time, so that's why most of these events are on a larger scale—even though he enjoys the smaller events very much. And it's very hard for him to say no, but he's getting better at it."

Because of Paula's experience and calm, efficient intelligence, Gene trusted her to step in and handle the greatly-increased volume of phone calls and emails. "The only piece of advice he gave me was, 'Remember anything you say or write is likely to end up on the internet somewhere,'" she said. "So when I respond to people I try to make sure it's very businesslike, and I answer their question or handle their concern as best I can, remembering that I need to be careful about what I'm saying,

Gene peeks through the conference room door at Diocesan House in Concord, New Hampshire.

because I could be quoted—and quoted incorrectly." She explained that, to begin with, confidentiality is the number one priority of the job, and after that, "it's just taking care in the way you deal with people. Everyone—those in the diocese as well as those from outside—is calling here for a reason, whether it's for information or assistance, or just to vent. And they all need to be treated with infinite respect. We all try to do that, and it isn't always easy. Some days you just don't want to answer the phone. But I think we all do it pretty well here."

The staff, of course, has had to accommodate itself to much greater security and to keep up a constant level of vigilance and awareness of potential danger. "After all, we live in Concord, New Hampshire!" Paula exclaimed. "We probably have all the problems of other small cities, but you just assume that nothing is going to happen, because that's the norm here in Concord."

Working so closely together in a small building that still feels like the house it once was, the diocesan staff functioned like a family even before it became the target for so much media attention. Paula has learned to be more aware of security upon arriving and leaving, just to see if anything seems different or amiss, but she worries the most when Gene goes off on a trip. She always talks to the contact people involved with the various events across the country, who often ask her about security arrangements. "I tell them he's not concerned so they shouldn't be, but I also tell them that if any calls or letters come in to indicate that there might be a problem at this particular location, I'll let them know. He's so well known now—he goes to places and he's still amazed that people recognize him! And sometimes I wonder, with all the traveling through airports and other places . . ." Her voice fell. "It would be so hard for me to hear that something had happened to him."

Although Paula had known Gene for several years, working for him as bishop turned out to be different than working for Doug Theuner. "They're totally different personalities," she said. "Doug is A+++, I think! We used to joke that you knew when he came into the building because the building vibrated. With Doug there was always a lot of energy—I think it was the coffee he drank! Gene is different. He has tons of energy, but it's a different kind of energy. Doug is like a thunderstorm. Gene is more like the crack of dawn: there's lots of energy and light, but it's quieter." She said that both men were charismatic, but in different ways. "With Doug you feel like there are all these neutrons and electrons bouncing all over the place. With Gene it's . . . deeper. I used to sometimes think Doug was going to burn out on me. Gene is more like—*simmering*. They're very different," Paula repeated, "but there are some things about them that are the same. They both seem to have a gift for focusing very well, giving each thing the attention that it needs, in spite of having so much going on. And they both have a deep pastoral concern for everyone. I guess that is part of their commitment to their vocation. Both are very clear not only about their call, but also about their faith."

After the consecration, Gene's entire schedule and routine changed. He had always taken very good care of himself, being sure to keep physically active, but with all the travel, he found he was getting off his schedule and his normal diet was disrupted. He had several minor illnesses and then a bout of pneumonia. Paula said that the staff became worried, and he did too. "So he put the brakes on and said, 'We've got to get back on track here.'" She shook her head and smiled. "It all happened so quickly. We were all sort of swept away with what was going on, the phones and the mail and all the attention being focused here, and everybody going crazy. And even on our craziest days we've been able to look at each other and laugh and say, 'Well, it's been one heck of a day!' I think we do a good job of avoiding the things that lead to burnout, and keeping our sense of humor."

In his role as president of the diocesan Standing Committee, the Rev. Hank Junkin was responsible for making sure the diocese had a healthy bishop. He also became concerned and was glad when Gene ramped back. "Gene means it when he says he's having so much fun. But you know, my Labrador retriever has so much fun chasing tennis balls that he will literally chase them until he collapses. And he'll have fun the very last time he retrieves that ball before he collapses. Gene *is* having fun every minute of it, but that doesn't mean it won't lead to his collapse. So I said to him, 'I want this to still be fun for you five or ten years from now, too.'"

Tim Rich, then the rector of St. John's Church, Portsmouth, and Gene were already good friends when Gene invited him to become his canon to the ordinary, a fact that Tim pointed out to his potential boss as a possible stumbling block. Gene had an immediate answer: that he was going to need a good friend. He told Tim he needed someone whom the clergy in the diocese were going to

The Rev. Canon Tim Rich.

trust and relate to from day one. This was not only because the clergy in the diocese had to deal with the fact that their new bishop's election was causing stress in their congregations, but also with the fact that the person to whom they would normally have turned for help was the canon to the ordinary—who was now bishop. "They were dealing with a collision of things," said Tim.

I first visited Tim on a spring day in 2004. On the coffee table in the Diocesan House lobby were the latest issue of *New Hampshire Episcopal News* and an issue of the *Daily Sun* from "Paper City," the northern paper-mill town of Berlin in the heart of New Hampshire's rugged White Mountains. While I waited for Tim to finish a phone call, I read the front page article in *Episcopal News* about the new bishop's involvement as a board member with the New Hampshire Endowment for Health, a group that works for access to health care for the state's neediest citizens, and his continuing work with the New Hampshire Community Loan Fund, which helps fund affordable housing and micro-enterprise. On the inside, Gene's pastoral letter, entitled "One Year Later," spoke about diocesan issues during the year since his election. It was printed across from an essay by the Rev. Susan Buchanan, entitled "Moose Crossing," about how we often disbelieve the signs telling us to watch for the sudden appearance of moose—or of God. The Berlin paper's front page had a color picture showing the bishop, in a t-shirt, baseball hat, and shorts, volunteering with a group of Episcopal teens at a food pantry. Inside was a story about a young Boston hiker who had died after being frightened by two encounters with a bear.

Gene's Kentucky background and log cabin/organic gardening days at The Sign of the Dove make him feel right at home in this folksy, rural atmosphere of most New Hampshire parishes—and it's part of what he loves. In fact, when diocesan needleworkers made him a finely-detailed needlepoint stole, he asked that they include a cloud of blackflies in addition to the fall leaves, purple finch and lilacs, Episcopal and diocesan seals that are the "official" symbols of his state and office.

Tim Rich came to New England much more recently, from Pittsburgh. Unlike Gene, Tim, with his wife, Megan, and two young daughters, fits the profile of the increasingly rare but most sought-after clergy type in America. Prior to becoming canon for the new bishop, he was rector of St. John's, Portsmouth, the oldest church in the diocese. "I think Portsmouth decided they were in danger of becoming a museum," he said, grinning, "so they called this young guy—me." Like his new boss, Tim is relatively small in stature, but younger, with dark hair and bright, flashing eyes.

When I asked why he and Gene had become such good friends, he immediately joked, "Maybe because we have the same twisted sense of humor." But, more seriously, he went on to speak about Gene and Mark's hospitality when he and his family first came into the diocese. "You can reach a point in life where even if you don't say it out loud, you feel like, 'I have all the close friends I need, or am able to develop.' To Gene and Mark's credit, they were willing to invite Megan and me into their home and their lives, get to know our daughters, and for us to know theirs." He said that he and Gene share a similar love for the church, for the Gospel as it relates to issues of justice and mission, and a similar energy level and passion about ministry.

Moving away from parish ministry to do this job had been a serious decision for Tim. "I love the opportunity that this role affords me to work more closely with my colleagues and around the diocese," he said. "And I miss the parish and that kind of intimacy every day. I think the role has made me more aware of the national church and the Anglican Communion. And some of that is probably going to result in a greater commitment, and some of it in a greater cynicism. I just had lunch with a friend who asked how the job was going. And I said, 'It's going all right so long as, in the grand scheme of things, I feel like I'm helping to build the Kingdom of God.' If I feel like that's what I'm doing, then I'm in for this. But when it feels like what I'm doing is more help build the institution known as the Episcopal Church, or helping prop that up, then that's the day I go back to the parish."

I asked whether Gene, having done Tim's job so successfully for sixteen years, had given him advice. He said no, that Gene hadn't had time! "To say we had to hit the ground running doesn't even begin to describe it. One very important thing that both of us have said at different times is that I can't be Gene, and I shouldn't put pressure on myself to *try* to be Gene. He has said, 'Don't try to guess what I would have done when I was canon to the ordinary, just do what you think is best.' And that's very liberating."

"I remember the final conversation we had at Chauncy's Lobster Pound on the day we were discussing the job. It's a great place, over on the coast. And it was Gene and Mark, and Megan and I, and Gene's bodyguard and the lobsters. So I'm asking Gene all these questions, and at the end I said, 'Did I leave anything out?' And then Mark said, 'Yeah, I have a question. Gene, I want to know how you're going to stop being canon to the ordinary, and let Tim be canon to the ordinary!'"

Because Tim was constantly listening to the clergy, he had a particular ear to the ground when it came either to serious storms in the diocese over financial problems or dropping attendance due to Gene's election, or to rumblings of discontent about electing Gene and ending up with a celebrity bishop. By that spring, he said that things were settling down. Attendance had come back in the parishes that had experienced a drop-off, and that rebound was attributable both to the return of some people who had left and to some new people coming in.

"The other way I'm sensing that things are back to normal is that we just aren't talking about it in such a consumed way any more," he added. "Most people are proud of who Gene is, and how Gene is, and have no problems with all the attention because Gene himself has stayed grounded. Some people were predisposed to being sensitive to how much the bishop is flying away . . . but I think most people realize that these first couple of years are a really rare evangelism opportunity, and we have to be generous with our bishop's time."

Tim freely admitted that they were all blindsided by the amount of attention the New Hampshire election had received. "Frankly, any diocese elects a bishop for the whole church, but—not like this! 'Cause we weren't electing him because he was gay, we weren't electing him to break down barriers, we were electing him because we had known him for seventeen years, and knew his gifts and his experience, and his faith and his presence. But after the election, when the media just went nuts, we realized, 'Oh, we aren't just electing someone for

Mark Andrew and Gene Robinson at their house in New Hampshire.

ourselves, but for the whole world.' I mean, let's face it: if Gene were straight, we wouldn't have media all over us, and I doubt if you and I would be sitting down talking about it, even though there is a great story to tell about Gene anyway. All the times I've spoken to the press, it's been about sexual orientation, or people's reaction to sexual orientation. So that's been a unique aspect to being canon to the ordinary for the first elected openly gay bishop. But for us, on the day that we elected him, and pretty much all the time since, it's just been business as usual, because Gene has been with us for seventeen years."

The first thing Gene always says about his partner, Mark, is what a private person he is: "I continue to be simply overwhelmed at the enormity of the gift that he has given me, and the church, by not just doing this with me, but doing it wholeheartedly—because it is simply the last thing on earth that he would ever hope for. So the fact that he would do this with me still takes my breath away."

Gene says it's merciful that this diocese doesn't have a lot of fixed expectations of the bishop's spouse—that New Hampshire is a long way from the priest's spouse being "the one who pours the tea and runs Sunday School and sings in the choir." Mark accompanies him on all his Sunday parish visitations. Gene remembered an early visit to one of the northern parishes near the Canadian border, when the rector said, "And this morning, we welcome Bishop Robinson, oh it's so wonderful to have him here, and his partner, Mark. Mark, do you want to stand up?" Mark stood up and people applauded, and then the rector went on with the announcements about the rummage sale next Saturday. Gene said, "And I was thinking, 'Oh my God, he just sat through that.' There was not a blip on the horizon. We went through that like we have done this for hundreds of years: 'And the bishop's partner is here—Mark, do you want to stand up?' It's like, oh my God!"

As a couple, Gene and Mark are complementary and compatible. Gene laughs about the differences between their outward personalities—his extroversion and Mark's apparent privacy and introversion—but says that Mark is actually a lot more extroverted than you'd realize at first. More than that, he admires—and is continually surprised by—Mark's communication style, which is very different from his own.

"I have never known him to interrupt anyone," Gene says. "That fact is Mark in a nutshell." Gene figures people can take care of themselves, and says that he himself will just "bulldoze anyone"—an exaggeration of his enthusiastic conversational style. At first, Gene worried that Mark's quietness came from a lack of self-esteem, but he gradually realized that it actually came from his deep respect for other people. "One of the ways he lives that out is that he will not trample on them. And if he's speaking, and someone interrupts him, he will stop speaking and let them say what they have to say. I get impatient with him sometimes: I know him so well, I know what he's about to say, and he'll start to say it, and somebody else will come in, and I'm sort of wishing I could say, 'Get in there, get in there, I know what you're going to say, and it's perfect!' But he'll wait—he just won't trample on anybody. It's such an honorable thing. I could never do it."

"I'm also hyperbolic about everything," Gene says. "I'll say, 'There were hundreds of people there!' and Mark will say, 'Actually, there were 167.' I don't care about the real number! If it *felt* like hundreds, then it was hundreds; but he will actually know the number. I go in for this Biblical language, like, 'It rained forty days and forty nights.' That's what the Bible says, but it might have rained five days: it wasn't forty days. But forty of anything means 'a lot'! I want to know that something was 'a lot,' and he wants to know 'how many.' To me, maybe we've been waiting for something *forever*, and for him, we've been waiting eight months. Well, if the eight months feels like forever, then it's forever! So that's allegorical language."

The couple's domestic life forms their core of sanity and their refuge. Gene says their house felt like 'our house' from the beginning, since he had had the plans with him when he first met Mark. Subsequently they worked on the design together, and in 2005 they completed a major renovation. They love to entertain, and the house is designed for that, with a bright, open kitchen, warm, beautifully-crafted cabinetry, and a huge dining table of polished granite in the dining room, ready to seat as many as twenty guests.

Gene had always been a big gardener, but Mark had never gardened before. "He loves to water, I love to weed," Gene laughed. One year, for Mark's birthday, Gene bought him a couple of orchids, and Mark became fascinated with growing them, discovering a green thumb he didn't know he had. A big east-facing window at the end of the dining room has a full-width, low shelf for orchids, and a tiled sun space is located on the south side of the house, also filled with blooming plants.

"Because our lives have become so busy, hectic and just full," Gene says, "we've gotten kind of minimalist at our house. We bought some new furniture: it's very modern, no arms on the sofas and chairs. Everything is super-clean. You go into my mother's house and there are ten million things to dust, and so forth. We don't do *tchotchkes,* little things, you know. When we go home, we don't want our house to be busy." Gene laughs and says he doesn't know if they'll ever be able to sell it to anybody because it is so personal and quirky, but they love it. "Now that we've made it handicap-accessible," he jokes, "we'll be able to stay a few more years."

"About the only time we really fight is when we're doing something handy around the house, and neither of us is good at it. But we each had fathers who taught us the right way to do it. And we *know* that *our* father knew the right way to do it. And we will both hold tenaciously to that way of doing it, even when we don't know anything about what we're doing. So we can just prepare for that, like, 'We're going to fix the bed today? Okay, great. Well, we'll hate each other at the end,' or just, 'Let's do it *your* dad's way. Before I even hear it, let's do it your dad's way. Today. My turn will be next time.'"

They both love to cook, although Mark is the more creative chef, while Gene describes himself as being pretty much "tied to the recipe." On Friday nights, they both go home from work and do their favorite thing, which is to cook dinner together, often from a new recipe, with Mark doing the directing: "This is going into the soup. Chop it." Then they sit down and watch the political pundit shows and "occasionally throw things at the TV." That's another way the two are alike: they're both political junkies.

"We always have public radio on," Gene says. "I was invited to interview for a special that was going to be done by Gwen Ifill and Bryant Gumbel. I adore Gwen—she's the African American woman who hosts *Washington Week in Review;* that's one of our favorite political pundit shows. So I said, 'Paula, you tell them that I'll do the interview if Gwen Ifill will do it.' Paula set up the interview to coincide with a trip they were taking to the Bishops' and Spouses' Conference in Philadelphia. The planned television special was to be shot at Independence Hall, with different segments on Constitution-related topics; Gene's was on gay rights. About three days before the interview, the producers called and said that Gwen Ifill wasn't going to be able to do it—Bryant Gumbel was going to do that particular piece. But they had arranged for Gene and Mark to meet Gwen.

"So we got to sit for an hour and a half with her, and it was a mutual admiration society. We just *loved* her. So now when we see her on TV, we say, 'That's our friend Gwen.'"

Gene grinned and then let out a wry laugh, remembering something else about that night. He said it was the only time he had allowed himself to be interviewed with an opponent of gay rights—this was an evangelical—beside him. "It's also the only time I've gotten kind of angry, which is why it's a good thing for me not to actually be debating somebody. At one point, he said something like, 'Yeah, well, if we let you marry, then you'll want to go in for polygamy, and probably animals, too.' And I said something brilliant like, 'Oh, stop it!' I was ready to send him to a corner. I said, 'Oh, stop it! That is so stupid, I can't believe that somebody like you said it.' Anyway, after the interview was over, this guy was totally taken aback because his grown daughter, twenty-eight years old or so, was there and wanted her picture taken with *me*. The man was just dumbfounded. He was like, 'Are you kidding me?'"

In addition to requests for interviews by the media, Gene began to receive awards, particularly from gay and lesbian groups, and to be honored at commemorative gatherings. Some of those events featured celebrities from the entertainment industry, and the bishop found himself sharing the podium with stars and Hollywood producers and being invited out to dinner with them afterwards. He told how he and Mark had been invited to Elton John's dressing room before a performance. After returning from an awards dinner in California, he laughingly claimed, "I opened for Janet Jackson!" and said she had been in the green room with him before going on stage. He had also met Ellen Degeneres's mother, who said her daughter "just loved him." "It's totally surreal," Gene said. "Totally."

"In the family," Ella Robinson says, "we all look back and we just can't believe this has all happened—that all this attention has been put on him and on the church." Ella, who works in publicity for Dreamworks Pictures, often

Sir Elton John with Gene and Mark.

Ella Robinson.

accompanies her father to various appearances and events. "It's so weird going places with him," she says. "Last year I went with him to the Human Rights Campaign Event down in Washington, D.C., where he was being honored. I work a lot with actors—we call them 'the talent.' When somebody comes into town, there is a person assigned to them and a car is sent to pick them up at the airport, all that kind of stuff. Well, at this event my dad was 'the talent': he was the star of this thing! *We* were the ones with the limousine and all the attention. And yet I look at him and say, 'Hey, he's just my dumb old dad!'"

Ella also can't say enough about Mark's influence and steady presence. "He is like the rock of our family," she says. "He would do anything for any one of us. Dad and I are so 'out there,' extroverted, and yet Mark had to do these press conferences, and people wanted to ask *him* questions. He was just there as support for my father, and not for the limelight at all, and he's had to do a fair amount of being paraded around as part of this process. But he's been such an incredible support for my dad."

Gene himself agrees. "I've always been astounded at how seriously bishops take themselves," he says, "and how they begin to believe their own PR. I want to guard against that. I do get all this praise, but all the negative stuff coming my way helps to not let that go to my head." He laughs and adds, "Look, let's be honest: I love having people tell me how wonderful I am all the time. So it gets back to Mark. Mark is just not terribly impressed, you know? I mean, he is, in the sense of being absolutely supportive and proud of me, but he also keeps me grounded and reminds me that 'Okay, so you're the big hotshot bishop, but you know what? The garbage needs to be taken out.'"

Ella says she doesn't know what her father would do without Mark. "He's been very influential in keeping it all in perspective and helping Dad keep focused on the right things," she says. "Because at the end of the day it's just the two of you. You leave behind the headlines and the TV interviews and all the attention: the two of you are sitting there having dinner together and that's really what matters. And I think Mark has kind of not let him change, not let it all affect him too much. They've been really strong throughout it all because of each other."

Coming home from the headiness of Hollywood, bright lights, fame and adulation to the extremely down-to-earth, often goofy diocese of New Hampshire was also good for Gene. He is fond of showing off some of the funky presents that various parishes have given him: the skiing teddy bear and a pair of green Incredible Hulk boxing gloves that growl when you hit them together. During one visitation, a parish presented Gene with a big ice cream float. He looked at it, confused. "The parishioners explained that, indeed, although it's called a visitation, it's not really a visit because all of the churches are mine here in the diocese, and so that I should feel at home there, rather than a visitation, it was more like a homecoming. And what would a homecoming be without a homecoming float?"

"Oh, my God," he exclaimed, laughing, as he recounted the story. "That's the sickness that is the Diocese of New Hampshire. Isn't that great?"

Gene is fond of telling audiences how grateful he is that he can go back home to New Hampshire, "the only place in the world where I am simply 'the bishop,' not 'the gay bishop.'" But as it did all over the country, the controversy surrounding his election did have ramifications at home. In every parish, there were a few disaffected people who either left or withdrew their pledges. But in one parish, Rochester, there was full-fledged opposition, and Gene, like other diocesan bishops, had to deal with it.

The Rochester congregation had already split once before. Seventeen years ago, the vestry had disagreed with the national church's position on the ordination of women and the revised Book of Common Prayer. The rector was loyal to the diocese, but the vestry wanted to take the parish out of the Episcopal Church.

The Rochester parish had a long history of fighting with the bishop: they had had disagreements with Bishops Hall, Smith, and Theuner as well as Bishop Robinson. As the argument heated up, someone from another church asked Gene, "Is this normal? Does it happen to other parishes?"

His reply could apply equally well to marriage: "Once you decide that leaving— that is, not staying at the table—is an option, once you ever do that, then it stays an option in everyone's mind, and when the going gets rough, it feels like an easier alternative than staying and working it out. So it's not surprising that the same thing would have happened in this parish seventeen or eighteen years later."

In the previous disagreement, the parish appealed to Canon 21 of the Episcopal Church's *Constitutions and Canons*, which concerns the dissolution of the pastoral relationship between the parish and the bishop—who was, at the time, a just-consecrated Douglas Theuner. Canon 21 puts the whole thing in the bishop's hands: it's the only time that a bishop has that kind of control over a parish. So Bishop Theuner fired the vestry. They and half the congregation went off and formed Trinity Anglican Church.

Now, nearly two decades later, the Rochester parish again clashed with the bishop. One would think that perhaps the present disaffected group would simply go and join those at Trinity who had previously left, but they didn't. Gene said he thinks that this group actually approves of the ordination of women and the new prayer book. One of the parishioners was asked about this by the press, and he replied, "Those people don't even believe in the ordination of women!"

"Once you've decided you can just leave," Gene reiterated, "there's no end to the things you can disagree about."

The bishop celebrates the Eucharist at St. Thomas Church, Hanover, after ordaining the Rev. Celeste Hemingson (to his immediate right) to the priesthood. The Rev. Canon Henry Atkins and the Rev. Louise Pietsch look on.

The Rochester controversy began to glow red immediately following Gene's consecration. When the Rev. Donald Wilson—the interim minister at Rochester who, along with a majority of the congregation, had opposed the consecration—refused to meet with Bishop Douglas Theuner to discuss their disagreement, Bishop Theuner removed him on grounds of insubordination. On November 9, 2003, the Sunday following the consecration, about half of the Rochester congregation walked out of the service in protest. The parishioners said that they could not accept Robinson's spiritual or pastoral authority because his sexual relationship with another man "went against Scripture" and "defied the will of God in their understanding." The Rochester parish was influenced and guided by the American Anglican Council (ACC) and the Anglican Communion Network of Parishes and Dioceses (ACN), which by then were working nationally to establish an organized network of opposing parishes, encouraging them to refuse to submit to the authority of consenting bishops. The statements by the AAC became increasingly combative: after the removal of the Rochester priest, AAC president Canon David Anderson called Bishop Theuner's actions "an act of war against a small church of 100."[3]

In late March, at his formal installation as bishop, Gene acknowledged the fact that two parishes in the diocese—the Church of the Redeemer in Rochester and St. Mark's in Ashland—were clearly opposed to the ordination of an openly gay bishop. In the emotional remarks he made after the formal investiture, he said that his intention was to "win them back one heart at a time." He repeated his call for infinite respect and radical hospitality toward all, including those who opposed his election. "God is always calling us out of our comfort zones and into risky places," he said. "If all our faith does is give us comfort, we have missed half of what God intends for us."[4]

In the months after the removal of their interim priest, two other priests, both supportive of Gene's election, came and went from Rochester parish. The opposing parishioners continued their protest by refusing to receive communion. After Gene took over from Douglas Theuner, he met with the dissenting parishioners on a Monday night. One of the parishioners, Lisa Ball, told reporters, "He asked a lot of questions last night. He said he's willing to do what it takes to make this work."

"We're trying to respect his office of bishop," she said, and then added, "On the other hand, we don't want anything to do with him."

The parishioners wanted to be placed under the oversight of a conservative bishop, one who agreed with their position on the issue of homosexual ordinations. This strategy of "alternative pastoral oversight" was being discussed nationally as a way of keeping dissenting parishes within the Episcopal Church but allowing them the freedom of their conscience while the church at large grappled with the issues. The local bishop of the diocese would retain administrative authority, and the parish would be required to accept his or her presence once a year. But the Rochester parishioners wanted no part of Gene Robinson's authority or presence, in spite of the fact that he was well known to them and had helped them during the previous crisis, when he was a young canon to the ordinary for Bishop Theuner. Gene left the meeting with a written list detailing their requests, and in return said he would give them a list of conservative bishops, acceptable to him, from whom they could choose.[5]

On a Wednesday evening in June 2004, Gene and the Rochester parish had a face-to-face meeting. Although he was still hopeful about salvaging a relationship—he had agreed to one of the few bishops they were willing to accept—he went into the meeting suspecting that the parishioners were more interested in a fight than an agreement. He was right.

"It was probably the worst experience I've had since I was elected," Gene said a week later. "If you could roll up all the hatred of the last year, Wednesday night would have exceeded it. It was as assaultive, hateful—evil is not a word I use very often, but evil—as anything I've ever been a part of. It was just unbelievable."

He was not alone at the meeting: Canon Tim Rich and the Rev. Hank Junkin went with him. The priest that Gene was willing to reinstate—the same one Bishop Theuner had previously let go—held forth in two tirades of about ten minutes each. "He was pacing back and forth, and shaking his finger at me, and screaming. It was just unbelievable. People were distorting things—it was just awful."

"Wednesday night was absolutely awful," Tim Rich said later. "I thought to myself, 'I know a little more now about how Peter must have felt when Pilate

225

was engaging the crowd with Jesus.' Hank and Gene were at the table with all the folks, and I had intentionally positioned myself up in the gallery. And what was so sickening about that was feeling the diffuse mean-spiritedness in the air. The most concrete and clearest example was at one point they said to Gene, 'You have a choice. Repent and be saved.' Gene said, 'I repent daily, and I believe I am saved,' and in the gallery there was this just appalling snicker—these sort of knowing glances exchanged. I mean, I didn't hear, 'He's going to burn in hell,' but I saw the glances and I heard the snickers. If you've ever been in a room where you feel like everyone else is on the same page except you and they're communicating by smirks and glances and the communication is not intended for you, it was that kind of experience. It was just . . . it was the force of darkness, bringing out the worst in people. That night brought out the worst in many, many of the people."

"Part of what perhaps made it worse was that these weren't faceless, unknown people saying all these hateful things to him. I mean, it stinks when you get a postcard with a picture of a cathedral on one side and on the other side it says, 'You fornicating lecherous pig, I hope you burn in hell'—that is pretty awful. But when you're sitting with people you've known for seventeen years—I mean, at the last blowup in Rochester, Gene went out there and did some amazing work with those people, to help them through that. So that's got to be even more painful."

Gene refused to give them a fight. He decided about halfway through that he was going to stay there till dawn if that's what it was going to take. "I think they wanted me to leave the table, so that I would be the one who was giving up. But I was not leaving the table."

So he called their bluff. "It was very interesting," he said. "I was prepared to give them everything they wanted, and they weren't willing to maintain even the slightest thread of a relationship. When it started to escalate—when it looked like they were about to do something dramatic, like walk out—the ACN advisor tried to steer it back to a compromise that had been proposed because he knew that if they walked out, it was over. But they weren't going to have any of it. In the end, their own anger and hatred just got the best of them. They all took their keys out of their pockets and slammed them down on the table, and stomped out."

Gene said to Hank, "Get those keys." They changed the locks on the church property the next morning, and put out the word around the diocese that there would be a service there on the following Sunday. After the meeting, which was closed to the media, Gene spoke to reporters and described himself as "a little bit shaken . . . and heartbroken."[6]

Afterwards Hank, Gene, and Tim were able to share the ride back from Rochester to talk about what had happened—but Gene was the only one of the three who slept that night. Thursday, however, was Clergy Day in the diocese. Its purpose was for the diocesan priests and deacons to meet and talk about their experiences over the last year. On the ride home from Rochester, Gene told his friends that knowing that was going to happen the next day was "like balm for my wounds." So within twelve hours, the three were telling the story to the gathered clergy and asking them to consider sending some parishioners to the Sunday service.

"That was a really healing thing," Gene said. "And after we'd told the story and processed it and everything, I knelt down, and all the clergy laid hands on me and prayed for me. So that was great, very healing, just wonderful."

Over 100 people attended the Sunday service at Rochester, including about 14 Church of the Redeemer parishioners who had been appalled by the hatred and bad humor of Wednesday night. Gene had invited other clergy to preach and celebrate so that he wouldn't be "in their face"—Tim Rich gave the sermon—but he and Mark attended the service, which he called "transformative." He left, hoping and expecting that the parish would be able to survive, despite the exodus of the majority of its already small congregation.

The split, predictably, made national headlines. A week later, Gene was upbeat and optimistic. He said that he had been receiving kudos from all over the church, including from conservative bishops, for the way he had bent over backwards to give the dissenting parishioners what they wanted. In fact, while I was in his office, he received a call from Bishop Ed Little, a conservative who hadn't voted for Gene's election but who knew him well, commending him for the way he had handled the situation.

As Gene told his colleagues, the Rochester rebellion had been directed from outside the diocese. "They literally read from scripts. They all had lines to read," he stated. This intentional move toward schism and the organized tactics of "flying bishops," extra-diocesan ordinations and other services, and threats of property fights in the courts were appalling to nearly all of the present American bishops. In spite of sincere disagreements, they were committed, as bishops are called to be, to the unity of the church. The church had stayed together during the controversy over the ordination of women, and they sincerely wanted it to stay together in spite of disagreements over homosexuality.

Doug Theuner, who had been a member of the House of Bishops for almost two decades, reflected on the future. He said he thought that ultimately most progressives hoped to see the normalization of the acceptance of homosexuality in the church and in the culture and the world at large, but that it was necessary to go through a period of upheaval before the achievement of normalization.

"It's as if people have to get it out of their systems, struggle with it, fight over it, both positively and negatively," he said. "If it weren't for people who were willing to come forward and take risks and be different, like Gene, it wouldn't happen, and if it weren't for people who would react to that negatively, it wouldn't happen either: it would just always be beneath the surface and never dealt with."

"But I really think we want to see it normalized: we want to see the day when people don't even raise the question of, 'Well, he only got elected because he's gay, or she only got elected because she's a woman, or he only got elected because he's black.' We're working toward the Kingdom of God here, folks, where all those distinctions are unimportant. So I think in the interim, in the short run, we need acceptance of different points of view, but that doesn't mean *hiding* or *ignoring* your point of view."

He felt that was what Gene tried to do in Rochester. "Gene told the congregation, 'You don't want me to be in charge here. But I *have* to be in charge, it's my responsibility, so what I *can* do is to delegate the authority to someone else.' Well, they didn't want that: they walked away. In other words, 100 percent or nothing at all. You can't do that. Gene was willing to compromise with them in a way that would be effective, that would keep them from having to deal with a gay bishop, even though he was there. It's like the issue of the ordination of women: if you don't want a woman in your parish, don't call one! The bishop doesn't decide the clergy in this diocese; we don't even assign the clergy in mission congregations. We let everybody choose their own clergy, so far as that is possible. But you know, if the people down the street want to have a woman priest, fine, let them have a woman priest. That's the New Hampshire way, by God. It's also the Christian way. But it's difficult."

At the diocesan Clergy Day, the participating clergy had been invited to tell stories in several categories: joys and rewards of the past year, difficulties and painful times, surprises. Gene said that it sounded as if not all that many people had left the church, and that a lot of those who did were coming back. There had been many stories of transformation: new people were coming, particularly Roman Catholic families in large numbers. "Even the negative stuff the clergy brought up was not in the context of, 'Oh, I wish we hadn't done this,'" he said, "but more that people simply felt they had permission to talk about the difficult stuff."

Gene and other self-aware priests and church analysts had said repeatedly, over the course of this controversy, that the tone in a particular congregation tended to be set by the rector. Much of the upheaval and anxiety that was driving the talk of schism nationally and internationally was coming not from the pews but from clergy and bishops.

One of the priests who spoke at Clergy Day said that this had been a real learning experience for her. "I thought we were in a very difficult place as a parish, and that this was touch-and-go, and I kind of laid it all out for my vestry. And the vestry said, 'Um, you know what? You're wrong! The parish is just fine. You're projecting all your own issues onto us, and we don't want it. So you find a good therapist, and work that out. But meanwhile, we're having a wonderful time.'" The priest said, "I realized that's exactly what I was doing. I was just projecting all that stuff. I was ignoring things like the fact that our pledge drive was oversubscribed, we're doing a building project, and we're about two years ahead on the fundraising for that. When I looked, I realized there were dramatic indications that things were really okay!"

A few days after all of these emotionally charged events, Tim Rich mused about his friend. "He's had this sustained period of pretty intense anxiety, I would think, but when I talked to him about it he said, 'I've got a therapist and a spiritual director, and I'm doing my prayers, and I have friends like you . . .' He's just really healthy in that way. He's very balanced, self-differentiated, self-reinforced, with an inner compass that he is staying with, but also he really appreciates and values the input and love of others. It's not that he doesn't need people, but I think it's the breadth and depth of his resources that have allowed him to cope with all of this."

The bishop found himself at the center of an escalating international controversy.

Chapter 14
Reverberations

"All this" was not, of course, confined to New Hampshire. Rather than dying down, as Gene had hoped, the controversy created by his election became more and more heated. It seemed inevitable that the debate would engulf the entire Episcopal Church in the United States. Like the Church of the Redeemer in Rochester, New Hampshire, some congregations in other states refused to accept the authority of bishops who had consented to the consecration, and broke away, triggering legal battles over church property and pensions. And despite Gene's initial optimism about what would happen in the Anglican Communion worldwide, strident voices from the bishops of the Global South made the threats of an international schism seem more and more real.[1]

In less than a year, the name "Gene Robinson" had become synonymous with religious controversy over homosexuality. "On This Day" almanacs from Australia to Scotland to South Africa listed the anniversaries of his New Hampshire election and consecration in their top-ten rankings on those respective dates. His name was repeatedly invoked as other denominations struggled with their own positions on homosexual ordination: at the General Assembly of the Evangelical Lutheran Church of America (ECLA) in August 2005, the upcoming vote on the ordination of non-celibate homosexual clergy was described as "ECLA's Gene Robinson moment."[2]

Gene's election, the passage of the first state laws allowing civil unions and same-sex marriage in Vermont and Massachusetts, and the passage of such laws on a federal level in Canada, along with the continuing scandals in the Catholic Church, propelled the issue of homosexuality onto the front pages of newspapers and into breakfast-table discussions in households across the country. The other mainline protestant denominations, deeply divided on the issue, found themselves facing open debates, trials, and votes they might have preferred to defer for a long time. A sexuality study/task force of the Evangelical Lutheran Church had recommended, early in 2005, that the church continue its present policy of not allowing the ordinations of non-celibate homosexuals or blessing same-sex unions. At the August 2005 ECLA General Synod, as a cautionary tactic, conservatives passed out leaflets describing the situation in the worldwide Anglican Communion and the possibility of schism.[3] They won, but only by a whisker: the final vote was 503 to 490.

Among the United Methodists the situation vis-à-vis gay clergy was complex. Gay ministers who were out, but celibate, were basically accepted, as were those who were non-celibate but successful in maintaining their closeted state. But those who were honest about both their orientation and non-celibate status were not considered acceptable to occupy positions in the ministry.[4] As progressives increasingly pointed out, it was one thing for the U.S. military to have a "don't ask/don't tell" policy. But was a similar, inherent hypocrisy an appropriate moral position for a church? Doug Theuner often made that point, saying, "We're focused on the wrong 'H' word. Everybody thinks it's 'homosexuality,' but it's really 'honesty.'"

In a highly-publicized and contentious trial in December 2004, the Rev. Beth Stroud, a United Methodist minister who was open about living in a committed, non-celibate lesbian relationship, was stripped of her ministerial credentials and no longer allowed to perform the sacraments of baptism and Holy Communion. The following April, a church appeals court reversed that decision, but in October 2005, the highest Methodist court, the Judicial Council, reinstated the original ruling. The Rev. Stroud is continuing to work within the church, and she and her partner have applied to become foster parents.

The United Church of Christ (UCC), which already had the most liberal policy toward gay and lesbian clergy of all the mainline denominations, strengthened its stated resolve to work for "open and inclusive" congregations and to allow the ordination of clergy regardless of sexual orientation or practice. In July 2005, the UCC passed a resolution affirming equal rights for all couples, regardless of gender. At the other end of the religious spectrum, the Southern Baptist constitution specifically excludes any local church that acts "to affirm, approve, or endorse homosexual behavior."

Amongst other monotheistic traditions, in the American Jewish community, acceptance of gay rabbis has been high among Reform Jews, less so in Conservative Judaism. Homosexuality is not generally approved by Orthodox Jews. Within Islam, homosexual relations are strictly forbidden, and in some Islamic countries, punishable by death. Neither the Hebrew Scriptures nor the Qu'ran mention lesbian relations at all; all the references are to male homosexuals and the prohibition is usually for the same reason as adultery: all extramarital sexual relations are forbidden. (Interestingly, like the Hebrew Scriptures/Old Testament, the Qu'ran also contains references to the city of Sodom and the story of Lot. For example, in Sura 26, Lot admonishes the people of the city, saying: "Do ye approach males of all the world and leave what God your Lord has created for you of your wives?")

The struggle to find ways to stay together in spite of stark internal differences over homosexuality is particularly difficult, though, in the mainline U.S. Protestant denominations. What to *do* about those differences remains the subject of enormous debate. "Our people are fed up with political jargon. They want more spiritual food," said conservative United Methodist pastor Chuck Ferrara in an interview about evangelical mainliners on BeliefNet. "If the mainline churches don't change and find new ways of doing ministry—

with the same message in a different way—we're going to see them be completely absorbed by nondenominational churches." His goal is to stay within the current structure and provide a different vision of Christianity for Methodists who are conservative and turned off by liberal theology. Others are looking elsewhere for support and a possible new home: over thirty conservative groups within the various mainline Protestant churches are members of the Association for Church Renewal (ACR), founded in 1996; some of those groups are also forming alliances with American and African evangelicals. Within all the denominations, liberals express willingness to live with the tension created by difference—but not if that means going backwards on issues of social justice and inclusion. Some conservatives are also willing to live with difference, as long as issues central to their theology are respected: faithfulness to Scripture and Biblical literalism, an emphasis on personal salvation through Jesus Christ, and evangelism aimed at converting others to Christianity. Other conservatives say it's become too difficult to share the same boat with people who they consider sinful, unfaithful, and misguided: they will only stay if they can successfully engineer a denomination-wide theological shift toward the right.[5]

When Pope John Paul died on April 2, 2005, liberal Catholics held their breath while the cardinals gathered in Rome and met behind closed doors to elect the next pope. Their worst fears were realized when the vote was announced: Cardinal Joseph Ratzinger had been elected and would become Pope Benedict XVI. For several decades, Cardinal Ratzinger had been one of the most influential clerics in the Vatican and a close aide of Pope John Paul II. He had been appointed in 1981 as head of the Congregation for the Doctrine of the Faith, the office charged with protecting the doctrine of the church. He had been a major opponent of liberation theology and grassroots involvement of the church in social justice issues. His opinion on women's ordination was strictly negative, and he held the view expressed in the Catholic catechism that people with "deep-seated" homosexual tendencies must live in chastity because "homosexual acts are intrinsically disordered." During the 2004 presidential and congressional campaign, Cardinal Ratzinger had said that pro-choice politicians should not be allowed to receive Holy Communion.[6]

As Pope, it was fully expected that he would continue his conservative policies and attempt to hold the line against liberalization, as represented by movements toward women's ordination, changing the rules on priestly celibacy and marriage, and the acceptance of gay clergy. Many observers were stunned in mid-September 2005, however, when the *New York Times* published details of a document, given to the paper by a priest, announcing the Vatican's plan to review all American seminaries for evidence of "gay tendencies" among students and faculty. The seminary review was undeniably a reaction to the sexual abuse scandals that had swept the church worldwide, but critics immediately condemned the implicit linking of homosexuality and pedophilia and slammed the Vatican for a blanket policy that was not only potentially devastating to thousands of gay clergy and seminarians, but extremely short-sighted. The Rev. Thomas J. Reese, Catholic priest and former editor of the Jesuit magazine *America* (he was forced by the Vatican to resign earlier in 2005), pointedly remarked that with the current shortage of priests, the church "could hardly afford to dismiss gay seminarians," but that seminary advisors who knew of a person's homosexuality would be asked to throw that candidate out, even if he was close to ordination, regardless of how mature the candidate's attitude might be. "It's much healthier if a seminarian can talk about his sexuality with a spiritual director, but this kind of policy is going to force it all underground," he said.[7] The actual numbers of gay Catholic clergy are unknown, but estimates range as high as 60 percent.

Following the papal election, the sense of defeat and hopelessness among liberal Catholics was palpable, and although reaction was not widely reported, for obvious reasons, one can only imagine the despair among gay Catholic clergy. While no one expected that gay rights would suddenly move toward the top of the agenda at the Vatican, activists for women's ordination had continued to press forward in recent years despite stony resistance from the church hierarchy. (In 2003, a Vatican directive even attempted to ban altar girls, who have generally been allowed to serve at the discretion of individual parishes.)

In July of 2005, the second Women's Ordination Worldwide International Ecumenical Conference was held in Ottawa, Canada. In addition to worshipping together, hearing speeches, and participating in seminars conducted by progressive Catholic leaders such as Rosemary Reuther, nine women (seven Americans, a Canadian, and a German) were ordained as Roman Catholic priests and deacons on a boat in the international waters of the St. Lawrence seaway. The nine were ordained by three other women who said they "had been ordained as bishops by male Catholic clergy in secret ceremonies." Most of the women said they planned to perform "quiet ministries as priests at their homes and give sacraments to those who sought them out."[8] The women fully expected to be excommunicated by Rome, as had a group of women who participated in an earlier irregular ordination.

The Rev. Joyce Sanchez of Christ Church Cathedral, Montréal, who is an activist for women and for gay rights within the Canadian Anglican Church, attended that conference and came home overwhelmed. "Being in the room with these Roman Catholic women, day after day," she said, "it was impossible not to feel their pain, their sadness, and their intense frustration. They are my sisters, and there was so little I could do in the present climate to help them, or offer them comfort or hope, if what they want is to remain Catholic." Joyce felt so uncomfortable about the difference between her position and theirs that she didn't wear her clerical collar the entire time she was at the conference.

The relationship between Catholicism and Anglicanism in Canada is interesting, with some significant differences from the United States. In the formerly French province of Québec, the Roman Catholic Church totally dominated religious and family life for centuries and had a major impact on the economy as well. Priests told parishioners that they could be farmers, teachers, priests, and notaries (lawyers who handle property transactions), but dissuaded them from entering law and business, and insisted that agriculture, not business enterprise, was appropriate for rural villages. As a result, English and Scottish merchants had free reign to develop businesses, educate their children, control resources, develop energy sources, and amass wealth. Large Catholic families were the norm, with women staying mostly in the home: of Québec women born in 1885, one in five had more than ten children. Even reading and libraries were controlled by the priests, and higher education discouraged, especially for women: why would they need it? Women's suffrage was opposed by the clergy; Québec women did not receive the vote until 1940.

When Québec's Catholics finally woke up to the fact that they had been living in an essentially feudal system, they threw off the yoke of the church in what has become known as the Quiet Revolution, from 1960-1966. Today, while most French Québeçois still self-identify as Catholic, they rarely attend church. Many of the huge Catholic churches and seminaries stand empty or have been converted into condominiums, senior housing, and community centers; some monasteries and convents still continue, but where young people once entered the religious vocation in droves, now one occasionally sees a solitary, elderly nun in the Montréal metro, holding a few brochures and a poster advertising the religious vocation.

The legacy of the past, however, does linger, as the story of one gay man illustrates. This thirty-something young man grew up in a large, conservative Catholic family in a rural Québec village. When he discovered his sexual orientation and spoke about it to his parish priest and to his family, hoping for acceptance, he instead received condemnation, was refused communion, and was told he should pray to be "changed." Eventually, at his mother's insistence, he journeyed to Eastern Europe on a pilgrimage to a Catholic shrine, where he promised to pray to become heterosexual. The "miracle" did not occur, nor did he receive any different counsel from the local priest when he confessed the reason for his pilgrimage. Upon returning to Canada, he moved to Montréal, living in the city's gay village. After a longterm relationship broke up, he became very depressed. One day he entered the Anglican cathedral in the center of the downtown commercial district and knelt in a front pew. The dean of the cathedral came in and found him weeping, but naturally the man was afraid, by then, of confessing his "sin" to priests, and refused to tell him why he was there. But when this happened a second time, the dean sat down beside him and insisted that he tell him what was wrong. The man was welcomed into the cathedral, where he eventually became a regular communicant and found support and friendship among the clergy and other parishioners, a number of whom were also gay. He also found himself finally free to explore his own strong call to ministry, which had been squelched by his earlier experiences, and to work with the clergy to bring a message of hope to other gay Roman Catholics who had experienced rejection and shame.

Along with British Columbia and its capital Vancouver, on the west coast, Québec is the now the most liberal province in Canada, with the most progressive politics and public attitudes in North America on issues such as gay rights, workers' rights, peace, and the environment. While church attendance and membership have fallen precipitously throughout Canada, as in Europe, church-based "family values" are strongest and most similar to their American counterparts in the rural, agricultural provinces of the central and western plains. But the Anglican Diocese of New Westminster (comprising Vancouver and its environs) voted to approve the blessing of "permanent, faithful same sex relationships" in June 2002. A year later, the bishop, Michael Ingham, issued a formal rite of blessing, and the first same-sex blessing took place shortly thereafter. According to the diocesan website, "The desire was to ensure that homosexuals who seek to be included in the Anglican Communion in New Westminster feel safe and respected . . . The majority of Anglicans in the Greater Vancouver area acknowledged their belief that homosexuality is a normative variation of human nature, morally neutral in and of itself, and that what is wrong is homophobia and religiously based prejudice."

In the United States, Vermont was the first state to allow legal civil unions between same-sex couples, passing that legislation in 2000. At a recent Convocation of Province I (New England) which focused on marriage, Bishop Tom Ely of Vermont said that his diocese was inspired by that civil union legislation to go back and examine its resources for couples who were preparing to marry. When those resources were found inadequate, a task force was established to develop parallel liturgies for holy matrimony and same-sex unions. The work of the Vermont diocese, conducted under the guidelines of the 2003 General Convention, has attracted little criticism or attention; the trial liturgies are available for download at the diocesan website,[9] and the report generated by the task force will be presented at the 2006 General Convention.

While America at large fought viciously over the legality of civil union and same-sex marriage bills, with the opposition led by the president himself and a coalition of conservative religious groups who clamored for a constitutional amendment restricting marriage to a covenant "between one man and one woman," the national legislature of Canada quietly legalized same-sex marriage on July 19, 2005. Some Canadians described the five-year national debate as "rancorous," but to this American observer it had an entirely different tone from what was happening in the United States. After the marriage bill passed, a Canadian website devoted to the issue wrote:

The language of debate over the past five years has reflected that at the heart of the debate was not just the question of a small wording change to a marriage law, but more profound questions: "Are individuals in same-sex relationships persons under the law or not?"; "Do we form families or not?"; "Are we deserving of dignity or not?" Finally the leaders of our country have answered those questions with "Yes."[10]

Later in 2005, same-sex marriage was also legalized in both Spain and South Africa. Michelangelo Signorile, journalist, radio host and author of *Hitting Hard*, a book on current gay politics, had some interesting observations on the apparent irony of the Spanish decision, coming in a country which had been so overwhelmingly Catholic—and these would apply to Québec as well:

> Catholicism is about the collective, the group, the family, and adhering to the church principles as handed down to the minions from a sole authority. The religious culture thus has always had a built-in dynamic that discourages individuality and personal pronouncements—such as "coming out" as gay—even as people secretly engage in gay sex. Historically, there was no need for the state in such countries to ban homosexuality, because Catholicism and religion did enough to discourage gay people from going public. The paradox is that, with no laws actually criminalizing homosexuality—and no discussion of it at all—there is often a disorganized gay movement in such places . . . [11]

(The same general cultural attitude applies to heterosexual marital infidelity—note the enormous difference between American attitudes and those in France, Spain or Italy.) Signorile argues that Protestantism, however, encourages the self-empowerment that has led to women's rights and gay rights movements in America, Canada, Britain, and Scandinavia, and that it also encourages people in those places to come out:

> The state in such countries often responded, long before such movements could even congeal, by crafting laws to control sexual behavior. This, in turn, has had people organizing fiercely and publicly to fight for their rights, and stressing the importance of "gay visibility."[12]

In Britain, though, closeted gay culture has had a very long history. It is so deeply entrenched in institutions—from government to education to religion—that the resistance to "gay visibility" is in some cases perpetuated, or even led, by closeted homosexuals who feel they have a great deal to lose by coming out.

Within the Anglican Communion as a whole, the action of the Canadian Diocese of New Westminster on same-sex blessings loomed very large and was considered nearly as great an affront to conservative Anglicans as the ordination of an openly gay bishop.

The Episcopal Church of the United States and the Anglican Church of Canada found themselves cast as New World upstarts. Not only were they causing problems for their British forebears by taking a stand on this particular social justice issue, rather than favoring the preservation of institutions and engaging in "further study," but their actions clearly demonstrated the vast gulf between the values of traditional patriarchal societies and twenty-first-century Western culture. It didn't sit well with moderate and liberal Canadians or Americans to be scolded, coerced, and censured by the Anglican hierarchy and imperial British authority both had rebelled against centuries before. Nor did they wish to be lectured on sexuality and sin by African bishops whose concept of Biblical interpretation and sexual morality came out of a very different cultural and religious context. On the other hand, most were genuinely distressed at the idea that this issue might split the Communion.

Unlike the Roman Catholic Church, the Anglican Communion has never had a central authority or control over the actions of the various provinces. The Archbishop of Canterbury is a symbolic head of the church, but he does not have the authority of the Pope, and there is no legal body that "rules" on matters of doctrine or has the power to enforce theological interpretation. The Archbishop of Canterbury functions more as a central hub, providing a link through which the thirty-eight Anglican world provinces are connected. Historically, widely diverging opinions on many matters have been held, albeit in tension, among the members of the Communion.

Rowan Williams, the relatively new Archbishop of Canterbury, a brilliant theologian who has a number of gay friends, holds liberal views on homosexuality, which he has expressed in his books, and has ordained at least one non-celibate gay man—facts that initially gave Anglican gays and lesbians hope when he was appointed, following the tenure of the much more conservative Archbishop George Carey. At the time of Williams's appointment in December 2002, the Reverend Richard Kirker, general secretary of the Lesbian and Gay Christian Movement in Britain, told *The Advocate* that he trusted the new Archbishop's instincts but that people should not have unrealistic expectations about how soon he might use his influence, or how far that influence might be able to go. "He's quite different from a Catholic bishop," Kirker said. "Any decisions in the Anglican Communion have to be reached at the end of the day by consensus."

In his very first year, Williams found himself with the unenviable task of trying to hold together an increasingly fractious Communion in which differences over homosexuality had made the vaunted "bonds of affection" extremely brittle. As the conservatives seemed to gain power and access and become increasingly emboldened, observers wondered whether the Archbishop was unable to exercise personal influence, or if he had made a decision to try to preserve the institution regardless of his own views.

When a BBC interviewer tried to probe this apparent conflict between the Archbishop's private views and public pronouncements, Williams said he was not in office "to advance personal views or a private agenda" but to see "what discernment the whole church comes to. If the whole church maintains its current discernment, well that is the church's right, the church's liberty." The interviewer pressed on, asking if he himself felt that a priest living in a "loving, committed, and physically expressed same-sex relationship" was living in sin. Williams answered that, as Archbishop, he had to maintain the view of the Communion and the Church of England bishops as a whole—which is that the church cannot publicly recognize this type of relationship as acceptable. The interviewer asked how he felt *privately*. The Archbishop answered, "Privately is privately, isn't it?"[13]

Responding to the outcry following Gene Robinson's election and its affirmation by General Convention, the Archbishop of Canterbury invited the leaders of the thirty-eight worldwide Anglican provinces to gather at the place where he lives and works, Lambeth Palace in London, on October 16 and 17, 2003, for an exceptional meeting to consider the crisis that would be provoked if the consecration went forward. Press photographs showed a smiling Archbishop welcoming Frank Griswold, the Presiding Bishop of the Episcopal Church, who had not yet confirmed that he would participate in Robinson's consecration a few weeks later. A meeting of conservative American Episcopalians had taken place earlier in the month in Dallas, and Pittsburgh Bishop Robert Duncan had said that their goal was to have the Episcopal leadership "severely sanctioned or disciplined." However, no one in the Anglican Communion, including the Archbishop of Canterbury, had judicial authority to discipline any of the member churches. Unbeknownst to most observers, the conservatives were also positioning themselves to try to change that.

At Lambeth, the most adamant opposition came from the Africans, led by Archbishops Peter Akinola of Nigeria and Emmanuel Kolini of Rwanda. After Rowan Williams announced that the meeting would begin with Holy Communion, Akinola and others said that to share in communion would "suggest a spiritual unity that had been broken by the Episcopal Church's actions." Williams said that either the meeting would begin with communion or it would not continue. The dissenting primates participated, but the incident was one of the first indications of how far Akinola was prepared to go. On a number of occasions over the next two years, he stated, "We do not have to go through Canterbury to get to Jesus."[14]

The most significant development that came out of the so-called Lambeth Summit was the appointment of the Eames Commission, headed by the Archbishop of All Ireland, Robin Eames, who had chaired a similar

Communion-wide study commission after the first women were ordained. The Eames Commission was to spend the next year gathering information, listening to input, and working to formulate a recommended path that would preserve unity within the Communion. Although it received little notice, separate work had already started with the goals of establishing a body of common laws for the Communion as a whole and of giving the Archbishop of Canterbury expanded power to intervene in churches outside the Church of England. Jamie Doward of the London *Guardian*'s Sunday edition, the *Observer*, described this action as the first step toward establishing "an overarching legal framework which would give the Communion more powers to discipline member churches that threaten to break ranks." Ruth Gledhill, religion correspondent for the London *Times*, pointed out that such an unprecedented change would have to be agreed upon by the various provinces. She also wryly quoted the communications director of the Anglican Church in Wales: "They are looking to have an Anglican version of the Holy Office and a Magisterium. They won't call the Archbishop of Canterbury a Pope but that is what he will be. If it looks like a duck and quacks like a duck, then it's a duck."[15] Lambeth may not have the secrecy of the Vatican, but its inner workings are quite obscure. It wasn't clear whether this consolidation of power was Rowan William's initiative or desire, how he personally felt about the crisis, or which other players might be behind the politics. People who knew him said that he seemed to be depressed and tired and was withdrawing more and more into his books and theological writing as the controversy wore on.

Whenever the Global South primates gathered, as the months passed, conservative American bishops such as Robert Duncan of Pittsburgh always seemed to be nearby, offering advice from the sidelines, hosting dinners, and issuing statements. Likewise, some of the African archbishops flew to the U.S. to speak and to perform ordinations and confirmations without the authority of the local bishops in liberal dioceses. The conservative American bishops, who minced no words in speaking about their desire to alter the structure of the Episcopal Church, were welcome at Lambeth. However, when the Eames Commission held a meeting in northern Virginia, the Standing Committee of the New Hampshire Diocese, representatives of the Search and Election Committees, and Gene Robinson himself all begged to meet with them, but those requests were denied. In the spring of 2004, after a private conversation between Rowan Williams and Frank Griswold that seemed to leave the possibility open, Gene wrote to the Archbishop requesting a personal meeting, telling him he would come "any time, any place, under the radar screen," or whatever would work—but that he would greatly appreciate a chance to meet with him.

Gene eventually received a reply from Canon Herman Brown, the Archbishop of Canterbury's Secretary for the Anglican Communion. A few days later, he read it aloud during an interview at his office:

Dear Bishop Robinson,

Archbishop Rowan was very grateful for your letter of 13 May requesting a meeting. As with requests of this nature, he has taken advice and on the basis of that advice, he has asked me to write. He apologizes that he does not feel able to make himself available for a meeting at this time in the life of the Communion. I realize how disappointed you may be with this reply, but I really do hope to bear better news on another occasion. With prayers and best wishes . . .

The bishop dropped the letter onto the coffee table. "I would have thought, just out of courtesy, that the Archbishop could have written those few sentences himself," he said, with deep woundedness obvious in his eyes and voice. For a moment the bishop looked small, sad, and alone, as he added, "It is very difficult to always be talked *about* and not talked *with*." As a bishop, he recognized that his first responsibility was to the clergy of the diocese: to listen to them, to try to understand their concerns, and to help them. Now he was an elected bishop of the Anglican Communion. Was this the extent of the Archbishop's compassion toward him, even as two fellow Christians in private, let alone as major players in this historical drama?

Gene straightened up, his indignation quickly winning out. He put his hands on his hips and tilted his head from side to side, his bright eyes flashing behind the wire-rimmed glasses. "They keep saying it isn't about New Hampshire, it isn't about homosexuality, and it isn't about me. Well, Archbishop Akinola of Nigeria gave an eight-page harangue in front of the Commission which was *all* about me and homosexuality, and how the Episcopal Church ought to be punished for it. And I don't think he was called out of order when he tried to go there. The Commission keeps saying, 'We're meeting with everyone who wants to speak with us. We're listening to every voice.' Well, it's just not true. So I don't know what that means."

One thing it meant was that Gene became even more appreciative of the firm support and leadership of the Presiding Bishop, Frank Griswold. At considerable personal cost, the Presiding Bishop had staunchly supported the legal process through which Gene had been elected, explaining it patiently to the foreign press when they didn't understand the considerable differences between American Episcopal elections and the appointments of bishops elsewhere. He had come back from the Lambeth Summit and presided over Gene's consecration; graciously and consistently fielded questions from the press and hostility from opposing bishops both within his own church and abroad; and charted a steady, calm course for the Episcopal Church. He had clearly grown in stature and wisdom through the course of a controversy that might have defeated him. Instead, it seemed to define him. Gene knew the force of the gales that blew, and he admired, respected, and thanked Frank Griswold.

The only nibble New Hampshire could get, as Gene put it, was a meeting with a small group of the Archbishop of Canterbury's close advisors. In early July 2004, the Rev. David Jones, the Rev. Hank Junkin, and Judith Esmay flew to London for a one-hour meeting at Lambeth Palace. Judith, who was the only woman present, said that Williams's advisors listened carefully and that the meeting was cordial, but the questions were pointed. "What it felt like they were saying to us was, 'How could you?'" she related. There were some sympathetic faces around the table, but the New Hampshire delegates felt the weight of representing a different worldview from that of the opposition: one where elections were democratic, where patriarchy was slowly but steadily being dismantled in favor of laity and clergy sharing strongly in decision-making, and where the church recognized the need to be responsive to the changing culture. Afterwards Judith said, "It is inherent in the Episcopal Church, as well as in the American form of government, that leaders derive their authority from the will of the people. People serve *by consent*. When a legal process for choosing a leader has been followed, that means that the people have spoken, and it's final: you don't turn around and change it! This is absolutely fundamental to how we do things! And it seems so difficult for people from other systems to truly grasp."

Could those world views coexist? Prior to the release of the Eames Commission's report, Canon Tim Rich said, "In this diocese we see it not so much as being about the one issue of sexuality but about 'how we are' within the Anglican Communion. A core part of our identity as Anglicans has always been living with ambiguity and tension. I think what's at stake here is whether or not we're going to find a way to stay in communion with each other, despite the tension. Personally, I don't want some pronouncement coming out of the Eames Commission saying, 'The Episcopal Church was *right* when it came to matters of human sexuality,' or, 'The Episcopal Church was *wrong*,' because I don't think that's what it's about. It's about whether people with different understandings of human sexuality should be held accountable for maintaining communion with one another. That honors the truth that good faithful Christians feel very differently about this one issue, and it honors the fact that Christ calls us to be at the table with one another."

But the ambiguity Tim spoke of was exactly what the conservatives objected to. They *did* want a pronouncement that stated unambiguously that one side was right and the other wrong. Rather than "moving the margins" wider, they wanted to define them more narrowly: not, they insisted, to throw out gay Anglicans per se (a constantly repeated phrase was "love the sinner but hate the sin"), but to return theologically to a much more literalist interpretation of Scripture which held certain things to be absolute, *never* to be subject to change as society and culture changed. Those who accepted that view would be "in," and those who did not—those whom the conservatives called "revisionists"—would finally be "out."

Speculation was rife in the days before the release of the Eames Commission's report. The September 21, 2004 issue of *The Christian Century* quoted the London *Times* and *Telegraph* as saying that "leaders of the Episcopal Church may be placed on quarantine by the rest of the Anglican Communion" and that new bishops everywhere in the Communion would be required to support official Anglican policy—whatever that was. These early leaks suggested that a decision would be taken at the next Lambeth Conference in 2008 to decide whether the entire Episcopal Church "would face exclusion from the Communion." Rumors also circulated that former Archbishop of Canterbury George Carey was behind the scenes, encouraging those opposed to the American and Canadian actions.

When the Windsor Report, as it was entitled, was actually released on October 18, 2004, Anglicans worldwide rushed to download and study the dense, long, complicated document. Clergy and congregations met to discuss the report or invited diocesan leaders to hold Windsor Report workshops for their parishes.

After the Anglican-ese had been parsed and the many pages thoroughly digested, several major points emerged. The American and Canadian churches were asked to "express regret" for the distress their actions had caused. They were requested to place a moratorium on any further ordinations of gay bishops or same-sex blessings until the next Lambeth Conference in 2008. Likewise, the conservative bishops were asked to cease disrespecting diocesan boundaries and participating in irregular ordinations, and procedures were recommended to allow alternative pastoral oversight for parishes unhappy with their local bishops, without changing the traditional and historical authority of local bishops for those parishes and property. Although the outlines were vague in the report, moves were made toward the establishment of greater central Anglican authority and toward an insistence on consensus among the members over matters of basic doctrine. And, finally, the American and Canadian churches were asked to refrain from participating for the next three years in the Anglican Consultative Council, the official gathering of Anglican primates, although they were both asked to make a formal presentations at the next meeting, including a Scriptural explanation of how they had arrived at their actions.

When he first read the Windsor Report, Gene Robinson was stunned. "The call for a moratorium on further gay ordinations took my breath away," he said. "I suddenly felt very lonely. I had hoped not to be the only person on the hot seat for too long." This isolation was rarely mentioned in the many statements made on the report. One exception was a statement by the Lesbian and Gay Christian Movement in England, which said, "We are particularly pained by the isolation suggested for Bishop Robinson from his Episcopal brothers and sisters throughout the world. This is an isolation many homosexuals feel all their lives." For that reason, Gene had been very appreciative when, shortly before the report's release, he received a personal phone call from Archbishop Robin Eames, chair of the Commission, who apprised him of its contents and asked him how he was doing.

Presiding Bishop Frank Griswold's statement on the report firmly reinforced the view of the Episcopal Church toward homosexuality and its context in American society:

> Given the emphasis of the Report on difficulties presented by our dif-
> fering understandings of homosexuality, as Presiding Bishop I am
> obliged to affirm the presence and positive contribution of gay and les-
> bian persons to every aspect of the life of our church and in all orders
> of ministry. Other Provinces are also blessed by the lives and ministry
> of homosexual persons. I regret that there are places within our
> Communion where it is unsafe for them to speak out of the truth of
> who they are.
>
> The Report will be received and interpreted within the Provinces of
> the Communion in different ways, depending on our understanding of
> the nature and appropriate expression of sexuality. It is important to
> note here that in the Episcopal Church we are seeking to live the gospel
> in a society where homosexuality is openly discussed and increasingly
> acknowledged in all areas of our public life.[16]

After Gene had studied the Windsor Report further, his natural optimism and desire for reconciliation bubbled back to the surface. He said it was a time when the Americans "needed to and could afford to be gracious." And he noted, for example, that the Episcopal Church had been asked to express regret for the *distress* caused by the New Hampshire election, not for the actual action. "It is a carefully-worded document that offers us a way forward if we all say yes to it," he said. "But we've got to stay at the table."

That assessment was shared by the Most Rev. Bernard Malango, Primate of Central Africa, a member of the Eames Commission, who said a common future would only be possible if all agreed, as the Commission had, to work toward the shared goals of healing and reconciliation. Not all the Africans felt that way. Nigerian Archbishop Peter Akinola immediately commented, "Where is the language of rebuke? It fails to confront the reality that a small, economically privileged group of people has sought to subvert the Christian faith and impose their new and false doctrine on the wider community of faithful believers."[17]

Exactly as had happened with Gene Robinson and the Church of the Redeemer in Rochester, New Hampshire, both sides professed (at least at first) their desire to remain together, but they maintained vastly different interpretations of what that would require. The requested expressions of regret and theological/Scriptural explanations of the actions were submitted, the moratoriums imposed, the vol-untary ostracism from Anglican gatherings reluctantly accepted. But this com-promise position seemed to be, in the eyes of the conservatives, only temporarily acceptable. What they wanted, and increasingly insisted upon, was nothing less than repentance and a full acceptance of the theological positions they themselves espoused.

An essay entitled "The Divorce is Under Way" had appeared in September 2004 in the Church of England newspaper. The author, the Rev. Prof. Stephen Noll, Vice Chancellor of Uganda Christian University and one of the original links between the African and American conservatives, wrote:

> Never once to my knowledge has any major official of the Episcopal Church suggested that the decisions of 2003 may have been a mistake and need rethinking. The Presiding Bishop has called for all kinds of dialogue, but repentance and reversal is one option that is clearly off the table. And let's be fair to the PB [Presiding Bishop]: the Episcopal Church has admitted winkingly so many homosexuals to the ordained ministry over the past decade or so that changing course would be as difficult a decision as that facing Ariel Sharon to uproot all the Israeli settlers from the West Bank. It's not going to happen.[18]

The "repentance and reversal" Noll described would most likely include the "best remedy" that the Most Rev. Drexel Gomez, Primate of the Church in the Province of the West Indies, suggested: an annulment of Gene Robinson's consecration. The bishops involved would be required to apologize and retract their support for homosexual clergy; same-sex marriage rites would be repealed; gay ordinations halted and possibly retracted; and the American and Canadian churches would have to cleave to a different theological path, based on the same Biblical literalism as that of the African and American fundamentalists. Archbishop Emmanuel Kolini of Rwanda stated this position bluntly: "The Windsor Report is not our Bible," he said. "Unity must have as its basis, its foundation, the authority of Scripture."

The Windsor Report, rather quaintly, stated that the Anglican Communion is held together by "bonds of affection"—and by the fact that its members periodically meet and talk to one another. The Episcopal House of Bishops, meeting shortly after the report was released, issued a clear statement honoring the legal action taken by General Convention, sent the requested expressions of regret, accepted most of the other conditions of the report, and, in a bold and innovative response, recommended a moratorium on *all* bishop elections until General Convention 2006; i.e., "If we cannot ordain any gay bishops, we won't ordain any bishops at all."

In most American congregations, a majority of members were exhausted with the issue. They wanted to move on and get back to normal after the anticipation and hubbub surrounding the report had died down, and they made an effort to do so. In many of the dioceses headed by aggressively conservative

Episcopal bishops, grassroots groups called "Via Media" sprang up, organized by parishioners and clergy who disagreed with their bishops' positions and sought to find a traditional Anglican "middle way" through the crisis. On many progressive Anglican websites frequented by politically-interested parishioners and clergy, discussion revolved around ways that unity could be maintained and what could or should be done to show good faith and good intentions. The tone was earnest, idealistic, sincere, optimistic, the suggestions well-meant and, it began to seem, extremely naïve.

For, on the higher political level, polarization rather than affection seemed to increase. The most dedicated opposition was not spending its time discussing the Windsor Report or theoretical possibilities for unity: they were taking actions aimed at realignment. In February 2005, the Anglican primates met again, this time in Ireland. In a move that indicated both their determination and a shift in the power dynamic, Archbishop Akinola and some of the Global South primates notified Rowan Williams that this time they refused to share Communion with the leaders of the American and Canadian churches. The Archbishop of Canterbury suggested another format that would still result in a shared Communion service, but Akinola again refused, and, according to press reports, a dozen primates joined him in refusing. Akinola stated that "unity of doctrine preceded unity of worship."[19]

The situation in the American Episcopal Church was more veiled, but gradually the layers separating rhetoric from intention began to be stripped away. At the House of Bishops meeting in March 2005, Gene and other progressives had expressed the desire to talk about how all the factions in the church could live together. One of the conservative bishops answered bluntly that he was not interested in reconciliation but in "divvying up the property from this divorce." Upon witnessing this degree of polarization, John Bruno, the bishop of Los Angeles, offered to host a private meeting of American bishops in Los Angeles that summer to talk about ways of approaching reconciliation. Gene attended but returned from that meeting deeply discouraged and convinced that the conservatives' position was fixed: if the church did not "repent," at least some of them were prepared to walk away.

One of the opposing bishops was Pittsburgh Bishop Robert Duncan, a founding member of the American Anglican Council (AAC) and moderator of the Network of Anglican Communion Dioceses and Parishes, developed at the suggestion of the Archbishop of Canterbury and officially launched on January 20, 2004 as a way of connecting dissenting parishes and providing theologically-conservative Anglican oversight as an alternative to local bishops.[20] On the AAC website, visitors can now download a booklet called "Equipping the Saints: A Crisis Resource for Anglican Laity," which contains a list of "frequently asked questions"; a timetable of events that have led to the present crisis; comparisons between "orthodox" and "progressive/revisionist" theological positions on various issues; and suggested actions that individuals and parishes can take. The AAC has also begun providing legal advice and referrals for conservative local parishes that become embroiled in court battles over church property after confrontations with diocesan bishops. Bishop Duncan told reporters that these actions did not represent "a power play . . . except in the sense that Bishop Robinson's position in the church is a total innovation in the life of the church and what we face are two positions that can't be put together." He said a resolution could only be found if church members joined together in "uniting around common beliefs."[21]

Gene had had enough experience by then to decode that phrase: the AAC and the Network were laying the groundwork for making a break with ECUSA and establishing an alternative Anglican province in the United States which they hoped would become the official embodiment of the Anglican Communion in America.

Another organization, the Anglican Mission in America (AMiA), under the sponsorship of African bishops, had already provided a home for disaffected priests and parishes who wanted to cut their ties with the Episcopal Church altogether. The AMiA continued to ordain new bishops, priests and deacons and was actively "planting churches." Some of those were new; some came from former Episcopal parishes and also from other denominations. "If there are defectors joining us because they cannot bear it any more, our arms are open. Our doors are open. They continue to come," said the Rev. John Richardson. "This issue of Robinson and human sexuality has not been the core issue," he said. "The real issue is the abandonment of biblical teaching. The word of God is no longer taken as the word of God."[22]

If one were to judge the extent of the rift by the publicity the opposition has received, it might seem the Episcopal Church was on its deathbed. The actual numbers say something quite different. As 2006 began, the AMiA said that it had more than 80 congregations and 15,000 members. The Rev. Jan Nunley of the Episcopal News Service reports current figures of 2.4 million members and 7,600 congregations in the national Episcopal Church. If there is a break in the Anglican Communion, or if the conservatives stage a walkout at the June 2006 General Convention, more dioceses and parishes will certainly leave and put themselves under the authority of one of the Global South provinces, but the numbers are likely to be disproportionately small compared to the attention the issue has received in the press.

In the fall of 2005, Gene Robinson decided to accept a long-standing invitation by the Oxford Union, the debating society of Oxford University, to participate in a debate about whether or not gay ordinations should be allowed. Mindful of both Anglican protocol and general courtesy, Gene requested permission from the local bishops before performing in any official capacity in their dioceses. He had originally been scheduled to go to England in March 2004 and was to be welcomed into the Diocese of Oxford by its Bishop, Richard Harries. In the middle of that earlier conversation, Harries had said he supposed he should check with "the powers that be." When Harries got back to Gene, he said that the word from Lambeth was that he was not to preach, celebrate or even speak in any church building in England. Gene's appearance at Oxford would be secular—he would not be participating in a service, preaching, or offering Communion—but sensing how volatile the situation was in the Anglican Communion, he decided not to go. In an official statement that was widely circulated in the British press, he wrote:

> I have thought and prayed long and hard about this wonderful invitation to speak at the Oxford Union. It has now become clear to me that for me to participate would not be in the best interests of the Anglican Communion at this delicate moment in its history. As St. Paul has said, "Not everything that is lawful is helpful." Indeed, in deference to the important work of the Archbishop's newly appointed Commission, I have decided to decline all public speaking engagements in provinces outside of ECUSA until the Commission has made its report. At that time, I will gladly join the international conversations about the full inclusion of gay and lesbian Christians as children of God and full members of the Church.[23]

In response, Oxford Union President Edward Tomlinson said:

> It has come as a great blow that Bishop Robinson will no longer be addressing the Oxford Union as part of the debate here on 11 March. From our point of view, it is a shame that the Archbishop's newly appointed commission should act as a gagging order, rather than as a catalyst for discussion. But, I understand that Bishop Robinson is a figure of totemic importance in this debate, and that his love for the Anglican Communion has meant that for the time being he believes silence to be the best course of action for him. However, as the President of the most famous debating society in the world, founded on the abiding principle of freedom of speech, and also as a committed Anglican, I look forward to the day when free discussion of this matter can and does take place.

By the end of 2005, though, the Eames Commission had long since made their report. Although the situation was not stable, Gene knew that his presence in England would not create the same waves it would have earlier. This time, in addition to the Oxford debate, he had also been invited to participate in a service for homosexual Christians at St. Martin-in-the-Fields in London, commemorating the tenth anniversary of the founding of Changing Attitudes, the British counterpart to the Episcopal Church's gay/lesbian group Integrity.

When the London Diocesan Evangelical Fellowship got wind of Gene's impending visit, its members began to pressure the bishop of London, the Rt.

Rev. Richard Chartres, to ban "the gay bishop" from visiting London or attending a church service there. Chartres refused and said that Bishop Robinson would be welcome to visit the city, attend the service, and speak to attendees afterward. Gene was told he could wear the "office" attire appropriate for a bishop at St. Martin-in-the-Fields, but not the cope and mitre which a bishop normally wears when participating in a service. In fact, he was not allowed to preach or participate in an official capacity in the actual service, although he would be able to address the audience afterwards.

When these plans had been made, Gene again approached the Archbishop of Canterbury, and this time it looked like a meeting was possible. The British press began speculating; the potential meeting was a front page story in several newspapers. Stephen Bates wrote in the *Guardian* that an Anglican Communion source involved in negotiations at Lambeth Palace said: "I know Rowan has no qualms about him coming and there have been no problems with his schedule while he is here."[24] Gene bought his plane tickets, still not knowing whether he would finally be meeting the Archbishop or not.

The bishop makes a point while debating in favor of the motion "Should gay people be ordained as bishops?" at the Oxford Union, November 3, 2005.

Chapter 15
In the Public Eye

"The Oxford Union debate was more fun than I've had in I don't know how long," Gene said, still excited to talk about it several weeks later. He had taken an overnight flight to England, gone directly to a meeting in London, and then proceeded to Oxford, where, late in the afternoon, he was met by the president of the Oxford Union Society, arguably the most famous debating society in the world. The student who is chosen to be president takes a year off from studies to do nothing but organize the weekly debates, which take place every Thursday night, often with a head of state or other major world figure as one of the debaters.

"It turns out that something like nine prime ministers of England were presidents of the Oxford Union when they were at Oxford!" Gene reported, his voice full of admiration and a touch of Kentucky gee-whiz. "And this young man who is the president now will absolutely be something! He was remarkable!"

After arriving, Gene quickly changed into his tuxedo and went to meet the other officers of the debating society: the men all dressed in black tie and tails, the women in long gowns. "First there were drinks. I didn't partake: I didn't want to be impaired in any way, and I had already been up for thirty-six hours. And then we sat down in this beautiful vaulted dining room." After dinner a photographer took the traditional formal portrait of the debaters with the members of the Society, to be added to those already covering the walls of the dining room. "I'm looking around the walls," Gene said, "and there's Bill Clinton, Mother Teresa, there's Margaret Thatcher—and then we're shown over to the debating hall, in this unbelievably magnificent building. We go in to thunderous applause. There are over 700 people there; they are almost hanging off the rafters. There's a balcony around the top with people standing five or six deep all around it. And the officers are up front and a secretary is seated at a desk in the center and the debaters stand on either side of that. You stand up and put your left hand on the side of the desk—and *orate!*"

There are always four debaters; Gene was joined in debating for the motion, "Should gay people be ordained bishop?" by Richard Kirker, general secretary of the Lesbian and Gay Christian Movement. The former bishop of Woolwich, the Rt. Rev. Colin Buchanan, and Andrew Goddard, tutor in Christian ethics, debated against the motion. Any one of the attendees has the right to interrupt at any point, which is done by the person getting to his or her feet and crying, "Point of information!" The debater can choose to recognize the person or not, and there is a set period of time for the interrupter to speak. Gene was not interrupted once during his speech.

At the end, the attendees leave the hall by one of two doors: one marked "Noes" and the other marked "Ayes." A steward posted at the doors counts the people. The final vote was 248 ayes and 156 noes; press reports said a large contingent from Wycliffe Hall, an evangelical school of theology and mission at Oxford, attended the debate, which probably accounted for the number of "no" votes.

"They had announced that people could come back and ask questions," Gene said, "and over 200 people returned. At 1:30 a.m. I just said, 'Look, I've been up forty-one hours, and I'm going to topple over! But then of course I had to go back to the president's chambers with three or four others to have port—that was my first port of the night—and then I went to bed, and he picked me up at seven for breakfast and had me back to Christ Church College at ten of eight, and I got into a BBC radio car that they had sent from London, and I was the first interview after the eight o'clock news, which is the prime news spot for the BBC. That piece is listened to by more people than any other BBC time spot." Gene had a quick meeting with the Bishop of Oxford, Richard Harries, and then took a train back to London. His media coordinator, Mike Barwell, was with him, and that day Gene did twelve or thirteen interviews, one right after the other. "While I was doing one interview in my room, Mike was setting up for the next one in his room, and when I was done I'd move to his room. It was just wild."

Immediately after landing at Heathrow the previous morning, Gene had gone into London and, as the papers had speculated, met privately with Archbishop Rowan Williams.

The *Guardian* had previously written that such a meeting would fuel the controversy at a particularly difficult time, just before Dr. Williams would be flying to Egypt to attend a meeting of bishops from the Global South, most of whom were adamantly opposed to Bishop Robinson's ordination. The paper quoted the AAC's comment that Robinson's consecration had been "a grievous day in church history" as well as the Archbishop of Kenya's response, which was that "the devil has entered our church." The week prior to Bishop Robinson's arrival in England, the Anglican Church of Nigeria had struck from its constitution all references to being in communion with the Church of England. That action had been taken after a decision by the English bishops that clergy living in same-sex civil partnerships could register those relationships so long as they vowed to keep them celibate. Discussing the possible meeting between Williams and Robinson, a conservative British evangelical, the Rev. Rod Thomas, said, "The Archbishop must not appear sympathetic to those who have caused the crisis," while the liberal dean of Southwark, the Very Rev. Colin Slee, said: "I think it is critical that Rowan meets him. This is a guy who has been legally, canonically, elected according to the statutes of his church and for the Archbishop not to speak to him would be a major injustice."[1]

Perhaps as a concession to the evangelicals, the meeting did not take place at the Archbishop's offices at Lambeth Palace but in a small room in St. Paul's

Cathedral. In a statement issued by Lambeth Palace afterwards, the meeting was characterized as "friendly but candid" and described as having "ended with prayer." Neither the Archbishop nor Bishop Robinson had anything more to say to the press about what was discussed, but some months later Gene said that the meeting had left him profoundly sad and that he was praying for the Archbishop.

In an interview with the *Guardian* later that week, Bishop Robinson was asked about the conservative voices in the Anglican Communion who were calling on him to "repent." He replied firmly that he was not ashamed of his sexual orientation and believed he had no reason for repentance. "It is not something of which I should repent and I have no intention of doing so," he said. "I have been led to understand that I am loved by God just as I am. That is not to say I am perfect but it is my belief that my orientation is value-neutral. It is what I do with my relationship that God really cares about. It has taken me the better part of 40 years to come to terms with all that. It was God that changed my heart about coming to accept myself. It was a very hard-won fight. I would be crazy to turn my back on that now."[2]

That message was welcomed by the large congregation at London's St. Martin-in-the-Fields, where Gene attended a special service commemorating the tenth anniversary of the Anglican gay rights organization, Changing Attitudes, and afterwards addressed the congregation. Jean Morris, a Londoner who attended the service, wrote this brief account:

> Members of Changing Attitudes read brief testimonials from gay Christians of their experience in the church. One in particular, an elderly woman, spoke very emotionally. Everyone spoke strongly and resonantly, but, following on the service sheet, I noticed many small omissions and reversals of word order, which suggested that everyone was nervous and emotional . . . The hour-long service passed very quickly, with an intense atmosphere of attentiveness and good-will and many waves of feeling.

> Then the Bishop spoke, from behind a table installed in front of the altar (remarking that he didn't usually speak from behind things). He looked very small, and seemed very large. He spoke very simply, recounting some of his own history, in life and in the church—his election and consecration, and his present feelings. Told a couple of jokes. Exhorted everyone to act normally and forthrightly, to assume their rights and their normality within the church, and to hope and trust in change and complete acceptance, though perhaps not in any of our life-times, since what it will take is nothing less than an end to patriarchy. I never thought I would hear an Anglican bishop evoke the end of patriarchy! He spoke for nearly an hour and a half and obviously went down wonderfully with just about everybody there. There was only time for a few questions, and these were friendly, concerned and supportive. It was an immensely warm and positive occasion.

"I've been to a lot of events with Dad, sometimes where he's giving the speech and sometimes where there's speeches being made about him." Gene's daughter Ella sat back in her chair and laughed, her round, happy face reminiscent of her father's. "We've joked that I've been to so many of these things that I could give his speeches for him. He has this one phrase, 'beyond my wildest imagining!' Haven't you heard that from him four million times? I always chuckle in the pew when I hear that: 'God loves me beyond my wildest imaginings.'" She shook her head, smiling affectionately as she replayed that mental tape. "But even hearing the same questions asked, and hearing him repeat the same thoughts and topics and phrases, there are two things that still surprise me. Number one: I'm still amazed at how good he is. He's so clear, and so funny, and so engaging. It's like he was just put here to do this. It's not an ego thing, it's not anything other than faith. I am always just bowled over by his faith, it's so strong. I hear him talk about it, and I still get tears in my eyes."

"And the second thing that keeps amazing me is the way people react to him. It's different from fans and stars, which I see in my work all the time." (Ella works in public relations for Dreamworks Pictures.) "What Dad has is kind of a mix between celebrity and faith and church . . . I just think there aren't many people who have such a profound presence in front of other people."

Another difference between Gene and other well-known public figures was the suddenness of his celebrity status. "The thing that makes it really different from an entertainer or a politician is that there was no ramp-up," he says. "On June the sixth I was nobody, and on June the seventh I became this other thing. Well, I suppose my whole life was a ramp-up, but in terms of the pace and the notoriety and the demands, it just went from very little to this whole other thing."

When he first became a bishop and a public figure, Gene seemed almost abashed by the praise that came his way from the outside, not just from people who already loved him. He tried to gracefully deflect it, along with the inevitable comparisons to other barrier-breaking figures. Not long after his consecration, during a speech on Martin Luther King Day, he said that one thing he had learned from people of color was that all of us "are standing on the shoulders of so many others who have gone before." He described a sculpture in the National Civil Rights Museum in Memphis, Tennessee: "The figures go around and around: this countless throng of people, making their way upward—to what? To heaven, to freedom, to liberation—and everyone is standing on the shoulders of someone else. And as you work your way through the museum, you get to sit on the bus. There's Rosa Parks sitting on the bus with you. And, I'm happy to say, Jackie Robinson is there too, in that museum. And one of the greatest honors of this last six or seven months has been some people writing in the press about the similarities between Jackie Robinson and Gene Robinson, an honor I don't deserve, but I can assure you, I am honored by."

But as time went on, and the award plaques continued to pile up in his office, awaiting their place on the wall, and the invitations to give keynote speeches kept coming, and the crowds continued to throng to his public appearances, Gene seemed to become more comfortable with his new role, although he continued to call much of it "surreal." He *is* a natural extrovert and was able to adapt to the whirl of appearances and connections and invitations, often from gay and gay-friendly members of the entertainment industry. He became close friends with some other famous people, including a Hollywood producer who continually urged him to make a guest appearance on his television sitcom, something Gene is unlikely ever to do. He worked to find ways to handle the notoriety and the demands on his time and energy without compromising his faith, his integrity, or his responsibility to New Hampshire.

Gene, Jamee, Ella, and Mark with Judy Shepard, the mother of Matthew Shepard, on the night Gene received the National Equality Award from the Human Rights Campaign.

Gene's schedule would make Bill Clinton tired, and yet he seems to thrive on it. "It's been quite a ride," says Ella. "And he's so happy being the bishop. He just loves it. Going and greeting people every Sunday morning? We're both extroverted, but I'd never be able to do that: I like my quiet Sunday mornings! But he lives for it. He likes being in the spotlight."

Her father agrees, a little sheepishly: "Well, it helps that I enjoy it, and frankly, it helps that most of the people in New Hampshire know and care nothing about all those awards and public appearances. The diocese keeps me sane and centered. As for the other stuff, I try to do the very best I can, but of course I still make mistakes."

Gene's nature is to be spontaneous, direct, and honest. Having an informal conversation with him is a fast-paced affair: he is very quick and eager, jumping in to make a point, and he doesn't hold back with his quick wit and off-the-cuff remarks. If his media coordinator Mike Barwell is in the room, he often cringes in mock horror at some of Gene's quick comments that could easily be taken out of context.

Because of his longtime work as a facilitator and counselor to clergy and parishes, Gene also has another side to his personality, easily becoming a quiet listener whose responses are few and carefully considered. In public, he has become better and better since his election at gauging his audiences and responding carefully to questions, mindful that any remark he makes may be taken out of context and used against him by his detractors. Being measured and sometimes circumspect is something he has to do consciously, because his natural instinct is to say quite honestly and directly what he thinks: he thrives on forming connections with people and bridging the distance between speaker and listener, turning formal exchanges into more of a conversation. "It's just impossible not to say something that someone will try to use against you," he admits. "Everywhere I go there are people with laptops trying to take down every word I say so they can use it. I mean, I'm used to it by now, but there is just this constant pressure."

Many of Gene's public appearances don't attract a lot of press attention, perhaps because they involve predictable circles such as progressive religious organizations or gay and lesbian rights groups. When he speaks to the national media or addresses large, constituency-spanning organizations it is a different story. In April 2005, he was the keynote speaker at Planned Parenthood's fifth annual interfaith prayer breakfast in Washington, D.C., and prior to his appearance, he did an interview that appeared on the organization's website and was widely quoted. In the interview he expressed the progressive views he has always held about reproductive rights and sex education:

> I don't find any disconnect between science and faith. There are ways of incorporating all of faith with all of what we know about science. [Right-wing politicians] and the so-called "pro-life" movement focus on all this as a great way to raise money, solidify their base, and get people all whipped up. If they can keep people whipped up about abortion, stem cell research, and gay marriage, then we don't have to talk about the things that really matter, like this illegal and immoral war in Iraq, the economy, the some 45 million people without health insurance in this country, and balancing the budget so that those least able to take care of themselves don't lose Medicaid. I think it was Senator Barbara Boxer (D-CA) who called all of the folderol about gay marriage a "weapon of mass distraction." That's what I think is going on here. I don't find anything in Scripture that says we shouldn't be doing these things.
>
> I've been involved in AIDS education for both young people and adults for a long, long time, and I think it's cruel beyond belief to be advocating abstinence-only sex education. This is the real disconnect—if you are against abortion, how can you not be for full and sufficient

education about birth control? It's something that would stop unintended pregnancies to begin with. It also exhibits a very low opinion of humankind. It says we can't make appropriate choices for ourselves, so somebody has to make those choices for us.[3]

His invitation to be the keynote speaker at the Planned Parenthood breakfast was, predictably, applauded by pro-choice progressives and criticized by "family values" conservatives. Ignacio Castuera, the national chaplain for the organization, called the bishop "an inspiring religious leader and a compelling moral and ethical force in the struggle for reproductive rights, human rights and sexual equality," adding that "his work mentoring everyone from youth to clergy on issues ranging from healthy sexuality to conflict mediation has shaped generations of believers who share his progressive spiritual values."

But after the speech, Tony Perkins, president of the Family Research Council, said, "Bringing together homosexual activism and abortion on demand hardly seems the best way to reach most people of faith in America."[4] Since then, the far right has continued to connect the bishop with Planned Parenthood. When a gay man, Chris Barron, was recruited from the Log Cabin Republicans to lead Planned Parenthood's outreach efforts to the Republican Party, Robert Knight, director of Concerned Women for America's Culture and Family Institute, remarked, "This should be a seamless transition, given that both organizations [Log Cabin and Planned Parenthood] pursue an anti-family agenda that's right at home in the culture of death. Recall, for instance, that V. Gene Robinson, the openly homosexual Episcopal bishop, spoke at a Planned Parenthood event . . . After all, both Robinson and Planned Parenthood have rejected the natural family and pursued sex outside marriage and abortion as a reasonable, logical response to an unintended pregnancy."[5]

One of the biggest flaps, however, happened because of remarks Gene made at a forum on sexual issues at a small venue, Christ Church of Hamilton, Massachusetts. He had been asked a leading question, aimed at the idea that Jesus affirmed the nuclear family as "the only way a family can be." "I happen to think the traditional family is a wonderful thing. I'm a product of it," Gene answered. "I dearly love my family, and I love my own family, with my own two kids. It just looks a little nontraditional. But this Jesus—when you ask, 'Who is Jesus?'—he was not terribly mainstream, was he?" Gene pointed out that Jesus himself lived a pretty non-traditional lifestyle: "This man that we follow . . . was single as far as we know; traveled with a bunch of men, although there were lots of women around; had a disciple who was known as 'the one whom Jesus loved'; said my family is not my mother and father, my family are those who do the will of God—none of us like those harsh words. That's who Jesus is, that's who he was, at least in his earthly life." Gene's remarks had come after his sermon, when he abandoned his notes and was speaking spontaneously and less formally with the audience. He had also shared some of his memories about what it was like to be homosexual back when he was young, when the slightest implication that you were gay might result in a savage beating, and the fear and repression this atmosphere created.

The next day, banner headlines in the conservative media, from the Manchester *Union Leader* to FOX News, were proclaiming that the "gay bishop" had implied that "Jesus was gay." The story was picked up on the conservative Anglican website of David Virtue, who had fanned the fires of the sexual allegations at the 2003 General Convention. The Diocese of New Hampshire itself received many angry messages, prompting Gene to speak and issue a clarification.

"Jesus lived a very untraditional lifestyle," he said. "Which is not to say that I in any way asserted that he was gay, or anything about his sexual orientation."

Gene's appearance at St. Martin-in-the-Fields occurred shortly after the Vatican's announcement of a forthcoming review of all United States Catholic seminaries in an attempt to root out any gay candidates for the priesthood. In a question-and-answer session following his speech, a young gay man stood up in the back of the church and said, "I'm Roman Catholic. What advice can you give me about how to manage my life in the Catholic Church?"

"I said all the stuff that didn't get reported," Gene said later, "like you should live your life with such joy and you should so shine with the light of Christ that no one can deny your full membership in the Body of Christ—and then I said, 'However, this thing from the Vatican connecting homosexuality and pedophilia is an act of violence against all of us.'"

There was an immediate firestorm. His remarks were quoted as a lead story on the BBC, and a high official from the Vatican registered a strong protest with the bishop in charge of ecumenical affairs for the Episcopal Church, as if Bishop Robinson were a mouthpiece for the church at large. But this time Gene had no intention of backing down.

"Before Cardinal Ratzinger was elected pope, I think everybody was holding out hope against hope that maybe things were going to change," he said. "They're not going to change. And now they're saying to the gay people in the seminaries, 'You're intrinsically disordered.' What they're saying now is that if you've ever had any homosexual experience, or any homosexual feelings, you're thrown out of the seminary or not allowed in. It's vile that they are addressing the child abuse scandal this way. It's outrageous, and I *did* say that I feel this was an act of violence against us all, and I'll continue saying it. It's just unbelievable."

Theologically, there is a nearly black-and-white divide between those who accept homosexuality and those who do not. Much has been written about that topic, including *Gays and the Future of Anglicanism: Responses to the Windsor Report*, an anthology of essays by various Anglican priests and theologians which appeared in October, 2005. While the arguments on both sides can go on at length, focus on topics that range from Scriptural literalism to cultural tradition, and be presented in a range of styles from academic rhetoric to discussions of "the 'ick' factor," much of the actual divide comes down to a difference of opinion over whether homosexuality is a choice or an orientation that is part of one's intrinsic make-up—God-given, as it were.

This basic difference matters a great deal. In the three decades since the American Psychiatric Association removed homosexuality from its official manual of mental and emotional disorders, scientific research has come closer and closer to demonstrating that sexual orientation is neither a choice nor a disorder but the result of biological difference. In a long article in the *Boston Globe* in 2005 (to which I am indebted here), journalist Neil Swidey examined past and present research studies about what makes a person gay. These included the study of male twins by Boston researchers Pillard and Bailey, which found that, among identical twins, if one twin was gay, the other had about a 50 percent chance of also being gay, while among fraternal twins, the chance was closer to 20 percent. This would indicate an inherited tendency. In 1993, Dean Hamer, of the National Cancer Institute, discovered a more precise genetic clue: gay brothers share a specific section of the X chromosome at a higher rate than do gay men with their straight brothers. A Swedish study has found that the brains of gay and straight men respond differently to chemical compounds that are suspected to be human sexual stimulants. Austrian researchers have recently discovered a genetic "switch" that controls sexual orientation in fruit flies and found that they could cause genetically-altered females to attempt to mate with females rather than males, mimicking male fruit fly courtship behavior. And, as Swidey concluded, the National Institute for Health has recently funded a major five-year study of gay brothers in North America, which should help to shed more light on these underlying genetic questions.

Of course, as the creationism/evolution debate proves, some people will never accept scientific evidence that conflicts with Biblical passages that they consider to be the literal word of God. Bishop Paul Moore, whose attitude about homosexuality has been affected greatly by examining the scientific evidence, remembered a discussion he had with about a dozen bishops and a psychiatrist. He was quite incredulous that after convincing data and scientific arguments had been shared that showed homosexuality was *not* a choice, some bishops still insisted a person could change if he or she really wanted to.

A book issued much more recently by the Family Research Council, a conservative Christian think tank, states that a scientific explanation for people being born gay "would advance the idea that sexual orientation is an innate characteristic, like race; that homosexuals, like African Americans, should be legally protected against 'discrimination'; and that disapproval of homosexuality should be as socially stigmatized as racism. However," the statement stubbornly concludes, "it is not true."

Other conservatives are not so sure. One evangelical leader, the Rev. Rob Schenck, recently said he had been converted to a different opinion after studying the research and talking to scientific professionals. He now believes homosexuality is "deeply rooted" and not a matter of personal choice or decision. His present position is that homosexual behavior should be opposed, but that "many evangelicals are living in a sort of state of denial about the advance of this conversation . . . If it's inevitable that this scientific evidence is coming, we have to be prepared with a loving response. If we don't have one, we won't have any credibility."[6]

The gradual changes in attitude toward homosexuality in American society have come about for many reasons: biological evidence, gradually relaxed attitudes in the media, and greater openness and more frequent contact between the public and gay people who have "come out." Attitudes based on theoretical ideas as well as gut-level responses have had to give way to real relationship, often with considerable struggle. Lots of people have had to adjust—families from Gene Robinson's to Dick Cheney's, and institutions as well, including the church.

Dr. Louie Crew, the founder of Integrity, credits the Rt. Rev. Bennett Sims, the retired bishop of Atlanta, as one of the first church leaders to admit an about-face on the issue of homosexuality. Sims had been a chief architect of the 1979 resolution against the ordination of lesbians and gays. In 1991 in an open letter to the Episcopal Church, he explained: "When I wrote that Pastoral Statement in 1977, I knew only one homosexual person up close. He scared me to death with his penetrating challenge that he was as complete a human being as I was." Louie Crew was that person—and over time, Bishop Sims changed. At the 1995 General Convention, he was the chief celebrant at a service commemorating the twentieth anniversary of the ordination of women, and he celebrated the twentieth anniversary of Integrity as well. He explained that he changed his mind when he began to know lesbians and gays as persons, as sister and brother Christians, not just as issues. Bishop Sims was present, his elderly face full of joy, to participate in Gene Robinson's consecration.

Dr. Crew has received several honorary degrees from theological seminaries and often speaks on their campuses. "When I spoke at Virginia twenty-five years ago I was booed and hissed. It was the worst response I've ever received, and I'm used to tough audiences. It was an embarrassment to me—still is—that a seminary of the quality of Virginia wouldn't have communicated to their students that hissing was not an acceptable way to treat an invited guest. But when I went back last year, I couldn't have been treated more hospitably and respectfully. I usually ask the students to raise their hands if someone who is a close friend of theirs is lesbian or gay. At least 80 percent of the people in Virginia raised their hands. And I said to myself, 'Well, that's the difference between now and twenty-five years ago.' I wouldn't have asked the question twenty-five years ago. While there would have been people back then for whom it would have been proper to raise their hands, I would have put those friendships in jeopardy. I think the reason people are changing is that they have—without using the central sense of the word—more intimate knowledge of what we're talking about."

As Gene often points out, a priest's own attitude and anxiety level—or lack thereof—have a great deal to do with how individual parishes deal with potentially divisive issues. The Rev. Hank Junkin says that, in his earlier ministry, he never would have dreamt that he would be sitting down with anyone talking about blessing same-gender unions, marriages, and talking about gay bishops. He was cutting his lawn one day when a parishioner—a member of the vestry—came over with tears in her eyes and asked if she could talk to him. He said, "Sure," and she said, "I need to talk to my parents about me being a lesbian and I don't know how to do it."

Hank said it was like being hit with a ton of bricks—he didn't know what to say or how to help her—"but at that moment, the whole philosophical, theological, ethical issue of homosexuality seemed to be dwarfed next to the care for an individual. It was a 'road to Damascus'⁷ experience for me." They talked for a long time, and he told her he would try to learn from her, and that he would stand with her.

"Not long after that I called Gene, who was then the canon to the ordinary, on the phone and said, 'I need to talk to you. I need your help in reaching out to this person in my congregation.' And slowly he sat with me, talked with me, and I became less afraid, more knowledgeable, tried to examine some of my own feelings about it, because at the heart of it I don't think this is a Biblical issue. You can argue the Bible every which way—this is a gut-level reaction, at least for me. There's a visceral, physical reaction to homosexuality. And I don't know whether that comes from a cultural bias, or from growing up in a family with three other brothers, with some sort of gender straight-jacket that we all wear . . . the hardest part for me to understand was that there was quite a lot of misogyny also related to this. Fear of being like a woman. Well, what's the matter with being a woman? It took me a while to kind of unpack all those feelings. But it happened. And I guess I've come to the place where I feel this is a matter of *hearts* fitting together, not *parts*. And that has much to say to the world, let alone to the heterosexual community itself, which I don't think should have a lock on what relationships are about, anyways."

In Hank's church, the issue later faced the vestry: the daughter of one of the vestry members was a lesbian and wished to have her union blessed. Hank describes the father as "a rock-ribbed Republican, a kind of old-style Episcopal Republican" who came "with tears in his eyes" and asked the vestry to agree to bless his daughter's union. Hank, as priest, would not do covenant services without the vestry's approval, or without the bishop's approval, because he felt that the sacrament itself "was enshrined in community," not a decision for him to make on his own.

"And we struggled, boy, each of the members, God bless them. And I sensed that they were having the same 'road to Damascus' experience I described having—that suddenly this wasn't theoretical or theological, or just 'out there' somewhere. This was our *family*. What were we going to do? What was God calling us to do here? So that's how it's happened here: very gently, with lots of prayer, agreeing to disagree, and trying to be as open about it as we could."

The Rev. David Jones of St. Paul's Church, Concord, who had been interviewed by the national media after Gene's victory in the New Hampshire election and later served with Judith Esmay and Hank Junkin representing the diocese in talks at Lambeth Palace, originally came from an evangelical background and had been adamantly opposed to homosexual ordinations. "How do you ever know what's going to happen?" he said, with a wry smile. "If I had ever thought I'd be out front, in public, on this issue on television—if you'd asked me that in seminary, let alone five years ago, I would have said you're crazy."

Before David came to New Hampshire, he never had any interaction with someone he knew was gay. In Pittsburgh, he said, it was just not an issue: you didn't talk about it. And at that time it wasn't on the radar screen in the life of the church. "I had no motivation to think hard about this issue, so I was opposed! Because if you're theologically conservative, and you read the Bible, that's where most people end up."

In David's class at seminary were three women who were hoping to be ordained to the diaconate. At that time he was opposed to the ordination of women—he had never met or worked with any women clergy; in the parish he came from, they didn't even have girl acolytes. But after he was ordained, he saw that there was a woman in the Diocese of Pittsburgh who couldn't be ordained, and he watched what she was doing and realized, "She's doing exactly the same things I'm doing, God's using her exactly the same way. How in the world can we say she can't be ordained, and I can?"

"But that's because I met a person," he said, "and the issue suddenly became incarnational. Same thing for me with the issue of gays and lesbians in ministry. And it's Gene—he's the one I met who I saw doing all this ministry around here, and who did ministry to me, and I'm thinking, 'God, you're not allowed to use him, don't you know that? He can't be a priest, let alone anything else . . .' Eventually I could no longer just say, 'This is my position because the Bible says this.' I had to look at some of my foundational beliefs about Scripture and how it was interpreted, and that was part of this journey. But what motivated it was having experience and a relationship with somebody who made the issue more than an issue."

David said that he had done two baptisms in which the baby had two mothers. "I think both children had come about through artificial insemination, where one woman was the actual biological mother. The couples came to me and asked, 'Would you ever baptize a baby like this?' which told me they'd been elsewhere, where the answer to that question was 'no.' And then the follow-up question was always, 'And would we be welcome here as the parents?'"

Of course, he said, there have been some people in his parish who have been troubled by all of that, but he asserted that, for the most part, his congregation focuses on how to accept and acknowledge difference while still agreeing to worship together as a community. "What I always try to say is that I have no need to convince you that you're wrong, because I could be wrong. I know that. I always say that." He added that when the New Hampshire delegation was at Lambeth, they had said the same thing, and that it had almost stopped the conversation, because the admission was so "out there." "'We could be wrong,' we told them. 'And so could you.'"

In his memoirs, Bishop Paul Moore wrote about the struggle that happens when the church changes its long-held positions:

The criteria by which I try to test the validity of change in doctrine are: Does this change give us a larger understanding of God and bring us closer to an understanding of Him as revealed in Scripture? Does this change liberate our spirit to become more fully human and nearer to the image of Christ? Does it reflect more clearly the image of God in which we are made? Therefore, does this change make us more compassionate, more just, more loving, and more free? If the change in thinking or practice accomplishes these goals, it is of God. However, if the change makes us have a smaller or more shallow understanding of God, or if it makes us more narrow of mind and spirit, the change is not of God. We bring to bear on these new understandings the ethical criteria gleaned from Scripture.[8]

Of course, change is very difficult, especially for institutions as old as the church. On every single issue of inclusion that the church has faced—race, gender, or sexual orientation—the same rhetoric has been used, the same arguments trotted out, the same delaying tactics recommended: more study, the appointment of yet another commission, deferring votes until the next general meeting . . . and the next. When the Lambeth hierarchy reacted with such affront to the actions of New Hampshire and the Diocese of New Westminster, it was precisely because these dioceses had not waited and delayed any longer.

In answer to the contention that New Hampshire and the American church had "gone about this all wrong," Gene Robinson recently said, "Actually, we followed every jot and tittle: my election followed the canons to the letter. But isn't this how it always works? Eleven Episcopal women deacons got themselves ordained as priests in an irregular service in Philadelphia in 1974—and do you think for a minute that the American church would have voted for the ordination of women in 1976 if they had not done that? For all I know, we might *still* not be ordaining women. So it seems to me that for every step forward that we've taken, someone has just done it, and the church has then figured out why it is okay. If we had waited for everyone in this country to stop being racist before passing the voting rights act, we still wouldn't have it!"

Sadly, organized religion often hides behind both theology and protocol when the real issue is one of power. The dismantling of patriarchy—power consolidated, most generally, in the hands of white western males—has happened slowly and painfully and been accompanied by much ugliness, including hypocrisy that is very evident to observers from the outside. One of the most uncomfortable facts about human beings is our tendency to coalesce into groups who are like us, and then to make those groups exclusive, resorting to extreme measures to keep power in the hands of the "insiders"—including lying, especially to ourselves, about what we are doing. Jesus was well aware of this human tendency, and he not only preached about it, but lived his life as an example of another way of being. It was radical in his day, and cost him his life—yet this is the vision of the world that we are called to as his followers.

Archbishop Desmond Tutu emphasized this message with his characteristic directness in a sermon preached in Pasadena, California on All Saint's Day in 2005. He reminded all Anglicans to remember that their tradition is "comprehensive," saying:

> Jesus did not say, "If I be lifted up I will draw some." Jesus said, "'If I be lifted up I will draw all, all, all, all, all." Black, white, yellow, rich, poor, clever, not so clever, beautiful, not so beautiful. It's one of the most radical things. All, all, all, all, all, all, all, all. All belong. Gay, lesbian, so-called straight. All, all are meant to be held in this incredible embrace that will not let us go. All.

Gene, Ella, and Mark at the New York City Gay Pride Parade, June 2005.

In the spring of 2005, during Gay Pride Week, Gene, Mark, and Gene's daughter Ella met in New York, where Gene preached at a synagogue and was honored at a fundraiser for GLBT street kids. The next day he did a service and a question-and-answer session in Chelsea, and then got onto the Episcopal float in the Gay Pride Parade.

"Oh, my gosh, it was so fun," said Ella. "I spent two summers here through college, and lived near the seminary. My first summer down here I lived by myself and didn't know anyone, but I kind of stumbled on Pride Parade, and I remember calling my dad from Fifth and Twenty-third, right by the Flatiron Building, and saying, 'We have to come to this next year, it's so fun, I've never seen anything like this!' So then, three or four years later, we're on a float *in* Gay Pride parade!"

"I looked over and this guy on the street was kind of cheering, and Dad and he kind of locked eyes, and the guy just burst into tears and said, 'Bishop Robinson, thank you, thank you,' and just kept saying that as we went past . . . I was, like, standing there, waving my rainbow flag, and I was just dumbstruck. I forget what this means to people, whether they're Episcopalians or have no faith whatsoever. It strikes people on so many different levels. And it reminds me that this is a big thing, and an important thing, for so many people who have heard his story."

Gene also says he'll never forget that day. "We were on that float for three and a half hours, with about a million and a half people on the sidewalks, and at one point Ella turned to me and said, 'Daddy, I just had no idea.' There were people pushing and straining to shake my hand or touch me or whatever—people were crying—she was just blown away by it, as was I. As close as she had been to this, she just had no idea this meant so much to people."

The Rev. Randy Dales says, "In his media interviews, Gene comes across to people who don't know what to think of the Episcopal Church, or of bishops, or perhaps even of churches in general, as someone who expresses very well the love of God for all sorts of people who are considered unloved by society—and homosexuals are not always the most loved people in our society. They are misunderstood, feared and in some cases hated. In Gene, people see someone who society has rejected and labeled, and they see his compassion and his openness to others, and his willingness to feel the hurt of those who don't understand his being chosen as a bishop. That speaks volumes about how individual human beings might indeed reflect God's love, and it's made a difference."

Some of those people, of course, have become Episcopalians. One new parishioner said: "I'm attracted to this kind of a church and to people like Gene Robinson who are willing to stand for something. I wasn't attracted to the old model. I mean, you have a society where there's no moral force at all—certainly not the government—trying to do what is right, trying to move forward. I think in a climate like the present one, the church *should* play that role, and I admire it for doing so and am willing to support it. Of course, the people who oppose it think that *they're* the moral ones, and that Gene and the liberals represent the height of immorality. When you have sex involved, there's always going to be complications. But what's really going on is that the progressives represent positive change, and the conservatives are the ones who want the status quo, who want everything to stay the same. In the past, people have thought of the church as being allied with the conservatives, but this shows that not only is the church willing to take a stand, it's willing to lead. And that attracts me."

The bishop at prayer during a service.

Chapter 16

Accepting the Mantle

"Servant leadership" has been a touchstone of the progressive theological movement in recent years, spawning not only several influential books but schools, institutes and centers for people attracted to a less authoritarian and hierarchical style of ministry. Conservatives who are set on clerical hierarchy and preserving the top-down authority of the ordained ministry—and who are threatened by what they see as an erosion of that authority by women, homosexuals, and the laity—are less enthralled. The idea that priests actually *gain* authority by sharing both power and real-world Christian work with the congregation has become an important way to talk not only about the changing role of the clergy, but also about "the priesthood of all believers." The concept, however, is very old in Christianity, foreshadowed in the quotation from St. Augustine of Hippo that Gene chose for the service booklet at his consecration:

> For you I am Bishop, but with you I am a Christian; one is an office, accepted; the other is a gift, received. One is danger; the other is safety. If I am happier to be redeemed with you than to be placed over you, then I shall, as the Lord commanded, be more fully your servant.

The first time Gene saw this quotation was in 1986 at Doug Theuner's consecration. He smiled: "When people ask Doug what they should call him, he always answers, 'Doug. Because that's what I'm going to be called when I get to heaven. I certainly won't be called Bishop.'" The comment always stuck with Gene. "It goes with my theology: that the ordained 'orders' of ministry are actually *below*, not above, the ordination that we all have by virtue of our baptism, and that *that's* the thing that saves us. The traditional language has been that we 'set aside' deacons and priests and bishops, but lately I've begun to say they are 'being set more deeply within.' I think in some sense becoming a priest actually limits your ministry. What I mean is that the *real* ministry is to the *world*, but as a priest and as a bishop, you limit yourself to be minister to the ministers."

For Gene, the quotation (which Presiding Bishop Griswold actually presents, framed, to *all* new bishops) is a reminder that he was baptized, first and foremost, and that his baptism will always be more important than any ordained position he holds. He also loves the quote because it comes from such an early time in church history. "One of the things that drew me to the Episcopal Church was all its history. The church I grew up in dated back 150 years, but to be a part of a church that stretches all the way back to the apostles is a source of immense comfort, and it's really nice to know that someone of Augustine's stature was already thinking this way in 400 A.D."

At every ordination he now performs, Gene preaches on this theme of shared priesthood, thus including the congregation as well as the person about to be ordained. "I don't know how people can read the Gospels and not get the concept that being a Christian is about being a servant," he says. "But being a bishop is undeniably seductive—it's one of the difficulties of the office. You get to wear all these fancy vestments and the gold cross and the fancy hat—there's nothing in it that looks servant-like."

One young man, a former Roman Catholic now living in Japan, cited the Catholic church's pomp as a reason he had left the religion of his birth. His sentiments are certainly shared by many: "I very deeply question all the pomp and circumstance, the glittering gold, the titles, the—to me—pretentious rituals, the insistence upon portraying other human beings as higher and better than you, of making the congregation into something small and silent before the leaders. It goes against everything I believe in. Kings and popes, princes and bishops are no longer a legitimate part of my world. I bow to nothing but the simple spirit of another person and the spirit of all living things." This person now identifies himself as Buddhist. "I still find the teachings of Christ very important and continue to read and try to practice them," he said, "but without all the trappings of a huge money-making, corporation-like organization. Christ was a simple man and would have been incensed by what the church has become."

Gene, who is keenly aware of social attitudes as well as economic injustice, is aware that some people perceive the Episcopal Church that way as well. Of course, for some, the robes and color and ritual are part of the attraction, deeply imbued with meaning and history. But Gene's humble background— poor, determinedly Protestant, and mistrustful of anything Catholic or "high-church"—certainly contributes to his reluctance to "show off" and his desire to identify with the flock rather than to set himself apart. He shares that quality with former President Jimmy Carter: instinctively wanting to be part of the crowd, to come down from the pulpit into the sanctuary, and feeling more comfortable in a sweater than in robes. But, like Carter, he has found it's not that simple, that the act of "lowering himself" is viewed unfavorably by some people.

When Gene first became bishop he considered not wearing a purple shirt all the time because of the color's association with royalty. "Symbols are important," he says. "I believe these things ultimately need to be changed, but I've discovered that probably I am not the one to change them. That's because there's this other thing going on with me. If I were heterosexual, I would feel free to do that. But there are so many people who *don't* want to see me as a bishop. My detractors refuse to call me 'Bishop Robinson.' A lot of them write to me as 'Canon Robinson' or 'Father Robinson' because they don't want to acknowledge that my election and consecration are valid. So I haven't worn a black shirt since the day I was consecrated. I just have to wear the purple shirt. It's important that I do it, and it's especially important to gay and lesbian folks and to other people on the margins. They don't want me to be 'less than' other bishops. So I've really tried to listen to that. Even that's a ministry, you know? Even what I put on in the morning: it matters."

He did change one symbol, a year after taking office. Like most dioceses of the Episcopal Church, the Diocese of New Hampshire was represented by a coat of arms with a heraldic history: a shield with a sword and arrows, surmounted by a bishop's mitre, with a key and a bishop's crook crossed behind the shield. During Lent 2004, Gene wrote about it in his monthly pastoral letter to the diocese:

> The symbol that appears on every piece of stationery, the doors of Diocesan House, the *New Hampshire Episcopal News*, and every publication of the diocese is our coat of arms/shield. It is the face we give to the world.
>
> Perhaps you've never given it much thought, but what does our coat of arms say about us? In a time of war, our "face" to the world has arrows and a sword. In a time when we believe the Bishop to be a servant of the people, our shield displays a mitre bejeweled with precious stones. In an age when people are starving the world over, and the gap between rich and poor becomes greater every day, our "face to the world" looks like the coat of arms of a great and wealthy family. In these times which beg for our self-sacrificing love in the Name of Jesus, there is little in this coat of arms to communicate our warmth, our respect and our love for all of God's children.

In the same issue of the diocesan newsletter, he introduced a new logo as a replacement: a stylized pair of human hands, reaching upward, holding a flame—representing the Holy Spirit, perhaps—accompanied by the tagline, "Infinite respect for one another, radical hospitality for the world." He wrote:

> Symbols and words won't automatically change us into the servant community Christ calls us to be, but they can remind us of that so that we can work on it every day, and they can signal to the world our real intention: to be God's loving hands in the world, empowered by the Spirit of the One who first loved us.

Gene's physical presence also became a symbol. Often that presence was positive: when he showed up to play softball at the New Hampshire Women's Prison or rode on a float in New York's Gay Pride parade, he was expanding the traditional role of an Episcopal bishop. Sometimes his presence was perceived negatively: shortly after his consecration, at the Episcopal House of Bishops meeting in Navasota, Texas in March 2004, four conservative bishops boycotted the meeting entirely and five bishops insisted on staying offsite; another reportedly withdrew from participation when he and Gene Robinson were placed in the same small prayer and discussion group.[1] Likewise, the conservative African bishops threatened to boycott the next international Lambeth Conference, to which all Anglican bishops in the world are traditionally invited, if the North American bishops who had supported Gene's election were present. Gene, somewhat naively perhaps, wrote to the Archbishop of Canterbury, saying that if it would help get the conservatives to come, he would be willing to talk about attending with a reduced status: as observer, perhaps, rather than as a full participant.

"What was so very interesting to me were the people who were horrified that I did that, because to have 'achieved this,' and then to voluntarily diminish myself—which is how they saw it—felt like I was diminishing them as well." Gene didn't feel personally responsible for the troubles in the Anglican Communion, but he also felt he didn't need to add to them. "I thought it was time for those of us in the American church to make some gracious gestures. I can afford to be gracious, and it was a good time for that. And I was frankly trying to help Rowan out of a bind: if he doesn't invite me to Lambeth, there'll be people who won't go out of sympathy for that. If he does invite me, a lot of conservatives won't come. So rather than have him un-invite me, or demand that I come in a lesser status, I thought I would make the offer. Nobody could hold it against him for taking me up on that."

That was in the days when everyone was still talking about reconciliation. And it was also when Gene still felt that it might be possible to be simply "Gene Robinson, Bishop of New Hampshire," rather than a symbol with both negative and positive connotations for different people all over the world.

Gene's trip to England in the fall of 2005 seemed to be another emergence of sorts, a time when he fully accepted the mantle that people had been thrusting onto his shoulders ever since he was elected. His decisions, actions, and reflections afterward represented a further maturing, both of the person himself and of his understanding of his role.

"I was totally naïve at the beginning," he said, shrugging. "Totally. I was just plain wrong in thinking this would all blow over and I could just be the bishop of New Hampshire. Yes, I'm getting to do the stuff that bishops do, and I love it, but there's this other thing that history has handed me, and it would just be terrible stewardship not to try to do it as well—but it is a huge burden. I feel it all the time."

As his second year as bishop drew to a close, Gene looked healthy and cheerful, but sometimes there was a strain and fatigue in his eyes and manner that hadn't been there before. And he definitely was not as accessible as he once had been: it was harder for people to get an appointment, and emails and phone calls were returned more slowly. For the most part, the diocese accepted these limitations without grumbling, and because New Hampshire remained Gene's priority and the office was so well organized, the bishop's hectic schedule was not always obvious. Gene has a way of "turning on" in a meeting—a remarkable ability to focus on the people and the task at hand, regardless of how tired he is or how many other projects or responsibilities are on his plate. Nevertheless, he is not thirty years old but nearly twice that, and he is constantly faced with the necessity of making difficult choices so that he can conserve his energy.

"The demands of the role are affecting me mostly in terms of pace," he said, his brow furrowed, in December 2005. "There's so much to do. There are so many people hurting. The 'demonization' and the 'angelization,' if that's a word, continue. My enemies make me out to be the devil, but the people who are looking to me for support and inspiration and courage are blowing me out of proportion on the positive side. What's hard about that is that while I'm pretty defended against the negative stuff, I am totally *un*defended against certain appeals from the other side. I see what's happening, I hear people's stories, and it just breaks my heart."

Gene received two invitations to events during the same week in the summer of 2006. One was to be a keynoter at the World Pride gathering in Jerusalem. The other was to help lead a five-day retreat for gay Roman Catholic clergy in the United States. He decided to do the latter. "The organizing is done through one priest who knows everyone on the list, and the participants only know his name. They keep the location secret because they're technically not allowed to meet in any Roman Catholic institution. It's just extraordinary. The emails from this guy inviting me are heartbreaking. Can you imagine what it must be like to be one of these priests right now?"

"It will matter little what I say, you know. It's more a matter of my being there. It's the same with the prison work. We're doing services on Fridays at the men's prison as well, and even though there are just a few people attending right now, they were blown away that I was willing to come up on the 22nd of December to do a Christmas service for them. I've become so aware of 'the bishop as symbol'—that's true for any bishop, but with this other role I am playing, it's huge. It's wonderful, and a huge privilege, but the symbolic importance of the role is quite astounding and something I just didn't understand at first."

Part of the privilege of Gene's position is that he is able to observe and hear a wide variety of contemporary views about religion and the church. He speaks with people in secular venues as often as in churches and comes in contact with many who are spiritually hungry but have no current religious affiliation, often because they were rejected or grew disillusioned or alienated at some earlier point in their lives. Because people quickly perceive in him someone who is different from their preconceptions of a bishop, they are honest with him—hoping, perhaps, that this is a person who can help create change.

"Of my whole time in England," said Gene, "the debate at Oxford was the most moving thing for me, because I could sense so strongly this spiritual hunger and the way the students seemed to be hanging on every word I was saying. The room was packed, and anyone can interrupt you at any time, but I don't think I was interrupted once. You could have heard a pin drop. The last person to speak was the retired bishop of Woolwich, and he started talking about rules and canons and the protection of the institution, and how we need to go about this in an orderly fashion, and if we could get the canons changed then this would have been okay . . . and you could see the kids' eyes glazing over. They could have *cared less*. I had been talking about the living God, and then this guy started taking about rules and canons and they could hardly bear him. There were people jumping up to interrupt him, like they had been shot out of their chairs. These young people are skeptical and cynical about institutions, and feel they've been let down by the institutions in their lives. They are incredibly spiritually hungry, and yet the church is the last place in the world where they would look. What these students want to know is, 'How can I come to know God? How can I come to believe in the community of the church when it seems so irrelevant to my life?'" The highly-regarded theologian Marilyn McCord Adams, Regius Professor of Divinity at Oxford, was present; she told Gene afterwards that it was the most powerful preaching of the Gospel she had ever heard in a secular setting.

Louie Crew agrees with Gene's observations. "Every religion that is going to stay alive has to be in dialogue with its own culture," he said. "That's one of the things that's killing so much of modern Christianity, and maybe the parts that are dying should die, because it's so in thrall to the past. Many people—including many men—don't want to be part of a church that degrades women, for example. The church makes itself so dramatically irrelevant." He cited the Archbishop of Canterbury's recent edict that gay priests in the Church of England can register their legal domestic partnerships, as long as they swear to remain celibate. "In the real world of Great Britain! Actually it didn't get that much reaction over there, and I think that's because so few people in Great Britain go to church anymore. Well, you can see why!"

What *is* the purpose of religion? This is a crucial question facing the church of the future, as well as its corollary: what do people hope to find there, and is the church equipped to help them find it?

Gene reflected on those questions one afternoon in the conference room at Diocesan House. The winter was just ending, and the spring light filtered through the lilac branches outside the window and stretched across the dark mahogany table. Above the fireplace stood a set of colorful hand-drawn cards sent to the bishop by school children, and on the wall nearby was the large parchment from his consecration, bearing the signatures and seals of the forty-eight bishops who had been present. Gene crossed his arms over his chest and leaned back from the table. "There are two kinds of people, I think: those who see the purpose of religion as being liberation and joy, and those who see it as the only thing that is keeping the lid on. For some people, religion is all about right thinking and rules of behavior that, when followed, keep us in some sort of civil place. They feel that without those rules, we would be—God knows what. But it would be bad. So it's all about keeping uncontrollable desires in control, keeping the lid on, keeping the closet door shut, keeping Pandora's box closed. That the human spirit is this wild and snarling animal, just ready to pounce if you take your eye off it one minute."

"Which is just a wholly different place than 'Look at the gifts God gives us!'" His eyes lit up as he leaned forward, opening his hands. "Look what is possible if we open that up and let those gifts be free and responsive to the world around us. If we could learn to love ourselves just partially as much as God loves us, what kind of creative energies would be released? It's about the Exodus story, about being in slavery, and then being called out to this Promised Land. It's all this incredibly hopeful stuff, as opposed to (going back to my growing-up and that kind of evangelical thing) that kind of white-knuckle existence to see if you could make it to the finish line without screwing up and going to Hell."

Some people want religion to be a rulebook with promises attached: if you follow the rules precisely, you will receive the reward. Biblical literalism and fundamentalism appeal for those reasons, and they seem particularly attractive to people who are troubled by the ambiguities, choices, and uncertainties that permeate modern life. When a young woman asked Gene, "How can you know how to live your life if you don't take Scripture literally," she was voicing that anxiety. His answer, "You live your life not being sure," was certainly very disturbing to her, but it is not disturbing at all to people for whom religion is *not* primarily a rulebook pointing toward salvation in the next life (though they hope for that) but a guide for understanding and navigating the challenges and responsibilities of being human in a dynamic world. One of the major differences between these two types of people is that the former would like to stop or reverse rapid change and cites the rules of religion for justification, while the latter accepts change as natural and inevitable and sees religion as a way of coping with and understanding change. A religious life bounded by fence-like rules, clearly delimiting those who are "inside" from those who are "outside," is sure to be comforting to those who want assurance about their eventual salvation—but that same rigidity and lack of responsiveness to societal change and advances in scientific knowledge alienate many other people. The resulting attrition within organized religion is a fact, even in churchgoing America—but it does not necessarily mean that people do not believe in God, and it certainly doesn't mean that they lack spirituality. When Gene Robinson talks about a "living God" who moves along with humanity and who is "within" and supportive of our faltering attempts to eliminate racism, sexism, homophobia, ethnic prejudice, environmental degradation, war, and economic and social injustice, he is speaking not only to the people remaining in the pews, but to many who have left—but have not relinquished their hope for a life lived in relationship with God.

This fundamental divide can also be seen when people are asked what they see as the primary task of Christianity. Conservatives say it is evangelism: the creation of new "saved" Christians through evangelism and conversion, as expressed in the "Great Commission" of Jesus to his disciples to go out and make new disciples. Progressives are primarily motivated by what is known as the Great Commandment: to love God with all one's heart, soul, mind and strength, and to love one's neighbor as oneself. The difference between these views—and where they lead, both religiously and in one's political decisions and lifestyle choices—is so great that conservative Anglicans have observed that they seem to have more in common with conservative Baptists than they do with progressives in their own denomination. This seems to be the real "realignment" that is gradually taking place, even across former denominational lines, and which will reshape religious life over the decades to come.

Gene Robinson has said bluntly that organized religion in the Western world is at a crossroads. "Unless the church recovers its sense of what Jesus meant when he spoke of 'restoring sight to the blind and setting the captives free,' it runs the risk of either actually dying, or becoming hopelessly irrelevant."

That recovery, of course, would entail a considerable amount of change. "It could mean the loss of our buildings, it would mean the loss—if we started speaking up to the government the way we ought to—it would mean losing our tax-exempt status, and then we'd be in worse financial shape . . . I'm not suggesting that the churches should sell all their property and give it all to the poor, but I'm thinking that we should begin asking ourselves some tough questions about that. Douglas John Hall,[2] a theologian in Canada, has written about the 'humilitization' of the church. What he means by that is that we need to be humiliated—that is, to be made humble—before we're really going to remember what the church was meant to do. And I am so struck with how the Sadducees and Pharisees come off in the Bible. Remember, they were the seriously religious people of the day, and yet they come off as the villains in the stories that are told about Jesus. All the people they looked down on were the people that Jesus spent all his time with. We think and we say that we want to be Christ-like, and yet we don't seem to want to get our hands dirty."

Gene *had* been naive in the early days following his election, when he really believed that reconciliation would be possible in a matter of a few years. Two years later, it was clear that this wasn't going to be the case, either in the Episcopal Church or in the Anglican Communion as a whole, at least not in the foreseeable future. The happy outcome he had so much wanted for the

Church of the Redeemer in Rochester, New Hampshire, in his own diocese, did not come to pass either: on April 2, 2005, the final service took place and the church was permanently closed.

The church treasurer said he was convinced that dwindling finances would have forced the church to close eventually anyway, even if the congregation had not split over Gene Robinson's ordination. In his sermon there on the final Sunday, Gene said he didn't blame the remaining parishioners: "I bet you'd love to just go into church and think about God."

While the Rochester closing was a source of sadness for Gene, he accepted it. Increasingly, though, he found he could not accept and remain silent about hateful rhetoric about homosexuals coming from conservatives. Just as he had returned from England unapologetic for his remarks about the Vatican's plan to purge seminaries of gays, he also spoke out against the most strident voices coming from conservative African bishops and their American colleagues. He was deeply moved by the courage of the Nigerian homosexuals who met openly at the end of 2005, risking persecution, arrest, and torture, to form a chapter of Changing Attitudes in their country and voice their opposition to Archbishop Akinola and his anti-gay rhetoric. It was apparent to him that many Americans didn't realize what was being said, or its potential cost: these Nigerians were literally risking their lives.

"I'm really about to take the gloves off around what it means for people in the American church to be aligning themselves with Archbishop Akinola and his friends," Gene said. "You've got him saying that people like me are lower than the dogs. That's one step away from saying we're inhuman. And that's the kind of language that the Nazis used about the Jews that allowed them to perpetrate the Holocaust. Do people in this country who are part of the network and want to swear allegiance to Uganda and Nigeria—do they really want to align themselves with people who are trying to deny my very humanity? I think it's time we asked that straight out."

In fact, a clampdown in Nigeria was swift in coming. In February, the federal government of Nigeria passed a sweeping bill designed to stop any gay/lesbian progressivism in the country. It prohibited same-sex marriage, banned the official registration of all gay organizations, prohibited the public show of same-sex "amorous relationship" or its depiction in electronic or print media, and stated that offenders who registered such a group or displayed affection in public were liable for a term of five years' imprisonment.

The issue of homosexuality intensified clashes of cultures and values that already existed at the beginning of the millennium to an extent that no one, perhaps, had been able to predict. Douglas Theuner said he didn't think any of the North American progressives were prepared for the depth of the reaction. "But here it's symbolic," he added. "It's a different thing overseas. The Africans are coming out of real conviction and a real sense that they are standing in opposition to Western culture, and they have a real fear of their image in reference to Islam, where homosexuality is forbidden. But in this country it's basically the same old conservative guys who just really don't want to let go and don't want to see anything change and certainly don't want to see cultural change. It's a cultural thing. It has very little to do with the church, at least I don't think it does."

Theuner also sees this culturally inspired behavior reflected in the actions of the senior warden in Rochester who left because he said he had to be "true to the Gospel." "He's divorced!" Doug exclaimed. "Jesus didn't say anything about homosexuality, but he did say something about divorce. The church has come to accept divorce. The church has *changed its mind about divorce.* But how can someone who's divorced say you can't have a homosexual bishop because the Bible is against it? The Bible isn't *nearly* as against homosexuality as it is against divorce, but divorce happens all the time. It's irrational, totally irrational. For some uninformed people it may really be a matter of faith. But for most people, it's a cultural thing that they use the tools of faith to justify."

The renovations had been completed on Gene and Mark's house by the spring of 2005, but a dark cloud hovered: Gene still hadn't found his gold cross. While meeting with a group of Dartmouth students, he told the story of his loss. One of the students shyly raised her hand and said, "My parents own a gold mine . . ." Gene laughed and thought, "Well, yeah, my parents do too!" She saw his skeptical look and insisted, "No, they really do. And they have this machine that they take down into the mine, and it detects gold anywhere around." She told the story to her parents, and they shipped the device to New Hampshire from California.

Three Dartmouth students brought the machine to Gene's house and spent all day there. "We did every inch of the house except for the basement," he said. "That was too overwhelming. Some places where I thought it really was we went over three times, and we could not find it. So the next morning I went to the goldsmith here in town who had made the cross, because Mark and I talked about it that night, after this didn't work, and I said, 'I have agonized over this for fifteen months; there's not been a day that I haven't thought about it; I never put on the other cross that I don't think about it. I'm going to take the money out of my own savings and replace the cross.' I just couldn't take another Sunday when someone comes up and says, 'Oh, is that the cross that my grandfather's wedding band is in?' That kind of stuff—it's just been so painful." So Gene went to the goldsmith, Mark Knipe, and asked him what could be done.

The goldsmith gave him a funny look, and replied, "Can you keep a secret?" When Gene nodded, he said, "I still have some of your gold."

Gene was astounded. "What?" he said. "You paid us for that. I assumed you sold it."

"Something wouldn't let me sell it. Yes, I paid you for it, but I've still got it out in the back room." He took Gene back there and pulled out a file and opened a little bag with "Gene Robinson" written on it, and inside there were four flat pieces of gold.

"When we laid them down in the original configuration," Gene said, "there was the shape of my lost cross in the negative space in the center, where it had been cut out. For some reason he let the gold sit in his file cabinet for fifteen months and did not sell it."

The goldsmith melted the remaining gold down, made a mold and cast a new cross. There was enough, and because of the process that had been followed, a bit of everyone's contribution remained in the new cross.

Gene's eyes danced. "Is that not simply astounding? My feet didn't touch the ground for three days. I told him, 'You have simply made me the happiest person!' And what's funny is that Mark Knipe had started by saying that Judith Esmay had come in three weeks before me, and she and several other people were planning to quietly raise the money to buy me a new cross." Gene called Judith and said, "Don't you dare raise money for this, I want to remedy this myself." And it was Judith who, when she heard the story of the remaining gold, told Gene, "Don't you see the symbolism of this? Your new cross will be made up of the gold that came from the margins!"

Gene said, "I'm really not big on material things, but this is more than a 'thing.' This is the diocese: it's like wearing the diocese over my heart! It was driving me crazy." Now he felt released, and free to tell the story.

At Diocesan House on a bright winter afternoon in early 2006, the New Hampshire delegation to the upcoming General Convention was gathering for an organizational meeting, chaired by Judith Esmay and the Rev. Hank Junkin. The conference room and kitchenette buzzed with conversation as friends from all over the state picked up some coffee and greeted one other. Everyone knew that General Convention, in June 2006, would be momentous: a new Presiding Bishop would be elected to replace the retiring Frank Griswold, and there could be a decisive confrontation between the liberal and conservative factions of the Episcopal Church that would not only determine its future direction but that of the Anglican Communion itself. A significant complication had just been added: as had happened in New Hampshire three years before, an election for a new bishop would take place in the Diocese of California (San Francisco) in May and the result would come before the Convention for their consent. Bishop William Swing, a consistent voice for progressivism and interfaith dialogue, was retiring. On the shortlist of candidates to replace him were two non-celibate homosexual priests, one of whom was a woman, in spite of the moratorium requested by the Windsor Report on the election of any more gay bishops. In England, where a tempest raged over the recent decision to allow female bishops at all, let alone lesbian ones, the Anglican hierarchy seemed dismayed, and the conservatives indignant. The *Telegraph* mentioned a recent letter sent by Archbishop Rowan Williams to the Anglican primates speaking of "the bitter controversy over sexuality in the Communion," and Canon Chris Sugden, Executive Secretary of the conservative coalition group Anglican Mainstream International (which includes the AAC and has the Bishop of the West Indies, the Rt. Rev. Drexel Gomez, as its spiritual advisor) said, "It has been done during the moratorium deliberately. It is a clear challenge to the rest of the Communion and the Church of England."[3] Gene Robinson had voted with the rest of the House of Bishops when they decided to place a moratorium on *all* bishop elections, not just of gay candidates, in response to the Windsor Report. Still, nearly every news article about the ongoing controversy mentioned his name, election, and sexual orientation as the catalyst—just as they had for the past three years.

That day, as his colleagues gathered in Concord, Gene Robinson seemed to be his jovial, enthusiastic self. But unbeknownst to all but his closest family members and a handful of colleagues, the stress was adding up—and a few weeks later, it came to a head. In a telephone call on a Thursday in early February, Paula Bibber was cryptic and uncharacteristically evasive: "The bishop is away," she said. "I'm sorry not to be able to be more forthcoming; I'll be able to tell you more on Monday." Though delivered just as calmly and professionally as ever, this response was very unusual and created immediate concern: Was he ill? In the hospital? Had something happened to Mark or one of his children? On Monday afternoon, February 13, an explanatory statement was sent from Diocesan House to every New Hampshire parish and posted on the diocesan website:

> Brothers and Sisters in Christ,
>
> I am writing to you from an alcohol treatment center where on February 1, with the encouragement and support of my partner, daughters and colleagues, I checked myself in to deal with my increasing dependence on alcohol. Over the 28 days I will be here, I will be dealing with the disease of alcoholism—which, for years, I have thought of as a failure of will or discipline on my part, rather than a disease over which my particular body simply has no control, except to stop drinking altogether.
>
> During my first week here, I have learned so much. The extraordinary experience of community here will inform my ministry for years to come. I eagerly look forward to continuing my recovery in your midst. Once again, God is proving His desire and ability to bring an Easter out of Good Friday. Please keep me in your prayers and know that you are in mine.
>
> Your Brother in Christ,
> +Gene

Gene's letter was accompanied by a message from the diocesan Standing Committee and the request that the priests of the diocese be sure to share *both* letters with their congregations:

Dear Colleagues in Ministry,

The Standing Committee of the Diocese of New Hampshire joins its bishop in writing to you about his decision to seek professional treatment for his dealings with alcohol. The Episcopal Church, through its General Convention, has long recognized alcoholism as a treatable human disease, not a failure of character or will.

The members of the Standing Committee fully support and stand with our bishop and his family as he confronts the effects of alcohol on his life, and we commend him for his courageous example to us all, as we pray daily for him and for his ministry among us.

Randolph K. Dales,
President, Standing Committee of New Hampshire

The decision to seek treatment had happened rapidly, as the result of an intervention by Gene's daughters, partner, and a small group of colleagues. Gene had returned home early one day in order, he thought, to meet his daughter Jamee and watch her children for a few hours. When he drove up to his house, he saw cars parked along the road, some with out-of-state license plates. "I knew immediately what it was," he said. "And I put up no resistance. I was so ready." Led by a facilitator, each person read a prepared letter to Gene telling him why he should agree to treatment. After the first letter, he asked the facilitator if he could make it easy for everyone and just go, because the dominant emotion he was feeling was relief. "No," he was told, "you have to listen to what everyone has to say." Gene said it was difficult and emotional for everyone, but that, ironically, he thought he had gotten through it in better shape than the people reading the letters. In the end, everything happened very fast: he was whisked away to a treatment center in Pennsylvania where he spent the next month without his cell phone, PDA, or laptop, restricted to three ten-minute phone calls per week, and living a life in which each minute was structured. "It's a bit like dying must be," he said afterwards. "Everything just stops: all your appointments are cancelled, all those loose ends are simply left untied, and you have to face your life exactly as it is at that moment. And you also have to face the fact that life, in which you were so involved, goes on quite well without you."

The news blindsided most of Gene's friends and colleagues. From Randy Dales to David Jones, people who saw and worked with the bishop every day expressed their surprise. Even Paula Bibber admitted that she had had no idea anything was going on. Tim Rich, who had been part of the intervention, said that no one had seen the problem impact Gene's ministry in the diocese in any way. That may have been a result of the fact that Gene had not been a person who drank every night. He explained later that he was quite capable of not drinking when he knew it would impact his work; it was more that once he *did* take a drink, he had no idea how much he would end up consuming. This had led to an increasing fear about his inability to control his intake as well as a fear that he would eventually lose control in a more public way. Gene had been aware of this pattern for a number of years, but he had always seen it as a failure of will. It was only during treatment that he learned about the physiology of alcohol addiction, how alcohol affects certain people in a way that makes them lose the ability to make the decision to stop. "They speak of how instead of you drinking the drink, 'the drink begins to drink you,'" he said. "It's absolutely true—but I had no idea. I thought it was all my fault."

Although those close to Gene had worried about a negative reaction when this news became public, in fact most of his detractors seemed to take a step back, saying that alcoholism was a widespread problem, acknowledged to be a disease rather than a weakness or character flaw, and that the appropriate response was to pray for Bishop Robinson and his recovery. "It makes him seem even more human," said one non-Episcopalian sympathizer who, like many, had been amazed at Gene's apparent equanimity at the center of controversy and unrelenting media attention.

"People have tried to make Gene into a poster child for everything from gay rights to the problems in the Anglican Communion, and now some will try to do that for alcohol addiction as well," said Tim Rich. "What he has done is courageous and difficult, and what he needs to do now is recover. Those of us who care about him need to make sure that he has the space to do that." As Gene himself had reflected a month earlier, the demonization and blame were sometimes less difficult to bear than the weight of people's positive expectations. He knew himself to be neither angel nor devil, but merely a human being doing the best he could, with God's help.

When the bishop returned home in early March, he described himself as "refreshed, focused, clear-headed and happy," and that is indeed how he seemed a few days later at his home, surrounded by Mark's blooming orchids and the sunlight of the first few warm days of early spring shining on the still-snow-covered gardens at the back of the house. He spoke about how much he had learned during treatment, not only about alcohol addiction but about the creation of Christian community, lessons he said he hoped to write about at length and that would inform his ministry for years to come. Nevertheless, he immediately acknowledged that he was "a mere babe in the woods" in terms of addiction and sobriety and that his first task was to take care of himself. In a statement released to the press on his return to work, he expressed his gratitude for the letters and prayers he had received and also for people's support of the way he had chosen to deal with it:

Thank you also for your support in my being open about this struggle. I knew it was central to my own recovery to be honest about this with you and with the world. So much of my life and ministry has been served well by that kind of openness, it would have seemed inconsistent to attempt to hide it.

In the book that was so important to Gene Robinson's own journey, John Fortunato writes about the myth we all carry within us: the illusion that we are somehow in control of our lives. Many of us manage to maintain that illusion for a long, long time because we don't run up against boundaries that tell us otherwise. It is a lot easier to believe we are in control when we are not living on the margins and being forced to recognize, on a day-to-day basis, that we are not part of the center, the in-group, the people who are acceptable and hold most of the power in society. But when we do come up against those barriers, often through circumstances that are not of our own making, the toll can be devastating. Fortunato writes:

> It is no surprise, therefore . . . that gay people ask an inordinate number of spiritual questions. Either because they realize it when they come to therapy or discover it in the process, they come to grips with the frightening reality that they must give up the myth [of control] *forever* . . . whether or not they consciously grasp their yearning as a need for spiritual grounding, the cry into the abyss is an acknowledgment that the only way *out* is *deeper*.

At its root, this yearning for control and meaning can be described as spiritual hunger. As has been particularly obvious since 9/11, the devastating Pacific tsunami, and Hurricane Katrina, we live in a world which we clearly cannot control and where much does not make sense to us. Fortunato says that most people start out by trying to convince themselves that they actually are in control, and then move outward from the self to create systems that they can control. All of that effort is a part of our attempt as humans to disguise the truth that actually we control nothing.

Many people, especially the young, see through this illusion of control. One way of reacting is to turn toward alienation and nihilism, which are certainly on the rise among today's youth. But the fact that many young people are attracted to Gene and his way of speaking about faith and scripture and God working in our lives—and yet are so turned off by much of traditional religion—is an indication both of that universal yearning for a deeper understanding of what it means to be human, and of how urgently we need new ways of talking about the spiritual life.

For homosexuals, spiritual questions can continue to be extremely difficult, even when society at large is gradually moving toward greater acceptance and some of the barriers are being removed. Gene doesn't talk much about the many personal letters he receives from gays and lesbians and their families. After all, these are often very personal, and he is a priest. But being the privileged recipient of so many people's stories and tears—listening to what they have to say rather than merely talking at them from a point of "arrival"—has helped him understand the unique role in which he is placed: that of being not only a symbol, but the bearer of a crucial message.

Ella Robinson says, "It's something more than whether a person can be openly gay on the streets of New York, or go to a club, or make it to the executive level. We're talking about God here! The ultimate validation, the ultimate judge. And to be okay with God? Clearly there hasn't been that kind of example before. And because that's what Dad represents and embodies, and he has that connection—well, he is the right person to deliver that message to each person he meets. And it is a kind of personal delivery."

"But it's even more than that. For my father, it's not just because somebody is gay, or they're a woman, they're okay: it's that *everybody* is okay, because we're all God's children. And he believes that so strongly that he's very convincing about it and can make you feel it and believe it if you didn't before."

Her father says that the essential message he really wants to convey to people is very simple: "It's the thing you've heard me say ten thousand times, which is that God loves us beyond our wildest imagining. That's why I use a passage from Isaiah so often, about 'proclaiming the year of the Lord's favor.' There are so many people, including people in the church, who have no idea how favored they are by God."

"But for oppressed people, that message is harder to believe. I think for people of color, for women, for gay and lesbian folk, they've been told that they are 'less than' for so long that it comes as especially good news to them, but it's also harder for them to believe. They have been shamed, and if they had faith, it has been battered and eroded and picked at, which is why Jesus was always preaching to those types of people, bending over backwards to let them know."

"We've had some gay people who have done very well—Martina Navratilova, arguably the best tennis player ever, Ellen DeGeneres, Greg Louganis—people who have accomplished a lot. But maybe why there has been so much furor over me and what I've accomplished, or whatever God has accomplished within me, is because it goes beyond saying, 'I think I'm all right.' It says, 'I think God thinks I'm all right.' That's something new, and I think maybe that's why so many people are interested in this, or angered by it, because in the last decade we've had more and more people coming out, more and more people being self-affirming. Still, self affirmation only goes so far. But if I say, in a clerical collar, that God thinks I'm all right, it carries a different kind of weight: it means I have the audacity to say, 'Not only am I self-affirming, but God is affirming me.' And that is either good news or bad news, depending on where you are."

"It goes back to what I said in my investiture sermon: nobody will get on your case if you preach a judgmental, narrow, punishing God, but if you start preaching a God that is too loving, too merciful, and too forgiving, people will be all over you like a duck on a junebug. It makes people crazy. I think that is fascinating, that so many people would not see the idea of a loving, forgiving God as 'good news.' That's exactly what happened to Jesus. The people who didn't see God that way were the ones who crucified him."

Only a person who has lived through repression, rejection, and doubts and then emerged into a different, light-filled consciousness can carry that message convincingly to others. Gene Robinson was once in a very dark place, and God spoke to him. As Fortunato wrote, "Once you know, at the core of your being, that you have a rightful place in God's creation, and that nothing can separate you from the love of God, then it doesn't much matter what people say or do to you. Then you are free to give and love—anyway."[4]

Gene's life changed the day he read those words, and he eventually became a person filled with courage, able to preach about a world in which infinite respect and radical hospitality are possible. The message is intended for all of us: gay and straight; male and female; people of all colors and economic levels; those in the public eye and those whose priesthood is lived in relationship with family and friends. As Gene Robinson shows us through his own ministry, there is no need to wait for the Kingdom of God: every meeting with another human being is an opportunity to let love shine forth in the world.

Notes

CHAPTER 1

1 "Christian Church (Disciples of Christ)," the official website of The Christian Church, http://www.disciples.org (accessed May 3, 2005).
2 Nearly all Christian denominations have some form of symbolic "meal" as part of their services, in which bread and wine (or grape juice) are formally offered by the minister and shared by the members of the congregation. This ritual commemorates the "Last Supper," which Jesus shared with his disciples the night before his crucifixion; he took bread and wine and gave it to them, telling them to repeat the ritual "in remembrance of me." The early Christians did do this, and the ritual of a symbolic communal meal, or "communion," became part of the tradition. Later, Roman Catholics began to believe in the doctrine of transubstantiation, which meant that the wine, when consecrated by a priest, turned into the actual blood of Christ and the bread into His body. This belief became, for a time, one of the major dividing lines between Protestantism and Roman Catholicism. But in the latter part of the nineteenth century, some Anglicans began to move toward acceptance of this belief. Belief in "the Real Presence" of Christ in the bread and wine distinguishes Anglo-Catholics, or high-church Anglicans, from low-church Anglicans, who are more traditionally Protestant. In Roman Catholic and high-church Anglican churches, some of the consecrated bread and wine is often kept in the church after the Mass, with a perpetual candle burning nearby, as a sign that Jesus Christ himself is present in the sanctuary.
3 Part of the controversy about women (and gay) priests comes from the belief that only a male priest, who has been consecrated by a bishop in direct lineage from the apostles, can perform the sacrament of consecrating the bread and wine for communion, i.e., be a conduit for the miracle of transubstantiation. Jesus had only celibate male disciples, they believe, so therefore women and gay men are disqualified to serve as priests. Bread and wine consecrated by a woman or gay person is, to opponents of their ordination, not properly holy and therefore tainted.

CHAPTER 2

1 Gail Jarvis, "University of the S**th," http://www.lewrockwell.com/jarvis/jarvis66. html (accessed January 31, 2006).
2 Lionel Wright, "The Stonewall Riots—1969," http://www.socialistalternative.com/ literature/stonewall.html.
3 Ann Marie Timmins, "Years of rejection, now understanding: Bishop-elect has accepted his homosexuality," originally published in two parts on the website of the *Concord Monitor*, July 18 and 20, 2003, and currently available at http://www. deimel.org/church_resources/monitor_profile.htm.

CHAPTER 3

1 Paul Moore, Jr., *Take a Bishop Like Me* (New York, New York: Harper & Row, 1979).
2 Carter Heyward, *A Priest Forever* (New York, New York: Harper & Row, 1976).
3 Ibid., 28.

CHAPTER 4

1 Moore, *Take a Bishop Like Me*.
2 Louie Crew, "Changing the Church: Lessons Learned in the Struggle to Reduce Institutional Heterosexism in the Episcopal Church," in *Combatting Homophobia*, ed. James Sears & Walter Williams (New York, New York: Columbia University Press, 1997), 341-353.
3 Martin Luther King, Jr., "Letter from a Birmingham Jail."
4 *Integrity Gay Episcopal Forum* 3.5, March 1977. The letter quoted is from a from Bishop Moore to Bishop R. M. Trelease, Jr. originally published in *The Southwest Churchman*.
5 Ibid.
6 Kathleen A. McAdams, "A Chronology of Gay and Lesbian History in the Diocese of California and Beyond," http://www.oasiscalifornia.org/chron.html (accessed May 14, 2005).
7 Ibid. (Elision in the original).
8 Andy Humm, "Rev. Paul Moore, Jr. Dies at 83," *Gay City News* 2.1, May 9–15, 2003.
9 Susan Kinzie, "Inventing a Marriage—and a Divorce," *Washington Post*, April 19, 2005, http://www.washingtonpost.com/wp-dyn/articles/A50350-2004Apr4_2.html.
10 John Fortunato, *Embracing the Exile: Healing Journeys for Gay Christians* (New York, New York: Seabury Press, 1982), 18.
11 Ibid., 18.

CHAPTER 5

1 "Historic Anniversary forSame-Sex Adoption," *Gay Asbury Park*, December 17, 2005, http://adoption.about.com/gi/dynamic/offsite.htm?zi=1/XJ&sdn=adoption&zu=http%3A%2F%2Fwww.gayasburypark.com%2Fmore.tpl%3D1128.
2 GLAD, http://www.glad.org/rights/newhampshire_lgbt.shtml#adoption (accessed February 21, 2006).
3 Michael Paulson, "New rites for Vt. civil unions," *Boston Globe*, June 18, 2004.

CHAPTER 7

1 "Report of the Theology Committee of the House of Bishops of the Episcopal Church," www.er-d.org/documents/theologycomreport.pdf (accessed 2/19/06).

CHAPTER 8

1 The SBC has no formal hierarchy and is actually a loose affiliation of churches organized by state, rather than a denomination in the same sense as, for example, Roman Catholicism or the Methodist or Presbyterian Churches.
2 "Carter breaks ties with Southern Baptists," *Alabama Baptist Online*, November 2,

2000, http://www.thealabamabaptist.org/ip_template.asp? upid=6099.

3 Bugalo Chilume, "The Plight of African Christians," *Mmegi/The Reporter* (Gaborone), August 26, 2005. http://allafrica.com/stories/200508260241.html.

4 Jan Nunley and James Solheim, "Mixed reaction to New Hampshire bishop election," *Episcopal News Service*, June 08, 2003.

5 "The History of Anglicans United," http://www.anglicansunited.com/history.html (accessed on February 19, 2006).

6 Lewis C. Daly, "A Church at Risk: the Episcopal Renewal Movement," *IDS Insights*, December 2001, http://www.idsonline.org/art/Insights_Vol02Iss02.pdf. I am greatly indebted to Lewis Day and Lionel Deimel, who pointed this article out to me, for much of the background in this chapter and for helping me understand the history of the religious right's inroads into the Episcopal Church.

7 Canon Kendall Harmon, "TitusOnline," April 18, 2005. Harmon is canon theologian for the Diocese of South Carolina and the editor of *Anglican Digest*; he is a leading spokesperson for the Episcopal Right. The above comment by John Rodgers appeared in a thread on Harmon's blog following the death of Diane Knippers. In another post (January 24, 2004) Harmon discusses the relationship between Episcopal bishops and the AAC: "I'm never sure what people mean when they speak of 'the AAC bishops.' There is a fairly fluid group of bishops that has worked together over the past several years, often in conjunction with the AAC efforts at the last three General Conventions. However, there is no 'official' membership in the group, except for those who are on the AAC Board. (I was, for about a year, following the GC in 2000.)"

8 Daly, "A Church at Risk."

9 Lionel Deimel, "Positions on the Election of V. Gene Robinson," http://deimel.org/church_resources/vgr.htm (accessed on 1/25/2006).

10 Jan Nunley and James Solheim, "Mixed reaction to New Hampshire bishop election," *Episcopal News Service*, June 8, 2003.

CHAPTER 9

1 Bob Williams, "American Anglican Council offers 'Place to Stand' for traditional views," *Episcopal Life Convention Daily*, July 30, 2003, http://www.episcopalchurch.org/gcdaily_17441_ENG_HTM.htm?menu= undefined.

2 Nunley and Solheim, "Mixed reaction."

3 Lucy Chumbley, "Gene Robinson's ratification passes first hurdle," Washington Window, August 1, 2003, http://www.edow.org/news/window/ special/generalconvention/0801robinson.html.

4 David Skidmore, "Robinson consent sent to House of Deputies," *Episcopal News Service*, Friday, August 01, 2003. London's *Daily Telegraph*, for example, had published a story on January 6, 2003, under the headline, "Gay canon who left wife is favourite to be Anglican bishop." On February 8, the *Washington Times* wrote that he had "left his wife and children and now lives with a male lover." On June 19, 2003, David Virtue wrote: "Mr. Robinson left his wife and family to move in with his homosexual lover," allegedly quoting a Church of England newspaper editorial on his conservative Episcopal Church listserve.

5 Ibid.

6 Ibid.

7 Richelle Thompson, "Robinson exonerated: Investigation finds 'no necessity to pursue' allegations," *Episcopal News Service*, August 5, 2003.

8 "Report to the House of Bishops by Rt. Rev. Gordon P. Scruton, Diocese of Western Massachusetts," *Episcopal News Service*, August 5, 2003, http://episcopalchurch.org/3577_18260_ENG_HTM.htm.

9 Ibid.

10 "Robinson Approved as Bishop," *Episcopal News Service*, August 5, 2003, http://episcopalchurch.org/3577_18269_ENG_HTM.htm.

11 The final breakdown of votes is detailed in the Anglican Web pages of Louie Crew: "In the final tally of votes by both Houses, only 16 of the 100 domestic dioceses were negative by bishop, clergy and lay on both resolutions: Albany, Central Florida, Florida, Fort Worth, Northern Indiana, Pittsburgh, Quincy, Rio Grande, San Joaquin, South Carolina, Southwest Florida, Springfield, Texas, West Tennessee, Western Kansas, Western Louisiana. Seven of the ten dioceses outside the USA were negative by bishop, clergy, and lay on both resolutions: Colombia, Dominican Republic, Ecuador Litoral, Ecuador, Haiti, Honduras, Virgin Islands. In the House of Deputies, both issues were voted 'by orders'—a process in which evenly divided votes count as a negative. Alabama, Central Gulf Coast, Dallas, Fond du Lac, Georgia, North Dakota, Upper South Carolina, West Texas, and West Virginia all had divided votes in at least one order on at least one of these."

12 Michelle Gabriel, *Episcopal Life Convention Daily*, July 31, 2003.

CHAPTER 10

1 Ricor Norton, "A History of Homophobia," http://www.infopt.demon.co.uk/homopho2.htm. "Christians with no linguistic expertise assume that 'know' means 'engage in coitus.' But the term for 'know'—*yadha*—is used in the sexual sense only 10 times in the Old Testament and all of these cases are heterosexual. *Yadha* is used in the sense of 'get acquainted with' 924 times. Thus the odds against the homosexual usage of this term are nearly 1000-to-1, and many modern Biblical scholars have now abandoned this theory." Norton goes on to explain that many scholars now see the destruction as being "a moral allegory on the dire effects of inhospitality."

2 Genesis 19:4-5, New Revised Standard Version.

3 Modern archaeologists disagree as to whether the cities actually existed, but it is generally acknowledged that if they did, the described location is along a major fault line, the Jordan Rift Valley.

4 Ezekiel 16:49-50: "Now this was the sin of Sodom: She and her daughters were arrogant, overfed and unconcerned; they did not help the poor and needy. They were haughty and did detestable things before me. Therefore I did away with them as you have seen."

5 Jesus was crucified on the day that has come to be known as "Good Friday," and just before he died he despaired that God had forsaken him—a despair shared by his disciples, who had no way to anticipate his resurrection on Easter. In informal Christian terminology, a "Good Friday moment" means a time when a person despairs, out of ignorance of God's greater plan.

CHAPTER 11

1 The Rt. Rev. Krister Stendahl is Bishop Emeritus of Stockholm, Sweden (Lutheran Church of Sweden), and Professor of Divinity Emeritus at Harvard University, where he was Dean of Harvard Divinity School. He is a prominent theologian and the author of many books and is considered a pioneer in interfaith relations.

CHAPTER 12

1 Kathy McCormack, "Dissidents gather for alternative service," Associated Press, Boston.com News, November 3, 2003; Carol Costello, CNN, and Mark Ericson,

WOKQ, CNN Daybreak, November 3, 2003; and Douglas Belkin, "Raised signs, voices at UNH", *Boston Globe*, November 3, 2003.
2 Ibid.

CHAPTER 13

1 Paul Moore, Jr., *Take a Bishop Like Me*.
2 Ibid.
3 Katharine Webster, "Gay Episcopal bishop begins his ministry," Associated Press, November 9, 2003.
4 Jan Nunley, Episcopal News Service, March 23, 2004.
5 Mike Recht, "Tough times for Rochester church," *Portsmouth Herald*, April 8, 2004.
6 Brian DeKoning, Manchester *Union Leader*, June 28, 2004.

CHAPTER 14

1 *A Church at War: Anglicans and Homosexuality* is a detailed study of the history of the Anglican Communion and the reasons why this issue has precipitated a potential split. It was researched and written by Stephen Bates, religion reporter for the *Guardian* (UK) and published in October 2004, by I. B. Tauris. The book, which has a photograph of a pensive Gene Robinson on the cover, contains material on the American church but is written mainly from a British viewpoint.
2 Jim Brown, "ELCA Prepares to Vote on Issues Related to Homosexuality," August 5, 2005, http://www.crosswalk.com/news/religiontoday/1343825.html.
3 Rachel Zoll, "Lutherans reject easing gay clergy rules," *Boston Globe*, August 12, 2005.
4 Charles A. Radin, "Debate over gay clergy is testing many faiths, Vatican expected to announce ban," *Boston Globe*, November 29, 2005.
5 Jason Kane, "Evangelical Mainliners Vow to Stay and Fight," *Religion News Service*, January 7, 2006, http://www.beliefnet.com/story/182/story_18257_1.html.
6 "Profile of Pope Benedict XVI," BBC News, April 19, 2005.
7 Laurie Goodstein, "Vatican to Check U.S. Seminaries on Gay Presence," *New York Times*, September 15, 2005.
8 Doug Struck, "Nine Defy Vatican's Ban on Ordination of Women," *Washington Post Foreign Service*, July 26, 2005, http://www.washingtonpost.com/wp-dyn/content/article/2005/ 07/25/AR2005072501586.html.
9 Cate McMahon, "Convocation Looks at Unions," *New Hampshire Episcopal News*, January/February 2006. (The liturgies are available for download and trial use, provided the Diocese of Vermont is credited: www.dioceseofVermont.org.)
10 Kevin Bourassa and Joe Varnell, "It's a quiet thing: equal marriage is law—marriage receives senate approval & royal assent," July 21, 2005, http://www.samesexmarriage.ca/legal/qui210705.htm.
11 Michelangelo Signorile, "Can Catholicism be Good for Gays?," August 11, 2005, http:www.365gay.com.
12 Ibid.
13 "Archbishop of Canterbury, Rowan Williams on Homosexuality," BBC interview on March 2, 2005, aired November 17, 2005, http://socrates58.blogspot.com/2005/11/archbishop-of-canterbury-rowan.html.
14 Douglas LeBlanc, "Out of Africa," *Christianity Today*, July 2005.
15 Frank Kirkpatrick, "The Anglican Crackup," *Religion in the News* 6.4, Fall 2003.
16 The Most Rev. Frank Griswold, Statement on the Windsor Report 2004, *Anglican Communion News Service*, October 18, 2004.

17 Laurie Goodstein, "Gay Bishop Sees Glint of Hope in Church Report," *New York Times*, October 21, 2004.

18 Rev. Prof. Stephen Noll, "The Divorce is Underway," http://www.americananglican.org/site/c.ikLUK3MJIpG/b.564003/apps/s/content.asp?ct=854113.

19 Douglas LeBlanc, "Out of Africa."

20 "History of the Network," http://www.acn-us.org/about/history/ (accessed March 1, 2006): "The formation of the Network was originally suggested by the Archbishop of Canterbury, the Most Rev. Rowan Williams. Initial plans for the Convocation were laid at a gathering of mainstream Anglican leaders (including four Primates) in London in November 2003. A Memorandum of Agreement came out of this meeting and was ultimately signed by 13 bishops of the Episcopal Church. The Memorandum stated the intention of these bishops to begin taking steps toward organizing a network of "confessing" dioceses and congregations within ECUSA. The signing of the memorandum by a bishop did not indicate that his diocese had joined the network. Since then, a total of ten dioceses— Albany, Central Florida, Dallas, Fort Worth, Pittsburgh, Quincy, Rio Grande, San Joaquin, South Carolina and Springfield—have ratified their affiliation. The Network of Anglican Communion Dioceses and Parishes was officially launched on January 20, 2004, at the Network's Organizing Convocation held at Christ Church, Plano, Texas."

21 Anne Saunders, "Gay Bishop Predicts Anglican Church Split," *Washington Post*, September 23, 2005.

22 Greg Garrison, "Conservative Anglicans heading to Birmingham," *Birmingham News*, January 8, 2006.

23 Rebecca Paveley, "Gene Robinson Pulls Out of Union Debate," March 2, 2004, http://www.oxford.anglican.org.

24 Stephen Bates, "Williams may meet gay US bishop during London trip," *Guardian*, October 20, 2005.

CHAPTER 15

1 Bates, "Williams may meet gay US bishop during London trip."

2 "Gay US bishop meets with Rowan Williams," Ekklesia News Service, November 4, 2005.

3 Laura Lambert, "Bishop V. Gene Robinson Talks to Planned Parenthood," *Choice!*, April 6, 2005.

4 Erin Curry, "Homosexual bishop courts Planned Parenthood," *Baptist Press Culture Digest*, April 27, 2005.

5 Randy Hall, "Log Cabin Official to Lead Planned Parenthood's Outreach to GOP," Cybercast News Service, November 18, 2005.

6 Neil Swidey, "What Makes People Gay?" *Boston Globe*, August 14, 2005.

7 The expression comes from the life of Paul of Tarsis (St. Paul), who had been a persecutor of early Christians. While walking on the road to Damascus, Paul was struck blind and received a vision of Christ that led to his conversion. Paul regained his sight and became the apostle who was most responsible for the spread of Christianity throughout the ancient world, as well as the author of a number of letters to early Christian communities that form a major part of the New Testament and contributed significantly to later Christian theology as well as our knowledge of early Christianity. He died as a martyr, probably around 65 A.D.

8 Moore, *Take A Bishop Like Me*, 31.

CHAPTER 16

1 "Church of England article on House of Bishops meeting," March 15, 2004, http://titusonenine.classicalanglican.net/?p=715 (accessed March 12, 2006). Also, "The Hard Work of Reconciliation," the Rt. Rev. Pierre W. Whalon, D.D., March 26 2004, http://anglicansonline.org/resources/essays/whalon/ Reconciliation_ work.html. Bishop Whalon wrote, "The saddest part of these difficult decisions was that a number of bishops boycotted the meeting, or barely attended at all, choosing to stay somewhere away from Camp Allen. Some attended daily Eucharists but ostentatiously refused to receive communion. As these were some of those alienated by General Convention's actions, the work of reconciliation that should have happened was severely impaired. You cannot reconcile with someone who will not speak to you."

2 Douglas John Hall is Professor of Christian Theology at McGill University, Montréal, Que., Canada.

3 Elizabeth Day, "Election of lesbian bishop 'will cause Church to unravel,'" *Telegraph*, March 12, 2006.

4 Fortunato, *Embracing the Exile.*

Jonathan Sa'adah

Elizabeth Adams has been granted unique, extraordinary access to Bishop Robinson and the events and people surrounding him. She also has significant knowledge about the Episcopal Church gained through lifelong membership and active participation, and has been an observer, writer, and speaker for many years about the interface between religion and contemporary life and politics.